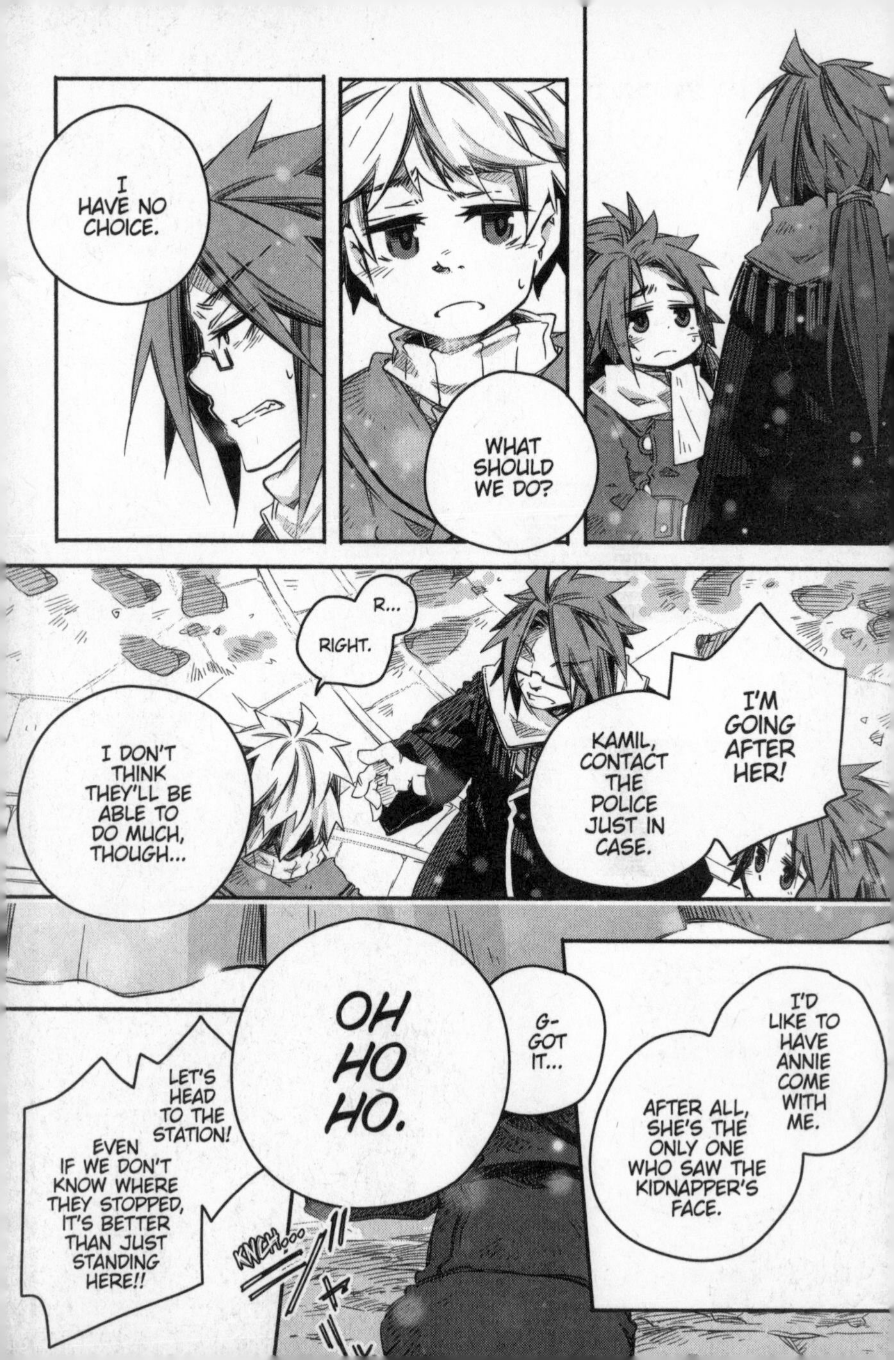
WHAT SHOULD WE DO?
I HAVE NO CHOICE.
I'M GOING AFTER HER!
KAMIL, CONTACT THE POLICE JUST IN CASE.
R... RIGHT.
I DON'T THINK THEY'LL BE ABLE TO DO MUCH, THOUGH...
I'D LIKE TO HAVE ANNIE COME WITH ME.
AFTER ALL, SHE'S THE ONLY ONE WHO SAW THE KIDNAPPER'S FACE.
G-GOT IT...
OH HO HO.
LET'S HEAD TO THE STATION!
EVEN IF WE DON'T KNOW WHERE THEY STOPPED, IT'S BETTER THAN JUST STANDING HERE!!

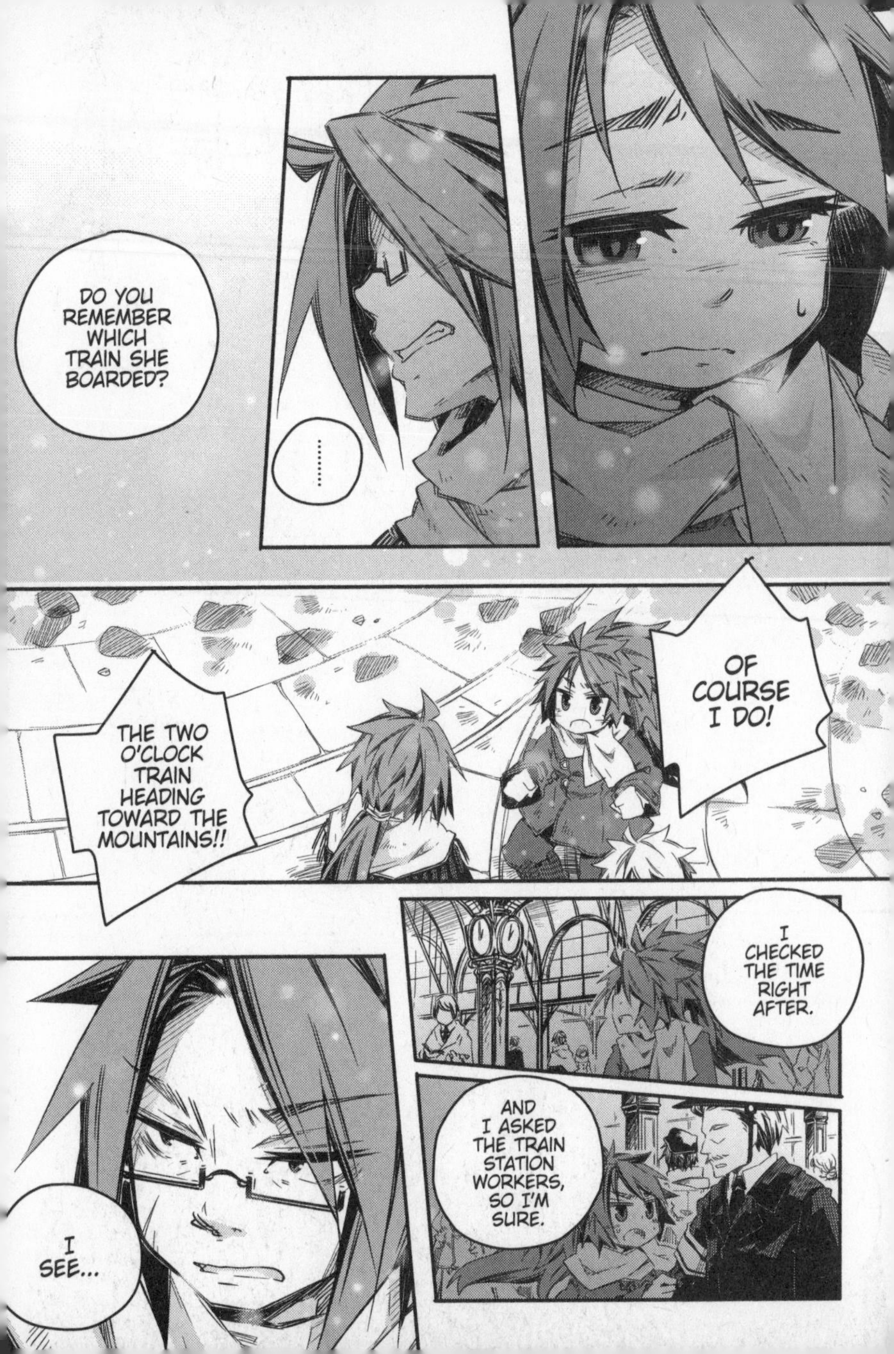
DO YOU REMEMBER WHICH TRAIN SHE BOARDED?
......
OF COURSE I DO!
THE TWO O'CLOCK TRAIN HEADING TOWARD THE MOUNTAINS!!
I CHECKED THE TIME RIGHT AFTER.
AND I ASKED THE TRAIN STATION WORKERS, SO I'M SURE.
I SEE...

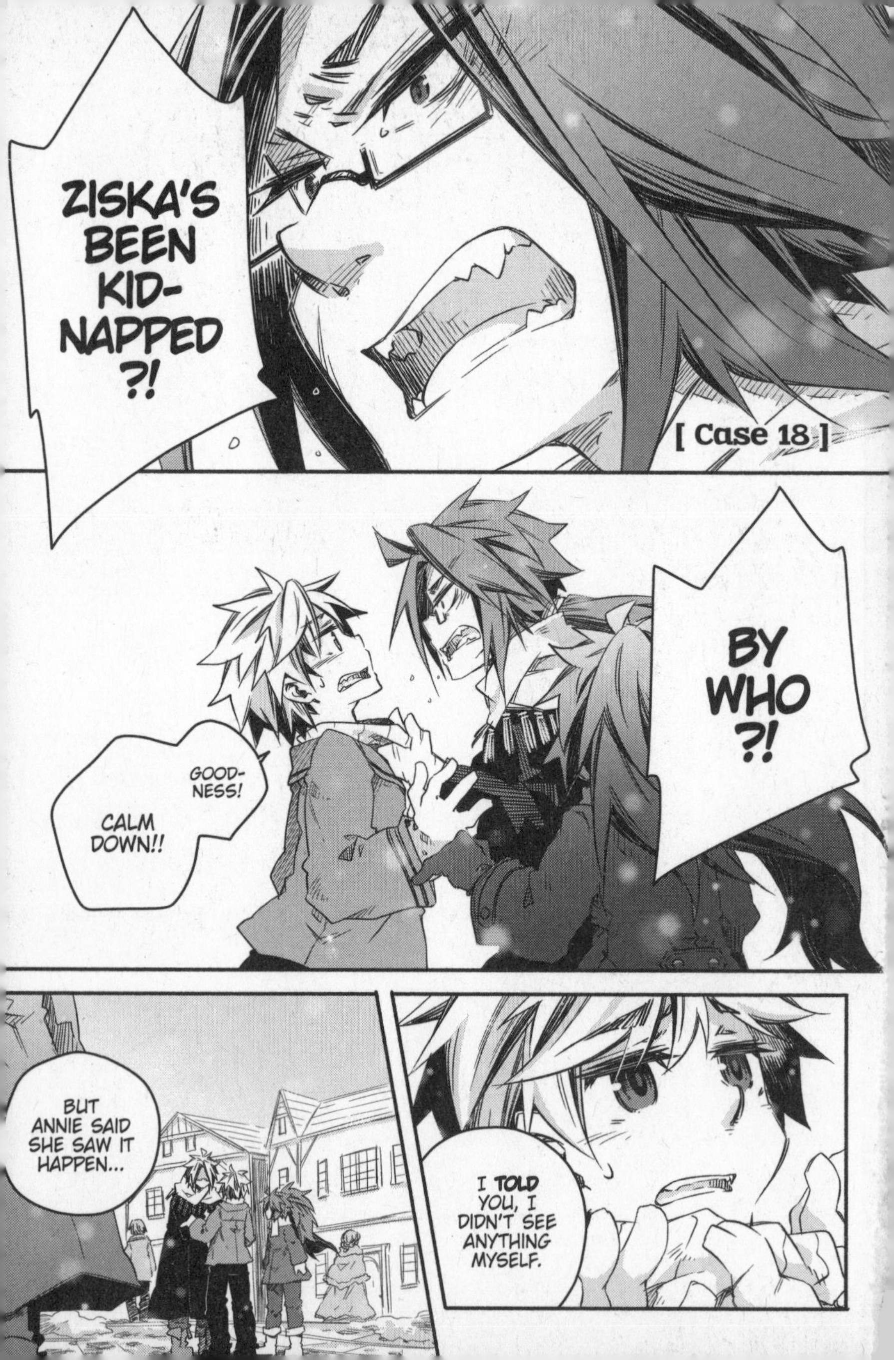
ZISKA'S BEEN KID-NAPPED ?!
[Case 18]
BY WHO ?!
GOOD-NESS!
CALM DOWN!!
I TOLD YOU, I DIDN'T SEE ANYTHING MYSELF.
BUT ANNIE SAID SHE SAW IT HAPPEN...

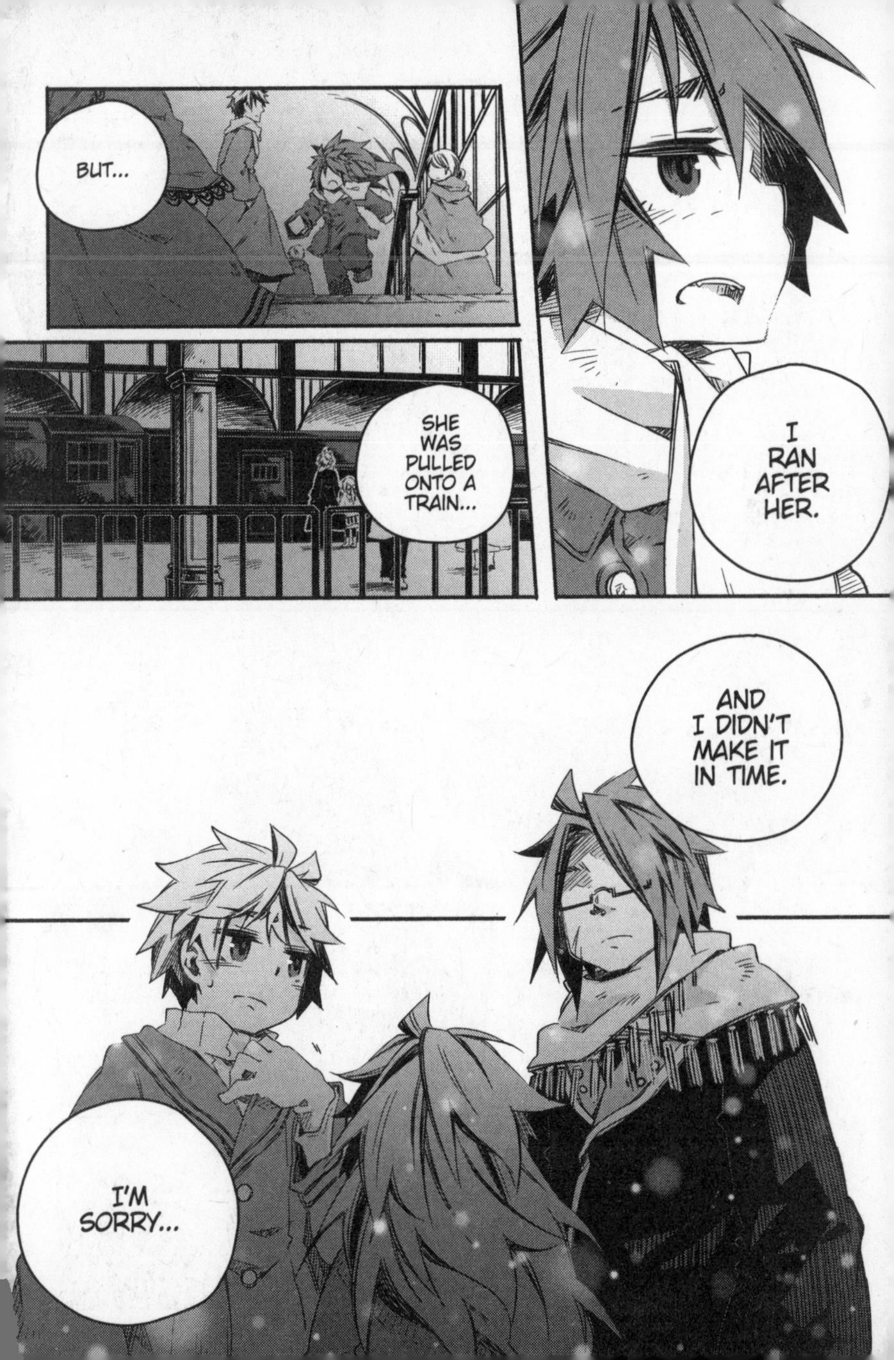
I RAN AFTER HER.
BUT...
SHE WAS PULLED ONTO A TRAIN...
AND I DIDN'T MAKE IT IN TIME.
I'M SORRY...

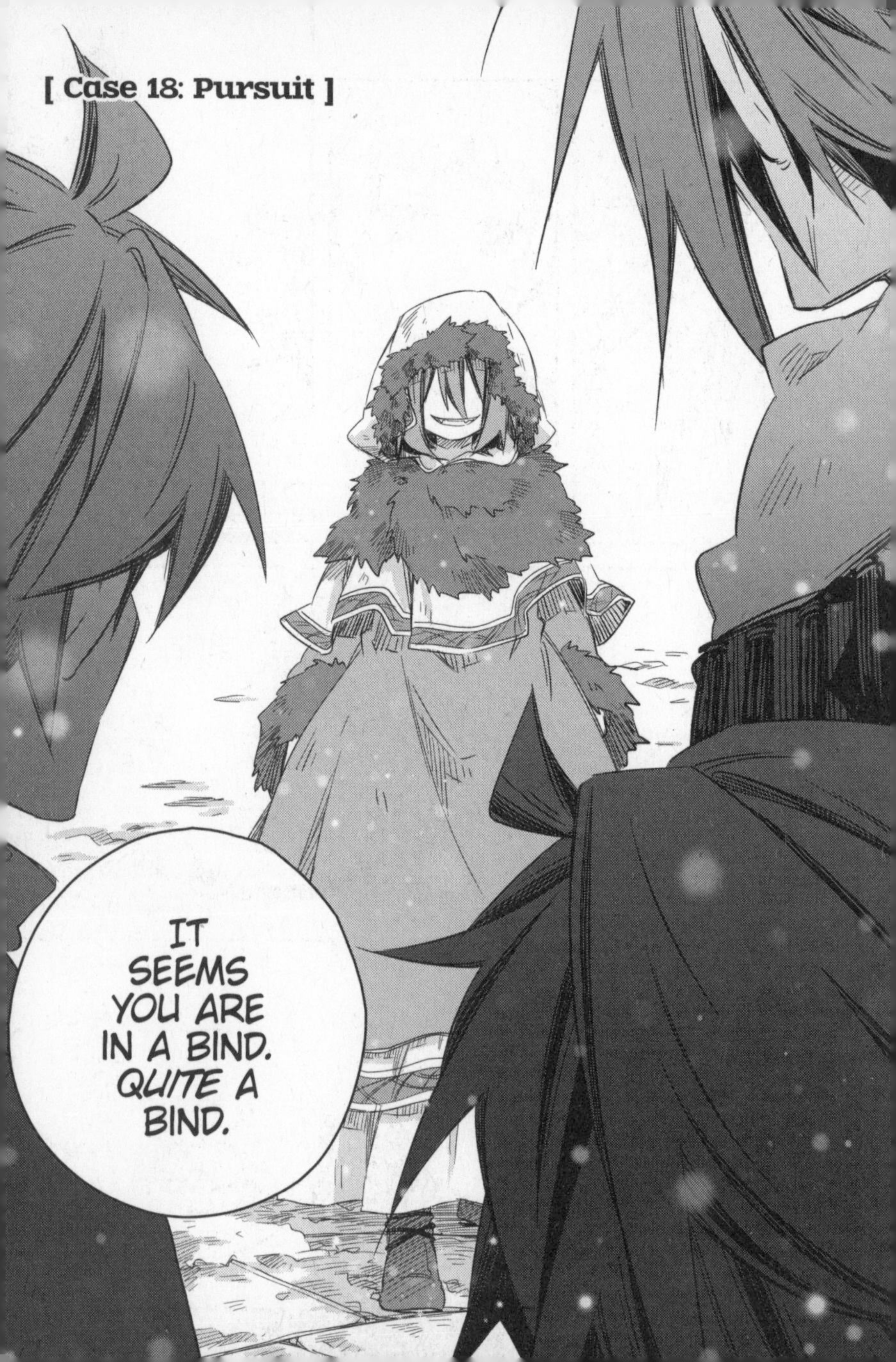
[Case 18: Pursuit]
IT SEEMS YOU ARE IN A BIND. QUITE A BIND.

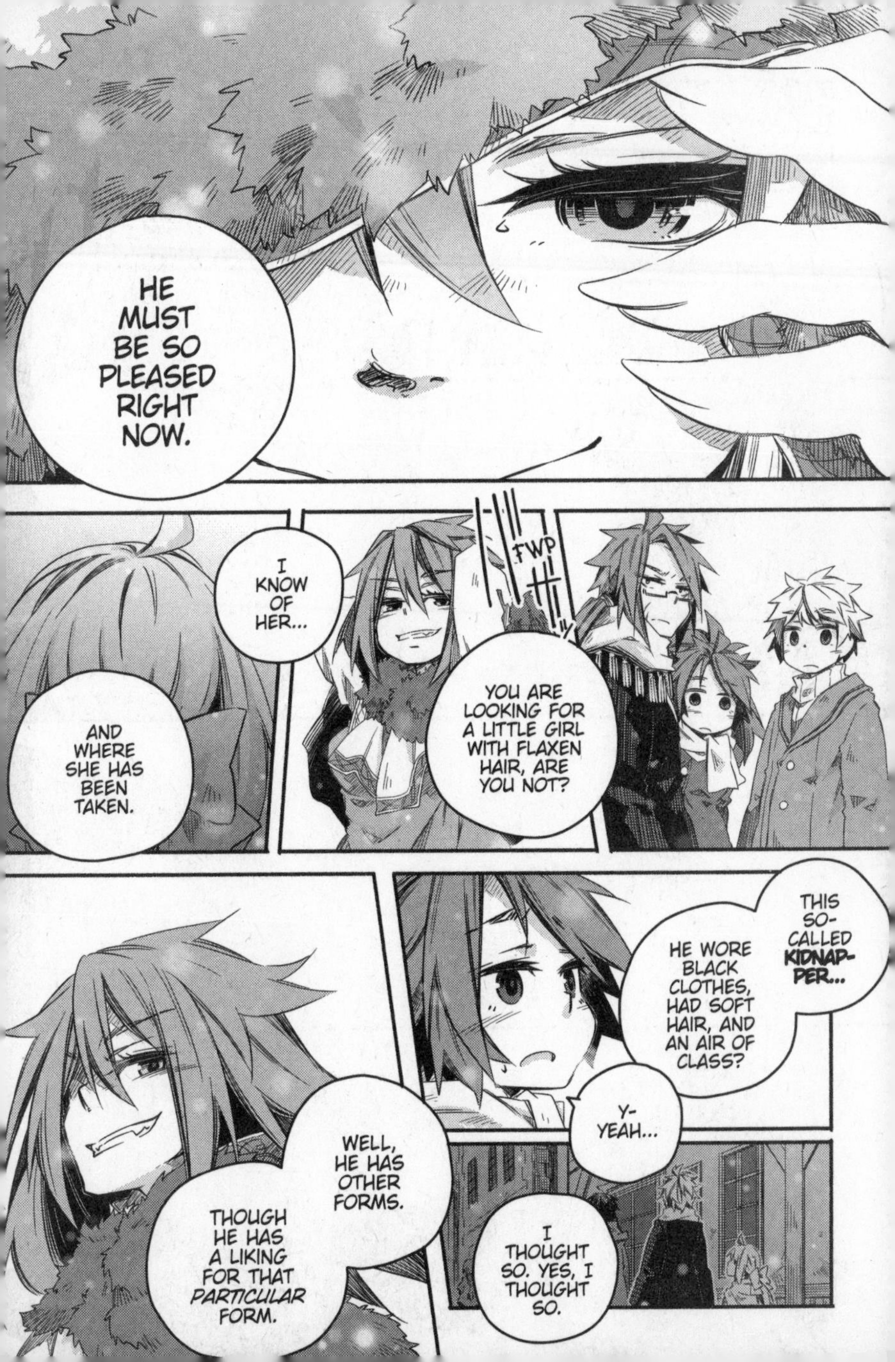
HE MUST BE SO PLEASED RIGHT NOW.
FWP
YOU ARE LOOKING FOR A LITTLE GIRL WITH FLAXEN HAIR, ARE YOU NOT?
I KNOW OF HER...
AND WHERE SHE HAS BEEN TAKEN.
THIS SO-CALLED **KIDNAPPER...**
HE WORE BLACK CLOTHES, HAD SOFT HAIR, AND AN AIR OF CLASS?
Y-YEAH...
I THOUGHT SO. YES, I THOUGHT SO.
WELL, HE HAS OTHER FORMS.
THOUGH HE HAS A LIKING FOR THAT *PARTICULAR* FORM.

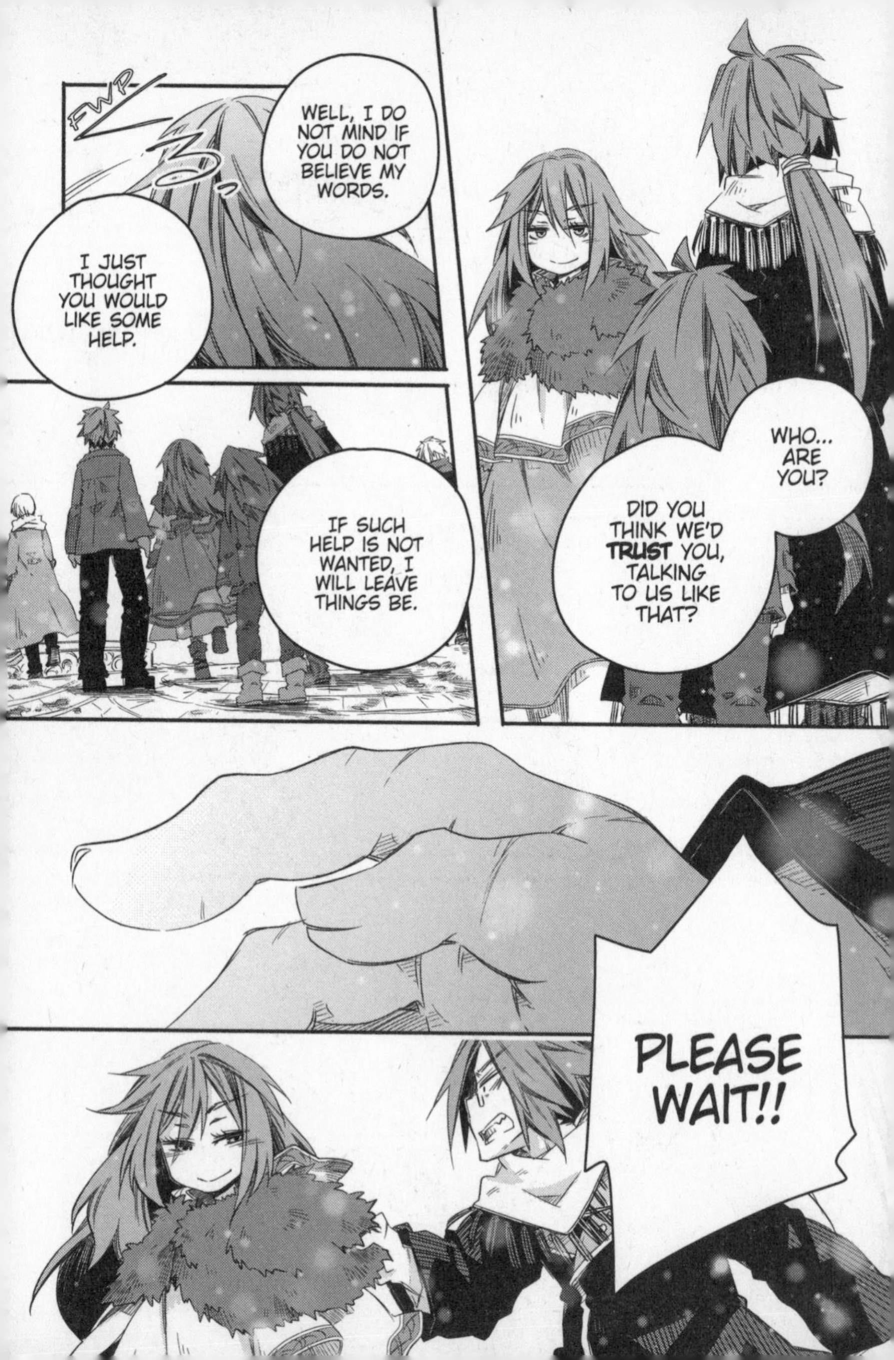
WHO... ARE YOU?
DID YOU THINK WE'D **TRUST** YOU, TALKING TO US LIKE THAT?
FWP
WELL, I DO NOT MIND IF YOU DO NOT BELIEVE MY WORDS.
I JUST THOUGHT YOU WOULD LIKE SOME HELP.
IF SUCH HELP IS NOT WANTED, I WILL LEAVE THINGS BE.
PLEASE WAIT!!

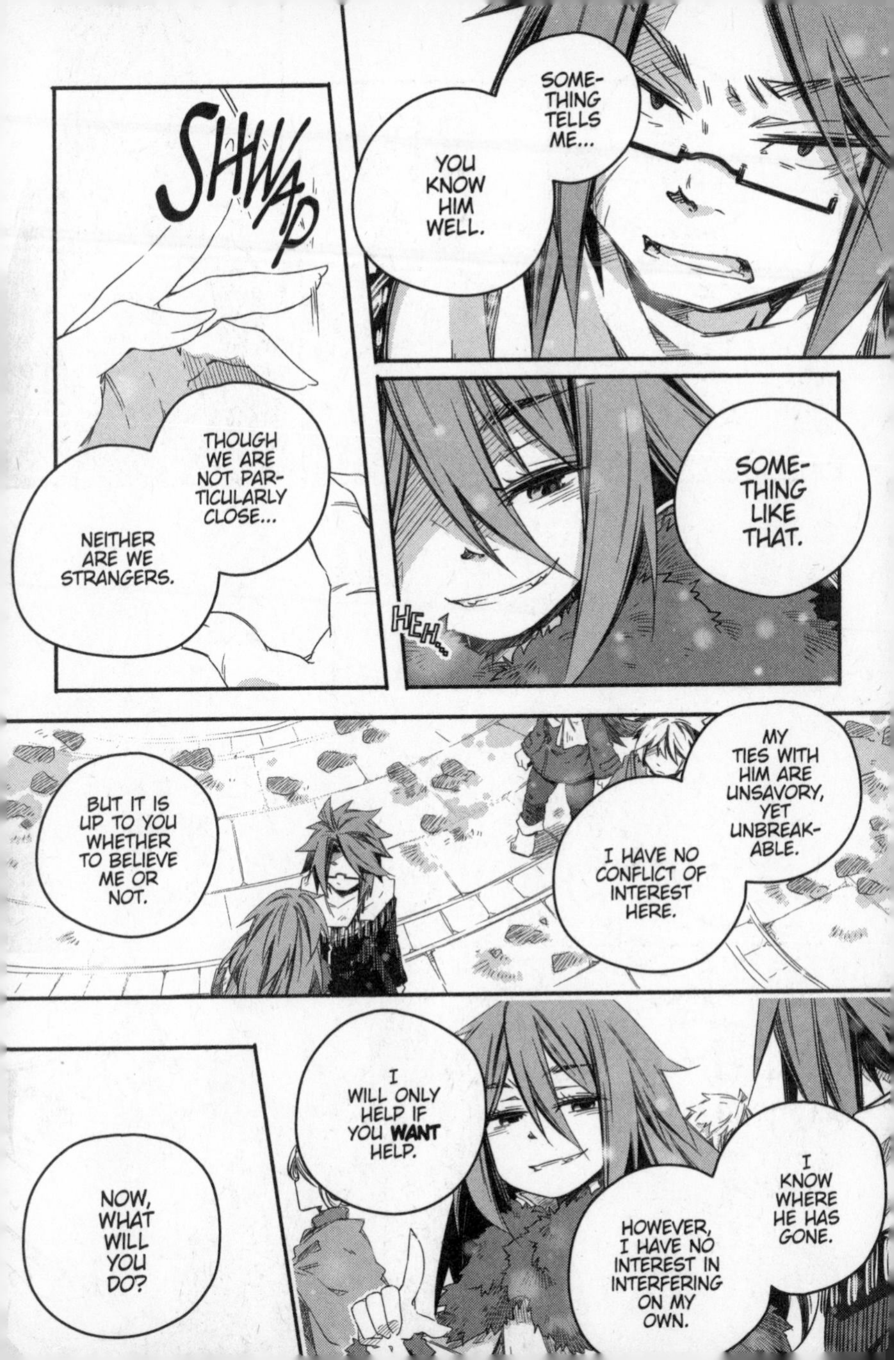

SOME-THING TELLS ME...
YOU KNOW HIM WELL.
SOME-THING LIKE THAT.
HEH...
SHWAP
THOUGH WE ARE NOT PAR-TICULARLY CLOSE...
NEITHER ARE WE STRANGERS.
MY TIES WITH HIM ARE UNSAVORY, YET UNBREAK-ABLE.
I HAVE NO CONFLICT OF INTEREST HERE.
BUT IT IS UP TO YOU WHETHER TO BELIEVE ME OR NOT.
I KNOW WHERE HE HAS GONE.
HOWEVER, I HAVE NO INTEREST IN INTERFERING ON MY OWN.
I WILL ONLY HELP IF YOU **WANT** HELP.
NOW, WHAT WILL YOU DO?

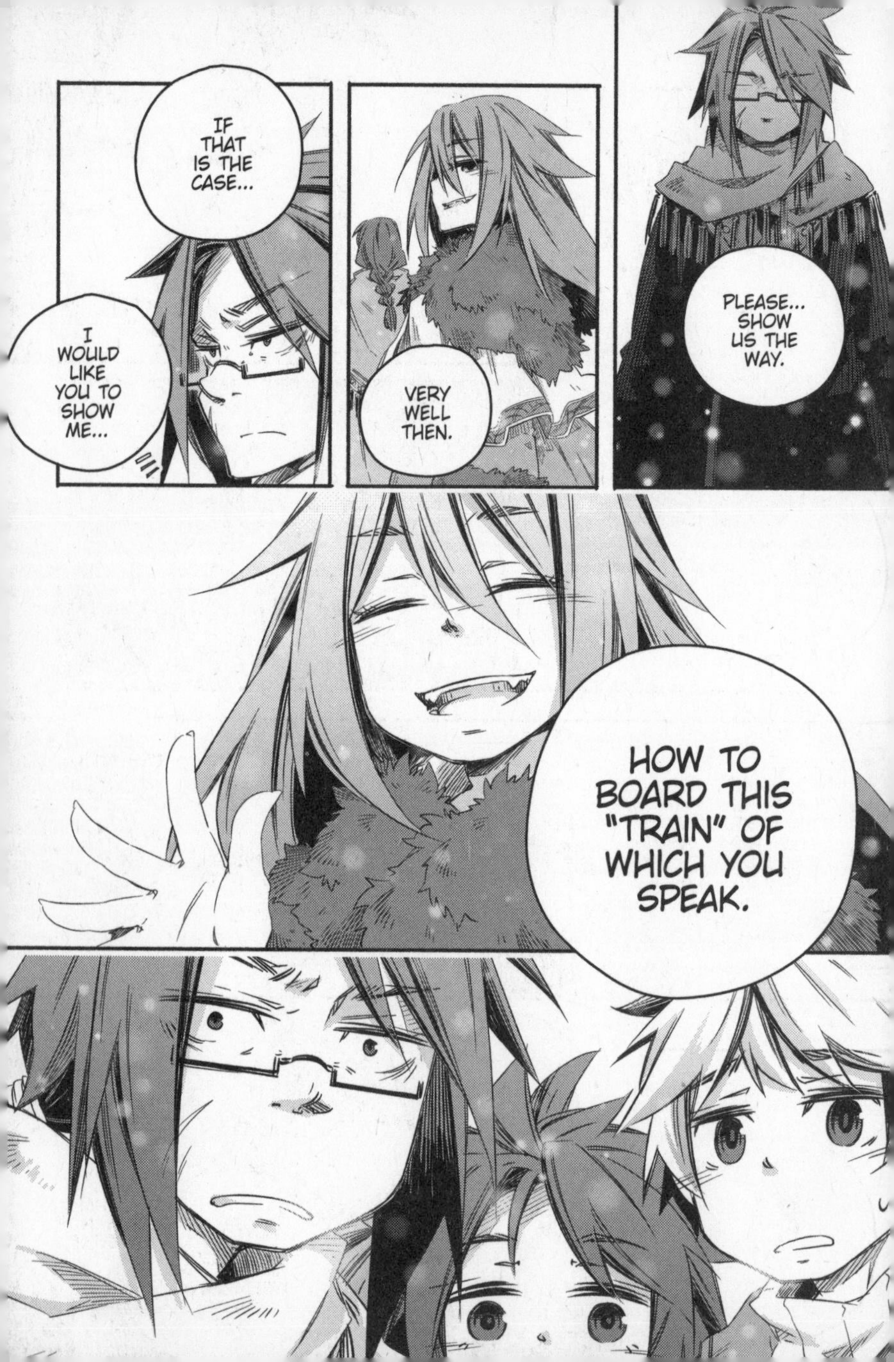
PLEASE... SHOW US THE WAY.
VERY WELL THEN.
IF THAT IS THE CASE...
I WOULD LIKE YOU TO SHOW ME...
HOW TO BOARD THIS "TRAIN" OF WHICH YOU SPEAK.

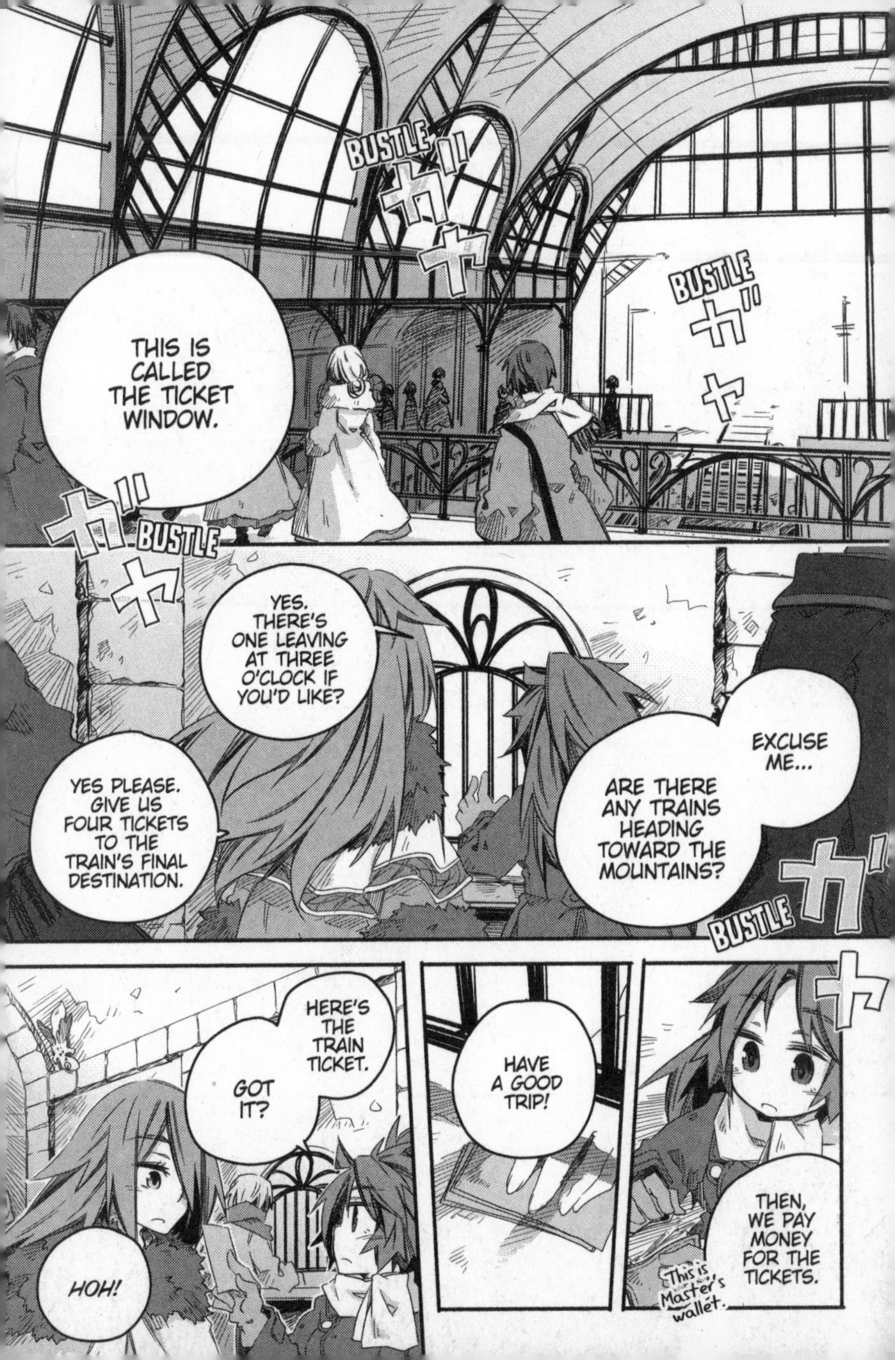

BUSTLE ガヤ
BUSTLE ガヤ
THIS IS CALLED THE TICKET WINDOW.
ガヤ BUSTLE
EXCUSE ME...
ARE THERE ANY TRAINS HEADING TOWARD THE MOUNTAINS?
BUSTLE ガ
YES. THERE'S ONE LEAVING AT THREE O'CLOCK IF YOU'D LIKE?
YES PLEASE. GIVE US FOUR TICKETS TO THE TRAIN'S FINAL DESTINATION.
ガ
THEN, WE PAY MONEY FOR THE TICKETS.
This is Master's wallet.
HAVE A GOOD TRIP!
HERE'S THE TRAIN TICKET.
GOT IT?
HOH!

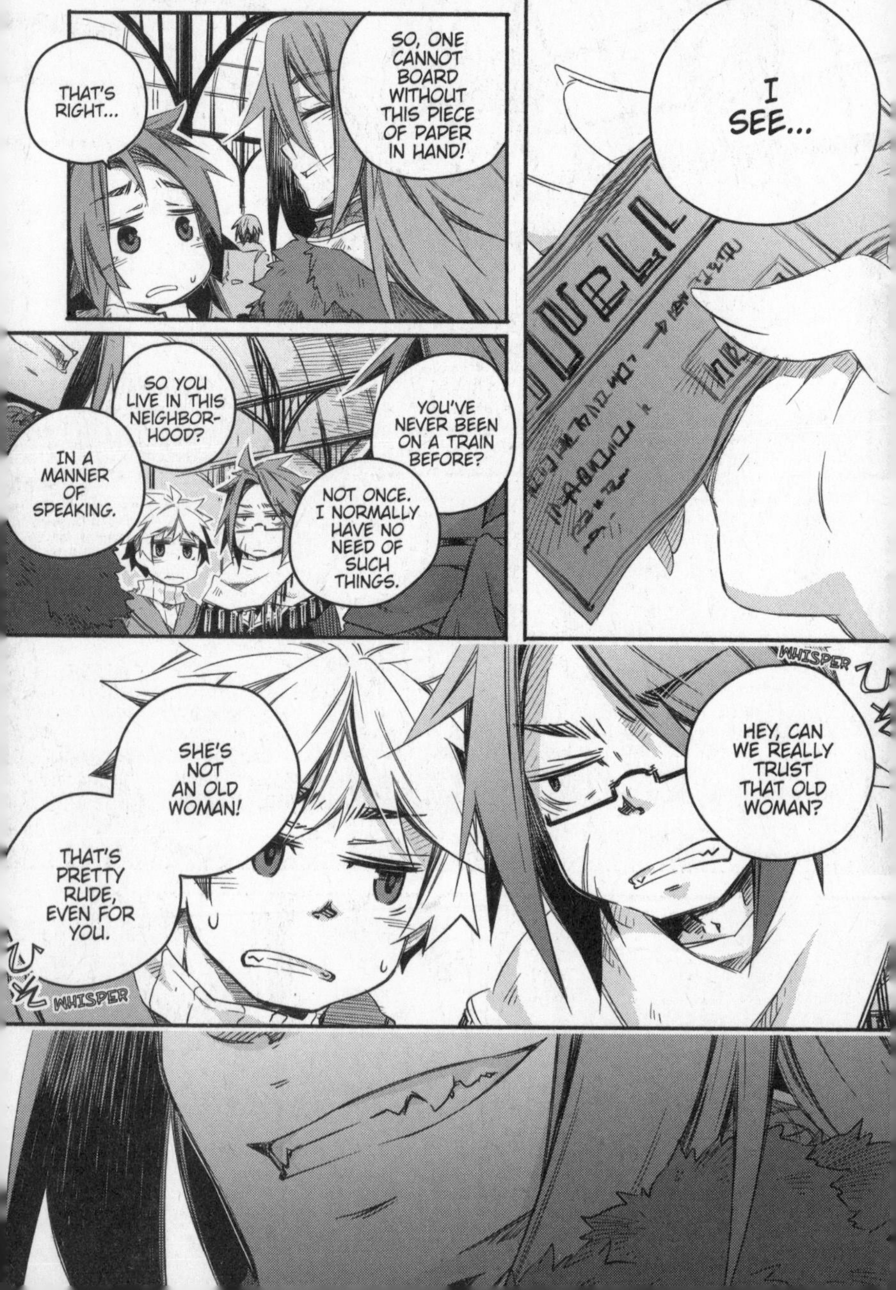
I SEE...
SO, ONE CANNOT BOARD WITHOUT THIS PIECE OF PAPER IN HAND!
THAT'S RIGHT...
YOU'VE NEVER BEEN ON A TRAIN BEFORE?
NOT ONCE. I NORMALLY HAVE NO NEED OF SUCH THINGS.
SO YOU LIVE IN THIS NEIGHBOR-HOOD?
IN A MANNER OF SPEAKING.
WHISPER
HEY, CAN WE REALLY TRUST THAT OLD WOMAN?
SHE'S NOT AN OLD WOMAN!
THAT'S PRETTY RUDE, EVEN FOR YOU.
WHISPER

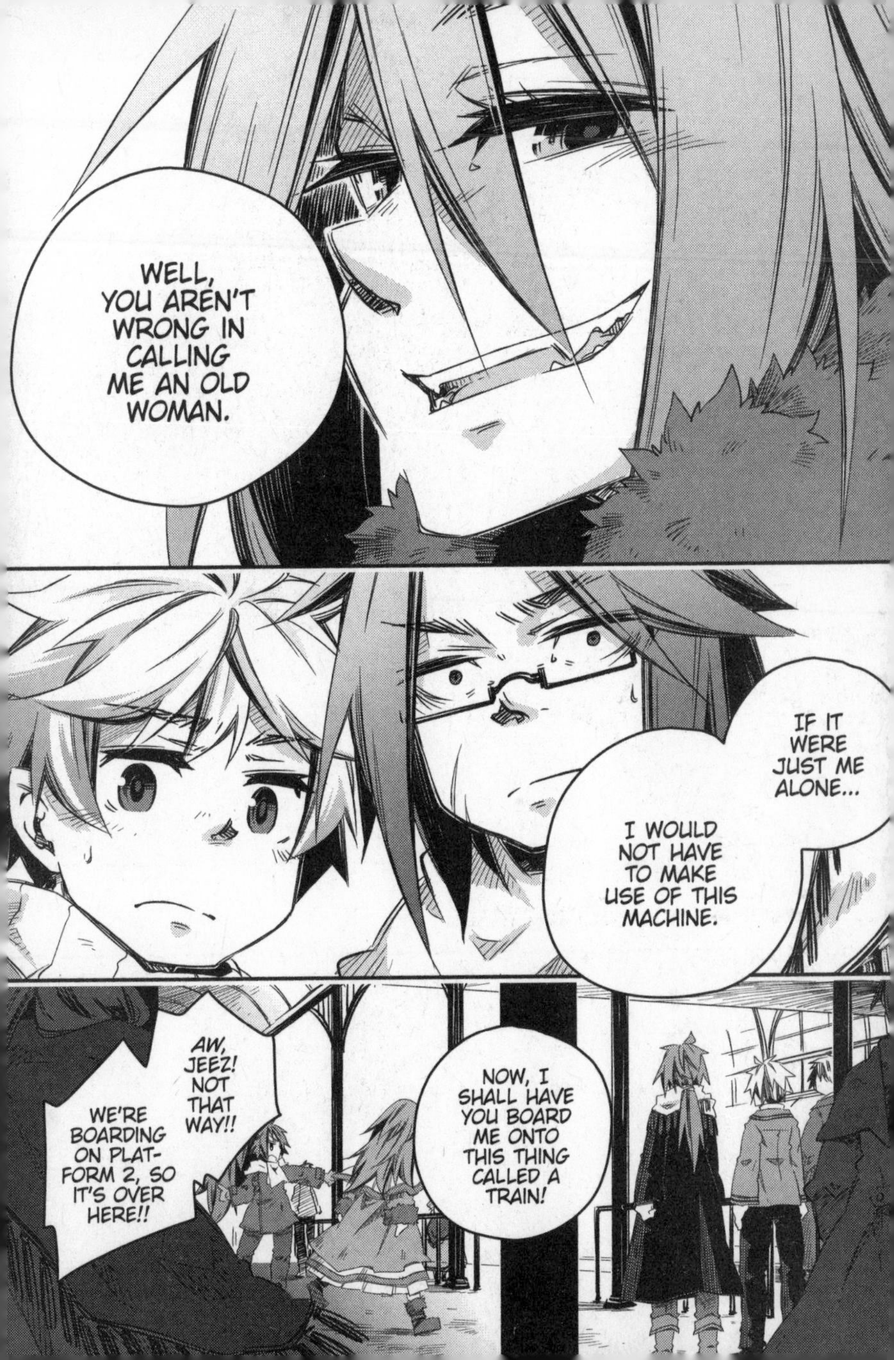
WELL, YOU AREN'T WRONG IN CALLING ME AN OLD WOMAN.
IF IT WERE JUST ME ALONE...
I WOULD NOT HAVE TO MAKE USE OF THIS MACHINE.
NOW, I SHALL HAVE YOU BOARD ME ONTO THIS THING CALLED A TRAIN!
AW, JEEZ! NOT THAT WAY!!
WE'RE BOARDING ON PLAT-FORM 2, SO IT'S OVER HERE!!

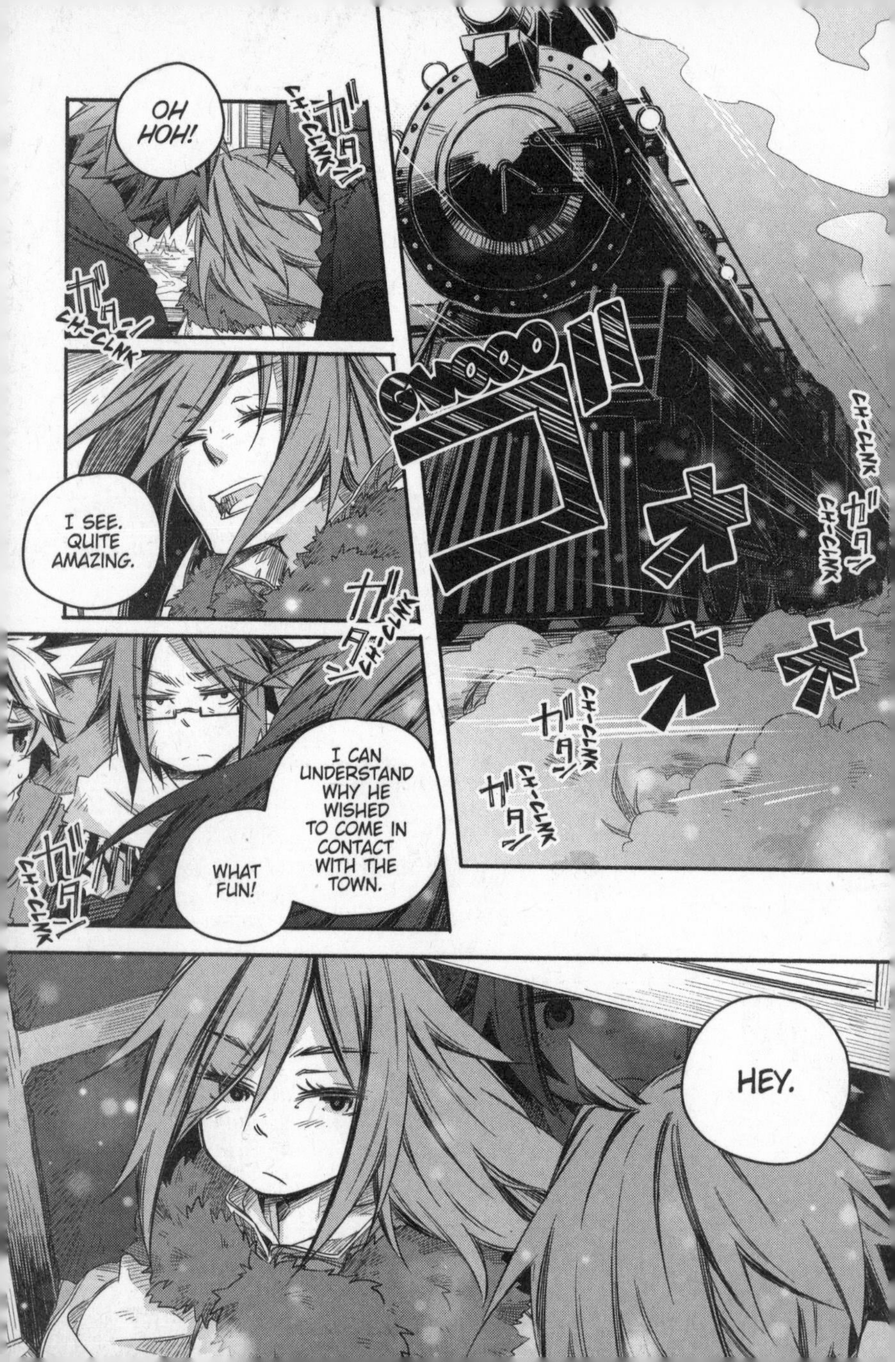
CH-CLNK
GWOOO
CH-CLNK
CH-CLNK
CH-CLNK
OH HOH!
CH-CLNK
I SEE. QUITE AMAZING.
CH-CLNK
I CAN UNDERSTAND WHY HE WISHED TO COME IN CONTACT WITH THE TOWN.
WHAT FUN!
CH-CLNK
HEY.

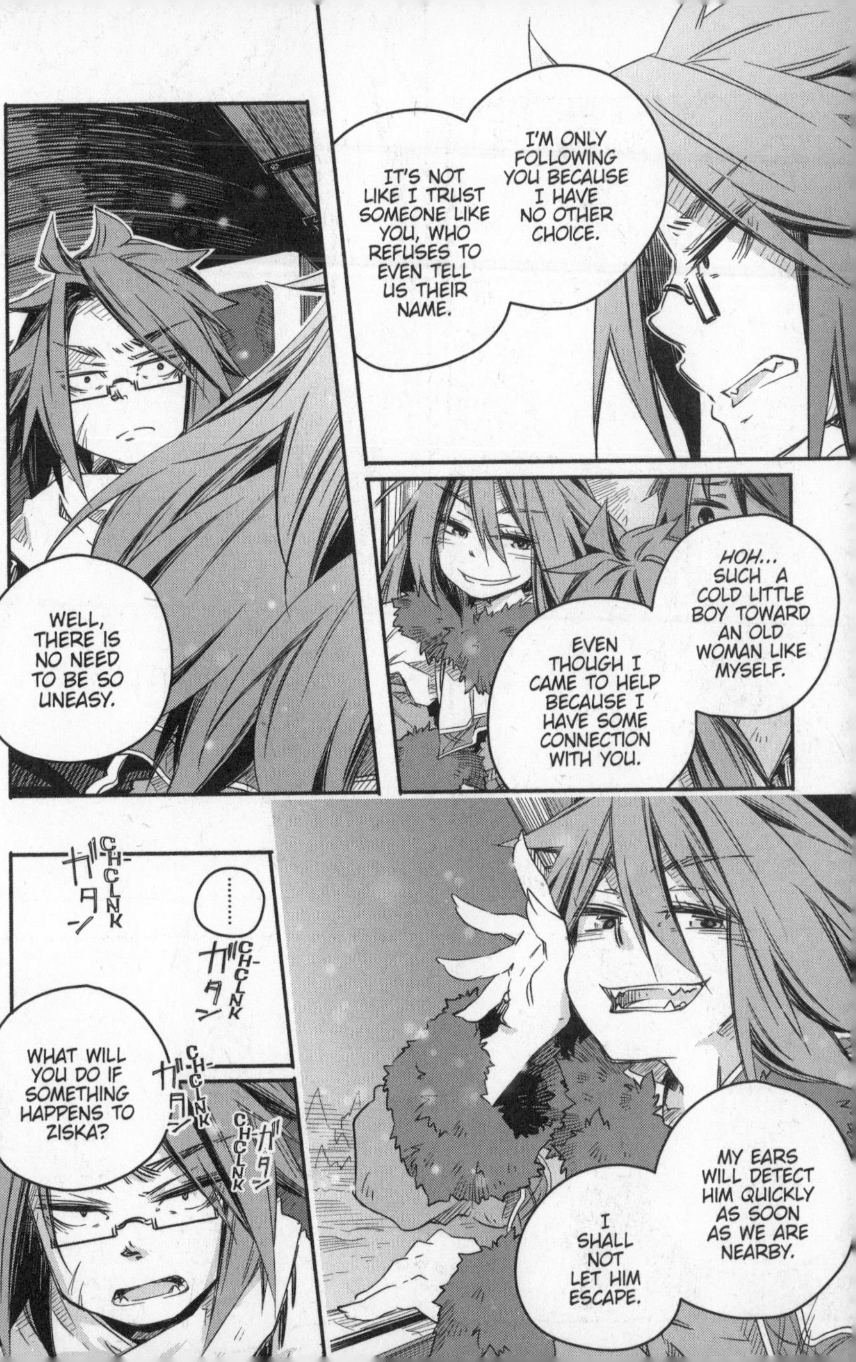
IT'S NOT LIKE I TRUST SOMEONE LIKE YOU, WHO REFUSES TO EVEN TELL US THEIR NAME.
I'M ONLY FOLLOWING YOU BECAUSE I HAVE NO OTHER CHOICE.
HOH... SUCH A COLD LITTLE BOY TOWARD AN OLD WOMAN LIKE MYSELF.
EVEN THOUGH I CAME TO HELP BECAUSE I HAVE SOME CONNECTION WITH YOU.
WELL, THERE IS NO NEED TO BE SO UNEASY.
MY EARS WILL DETECT HIM QUICKLY AS SOON AS WE ARE NEARBY.
I SHALL NOT LET HIM ESCAPE.
CH-CHCLNK
......
CH-CHCLNK
WHAT WILL YOU DO IF SOMETHING HAPPENS TO ZISKA?
CH-CHCLNK
CH-CHCLNK

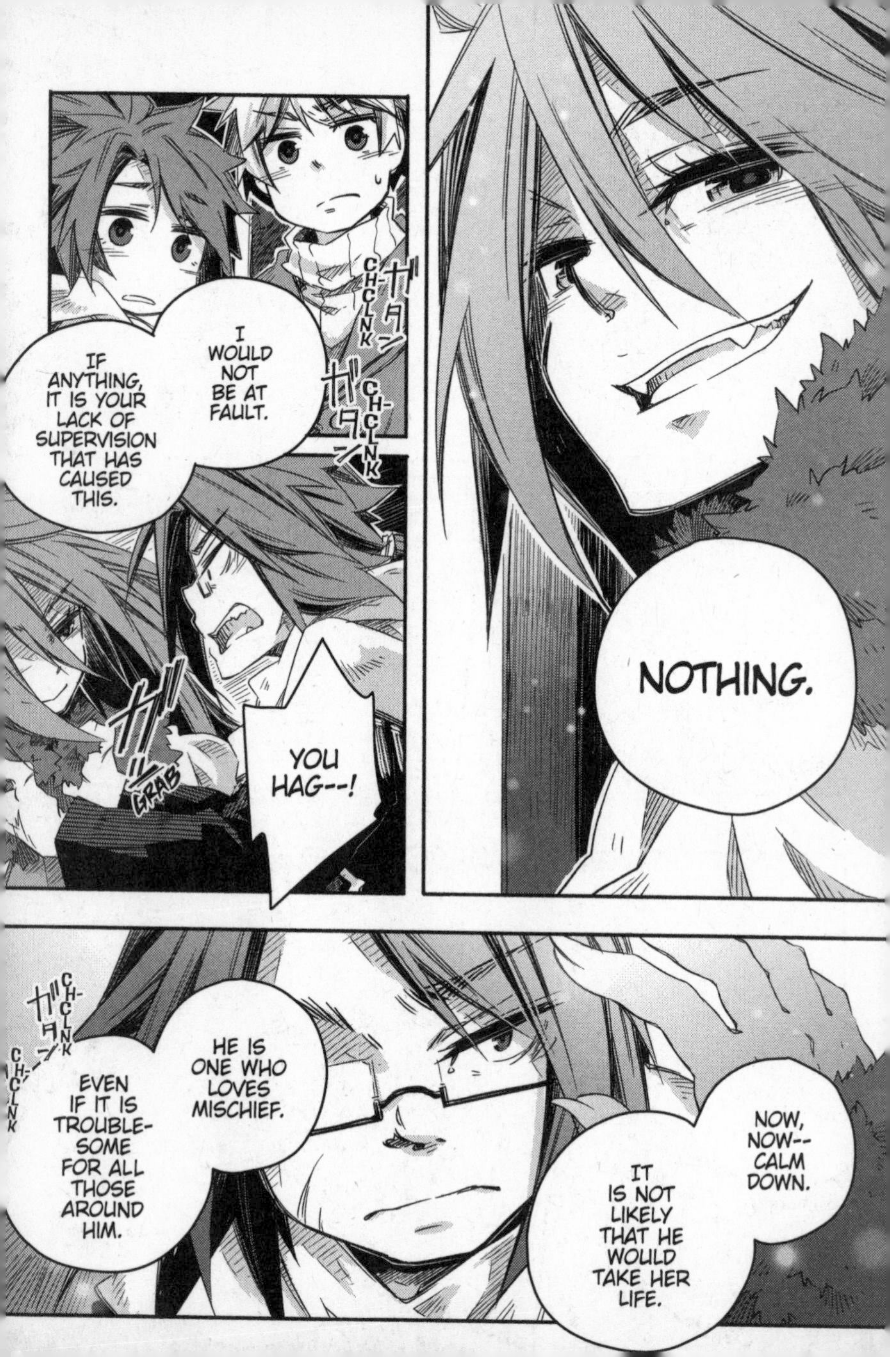
NOTHING.
I WOULD NOT BE AT FAULT.
IF ANYTHING, IT IS YOUR LACK OF SUPERVISION THAT HAS CAUSED THIS.
CH-CLNK
CH-CLNK
YOU HAG--!
GRAB
NOW, NOW-- CALM DOWN.
IT IS NOT LIKELY THAT HE WOULD TAKE HER LIFE.
HE IS ONE WHO LOVES MISCHIEF.
EVEN IF IT IS TROUBLE-SOME FOR ALL THOSE AROUND HIM.
CH-CLNK
CH-CLNK

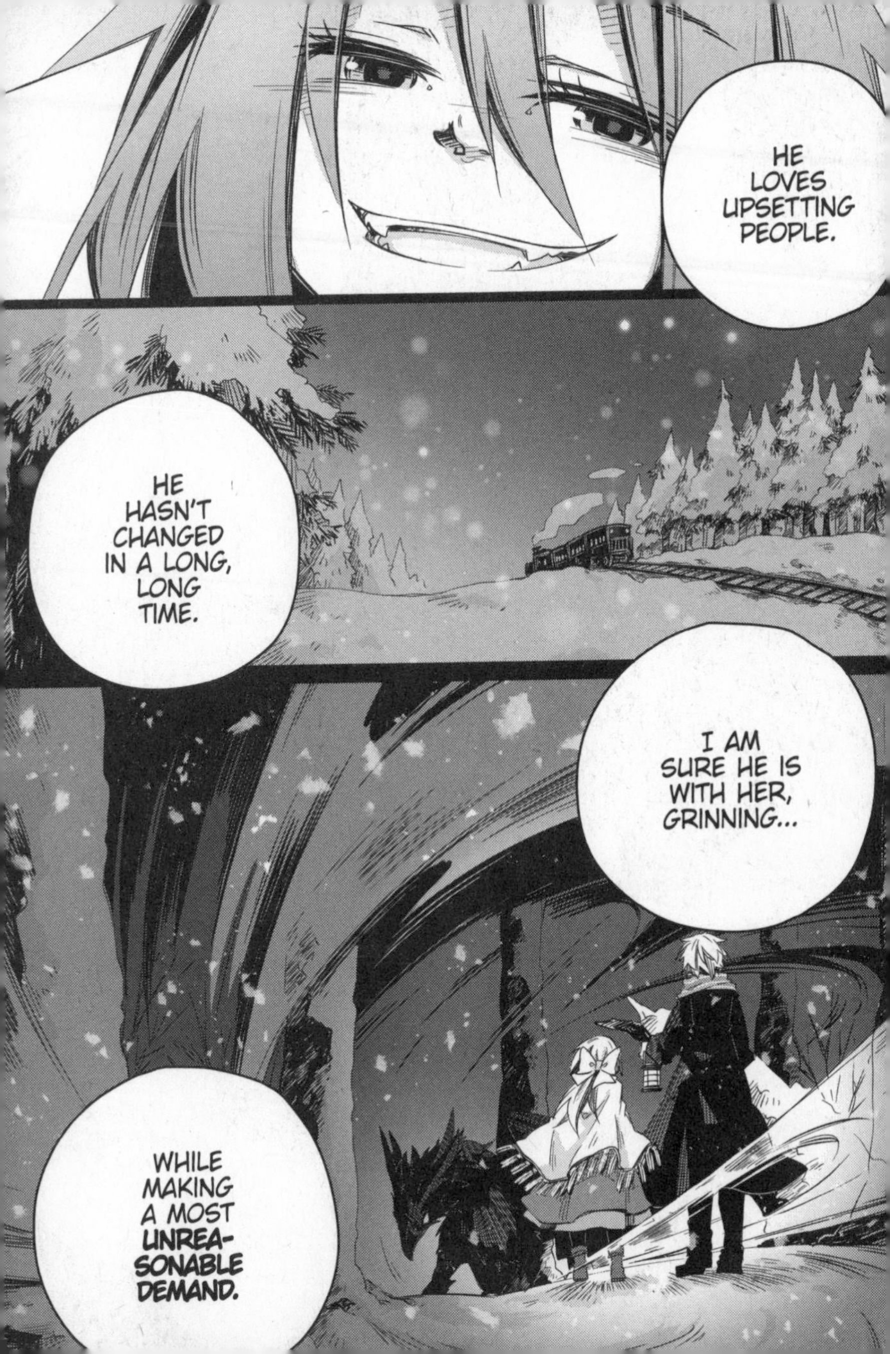
HE LOVES UPSETTING PEOPLE.
HE HASN'T CHANGED IN A LONG, LONG TIME.
I AM SURE HE IS WITH HER, GRINNING...
WHILE MAKING A MOST UNREA-SONABLE DEMAND.

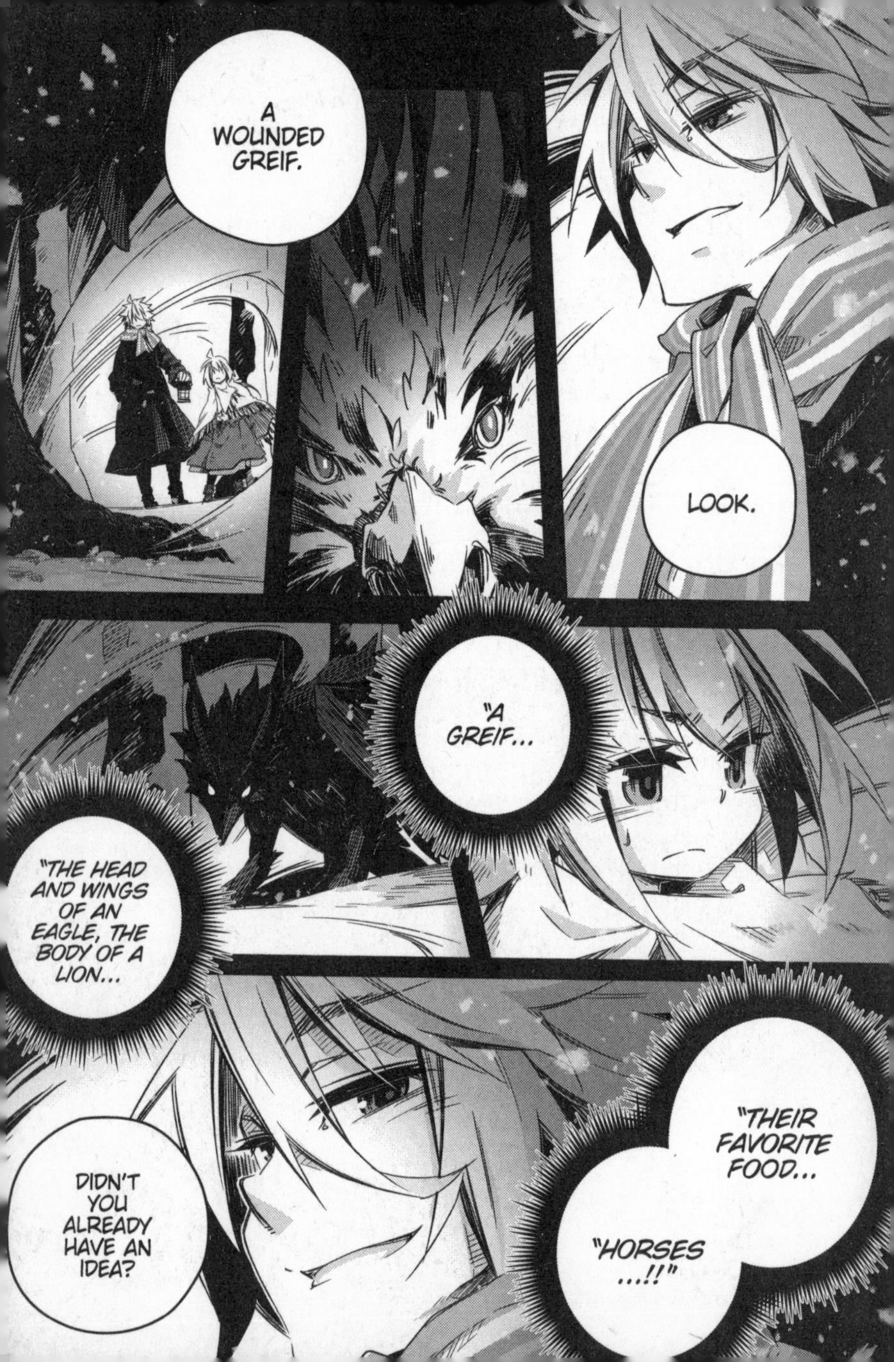
LOOK.
A WOUNDED GREIF.
"A GREIF...
"THE HEAD AND WINGS OF AN EAGLE, THE BODY OF A LION...
"THEIR FAVORITE FOOD...
"HORSES ...!!"
DIDN'T YOU ALREADY HAVE AN IDEA?

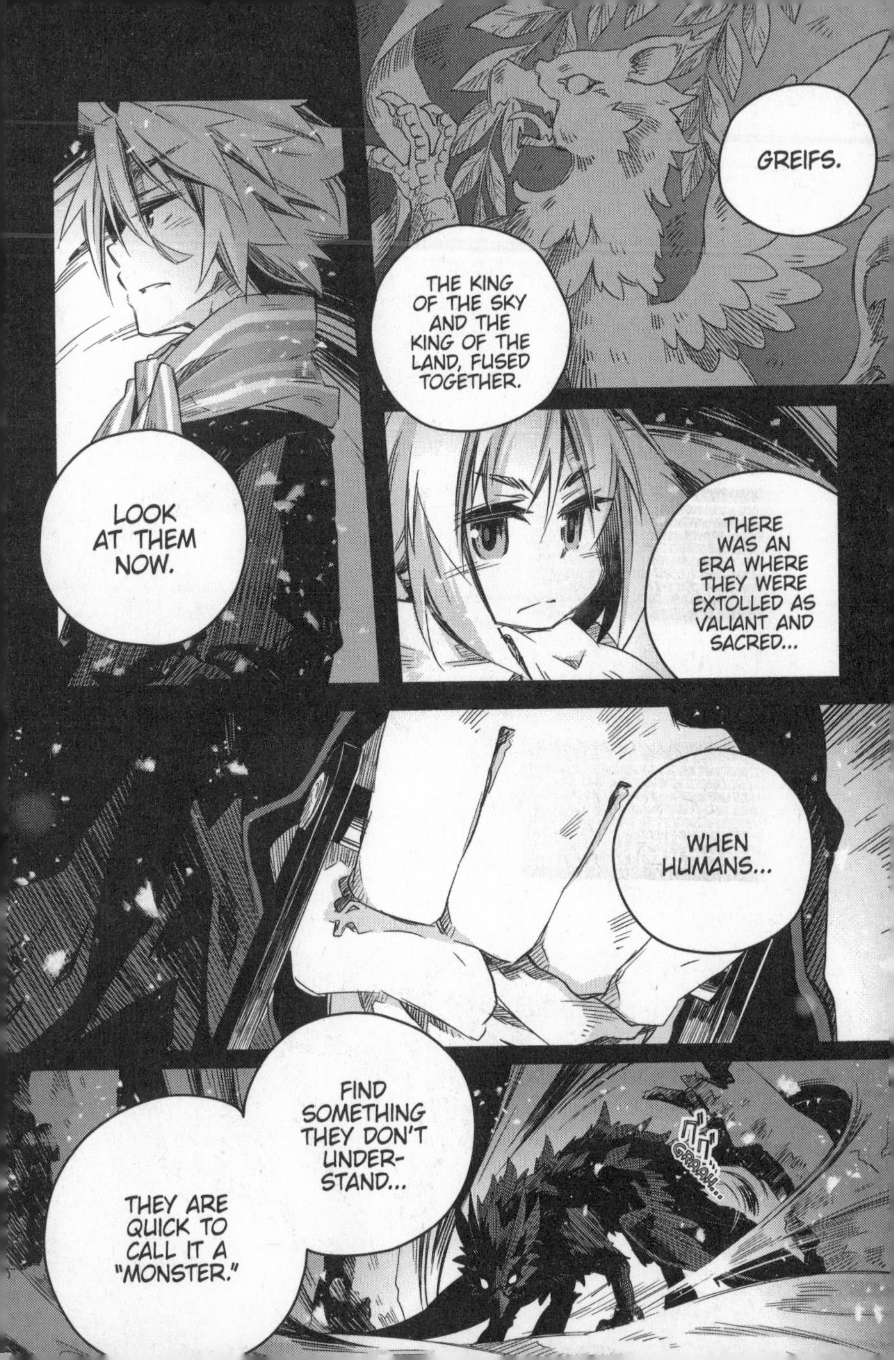
GREIFS.
THE KING OF THE SKY AND THE KING OF THE LAND, FUSED TOGETHER.
THERE WAS AN ERA WHERE THEY WERE EXTOLLED AS VALIANT AND SACRED...
LOOK AT THEM NOW.
WHEN HUMANS...
FIND SOMETHING THEY DON'T UNDER-STAND...
THEY ARE QUICK TO CALL IT A "MONSTER."
GRAAH...

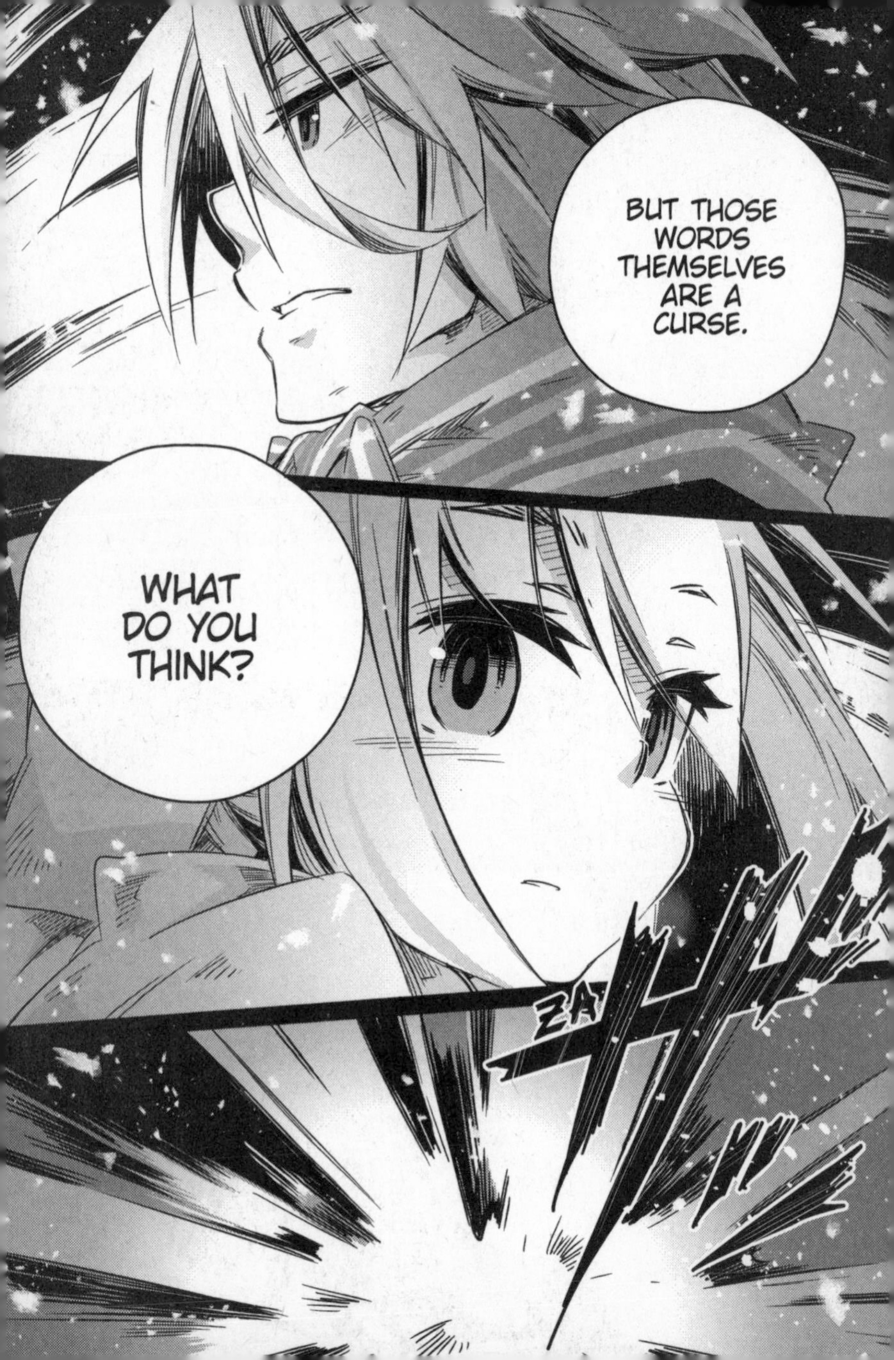
BUT THOSE WORDS THEMSELVES ARE A CURSE.
WHAT DO YOU THINK?
ZA

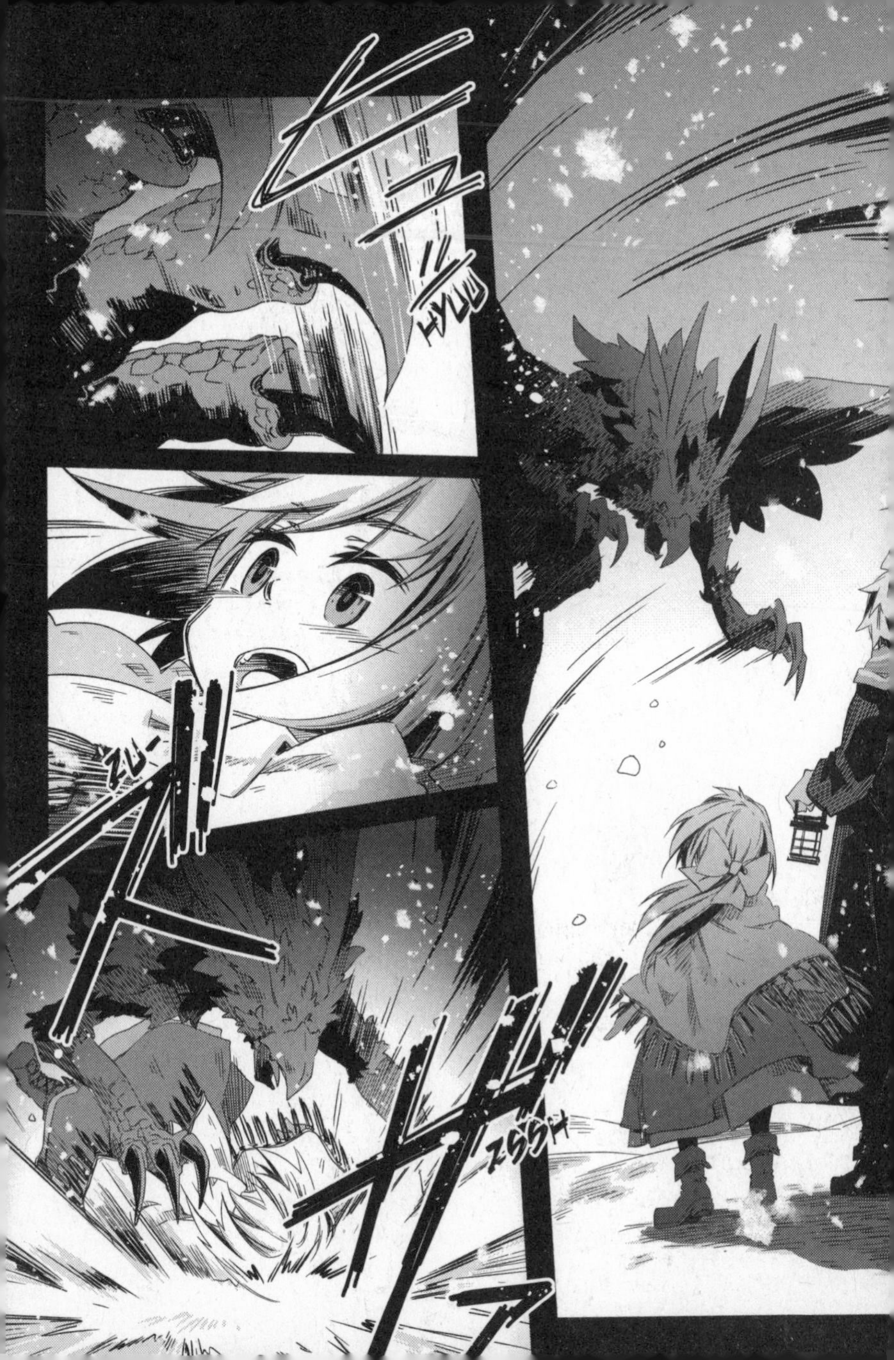
HYUU
ZU-
ZSSH

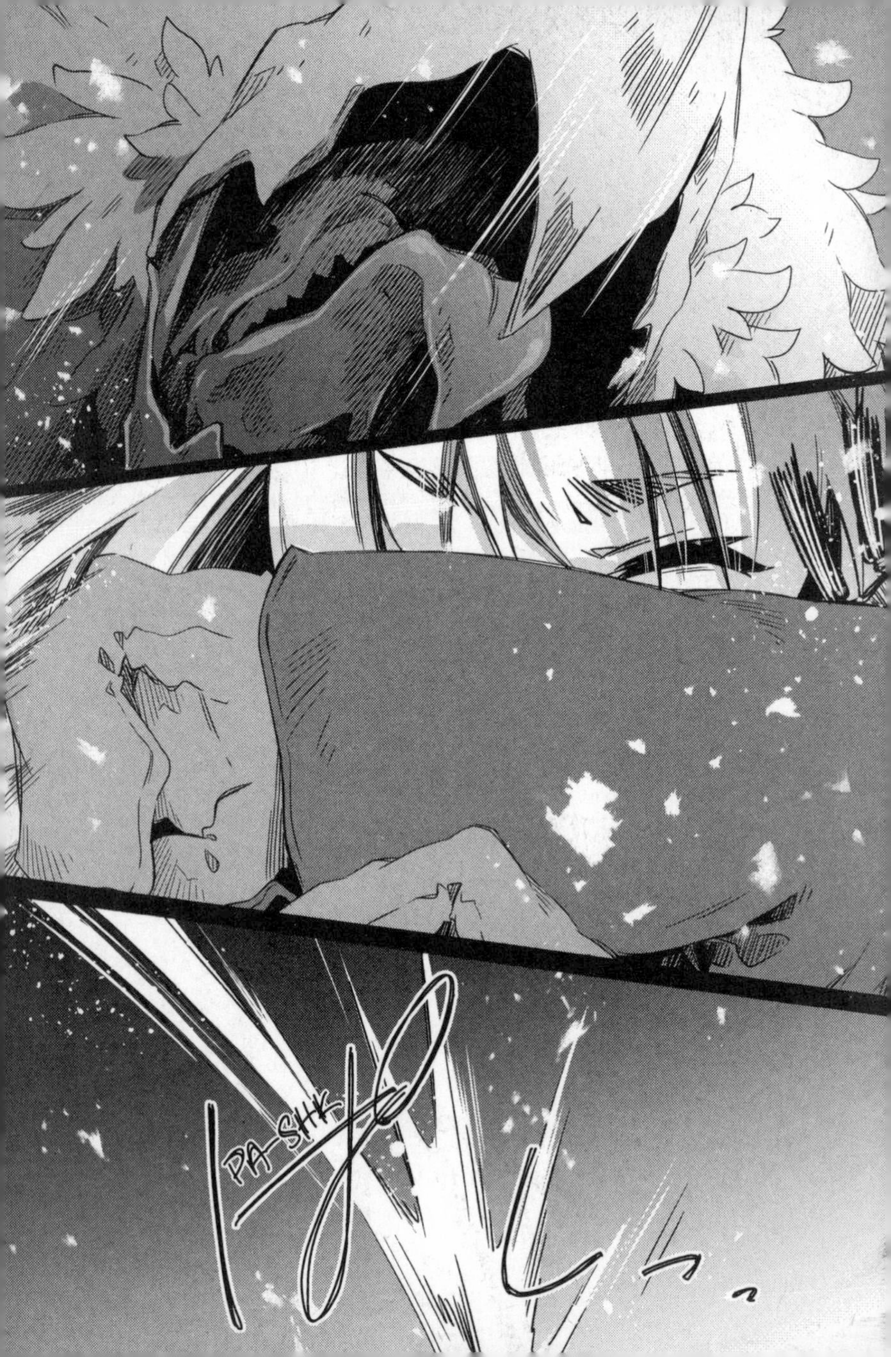
PA-SHK

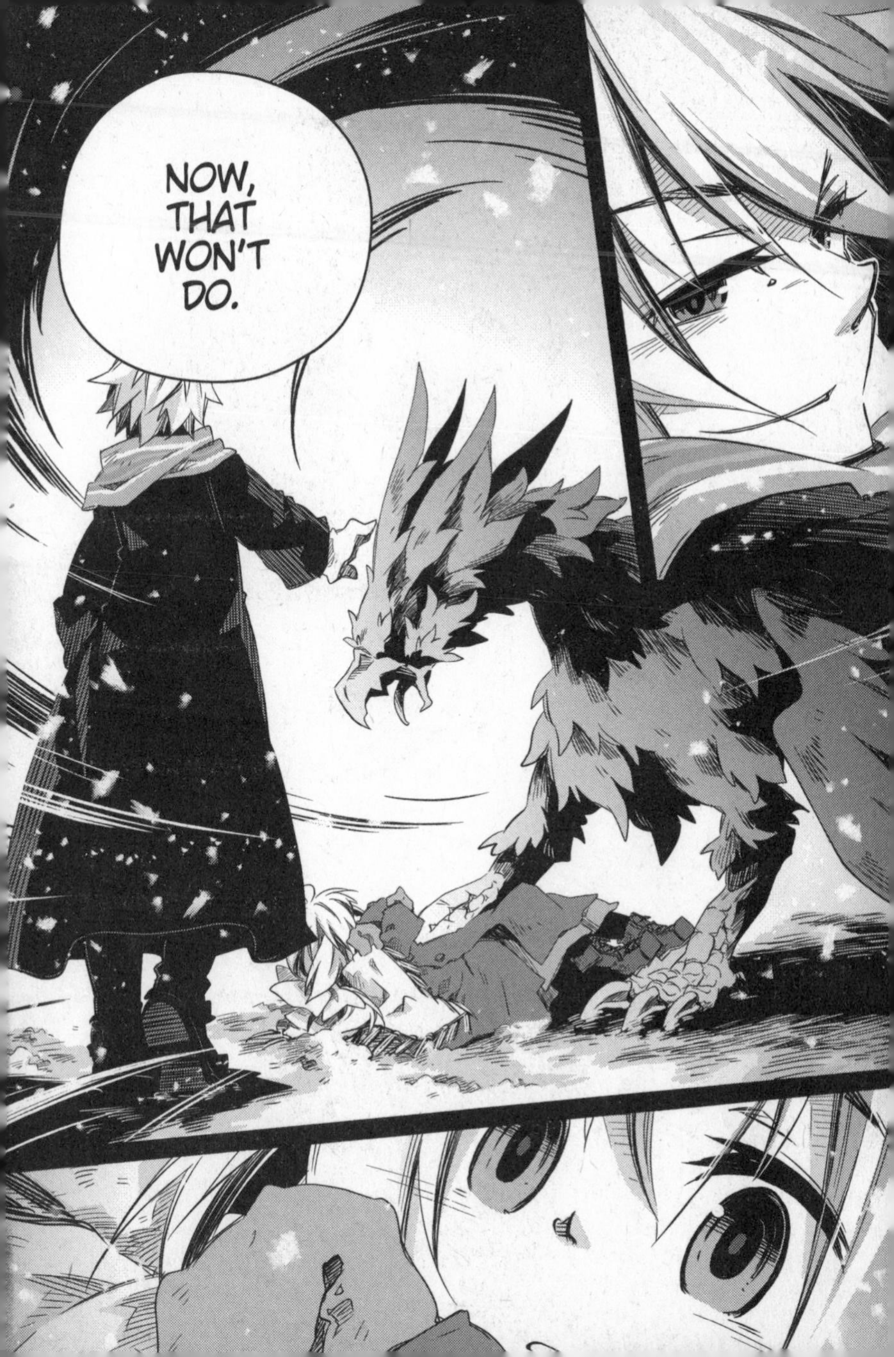
NOW, THAT WON'T DO.

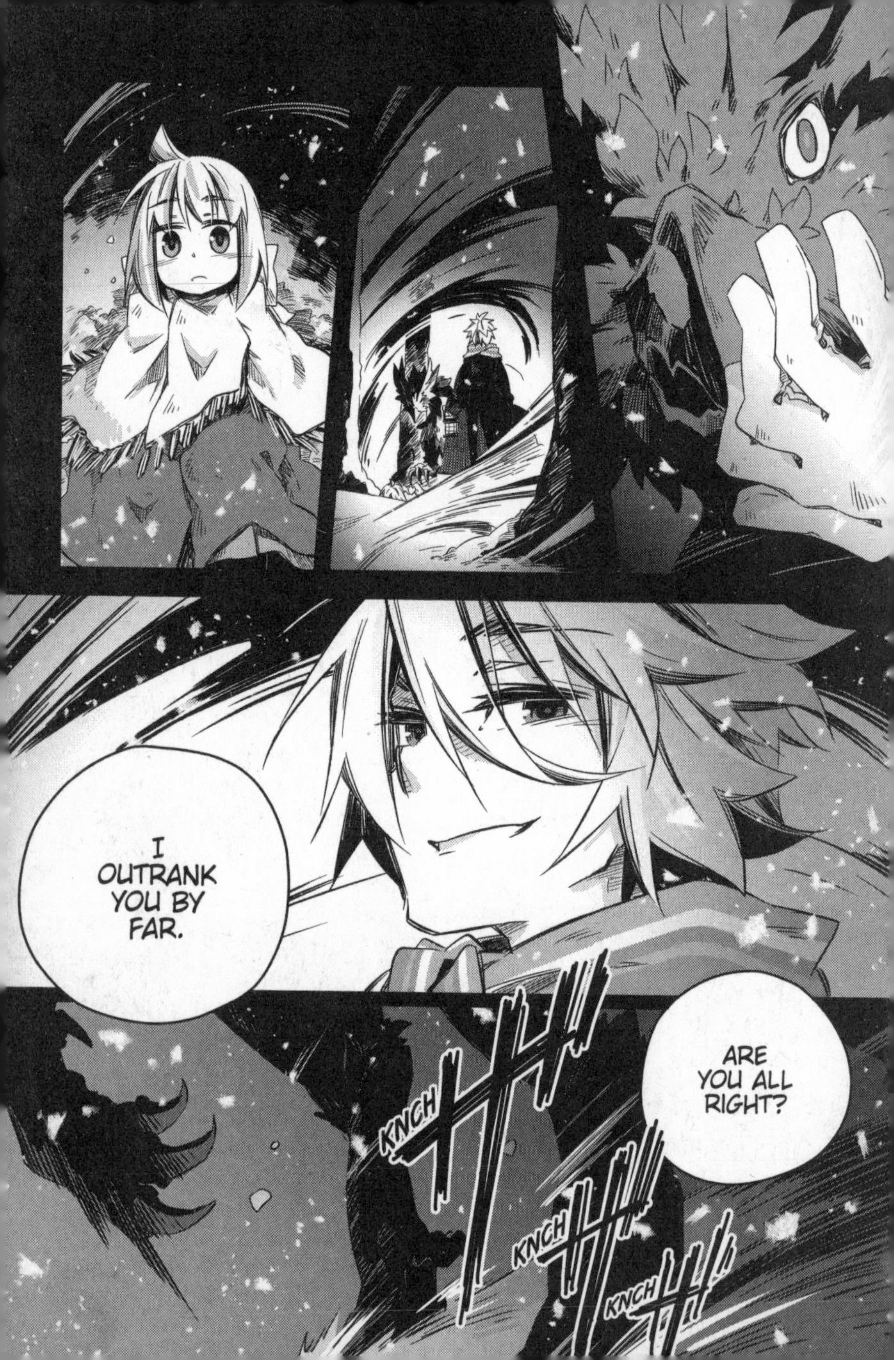
I OUTRANK YOU BY FAR.
ARE YOU ALL RIGHT?
KNCH
KNCH
KNCH

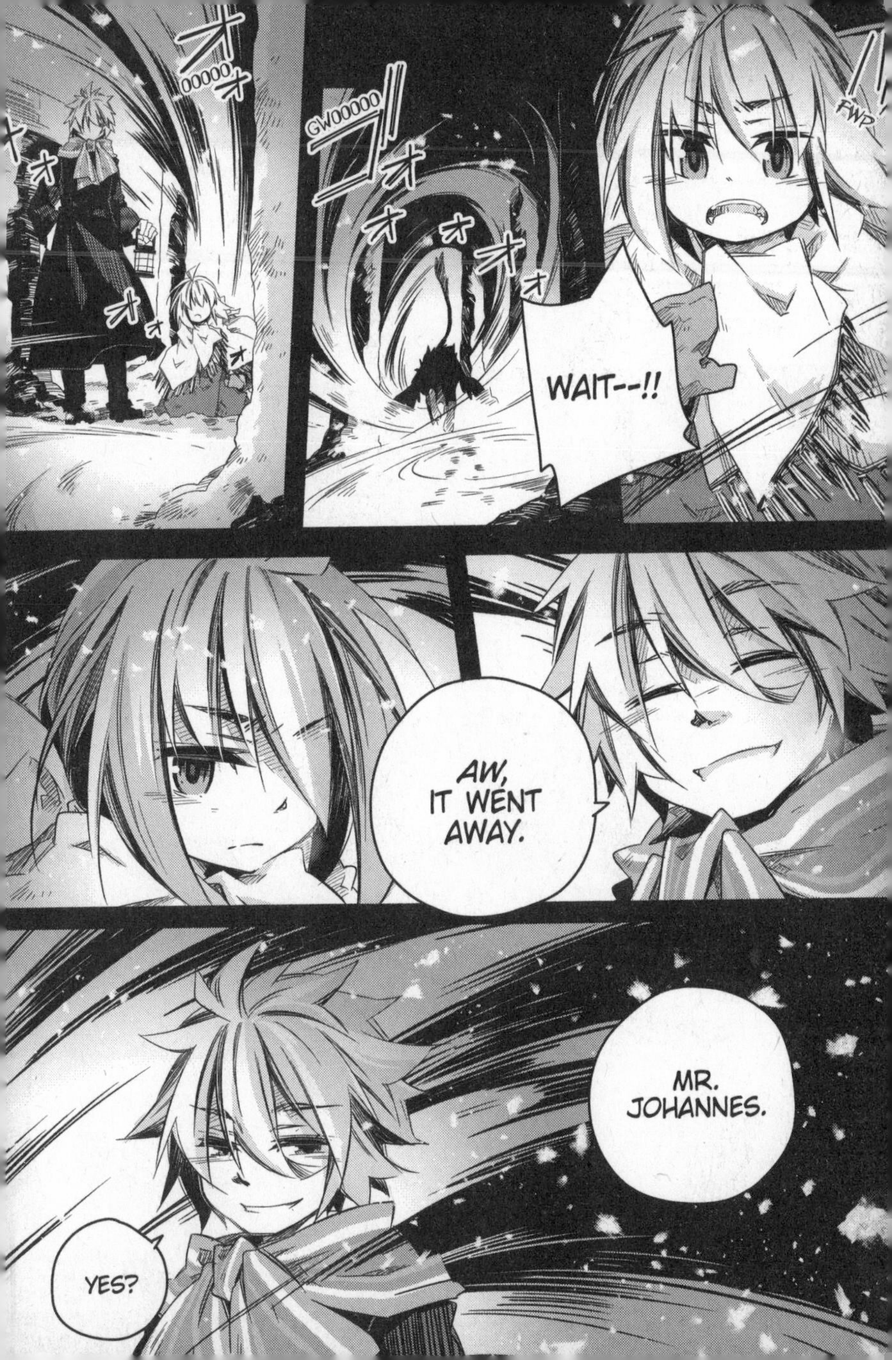
FWP
WAIT--!!
GWOOOOO
OOOOOO
AW, IT WENT AWAY.
MR. JOHANNES.
YES?

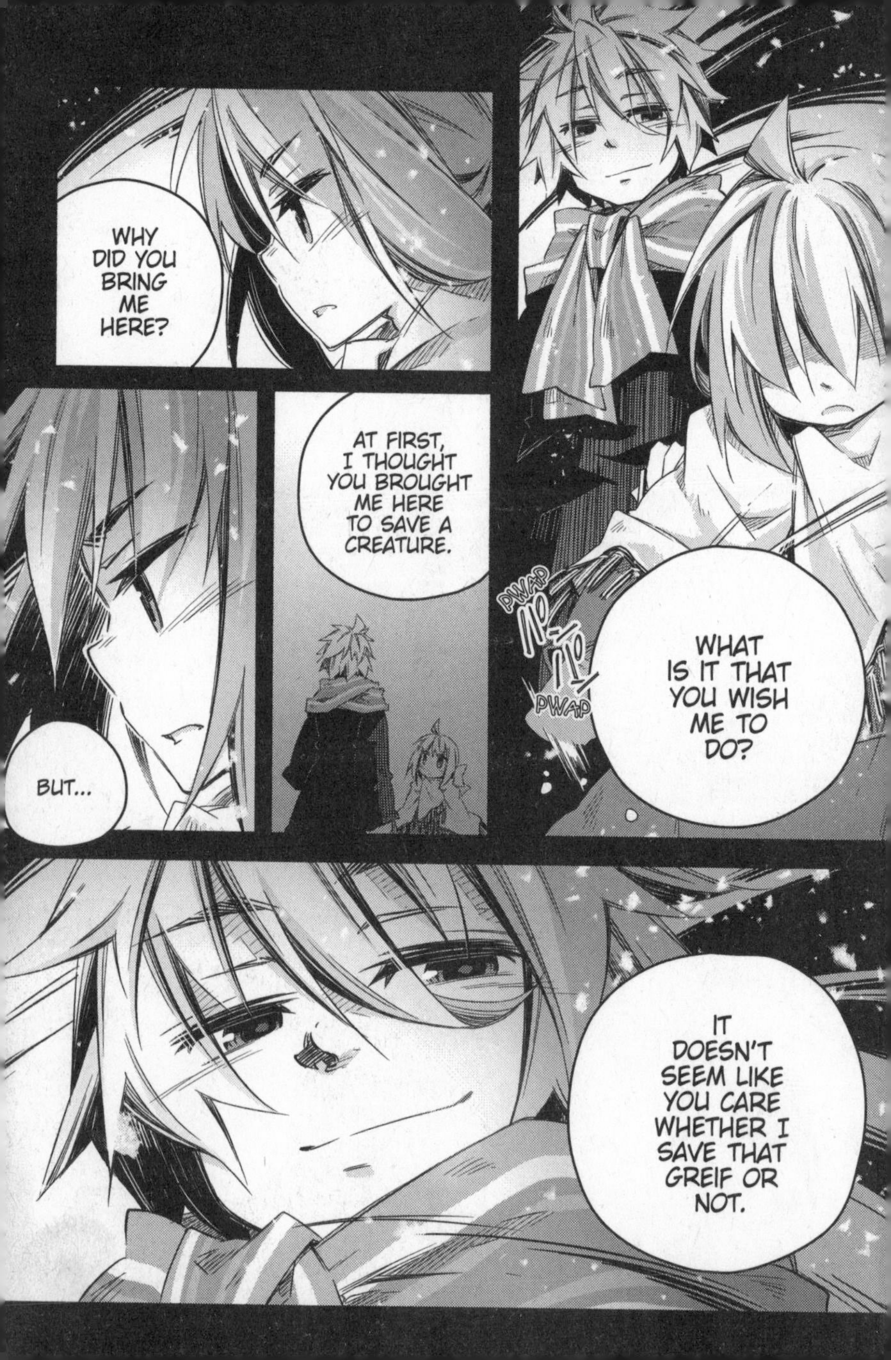
PWAP
PWAP
WHAT IS IT THAT YOU WISH ME TO DO?
WHY DID YOU BRING ME HERE?
AT FIRST, I THOUGHT YOU BROUGHT ME HERE TO SAVE A CREATURE.
BUT...
IT DOESN'T SEEM LIKE YOU CARE WHETHER I SAVE THAT GREIF OR NOT.

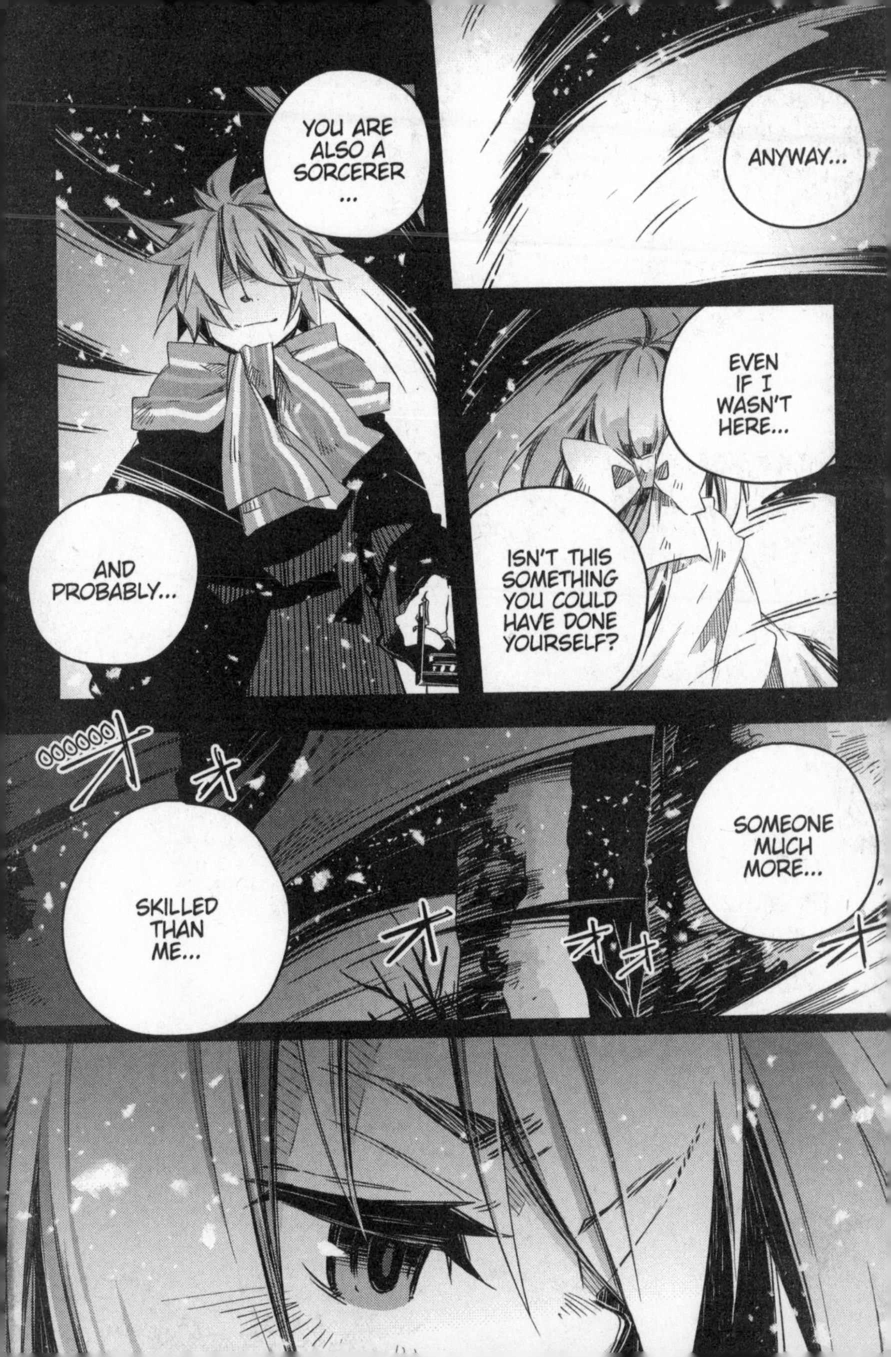
ANYWAY...
EVEN IF I WASN'T HERE...
ISN'T THIS SOMETHING YOU COULD HAVE DONE YOURSELF?
YOU ARE ALSO A SORCERER ...
AND PROBABLY...
SOMEONE MUCH MORE...
SKILLED THAN ME...
OOOOOO

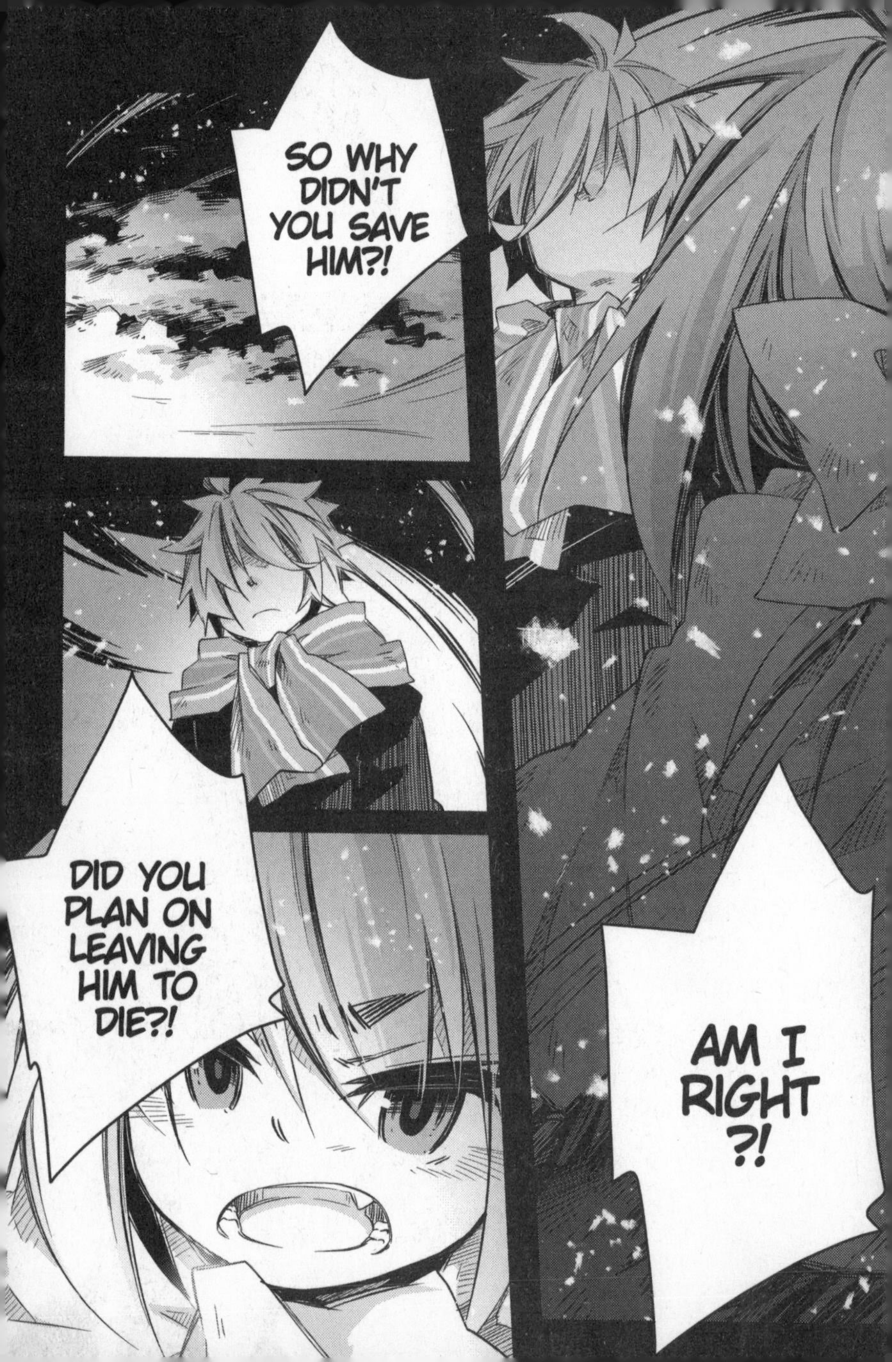
AM I RIGHT?!
SO WHY DIDN'T YOU SAVE HIM?!
DID YOU PLAN ON LEAVING HIM TO DIE?!

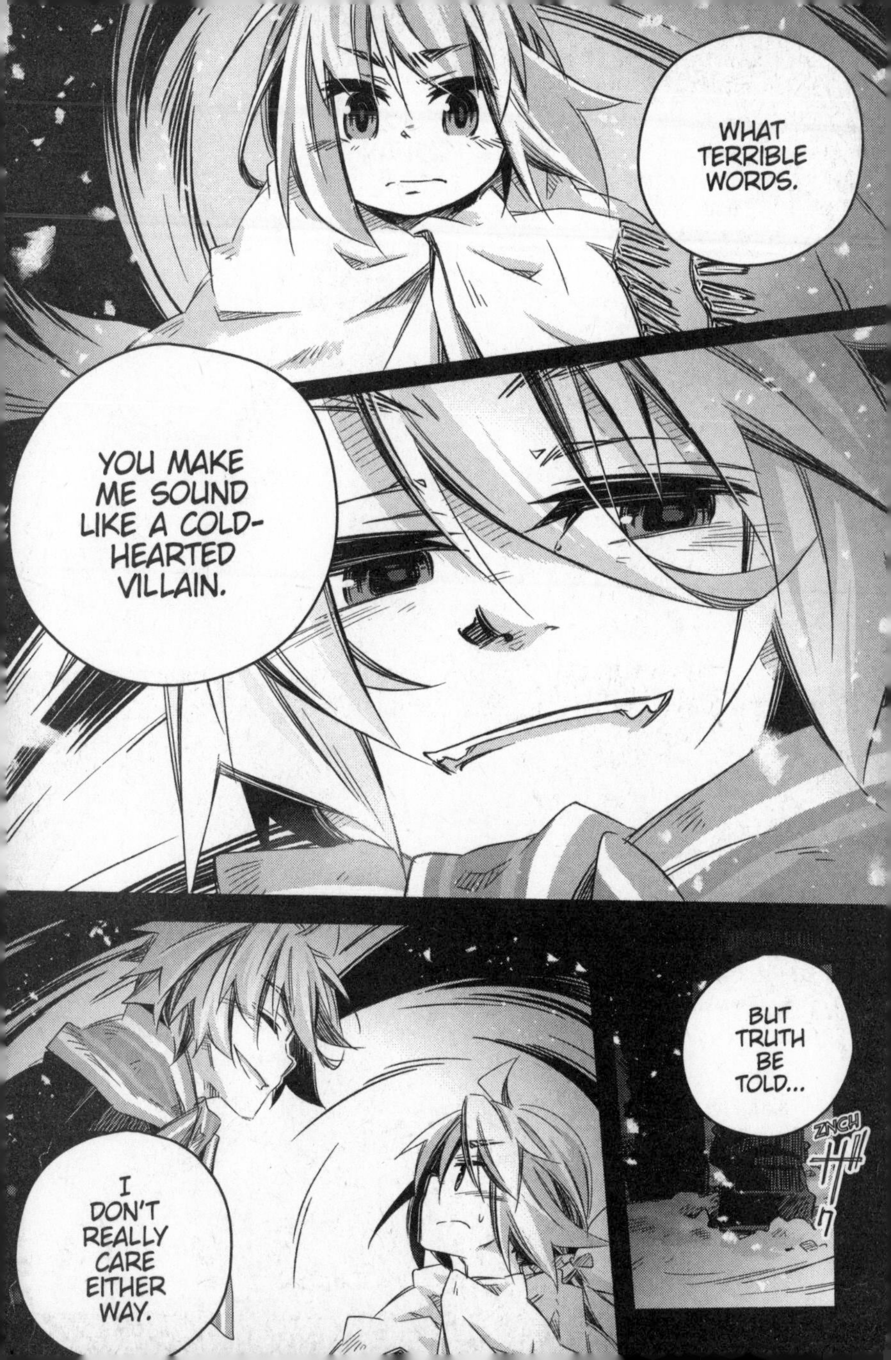
WHAT TERRIBLE WORDS.
YOU MAKE ME SOUND LIKE A COLD-HEARTED VILLAIN.
BUT TRUTH BE TOLD...
ZNCH
I DON'T REALLY CARE EITHER WAY.

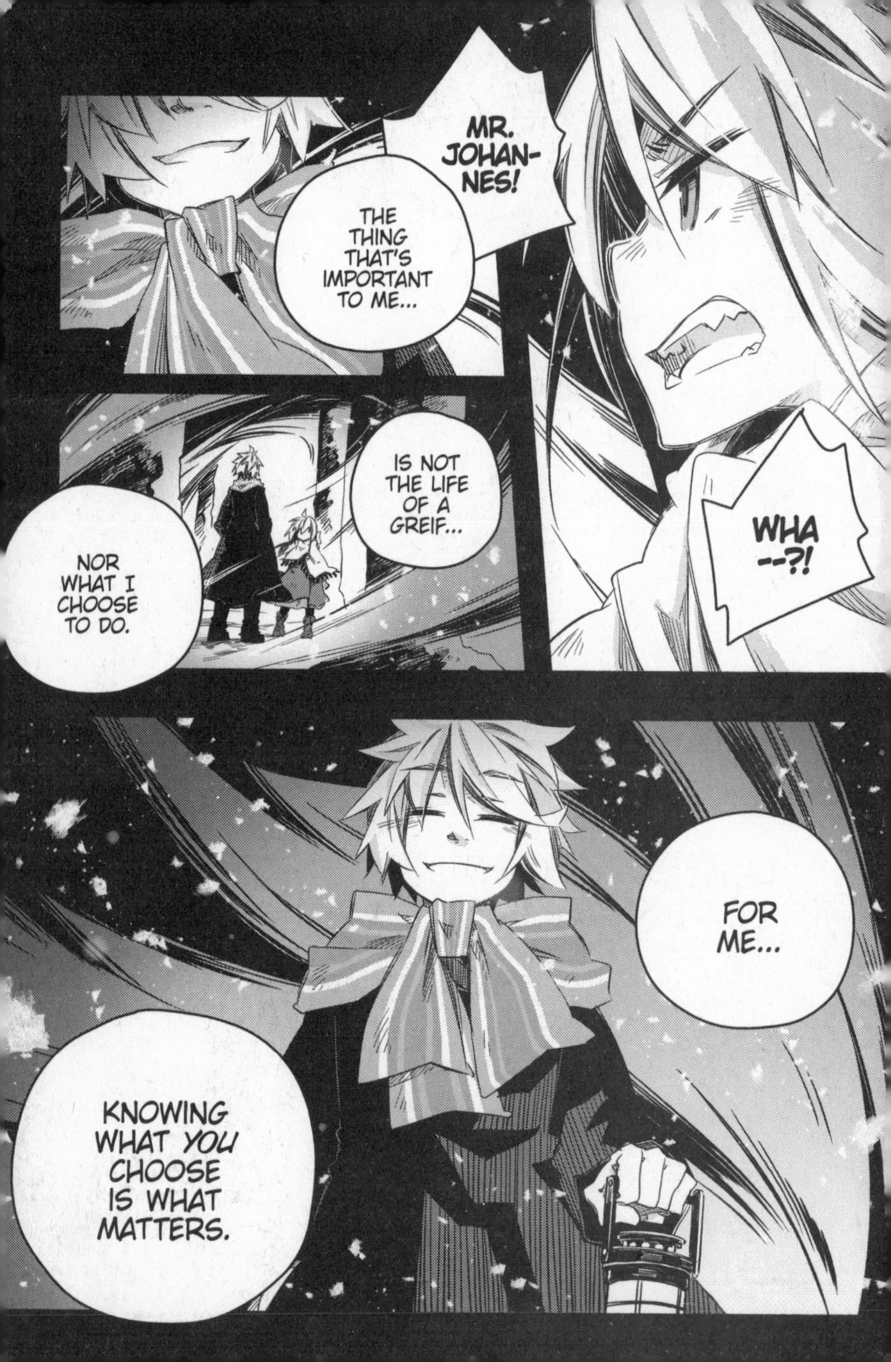
MR. JOHANNES!
WHA --?!
THE THING THAT'S IMPORTANT TO ME...
IS NOT THE LIFE OF A GREIF...
NOR WHAT I CHOOSE TO DO.
FOR ME...
KNOWING WHAT *YOU* CHOOSE IS WHAT MATTERS.

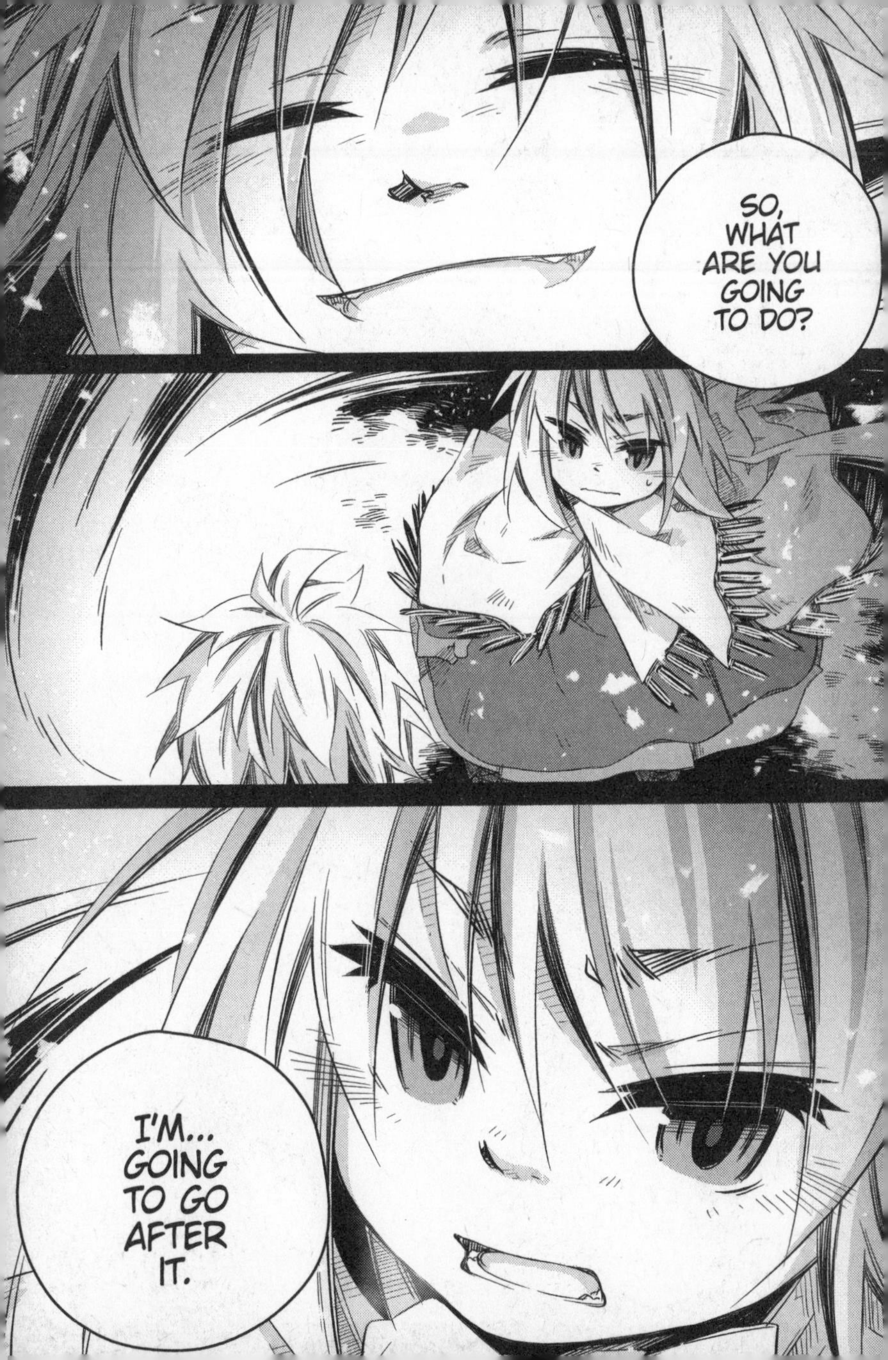
SO, WHAT ARE YOU GOING TO DO?
I'M... GOING TO GO AFTER IT.

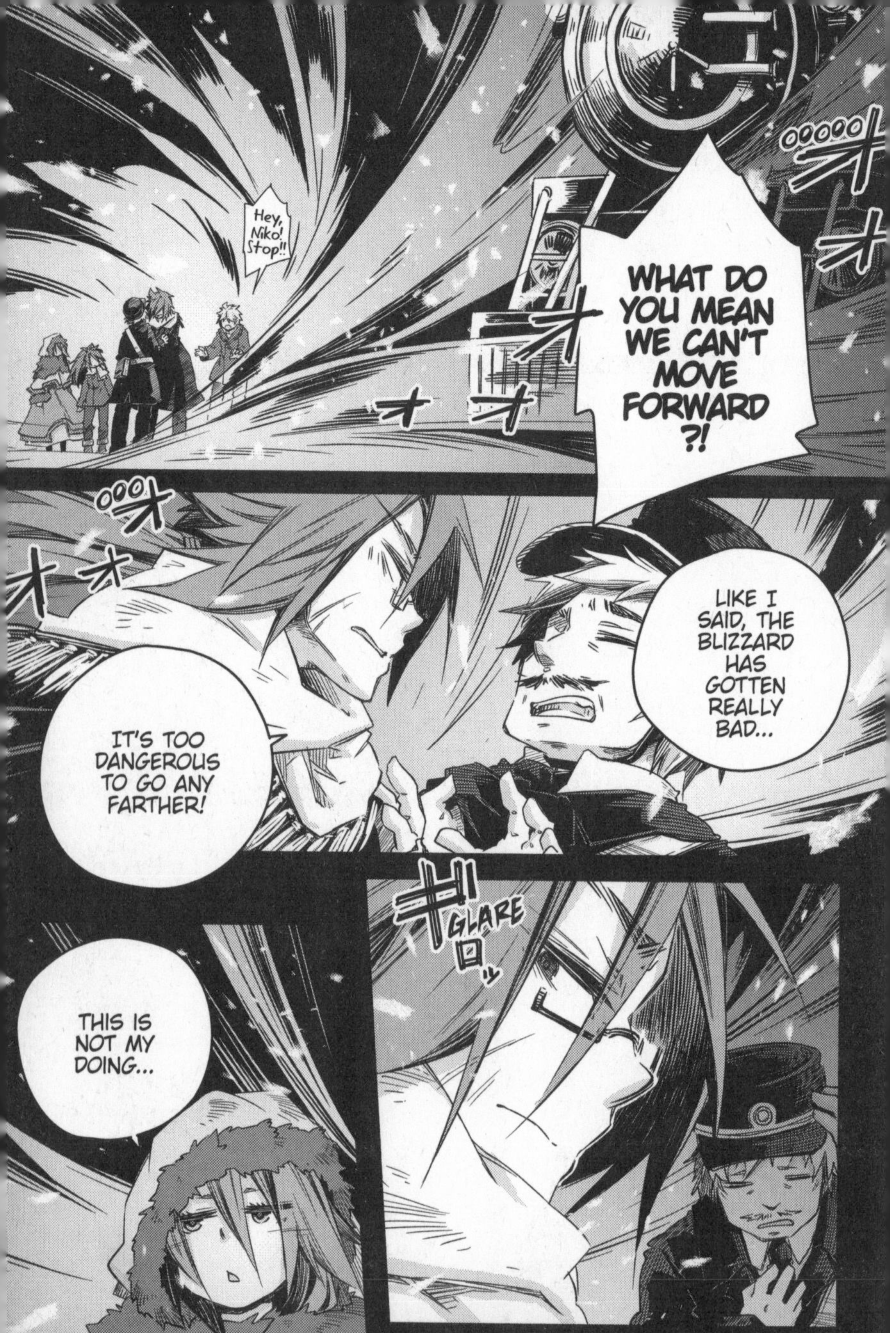
WHAT DO YOU MEAN WE CAN'T MOVE FORWARD ?!
Hey, Niko! Stop!!
LIKE I SAID, THE BLIZZARD HAS GOTTEN REALLY BAD...
IT'S TOO DANGEROUS TO GO ANY FARTHER!
GLARE
THIS IS NOT MY DOING...

[Case 19: Greif]

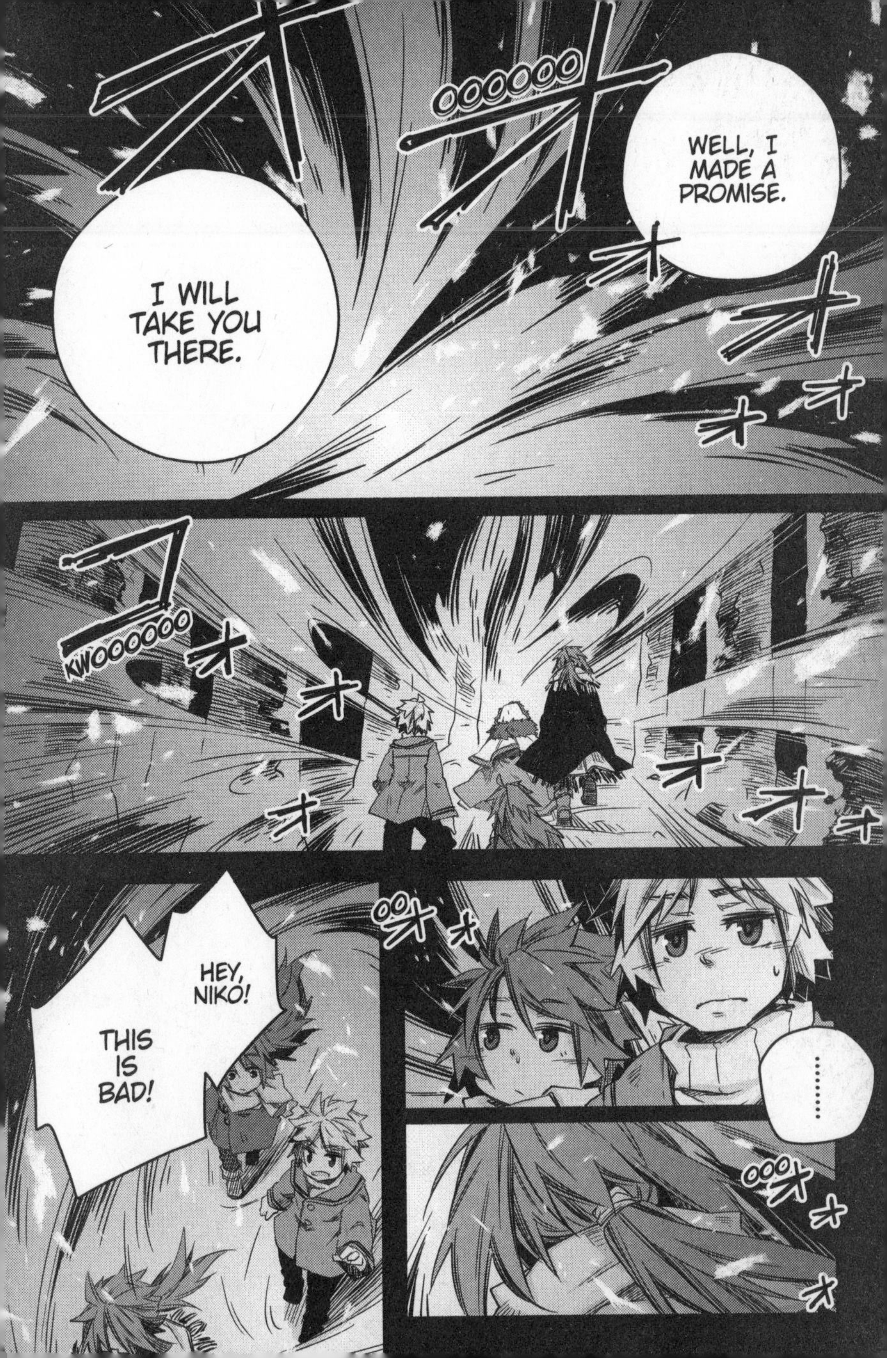
OOOOOO
WELL, I MADE A PROMISE.
I WILL TAKE YOU THERE.
KWOOOOOO
OO
......
OO
HEY, NIKO!
THIS IS BAD!

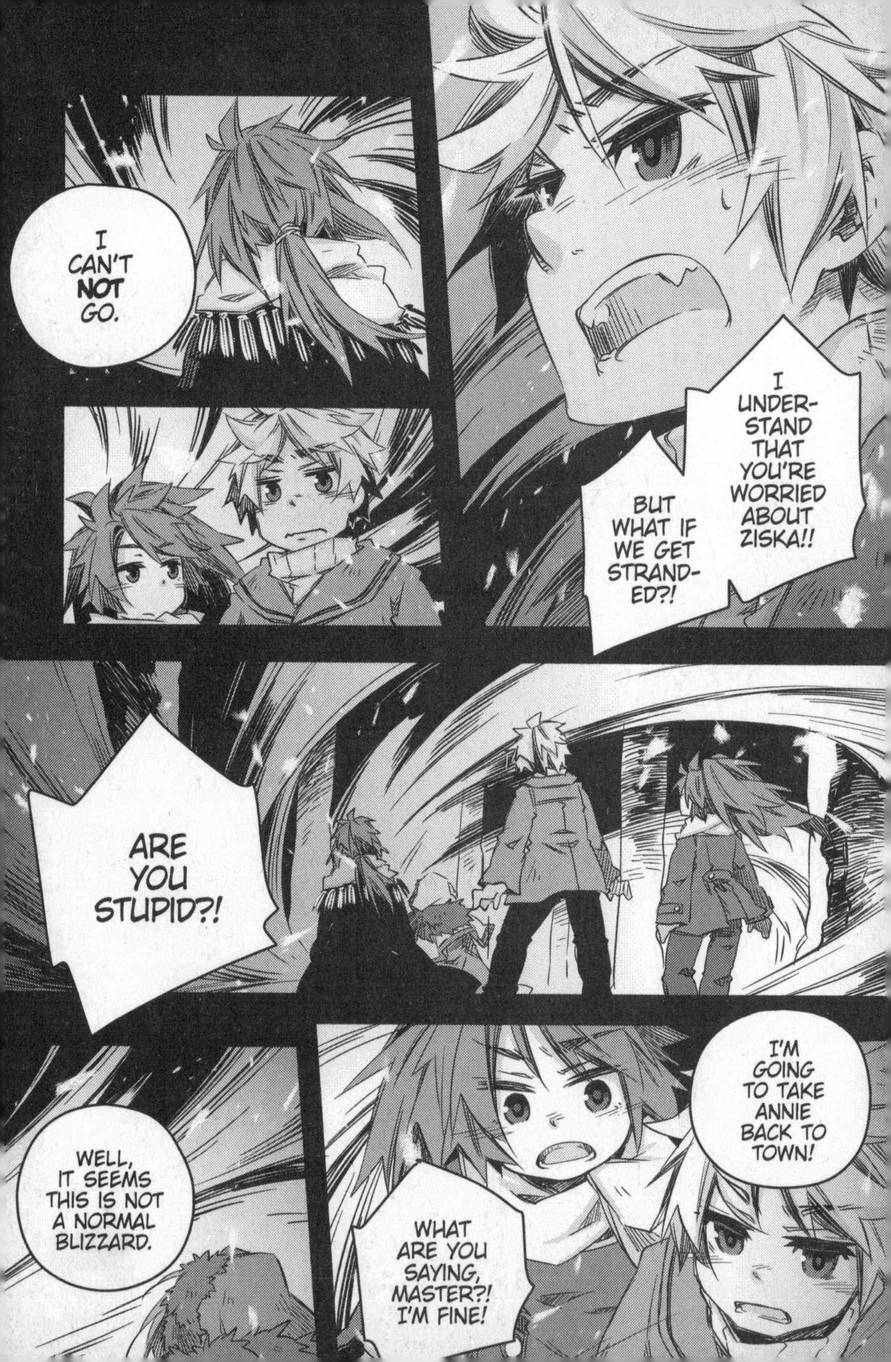
I UNDERSTAND THAT YOU'RE WORRIED ABOUT ZISKA!!
BUT WHAT IF WE GET STRANDED?!
I CAN'T **NOT** GO.
ARE YOU STUPID?!
I'M GOING TO TAKE ANNIE BACK TO TOWN!
WHAT ARE YOU SAYING, MASTER?! I'M FINE!
WELL, IT SEEMS THIS IS NOT A NORMAL BLIZZARD.

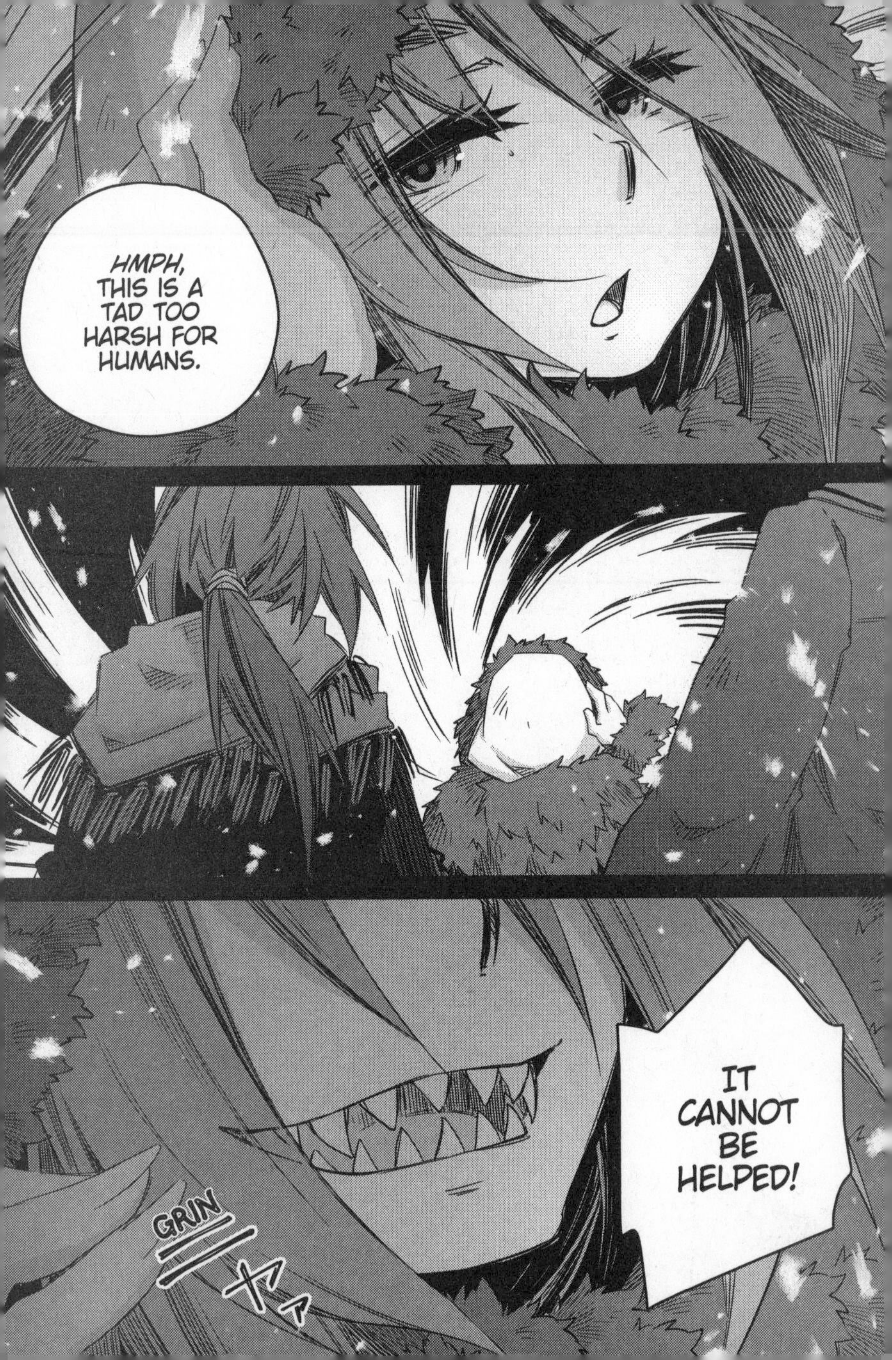
HMPH, THIS IS A TAD TOO HARSH FOR HUMANS.
IT CANNOT BE HELPED!
GRIN

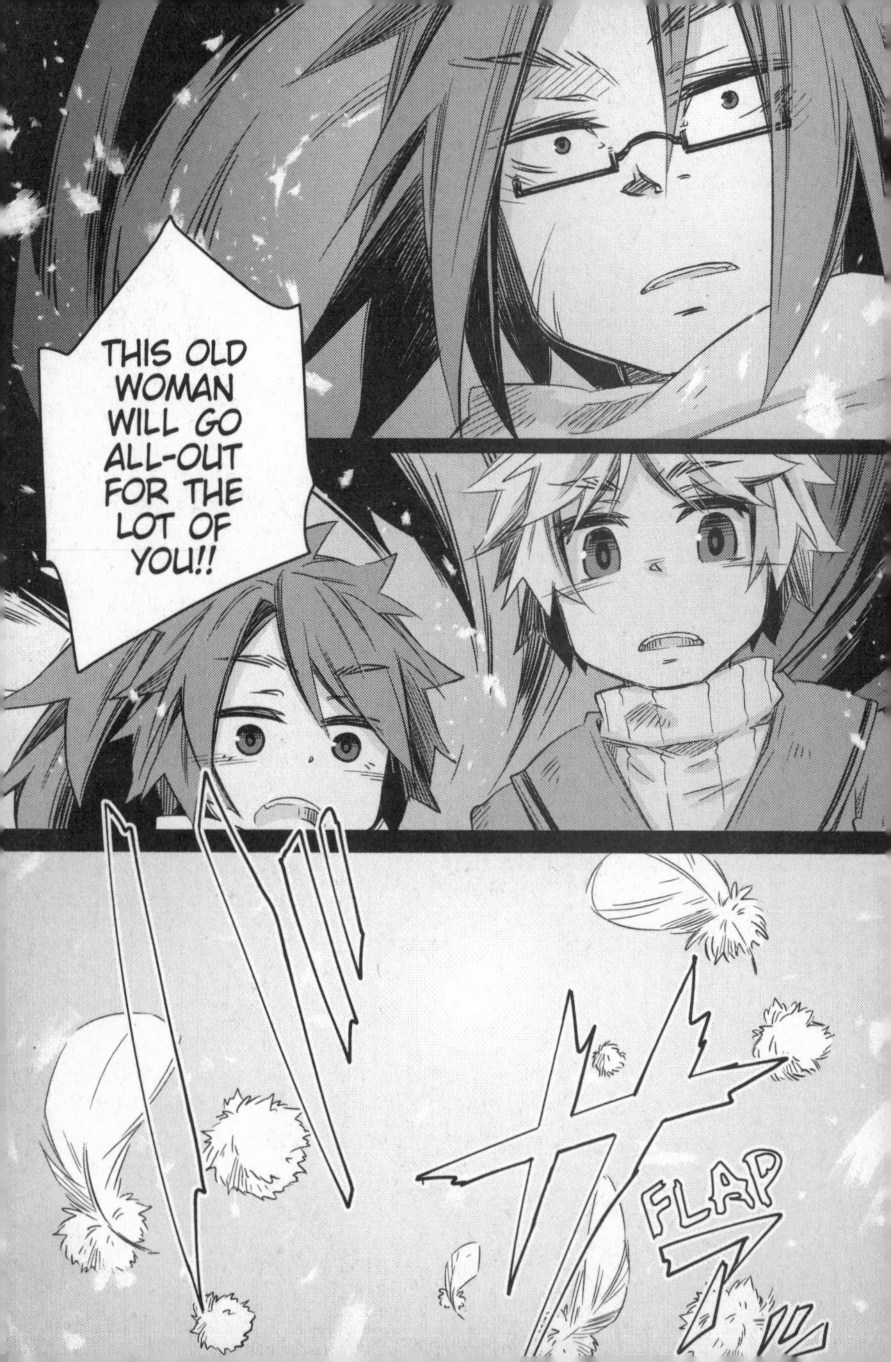
THIS OLD WOMAN WILL GO ALL-OUT FOR THE LOT OF YOU!!
FLAP

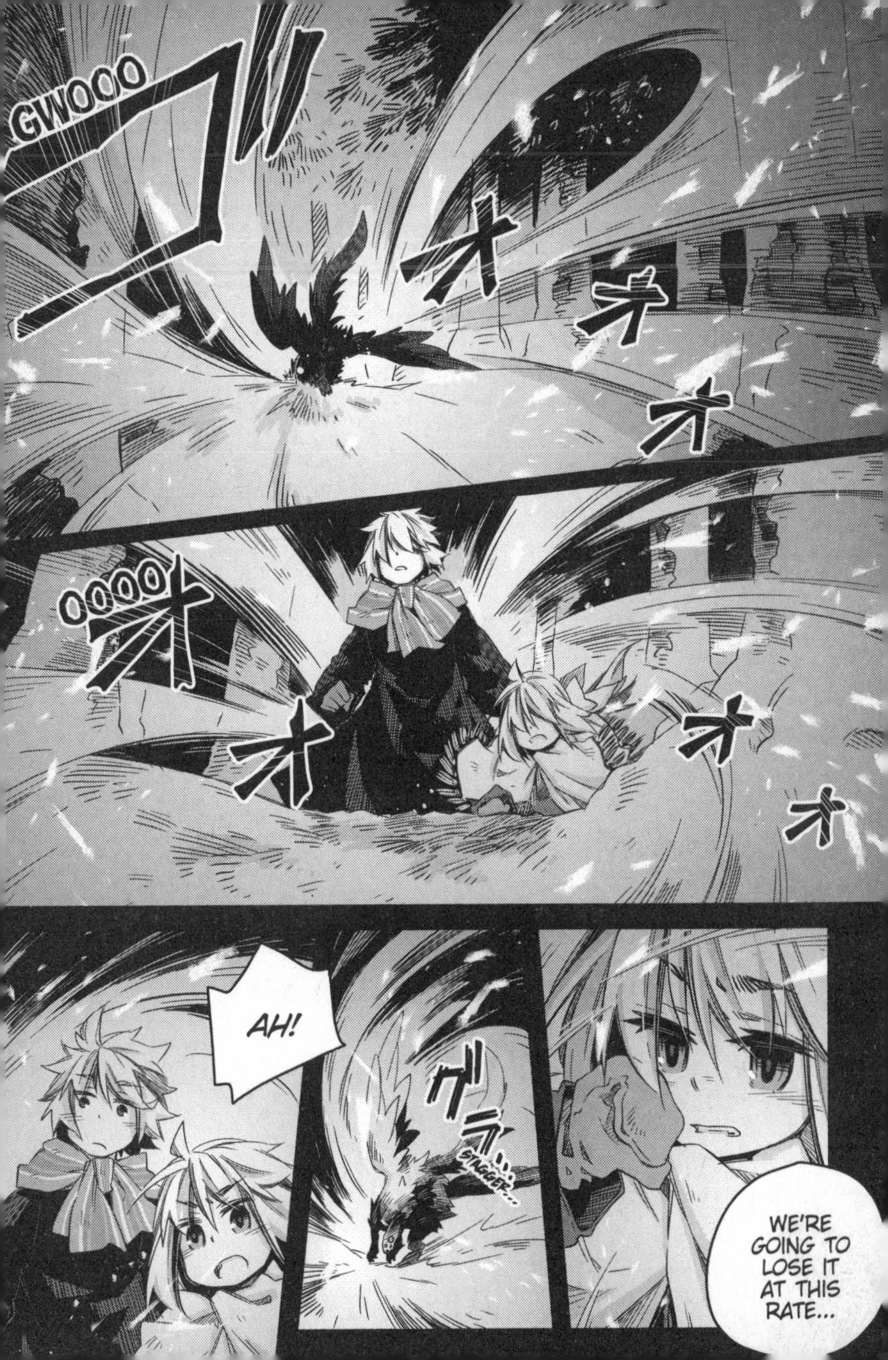
GWOOO
OOOO
WE'RE GOING TO LOSE IT AT THIS RATE...
STAGGER...
AH!

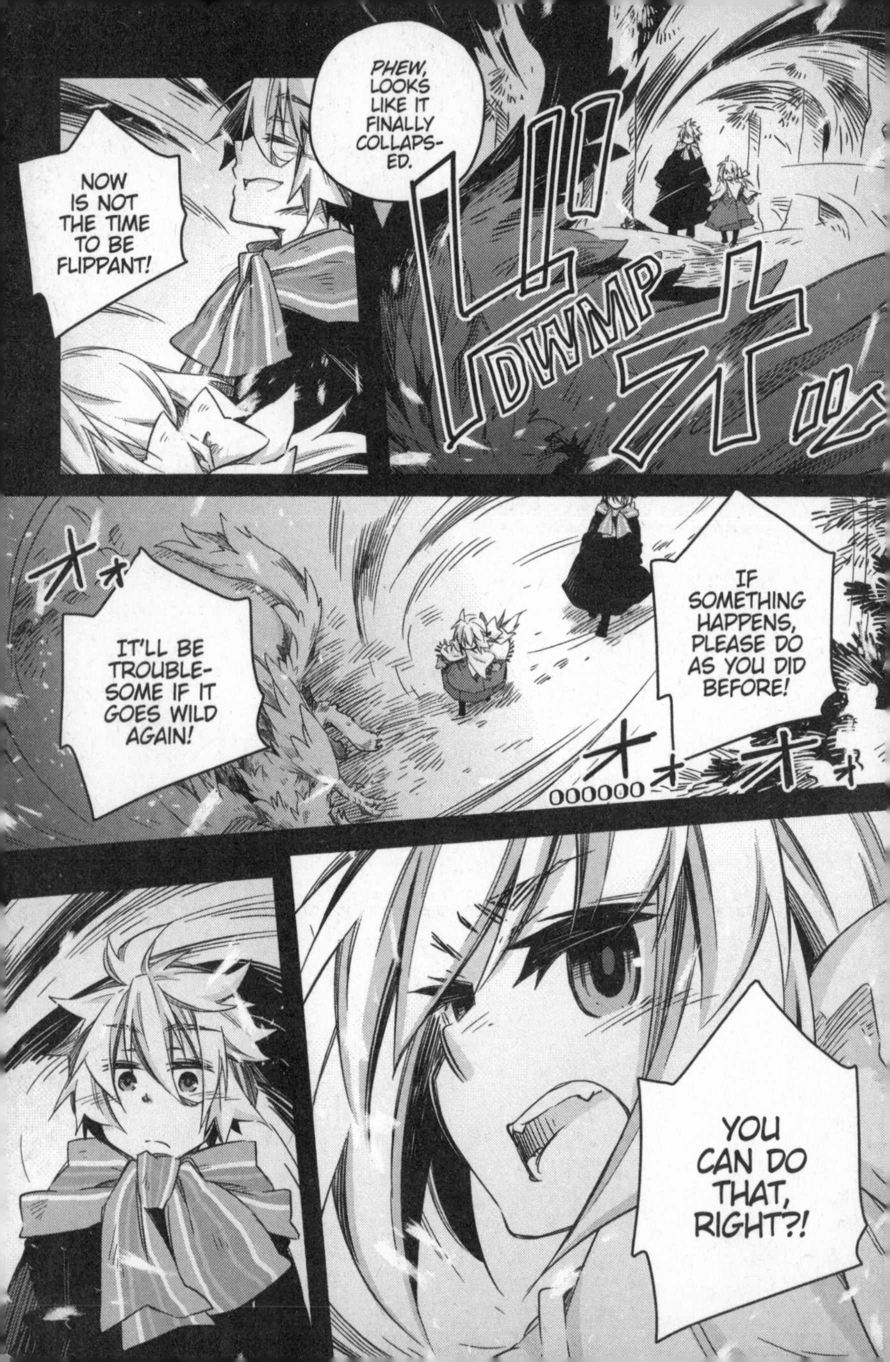
PHEW, LOOKS LIKE IT FINALLY COLLAPSED.
DWMP
NOW IS NOT THE TIME TO BE FLIPPANT!
IF SOMETHING HAPPENS, PLEASE DO AS YOU DID BEFORE!
OOOOOO
IT'LL BE TROUBLESOME IF IT GOES WILD AGAIN!
YOU CAN DO THAT, RIGHT?!

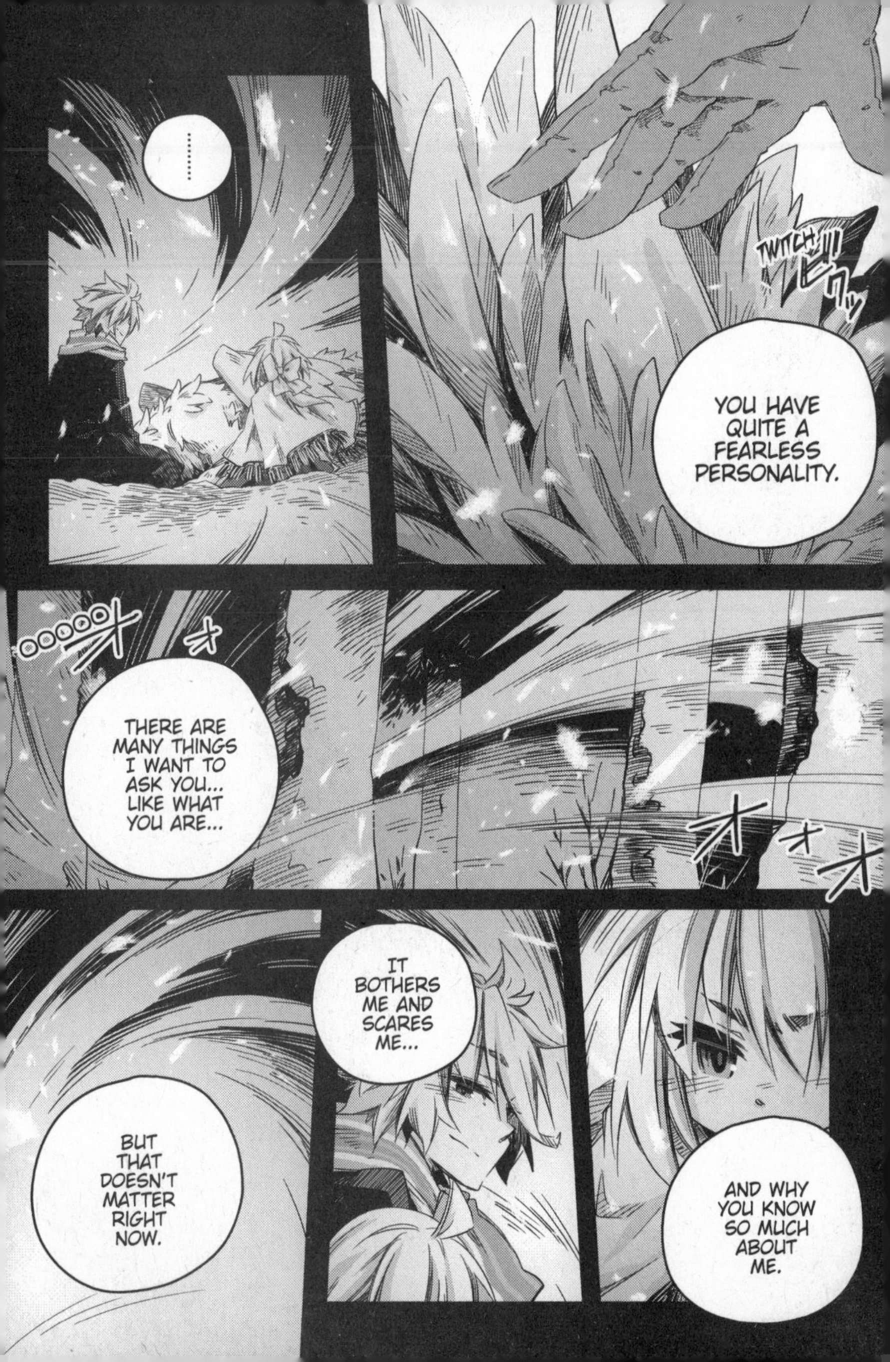
TWITCH!!!
ビクッ
YOU HAVE QUITE A FEARLESS PERSONALITY.
......
オオオ
...OOOOOO
オ
THERE ARE MANY THINGS I WANT TO ASK YOU... LIKE WHAT YOU ARE...
AND WHY YOU KNOW SO MUCH ABOUT ME.
IT BOTHERS ME AND SCARES ME...
BUT THAT DOESN'T MATTER RIGHT NOW.

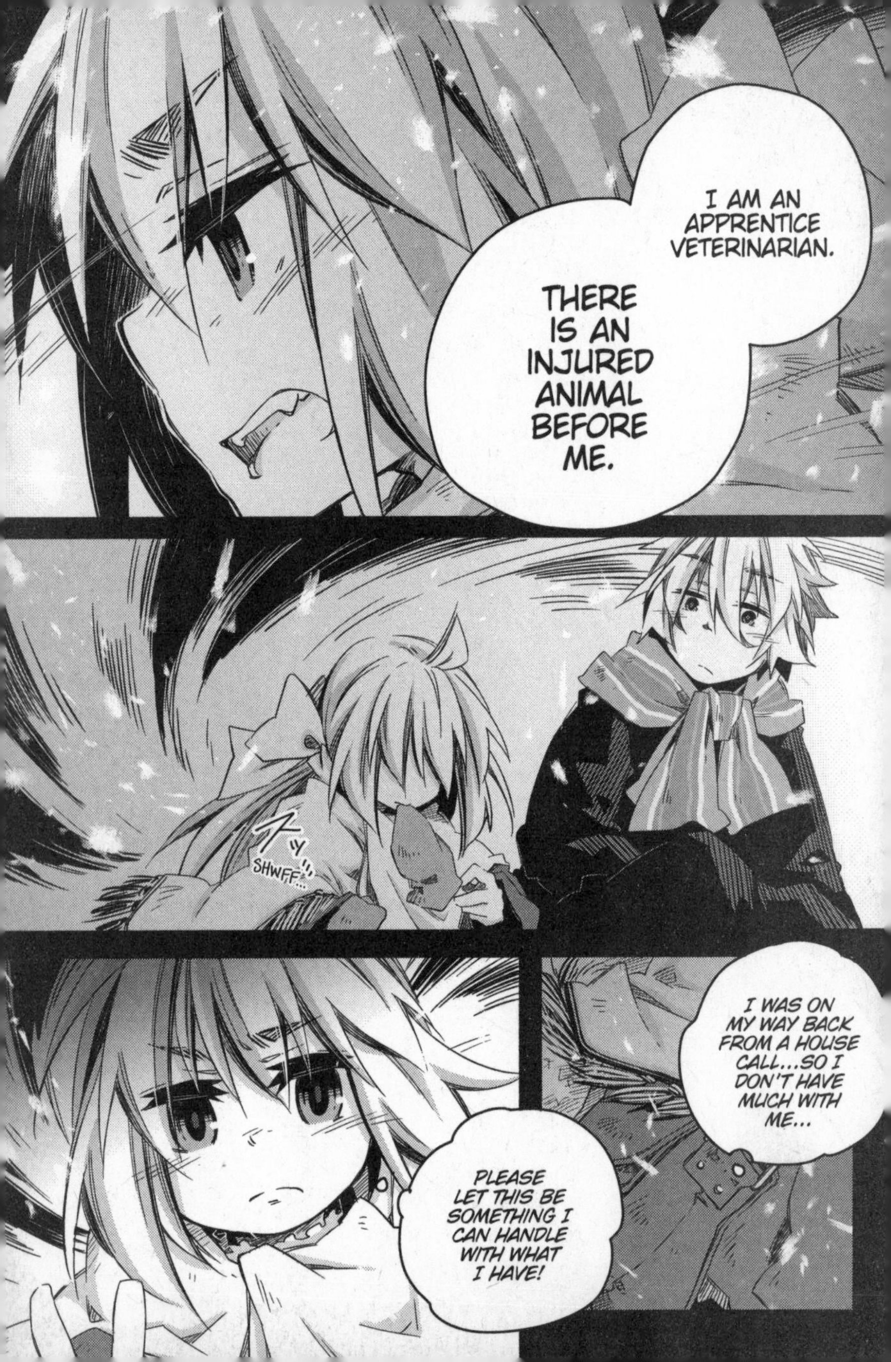
I AM AN APPRENTICE VETERINARIAN.
THERE IS AN INJURED ANIMAL BEFORE ME.
SHWFF...
I WAS ON MY WAY BACK FROM A HOUSE CALL...SO I DON'T HAVE MUCH WITH ME...
PLEASE LET THIS BE SOMETHING I CAN HANDLE WITH WHAT I HAVE!

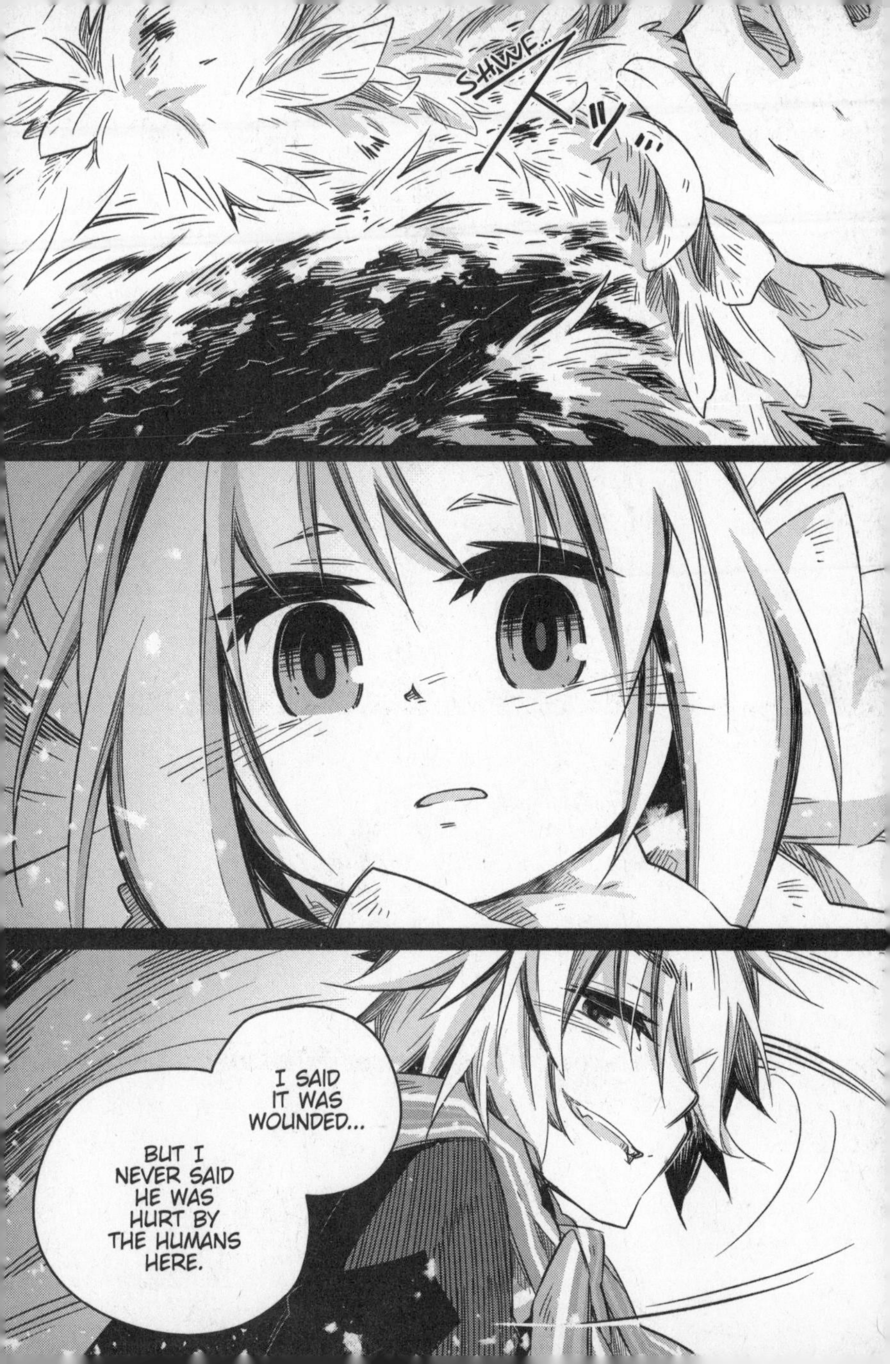
SHWF...
I SAID IT WAS WOUNDED...
BUT I NEVER SAID HE WAS HURT BY THE HUMANS HERE.

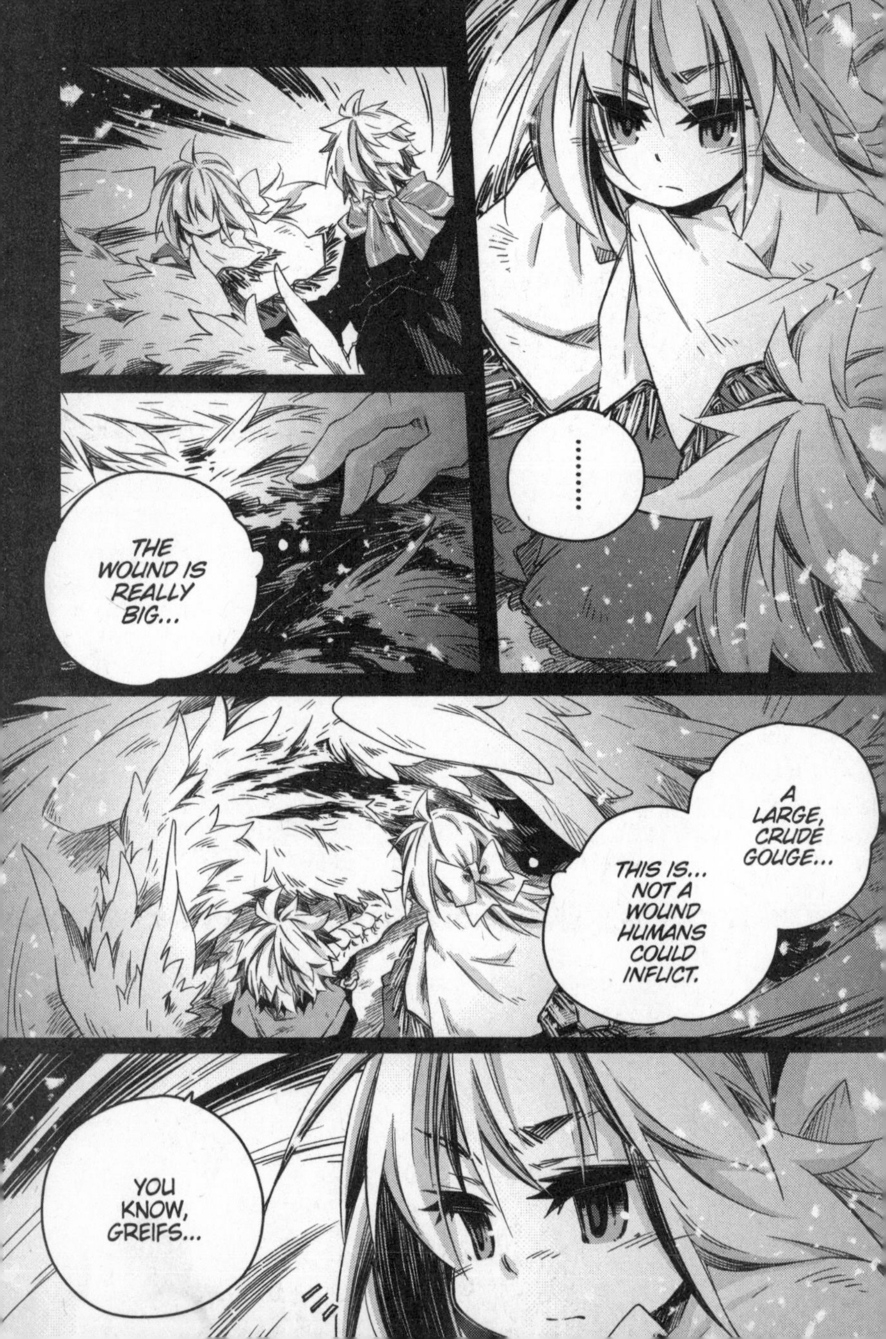
......
THE WOUND IS REALLY BIG...
A LARGE, CRUDE GOUGE...
THIS IS... NOT A WOUND HUMANS COULD INFLICT.
YOU KNOW, GREIFS...

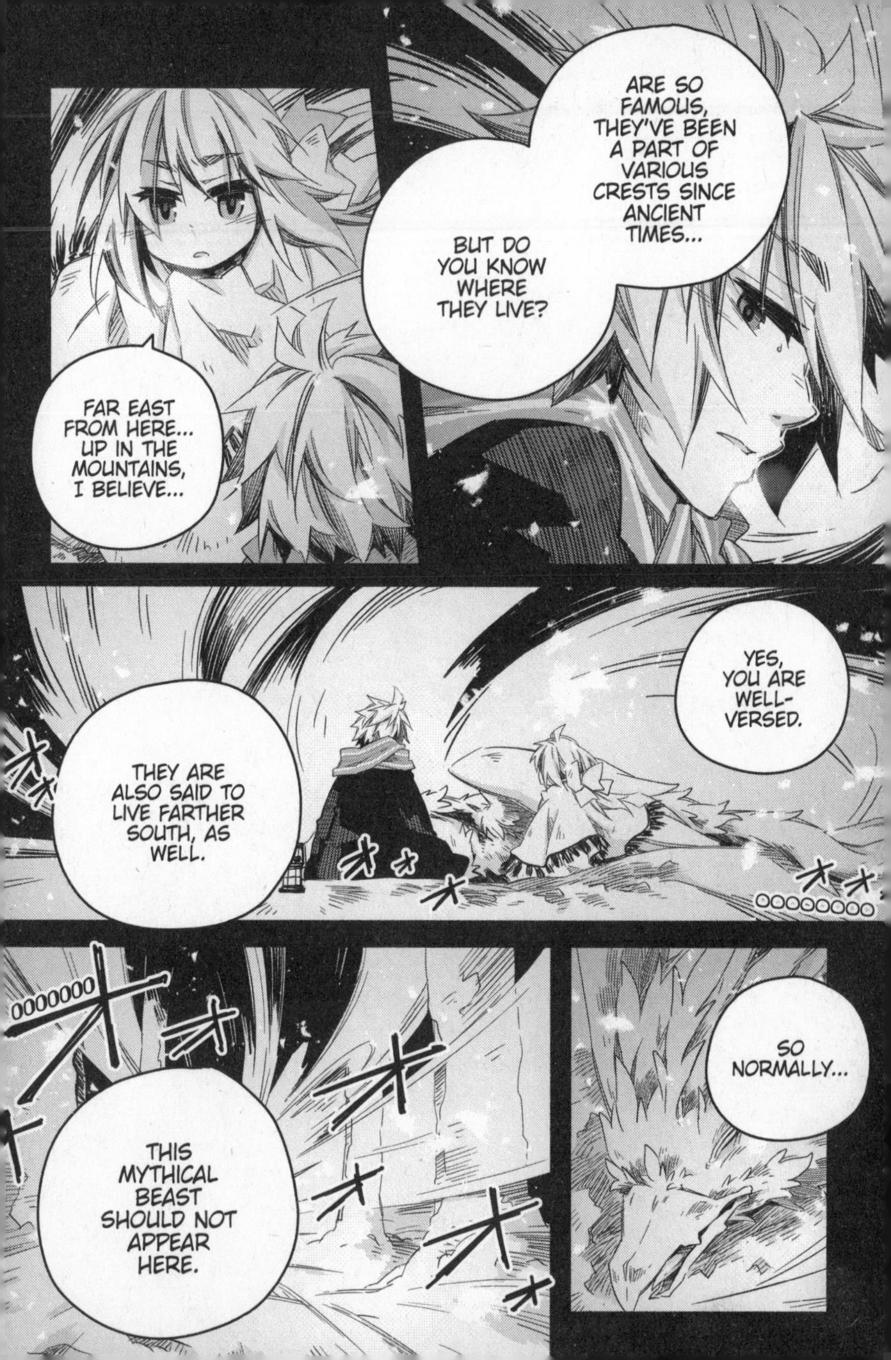
ARE SO FAMOUS, THEY'VE BEEN A PART OF VARIOUS CRESTS SINCE ANCIENT TIMES...
BUT DO YOU KNOW WHERE THEY LIVE?
FAR EAST FROM HERE... UP IN THE MOUNTAINS, I BELIEVE...
YES, YOU ARE WELL-VERSED.
OOOOOOOO
THEY ARE ALSO SAID TO LIVE FARTHER SOUTH, AS WELL.
SO NORMALLY...
OOOOOOO
THIS MYTHICAL BEAST SHOULD NOT APPEAR HERE.

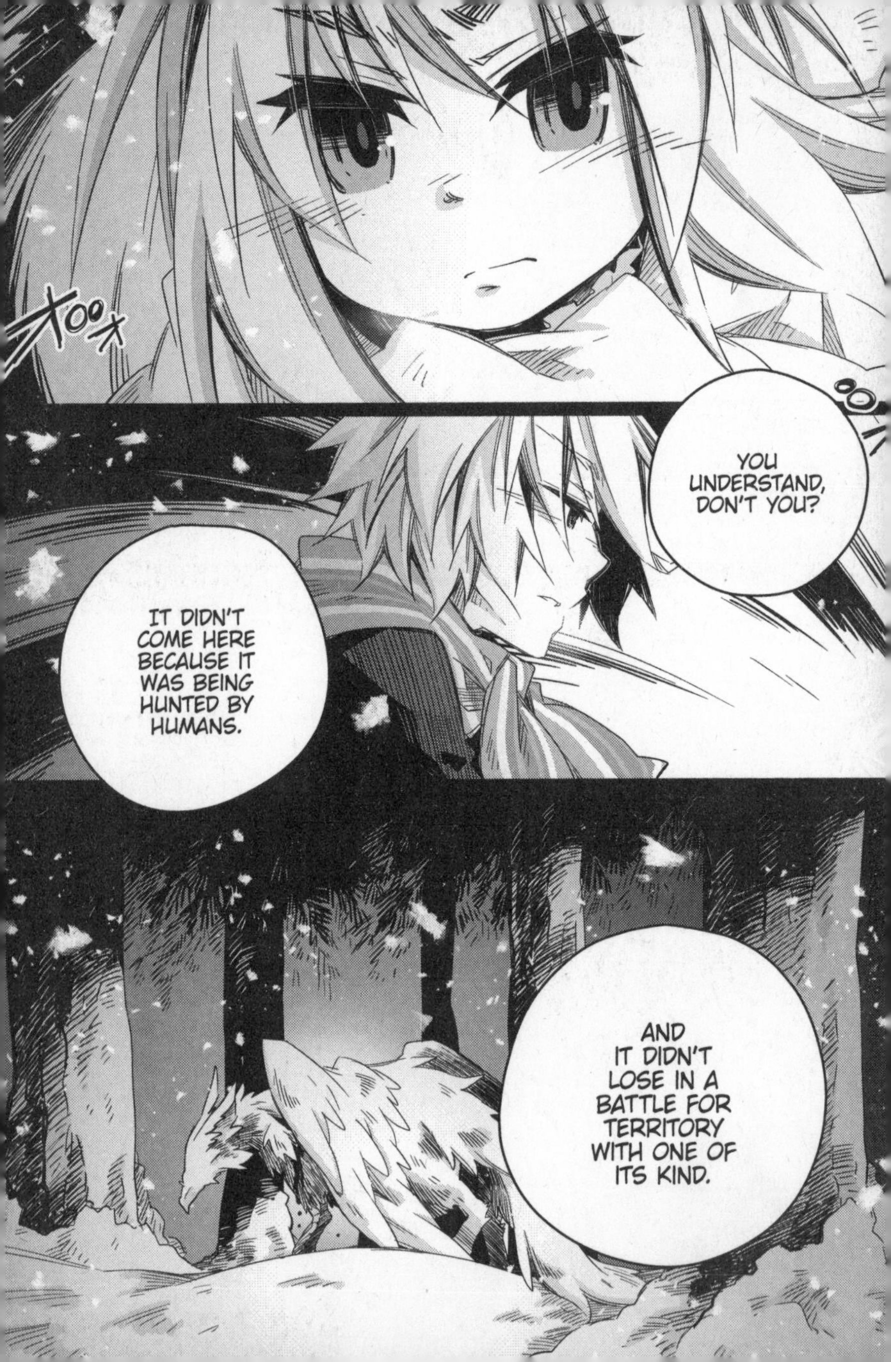
YOU UNDERSTAND, DON'T YOU?
IT DIDN'T COME HERE BECAUSE IT WAS BEING HUNTED BY HUMANS.
AND IT DIDN'T LOSE IN A BATTLE FOR TERRITORY WITH ONE OF ITS KIND.

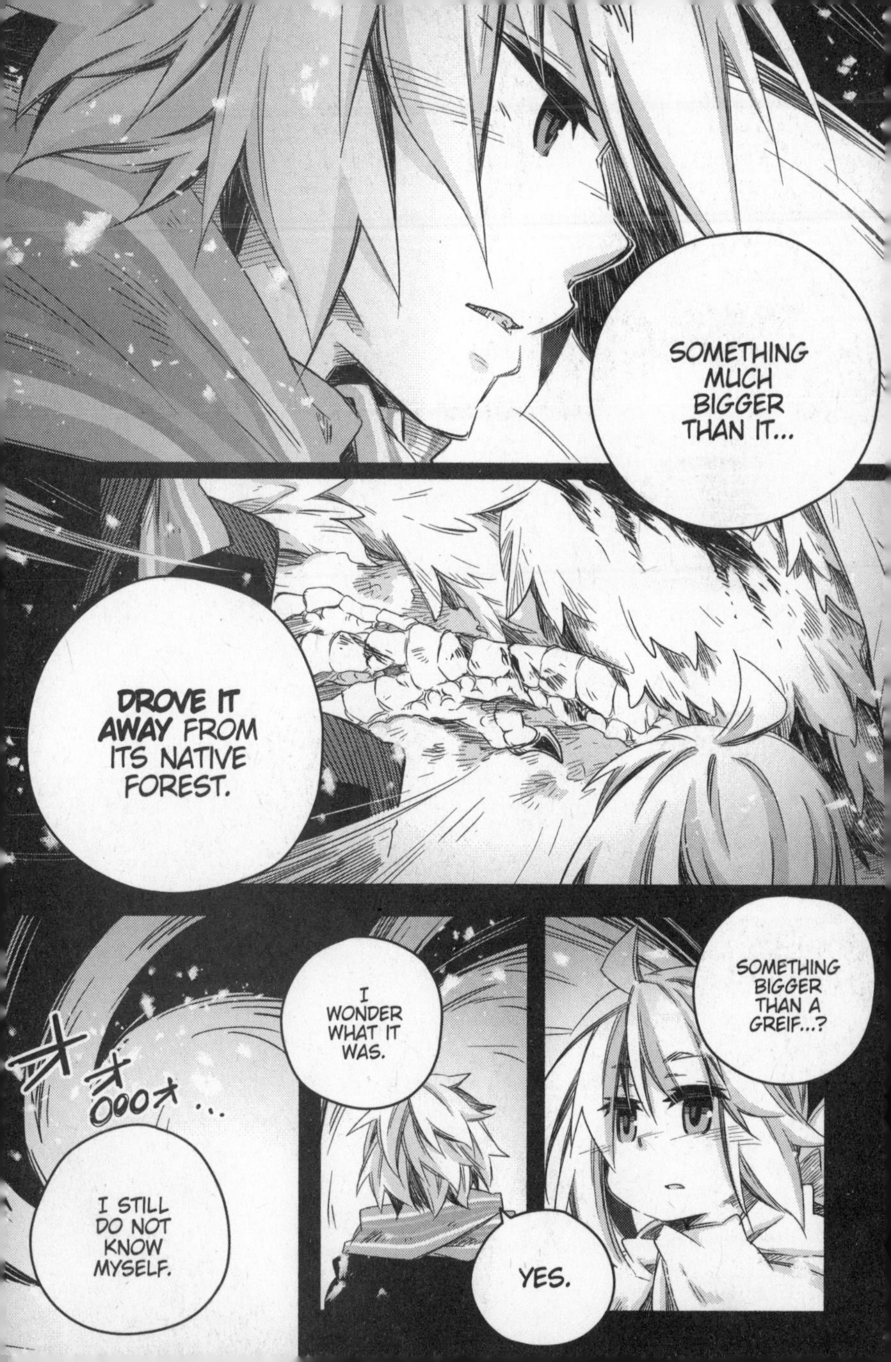
SOMETHING MUCH BIGGER THAN IT...
DROVE IT AWAY FROM ITS NATIVE FOREST.
SOMETHING BIGGER THAN A GREIF...?
YES.
I WONDER WHAT IT WAS.
オオ
OOOオ...
I STILL DO NOT KNOW MYSELF.

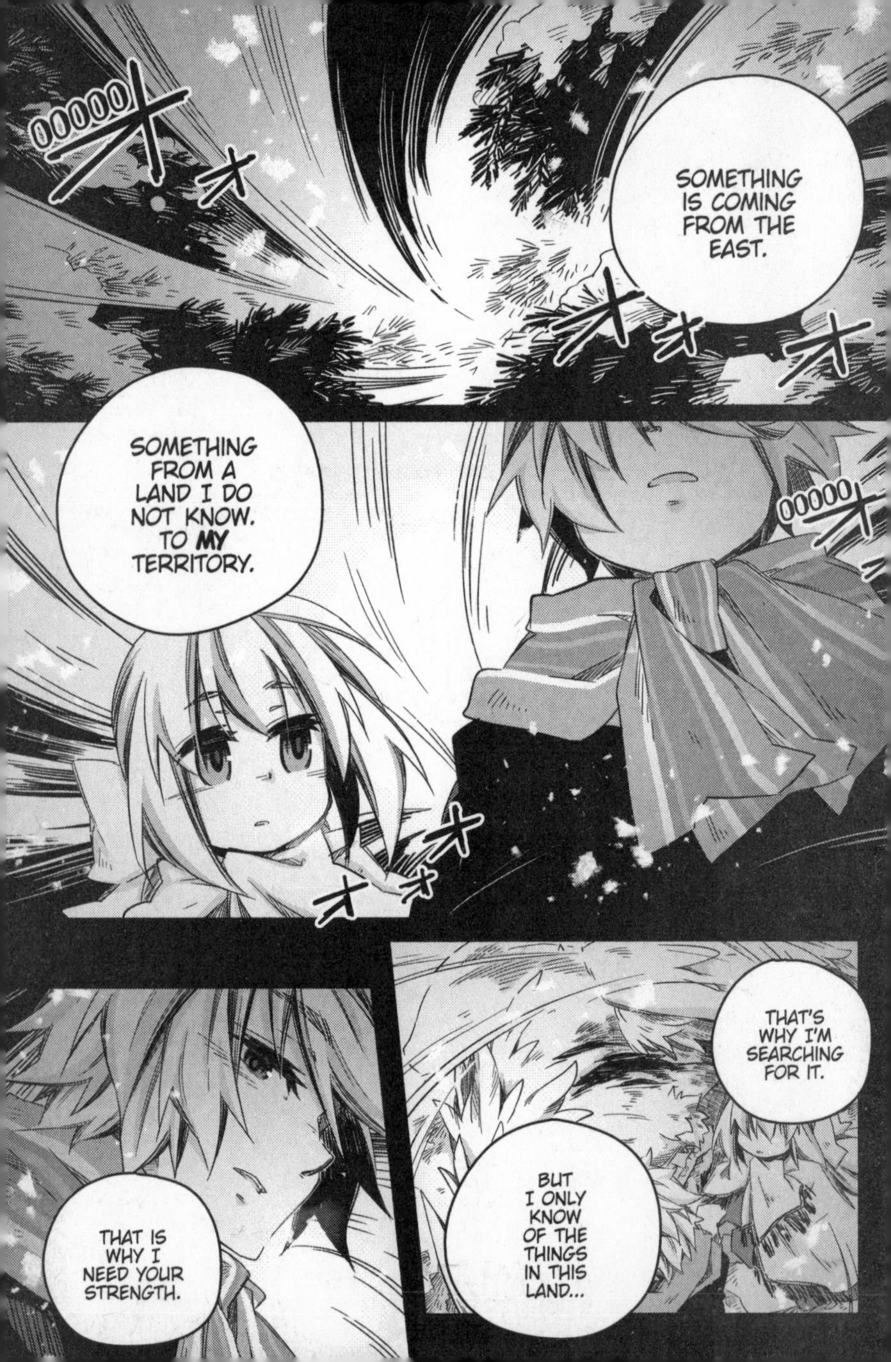
SOMETHING IS COMING FROM THE EAST.
OOOOO
OOOOO
SOMETHING FROM A LAND I DO NOT KNOW. TO **MY** TERRITORY.
THAT'S WHY I'M SEARCHING FOR IT.
BUT I ONLY KNOW OF THE THINGS IN THIS LAND...
THAT IS WHY I NEED YOUR STRENGTH.

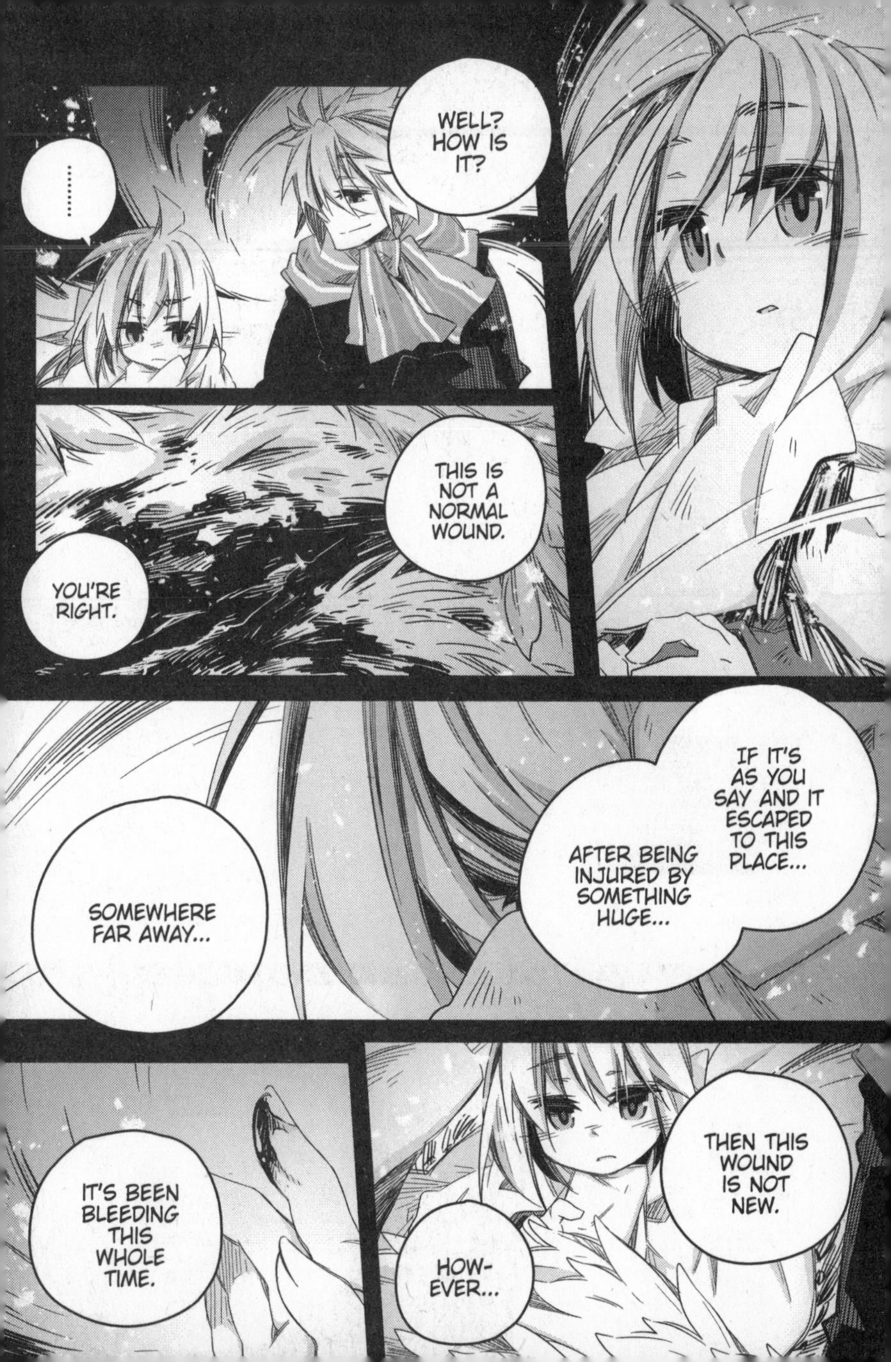
WELL? HOW IS IT?
......
THIS IS NOT A NORMAL WOUND.
YOU'RE RIGHT.
IF IT'S AS YOU SAY AND IT ESCAPED TO THIS PLACE...
AFTER BEING INJURED BY SOMETHING HUGE...
SOMEWHERE FAR AWAY...
THEN THIS WOUND IS NOT NEW.
HOW-EVER...
IT'S BEEN BLEEDING THIS WHOLE TIME.

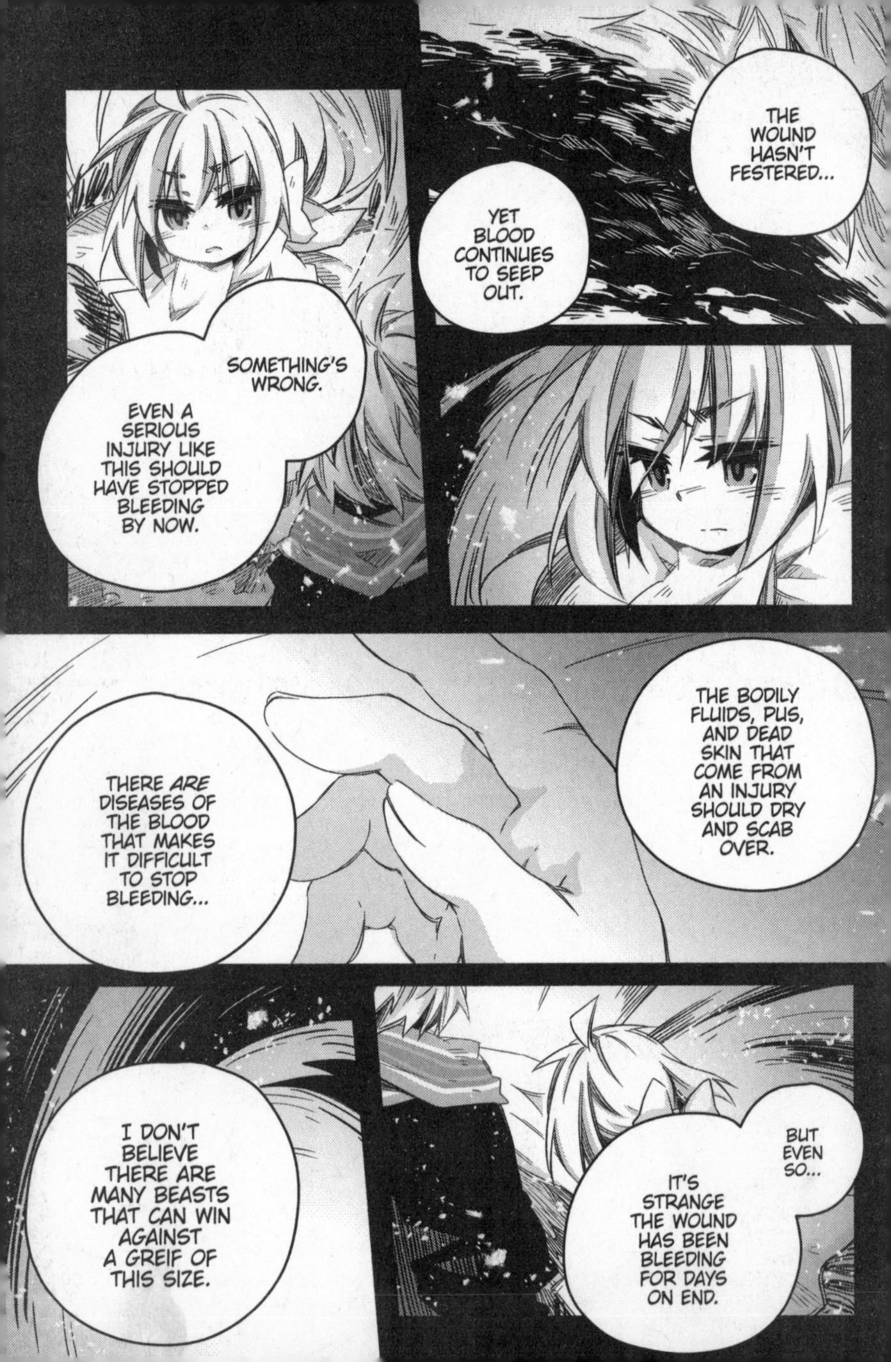
THE WOUND HASN'T FESTERED...
YET BLOOD CONTINUES TO SEEP OUT.
SOMETHING'S WRONG.
EVEN A SERIOUS INJURY LIKE THIS SHOULD HAVE STOPPED BLEEDING BY NOW.
THE BODILY FLUIDS, PUS, AND DEAD SKIN THAT COME FROM AN INJURY SHOULD DRY AND SCAB OVER.
THERE *ARE* DISEASES OF THE BLOOD THAT MAKES IT DIFFICULT TO STOP BLEEDING...
BUT EVEN SO...
IT'S STRANGE THE WOUND HAS BEEN BLEEDING FOR DAYS ON END.
I DON'T BELIEVE THERE ARE MANY BEASTS THAT CAN WIN AGAINST A GREIF OF THIS SIZE.

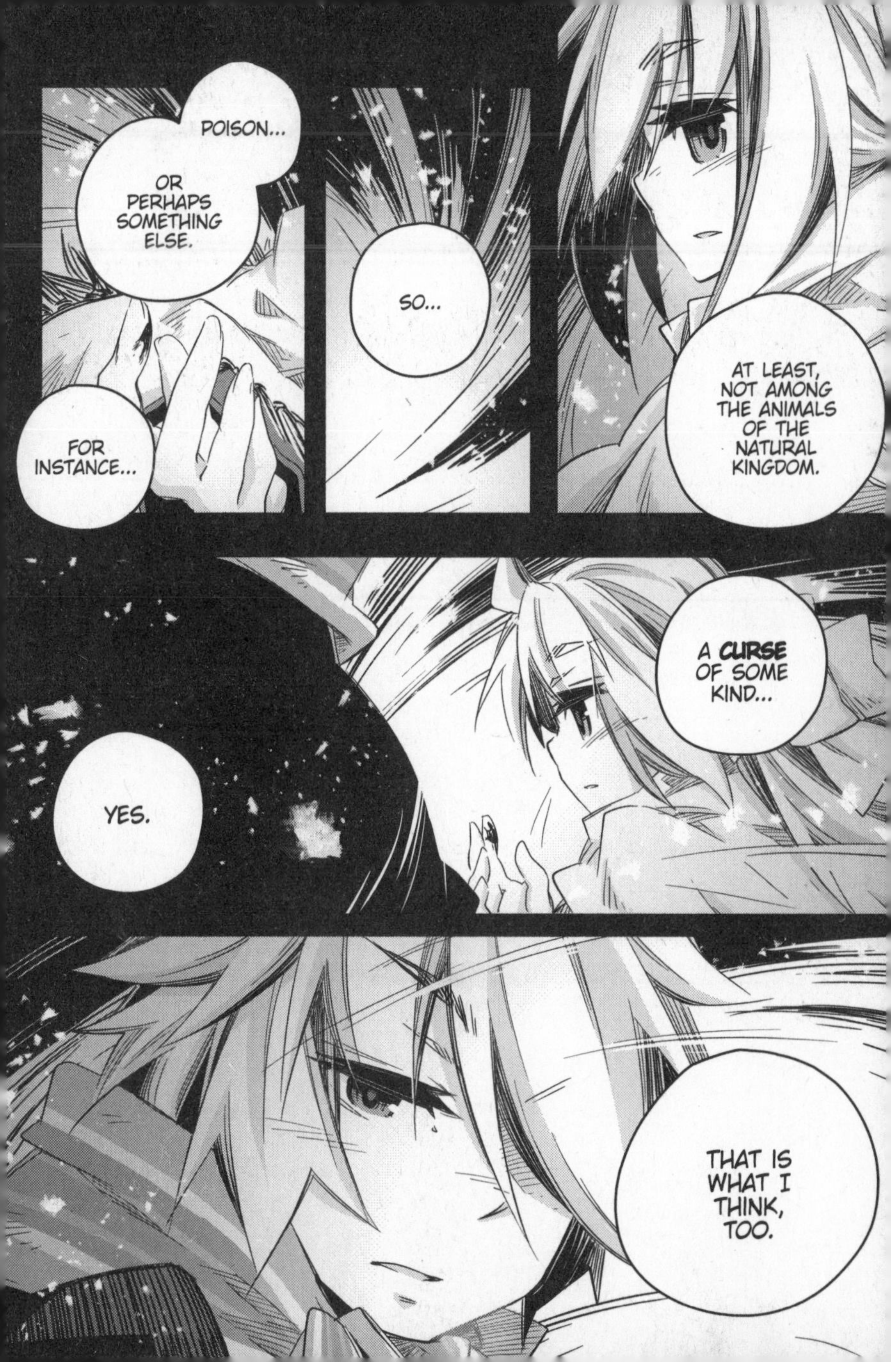
AT LEAST, NOT AMONG THE ANIMALS OF THE NATURAL KINGDOM.
SO...
POISON...
OR PERHAPS SOMETHING ELSE.
FOR INSTANCE...
A **CURSE** OF SOME KIND...
YES.
THAT IS WHAT I THINK, TOO.

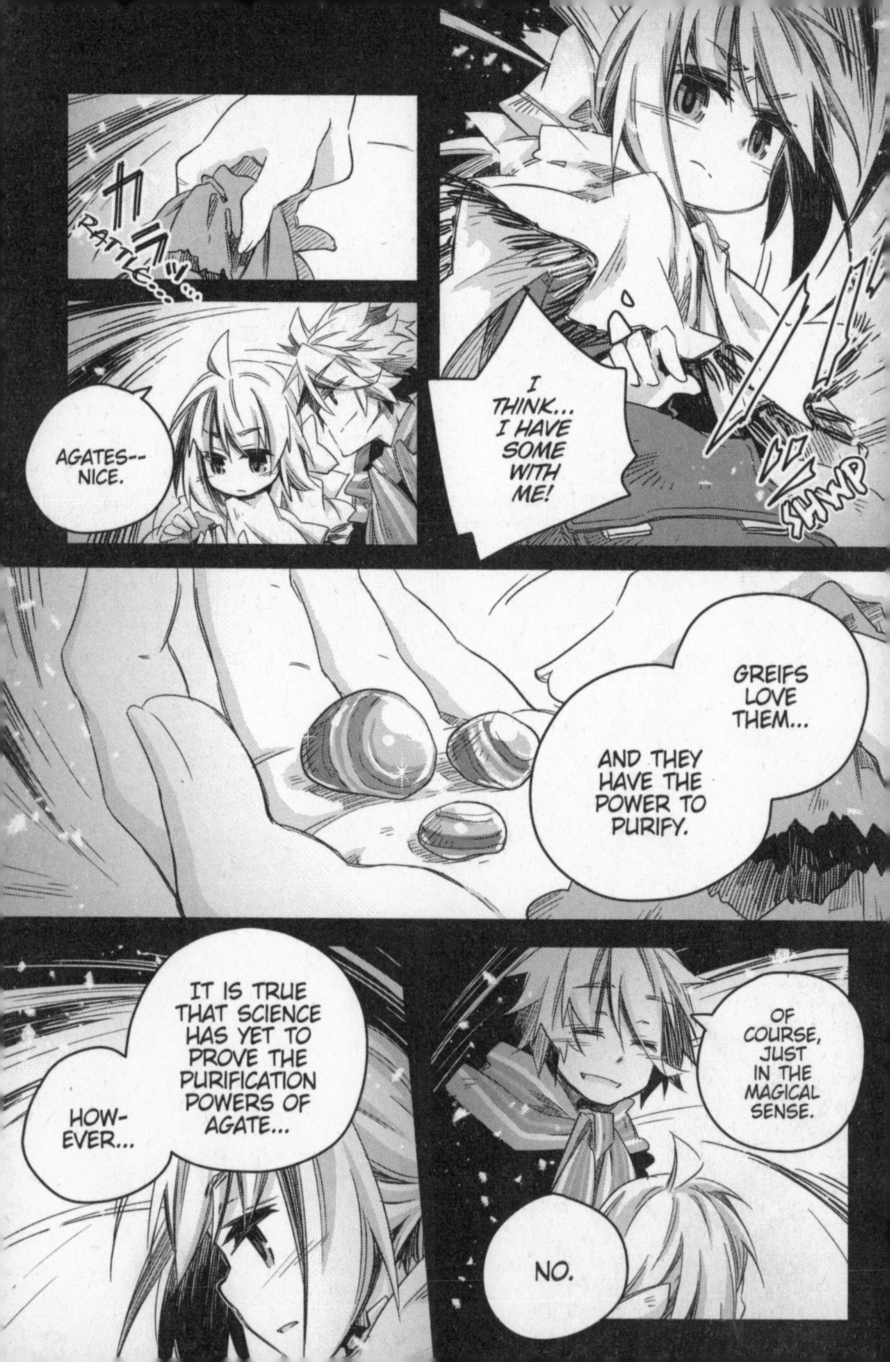
I THINK... I HAVE SOME WITH ME!
SHWP
RATTLE...
AGATES-- NICE.
GREIFS LOVE THEM...
AND THEY HAVE THE POWER TO PURIFY.
OF COURSE, JUST IN THE MAGICAL SENSE.
NO.
IT IS TRUE THAT SCIENCE HAS YET TO PROVE THE PURIFICATION POWERS OF AGATE...
HOW-EVER...

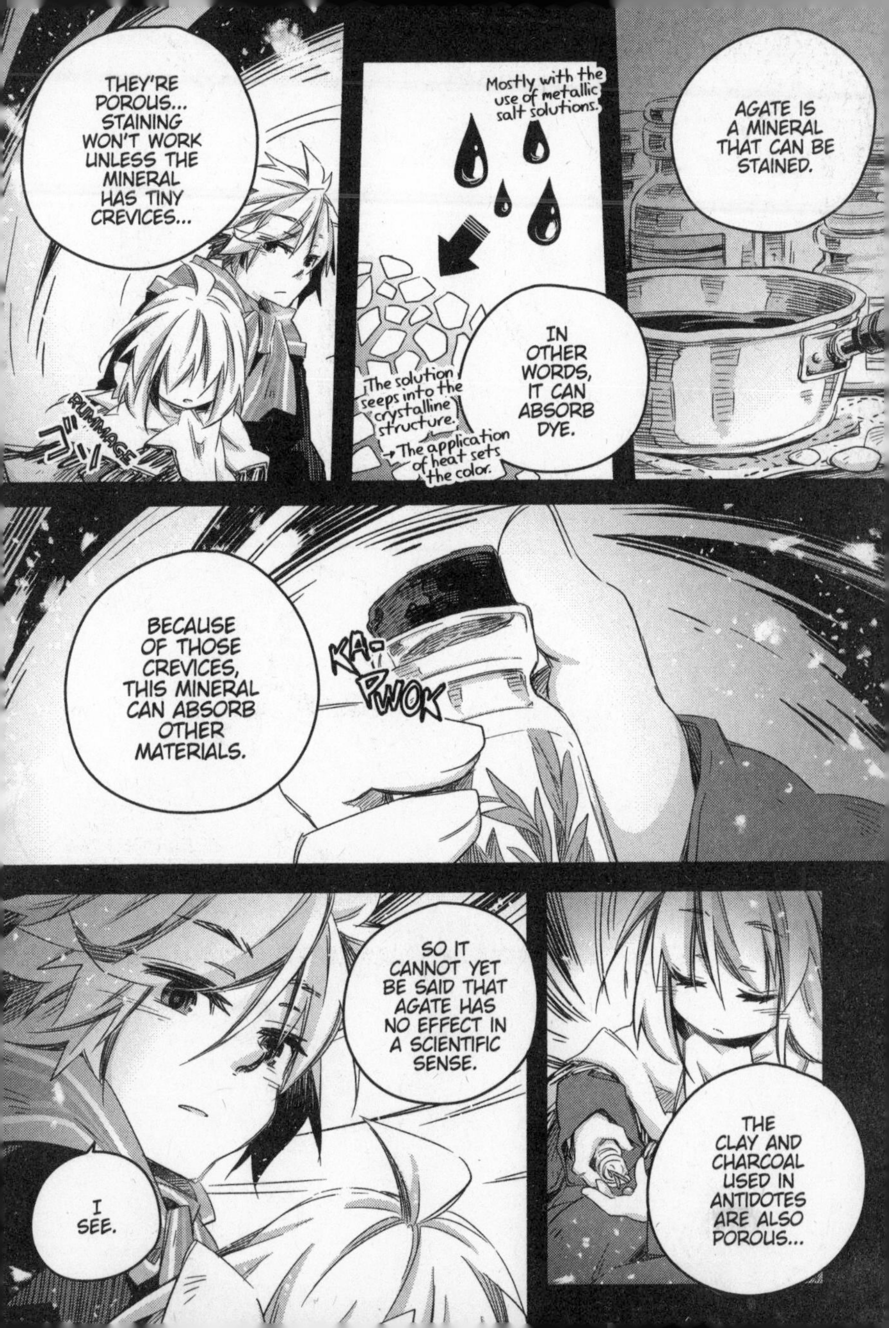
AGATE IS A MINERAL THAT CAN BE STAINED.
Mostly with the use of metallic salt solutions.
IN OTHER WORDS, IT CAN ABSORB DYE.
The solution seeps into the crystalline structure.
→The application of heat sets the color.
THEY'RE POROUS... STAINING WON'T WORK UNLESS THE MINERAL HAS TINY CREVICES...
RUMMAGE
BECAUSE OF THOSE CREVICES, THIS MINERAL CAN ABSORB OTHER MATERIALS.
KA-PWOK
THE CLAY AND CHARCOAL USED IN ANTIDOTES ARE ALSO POROUS...
SO IT CANNOT YET BE SAID THAT AGATE HAS NO EFFECT IN A SCIENTIFIC SENSE.
I SEE.

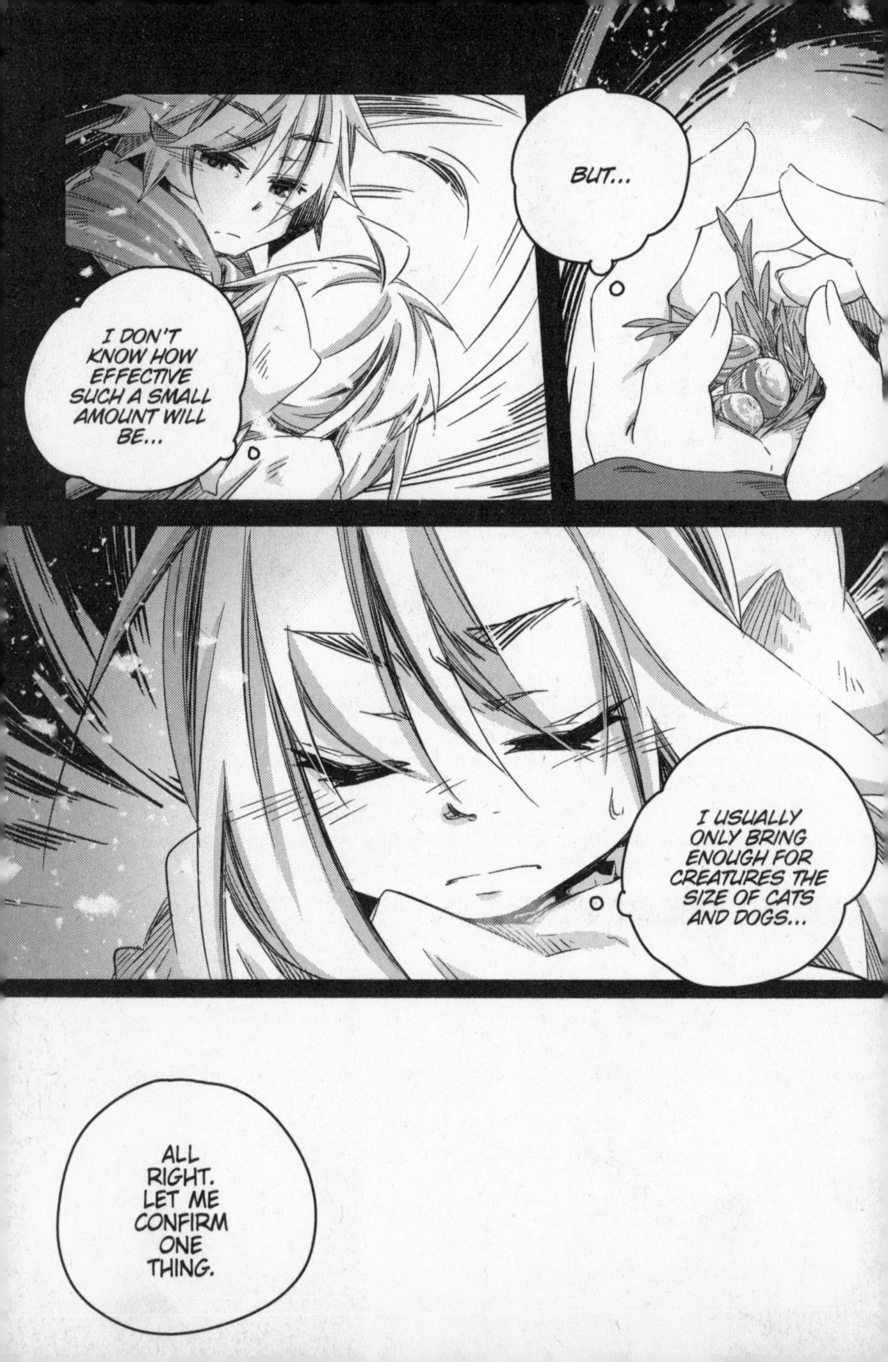
BUT...
I DON'T KNOW HOW EFFECTIVE SUCH A SMALL AMOUNT WILL BE...
I USUALLY ONLY BRING ENOUGH FOR CREATURES THE SIZE OF CATS AND DOGS...
ALL RIGHT. LET ME CONFIRM ONE THING.

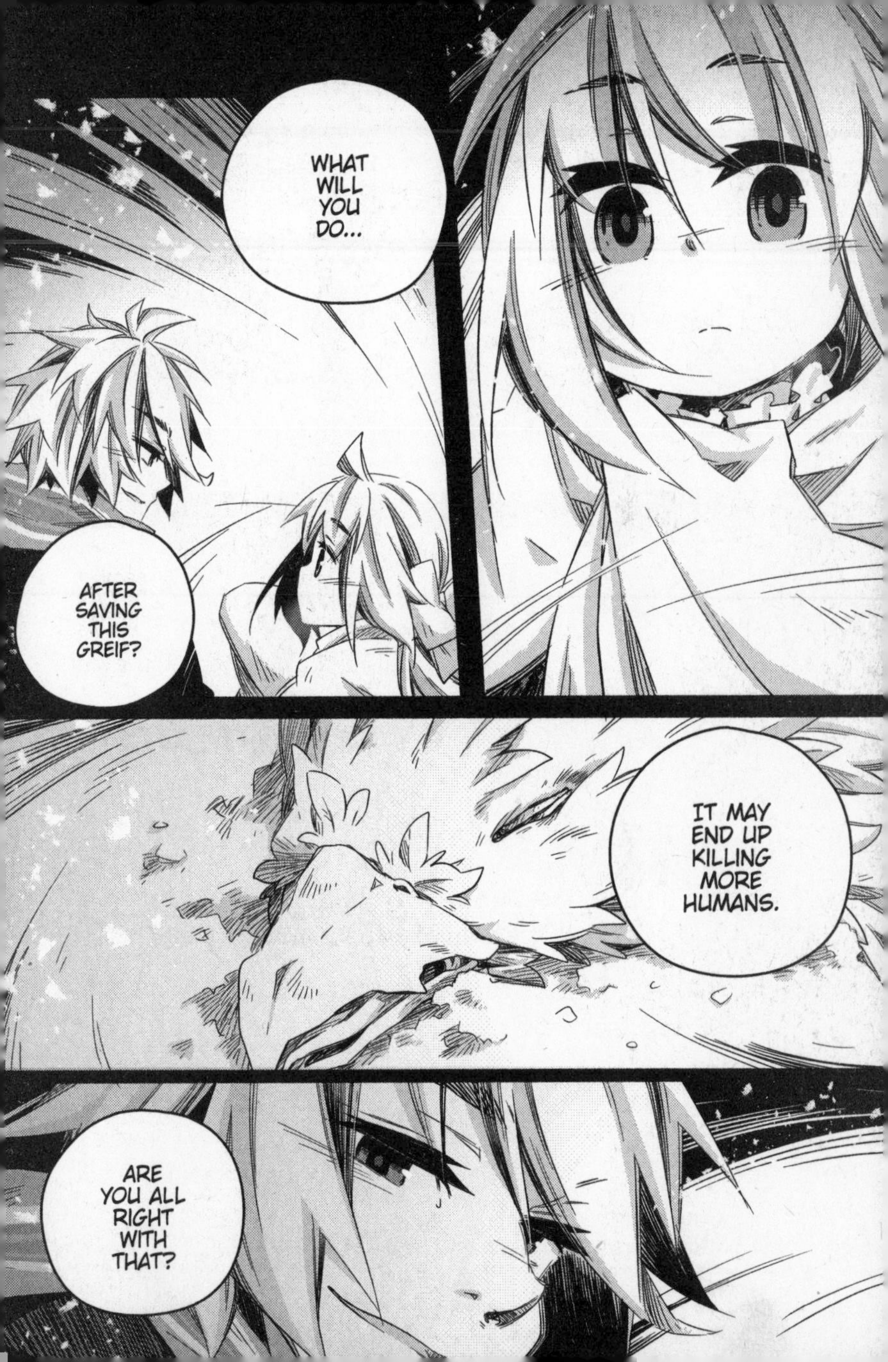
WHAT WILL YOU DO...
AFTER SAVING THIS GREIF?
IT MAY END UP KILLING MORE HUMANS.
ARE YOU ALL RIGHT WITH THAT?

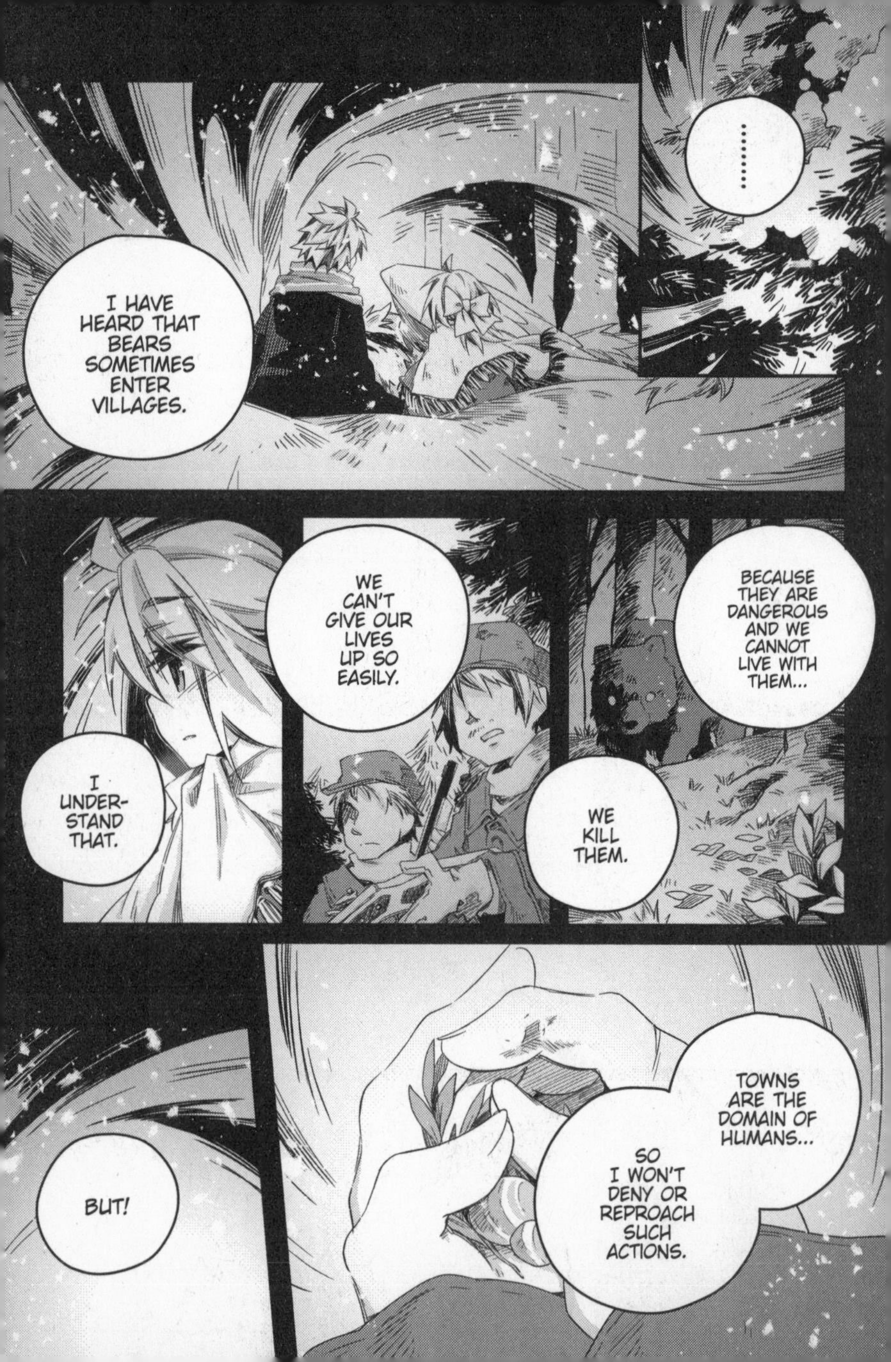
......
I HAVE HEARD THAT BEARS SOMETIMES ENTER VILLAGES.
BECAUSE THEY ARE DANGEROUS AND WE CANNOT LIVE WITH THEM...
WE KILL THEM.
WE CAN'T GIVE OUR LIVES UP SO EASILY.
I UNDER-STAND THAT.
TOWNS ARE THE DOMAIN OF HUMANS...
SO I WON'T DENY OR REPROACH SUCH ACTIONS.
BUT!

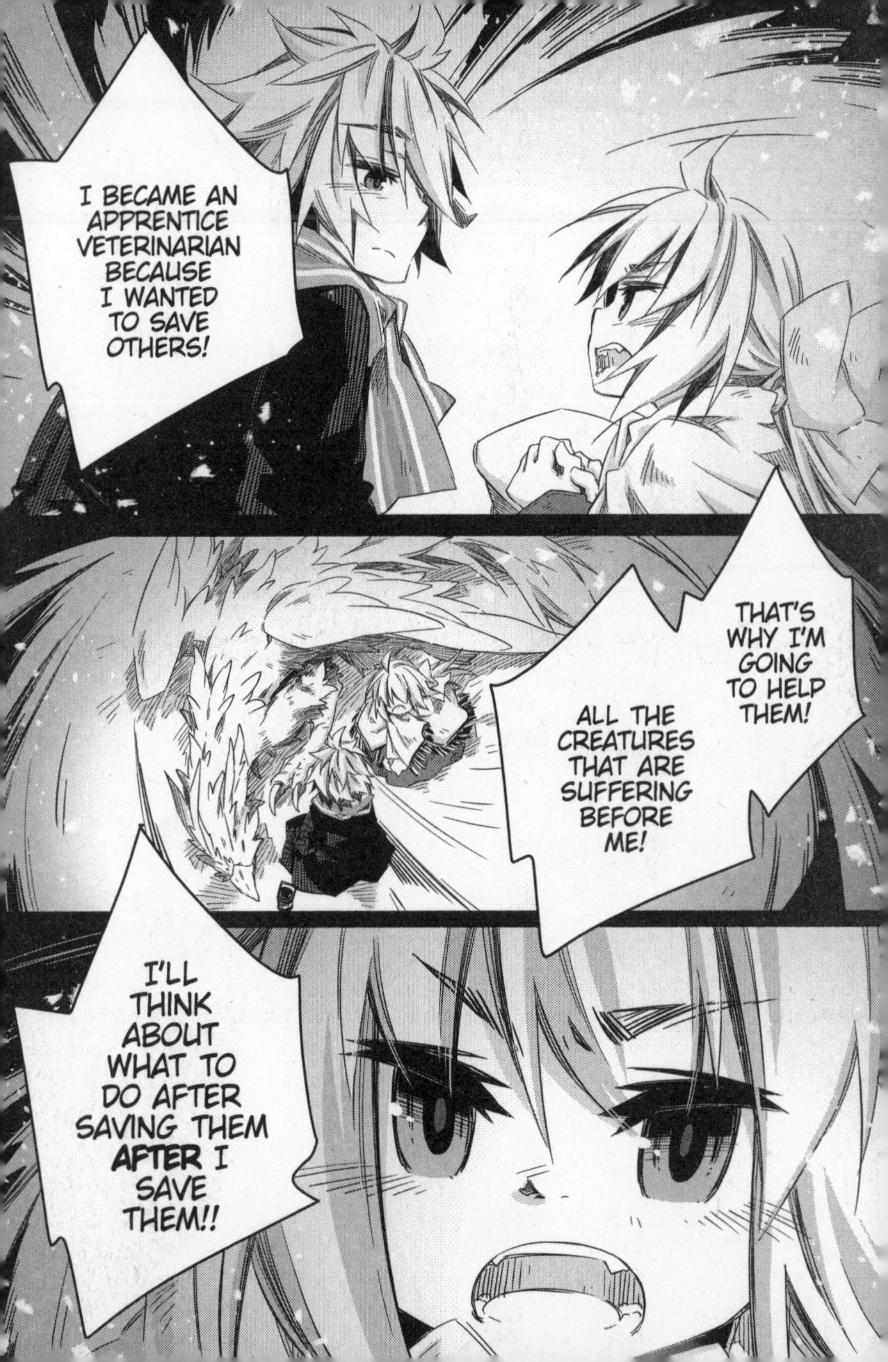
I BECAME AN APPRENTICE VETERINARIAN BECAUSE I WANTED TO SAVE OTHERS!
THAT'S WHY I'M GOING TO HELP THEM!
ALL THE CREATURES THAT ARE SUFFERING BEFORE ME!
I'LL THINK ABOUT WHAT TO DO AFTER SAVING THEM **AFTER** I SAVE THEM!!

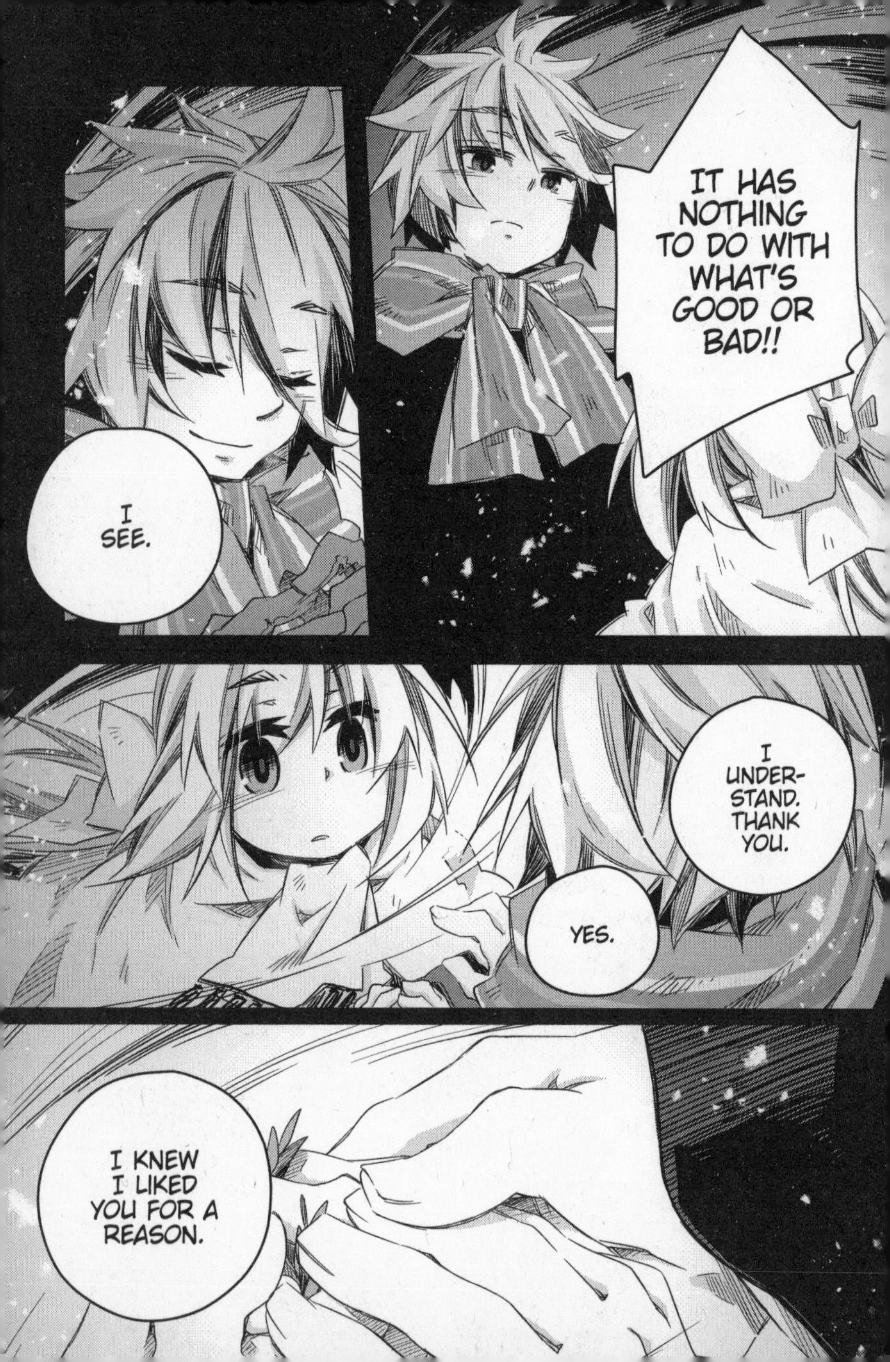
IT HAS NOTHING TO DO WITH WHAT'S GOOD OR BAD!!
I SEE.
I UNDERSTAND. THANK YOU.
YES.
I KNEW I LIKED YOU FOR A REASON.

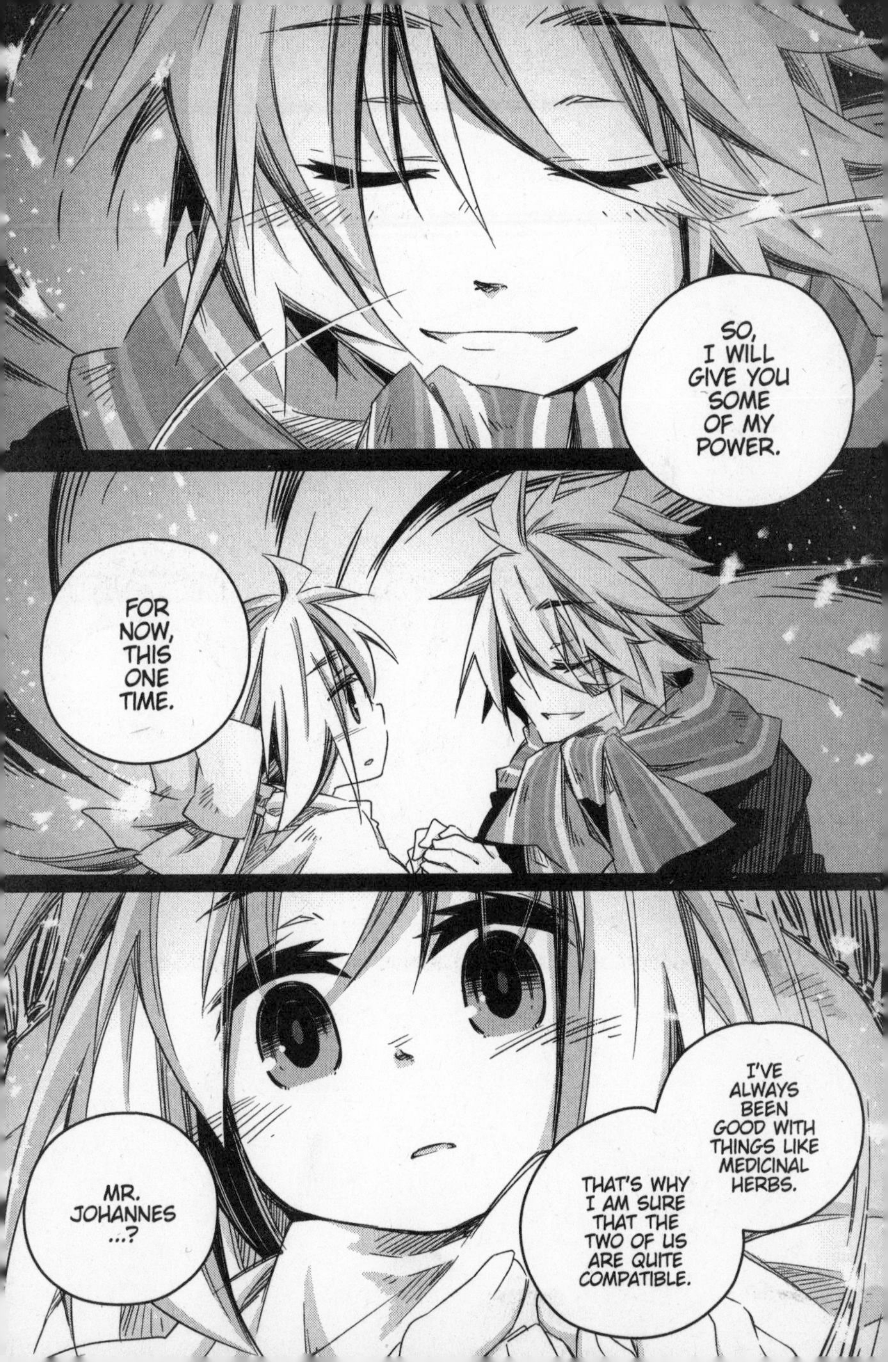
SO, I WILL GIVE YOU SOME OF MY POWER.
FOR NOW, THIS ONE TIME.
I'VE ALWAYS BEEN GOOD WITH THINGS LIKE MEDICINAL HERBS.
THAT'S WHY I AM SURE THAT THE TWO OF US ARE QUITE COMPATIBLE.
MR. JOHANNES ...?

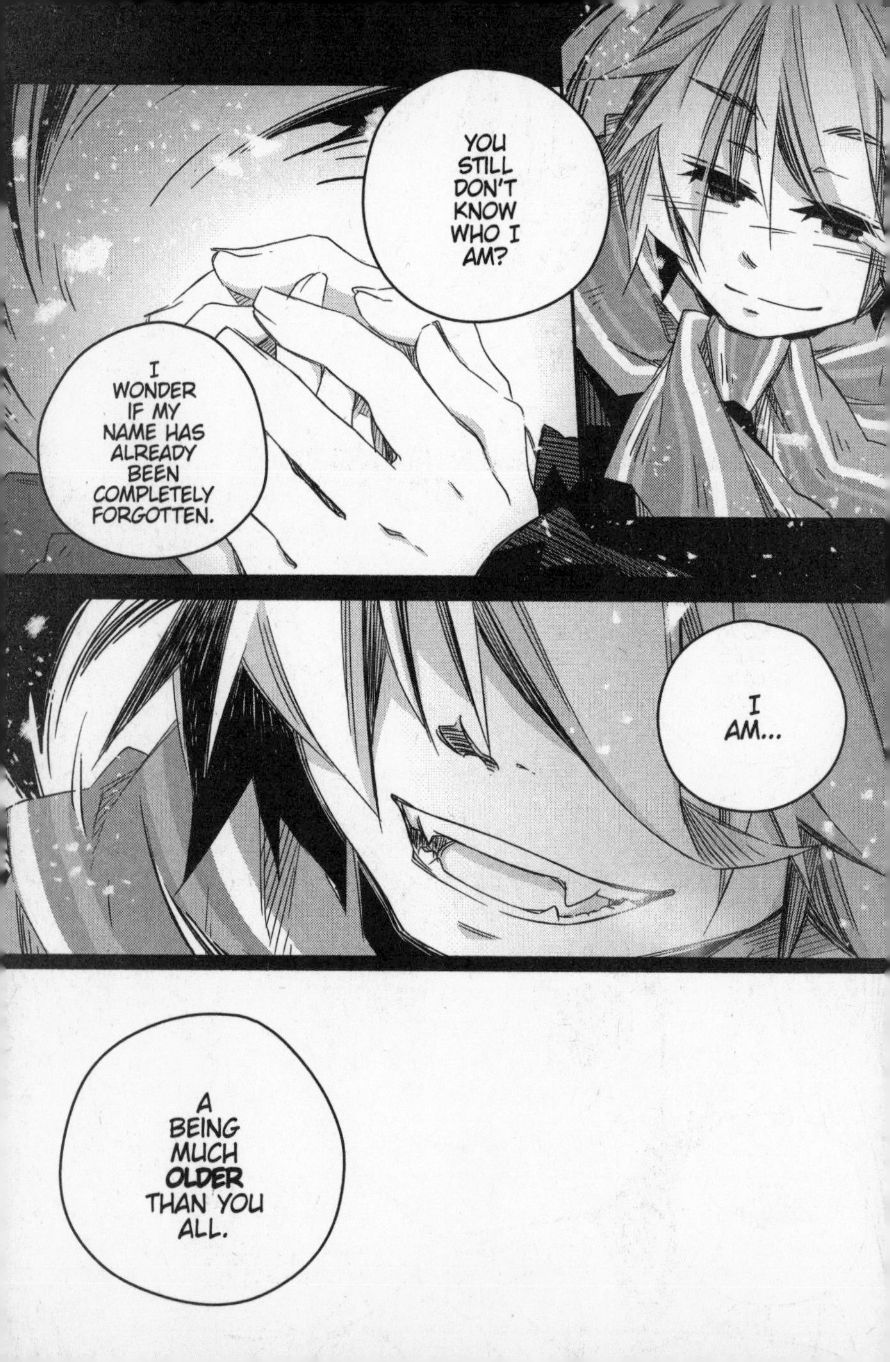
YOU STILL DON'T KNOW WHO I AM?
I WONDER IF MY NAME HAS ALREADY BEEN COMPLETELY FORGOTTEN.
I AM...
A BEING MUCH **OLDER** THAN YOU ALL.

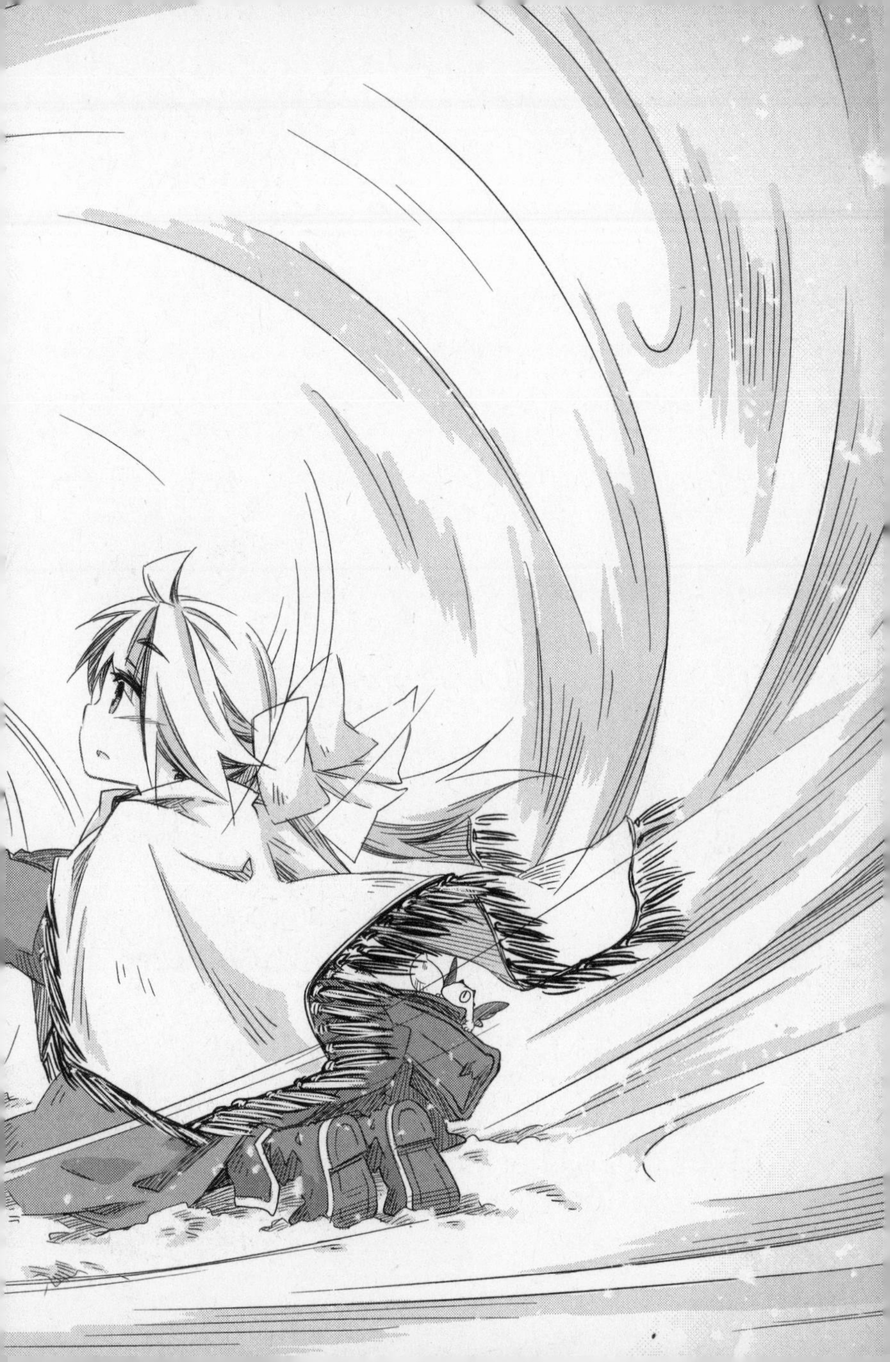

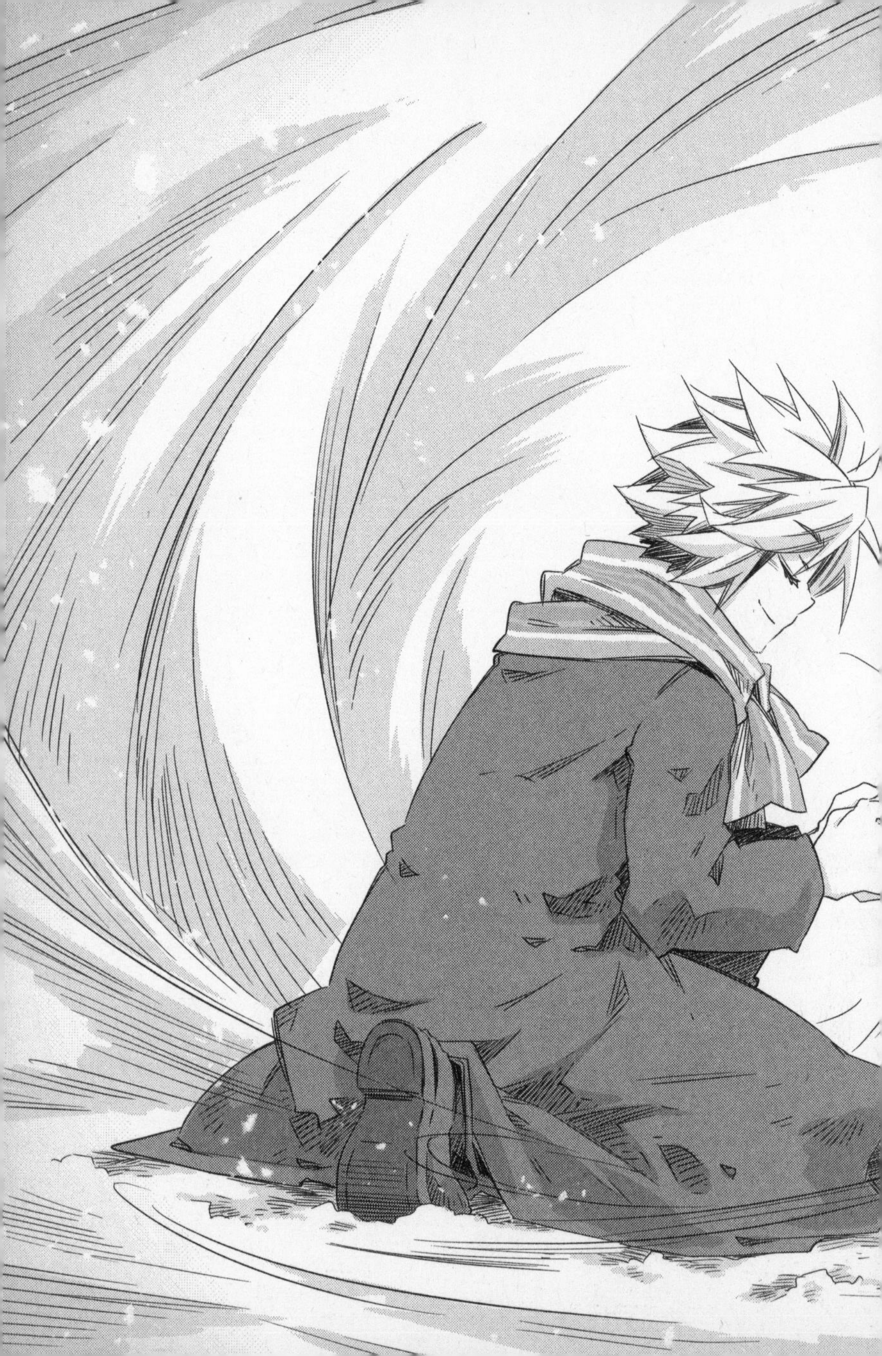

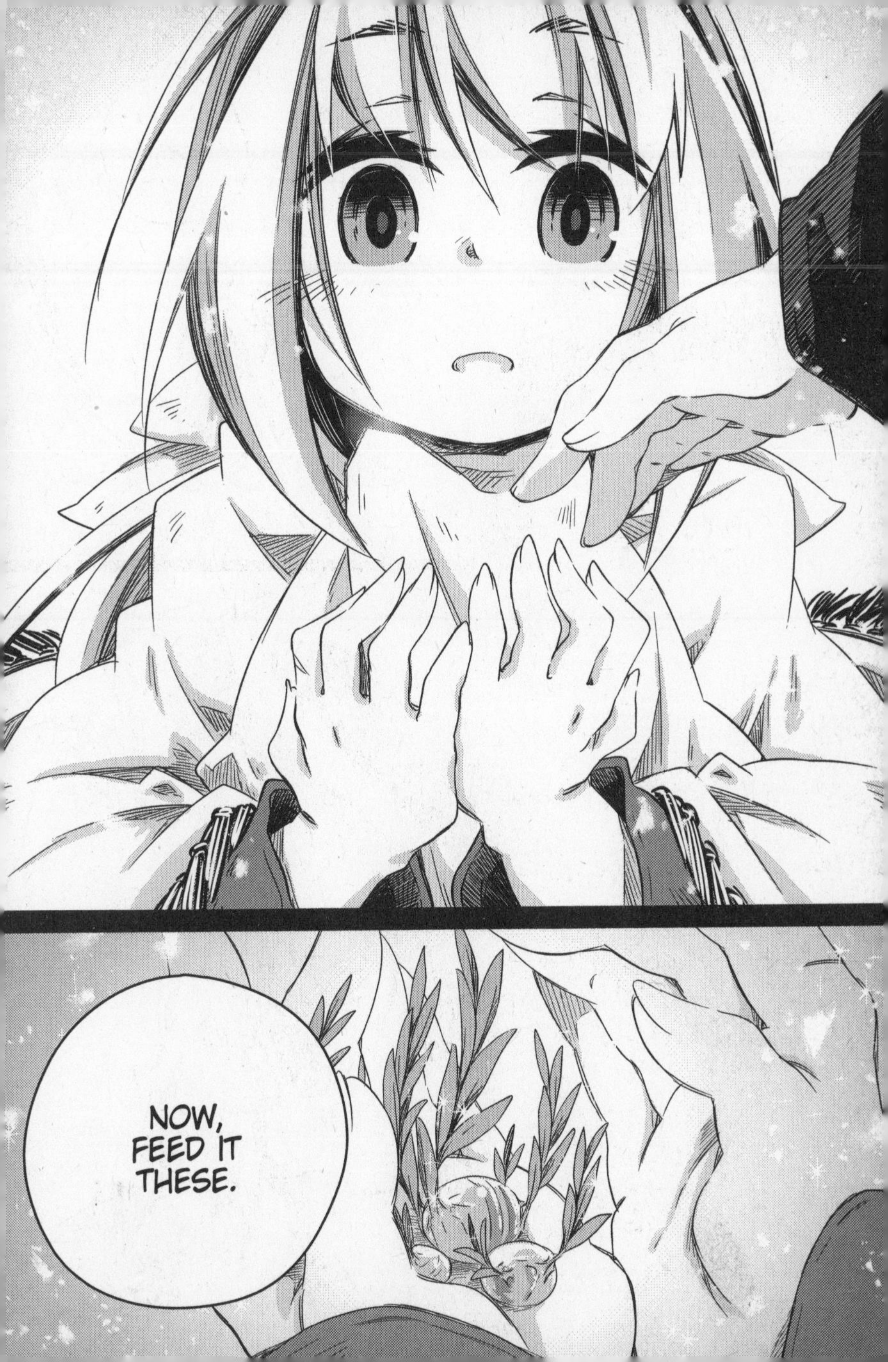
NOW, FEED IT THESE.

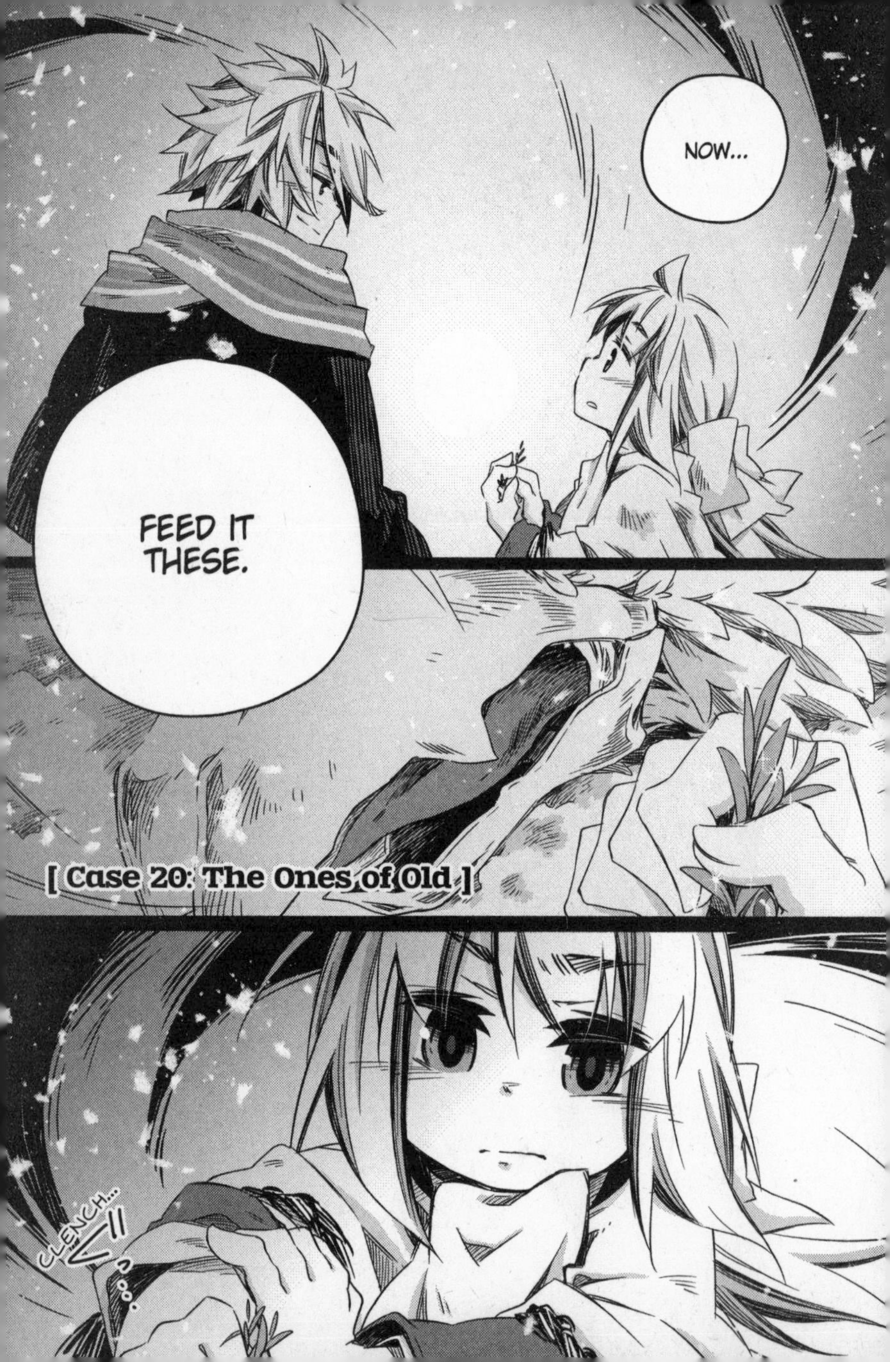
NOW...
FEED IT THESE.
[Case 20: The Ones of Old]
CLENCH...

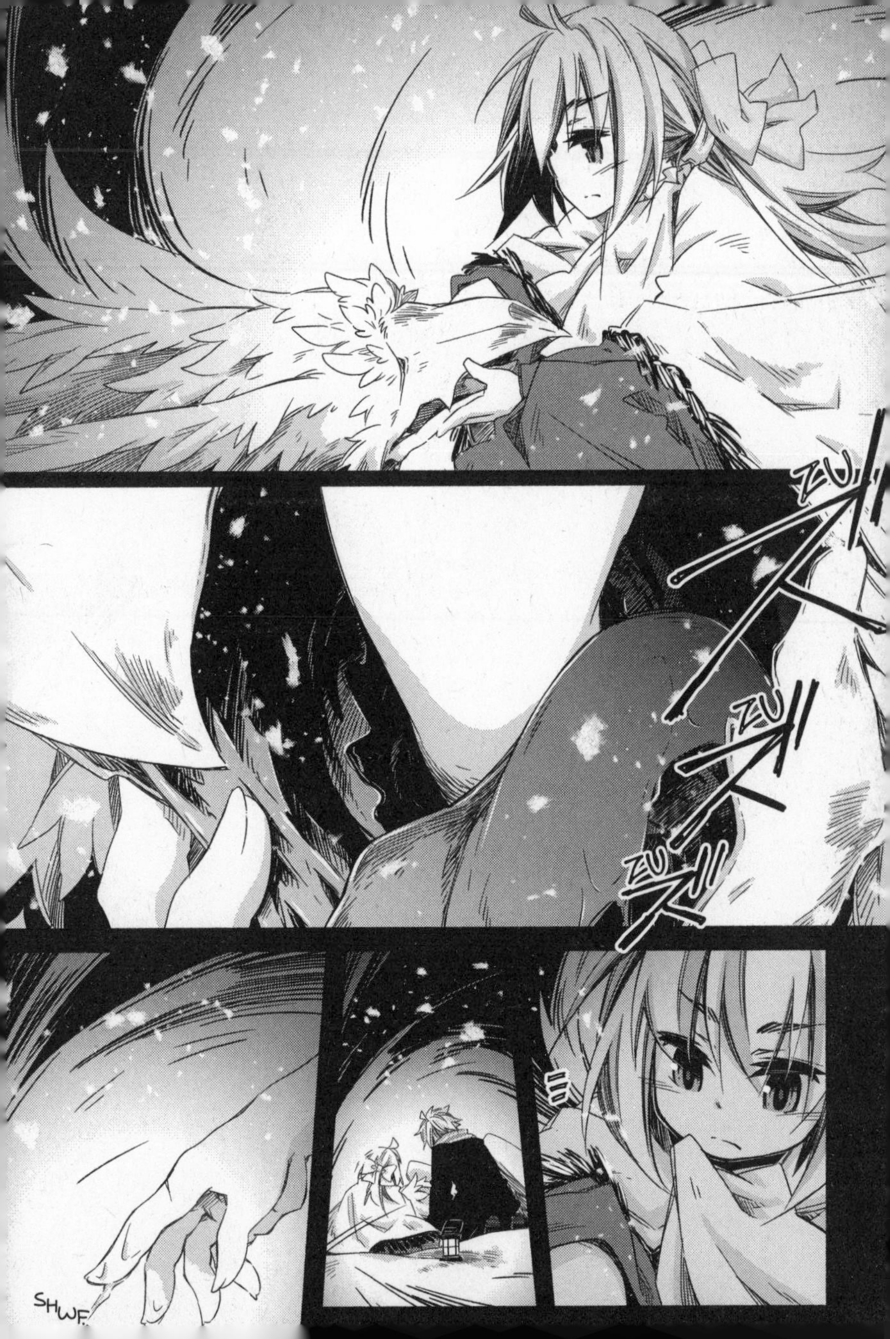
ZU
ZU
ZU
SHWF.

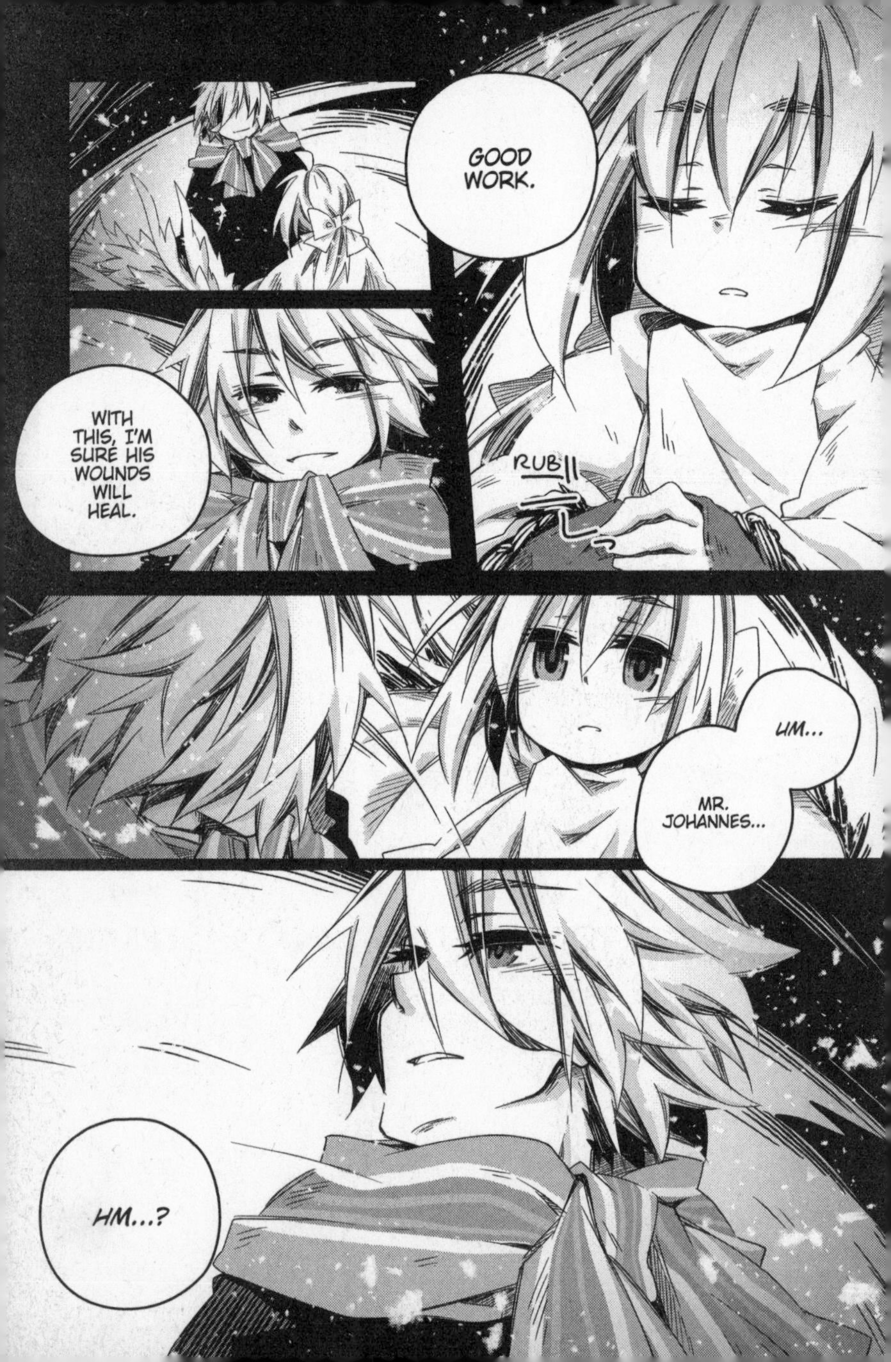
GOOD WORK.
RUB
WITH THIS, I'M SURE HIS WOUNDS WILL HEAL.
UM...
MR. JOHANNES...
HM...?

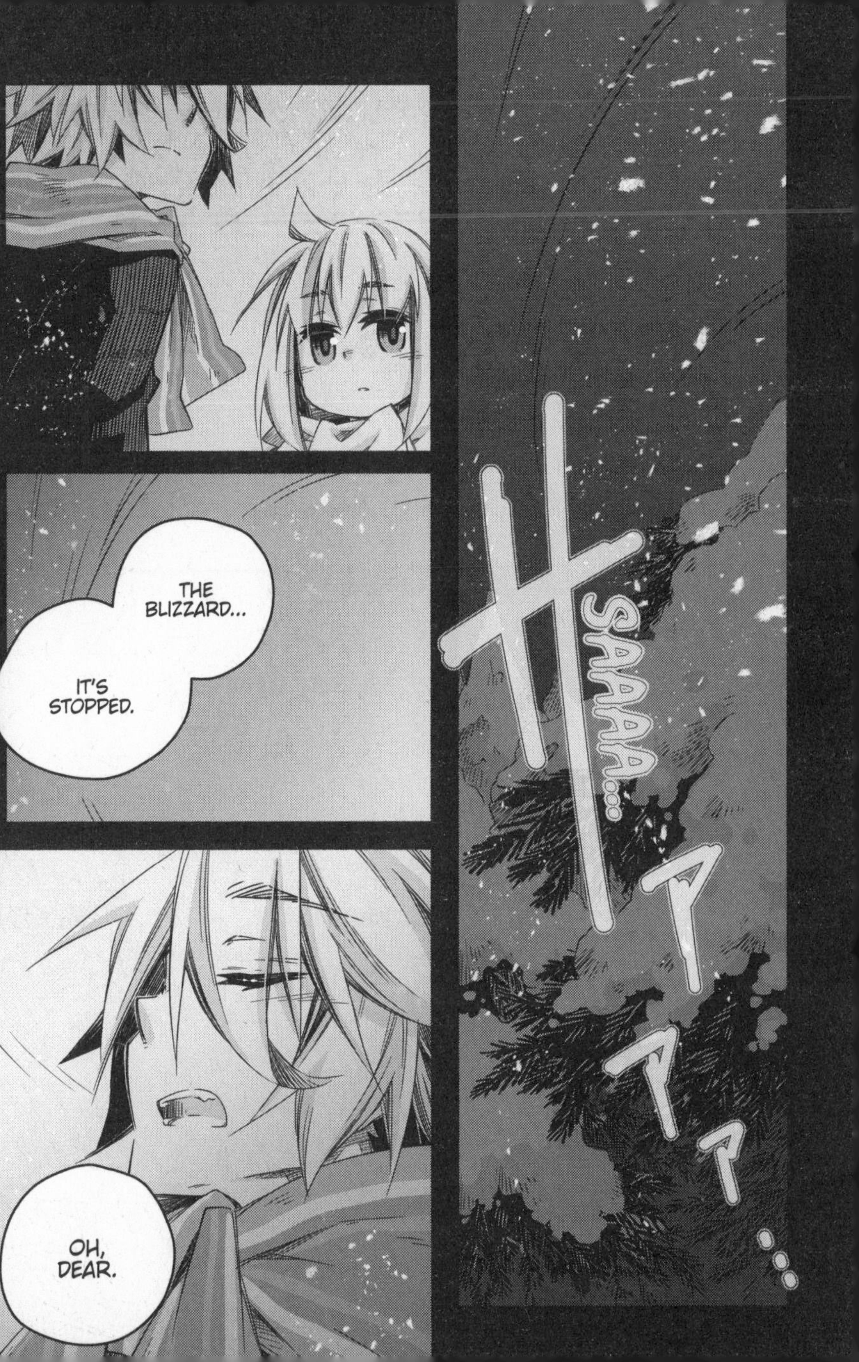
SAAAA...
THE BLIZZARD...
IT'S STOPPED.
OH, DEAR.

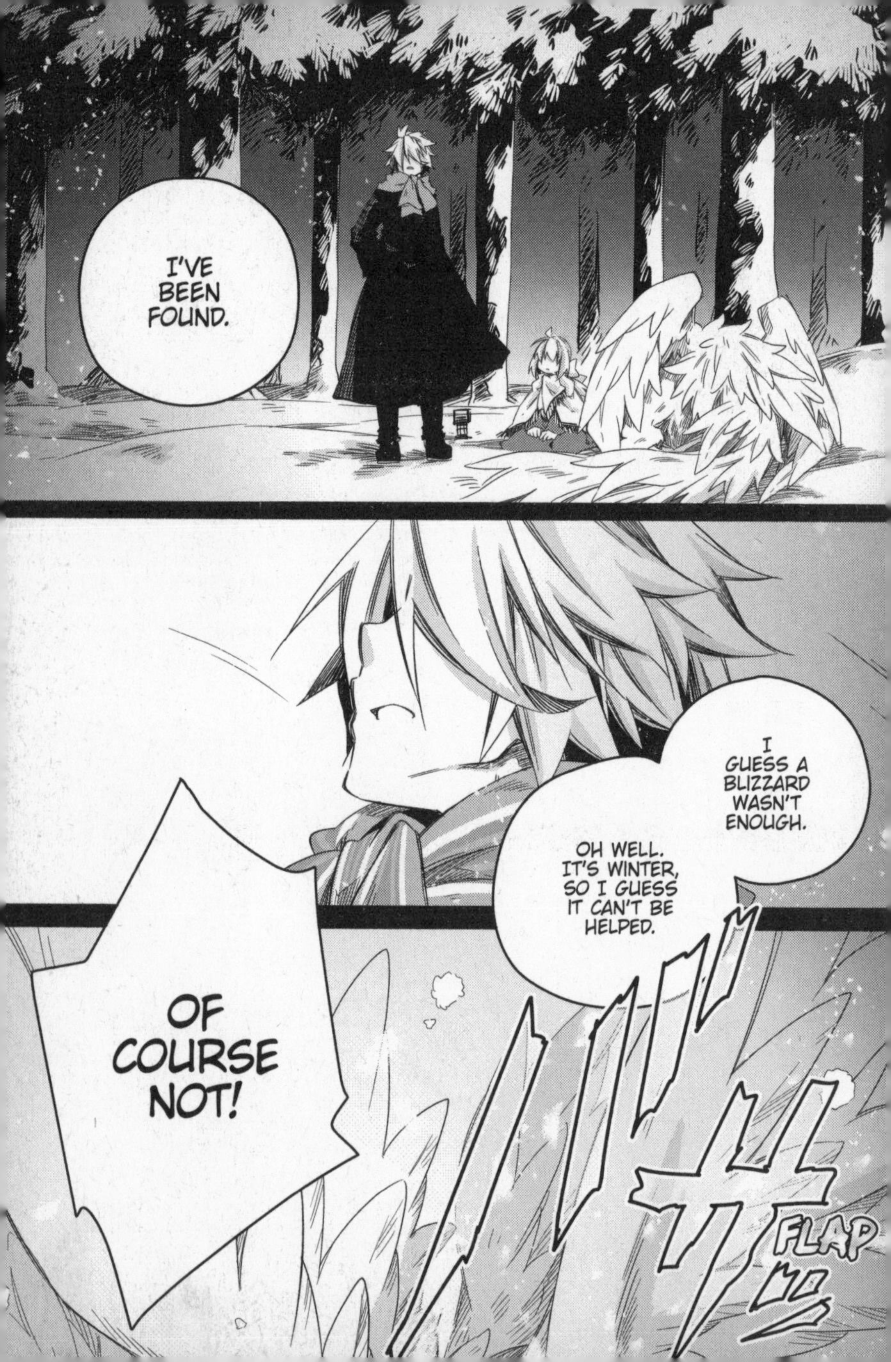
I'VE BEEN FOUND.
I GUESS A BLIZZARD WASN'T ENOUGH.
OH WELL. IT'S WINTER, SO I GUESS IT CAN'T BE HELPED.
OF COURSE NOT!
FLAP

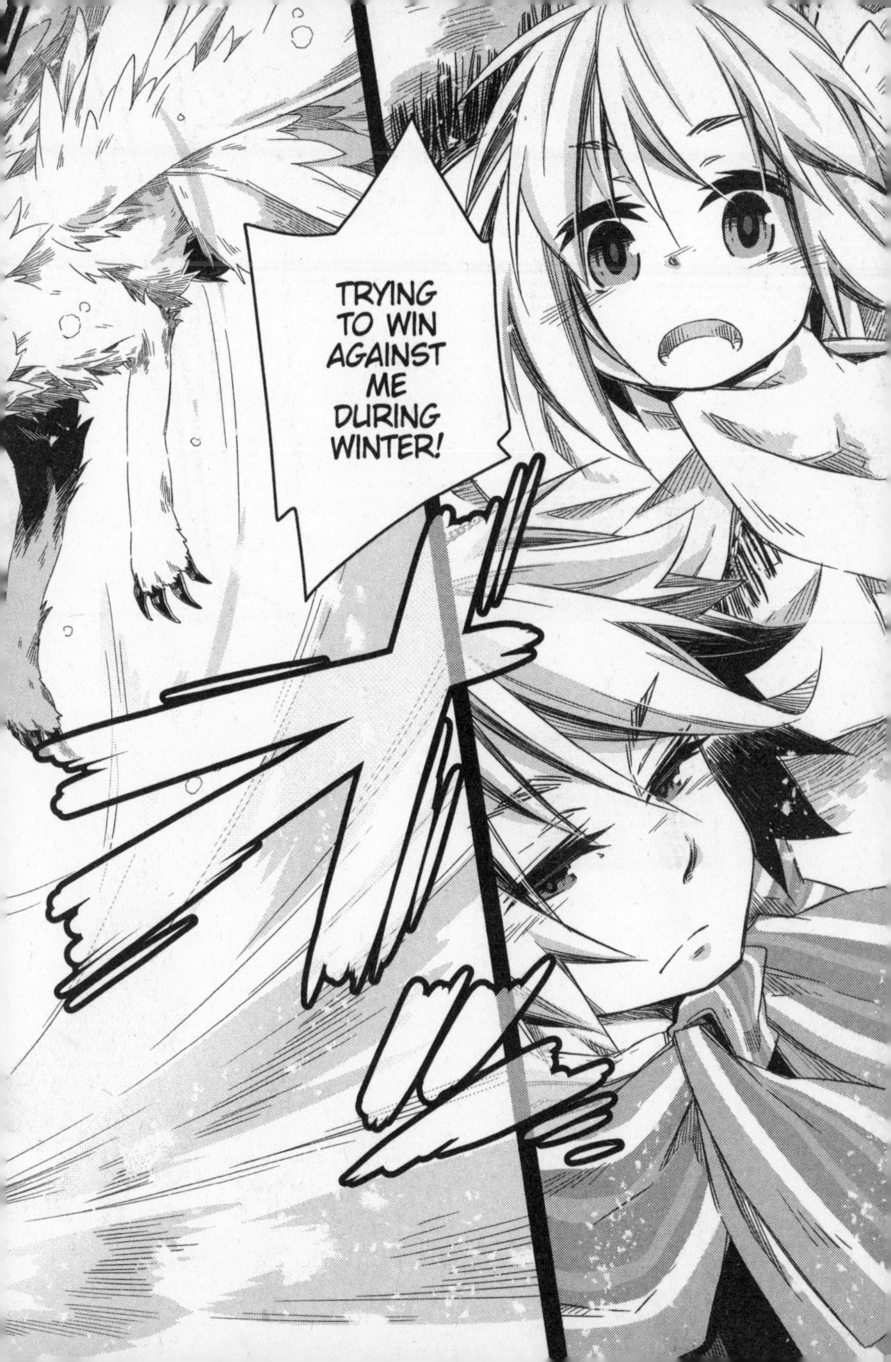
TRYING TO WIN AGAINST ME DURING WINTER!

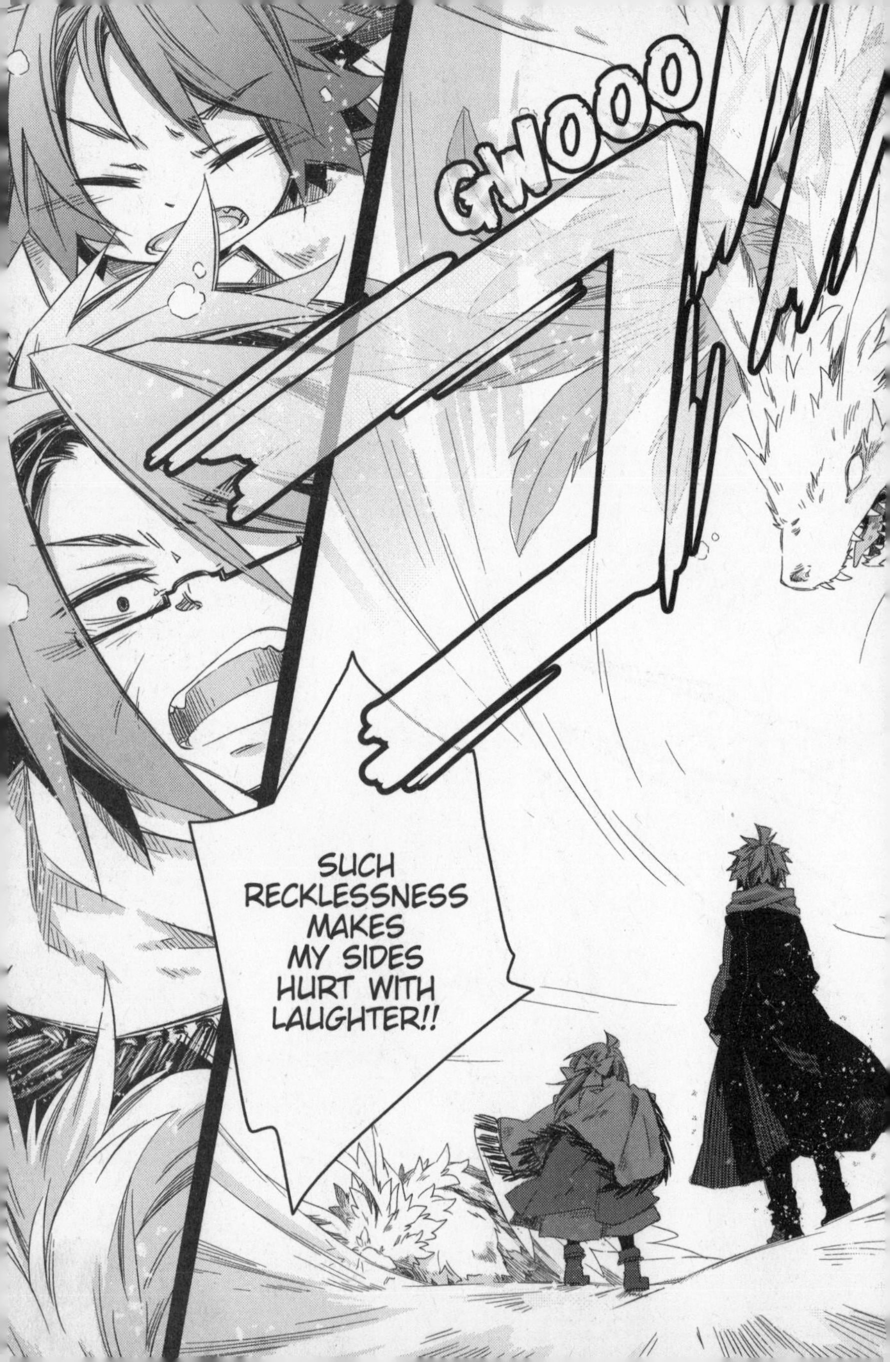
GWOOO
SUCH RECKLESSNESS MAKES MY SIDES HURT WITH LAUGHTER!!

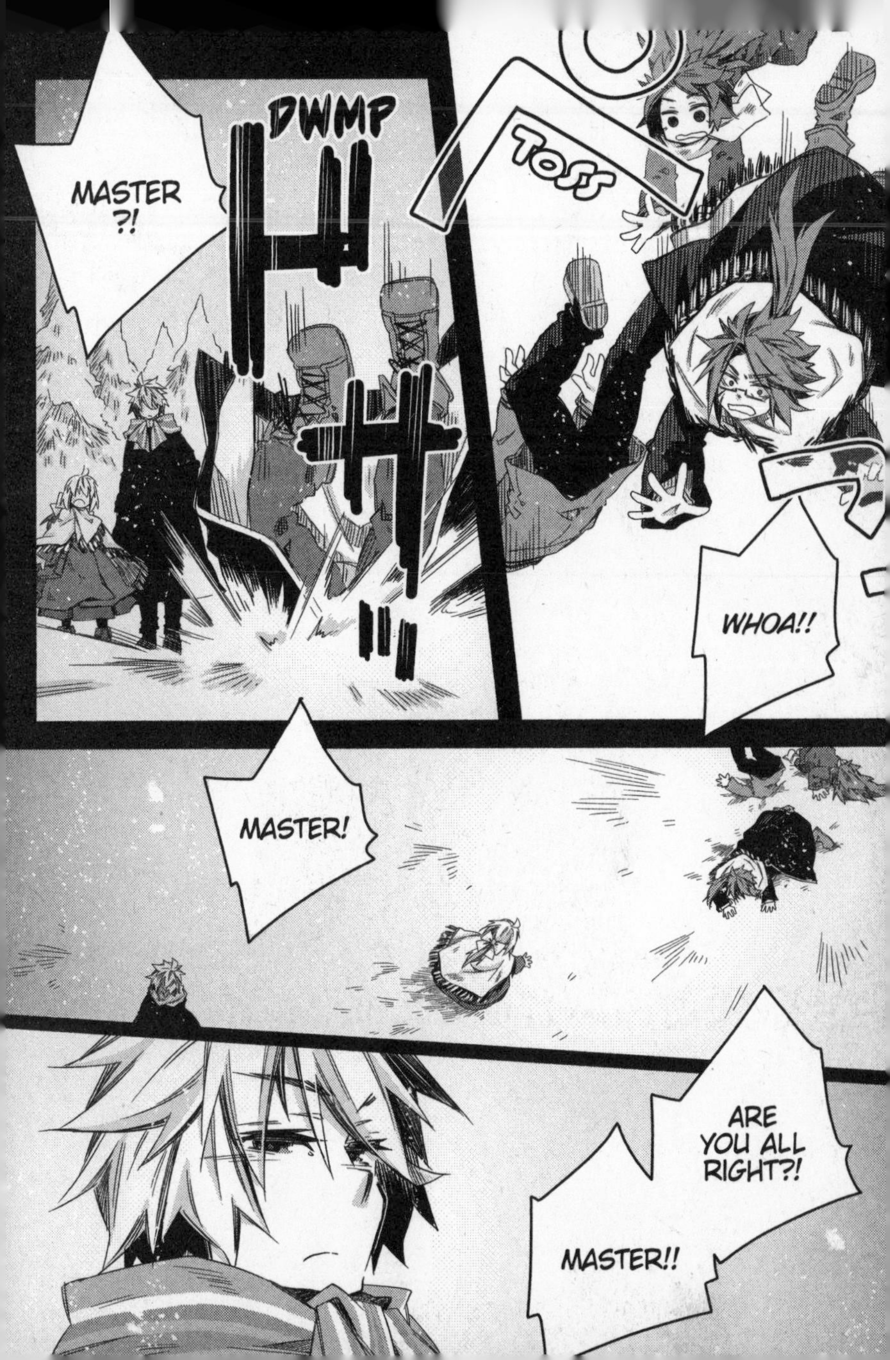
TOSS
WHOA!!
DWMP
MASTER ?!
MASTER!
ARE YOU ALL RIGHT?!
MASTER!!

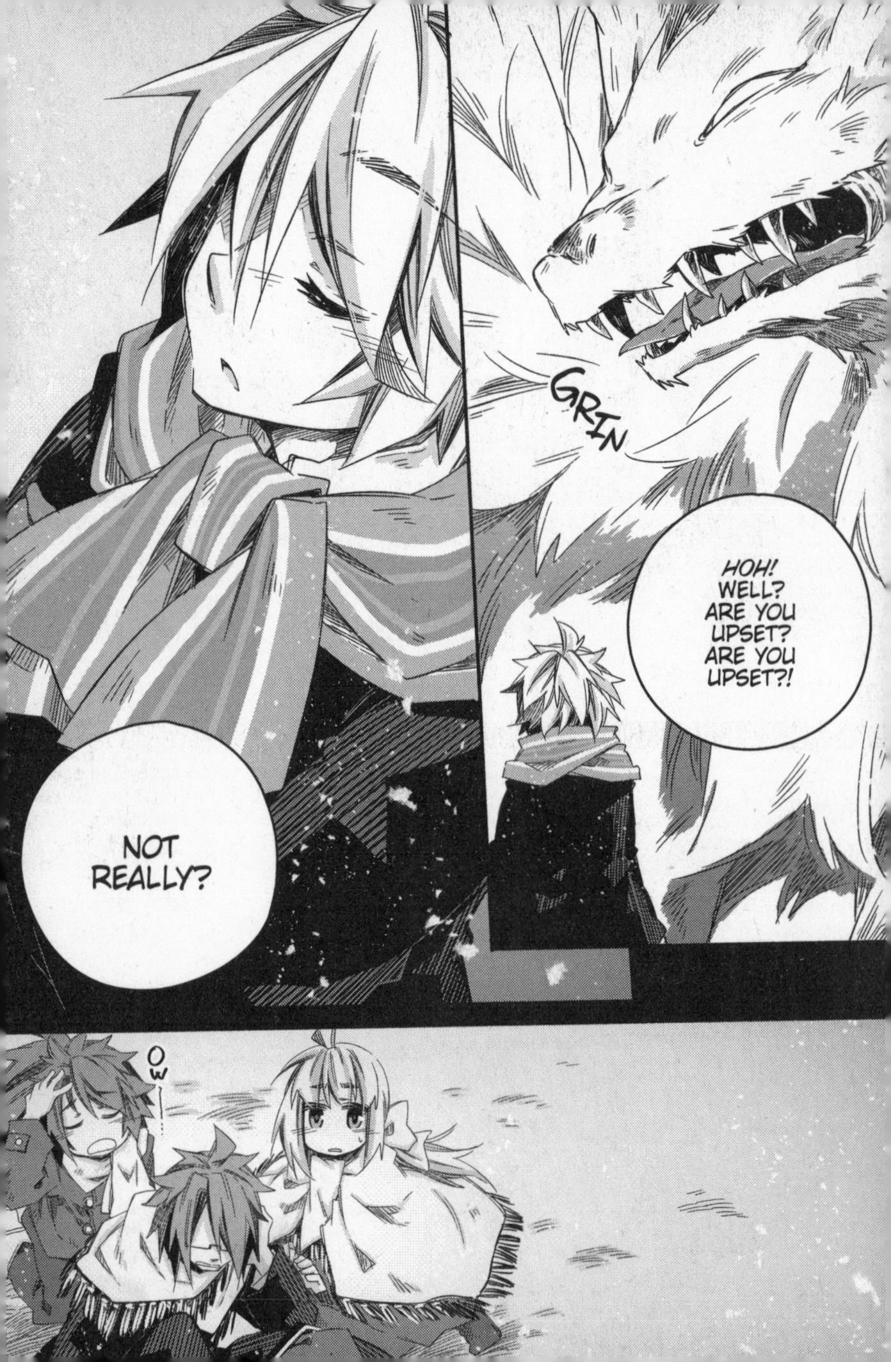
GRIN
HOH! WELL? ARE YOU UPSET? ARE YOU UPSET?!
NOT REALLY?
OW...

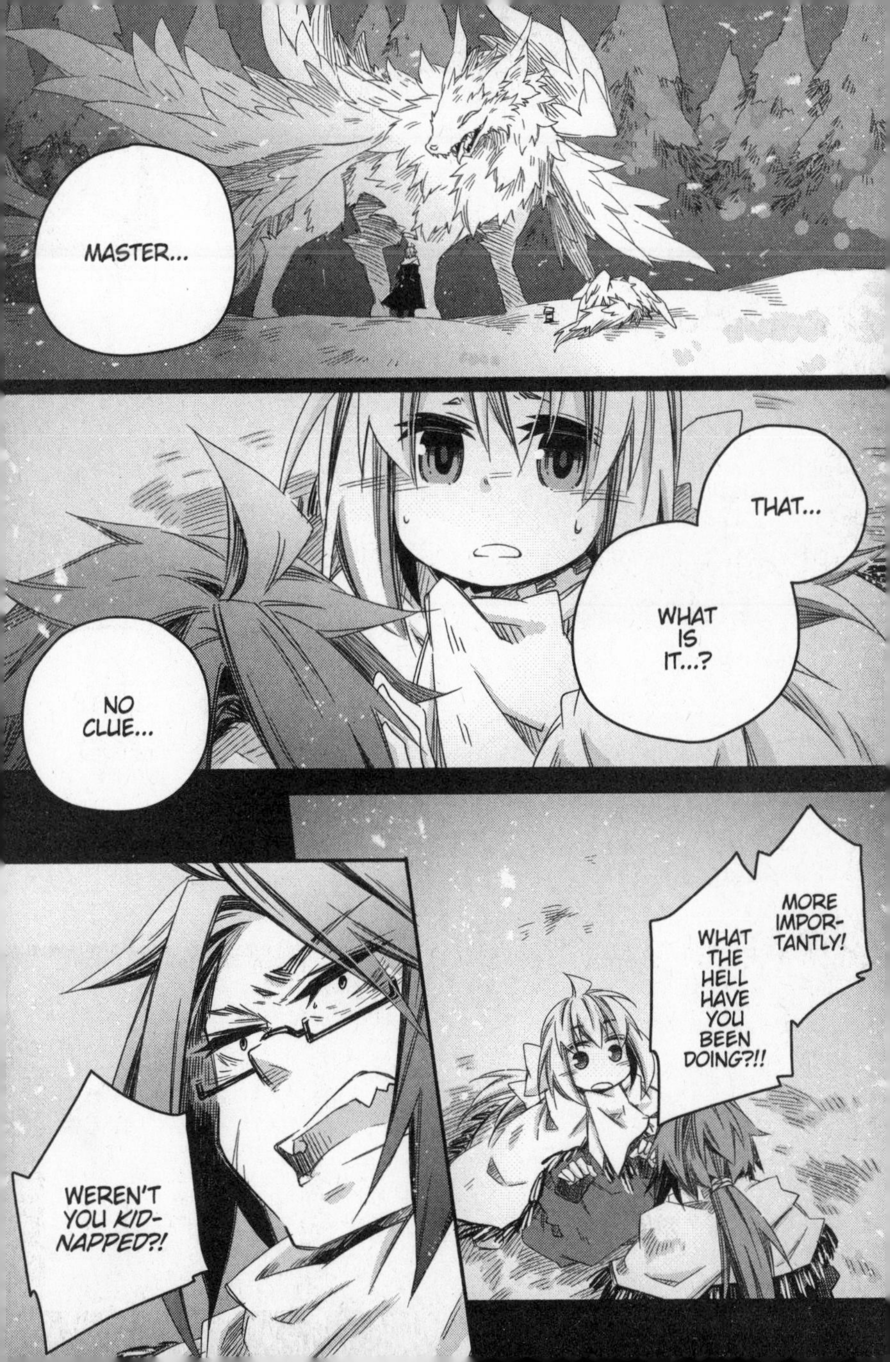
MASTER...
THAT...
WHAT IS IT...?
NO CLUE...
MORE IMPORTANTLY!
WHAT THE HELL HAVE YOU BEEN DOING?!!
WEREN'T YOU *KID-NAPPED*?!

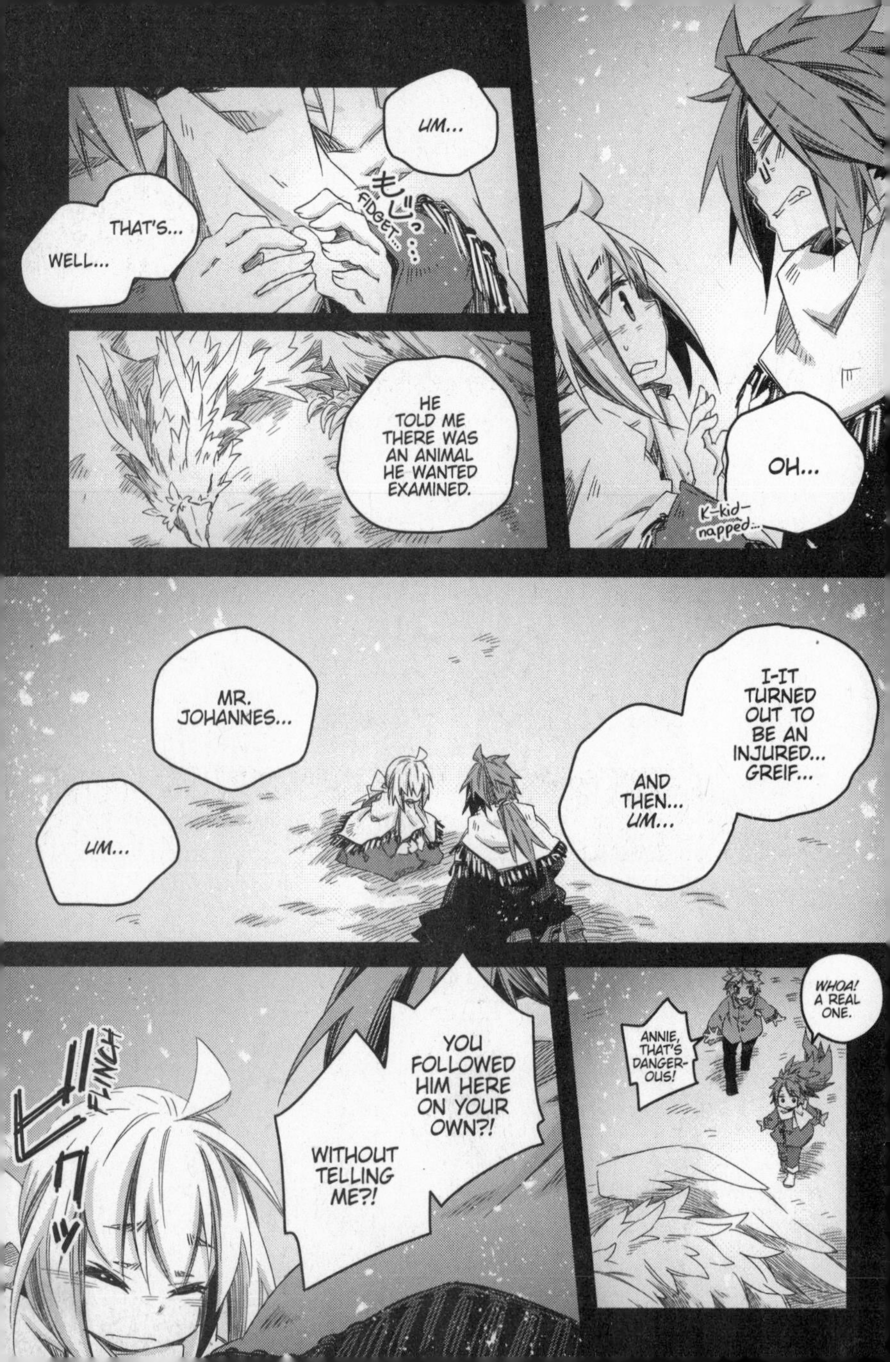
OH...
K-kid-napped...
UM...
FIDGET...
THAT'S...
WELL...
HE TOLD ME THERE WAS AN ANIMAL HE WANTED EXAMINED.
I-IT TURNED OUT TO BE AN INJURED... GREIF...
AND THEN... UM...
MR. JOHANNES...
UM...
WHOA! A REAL ONE.
ANNIE, THAT'S DANGER-OUS!
YOU FOLLOWED HIM HERE ON YOUR OWN?!
WITHOUT TELLING ME?!
FLINCH

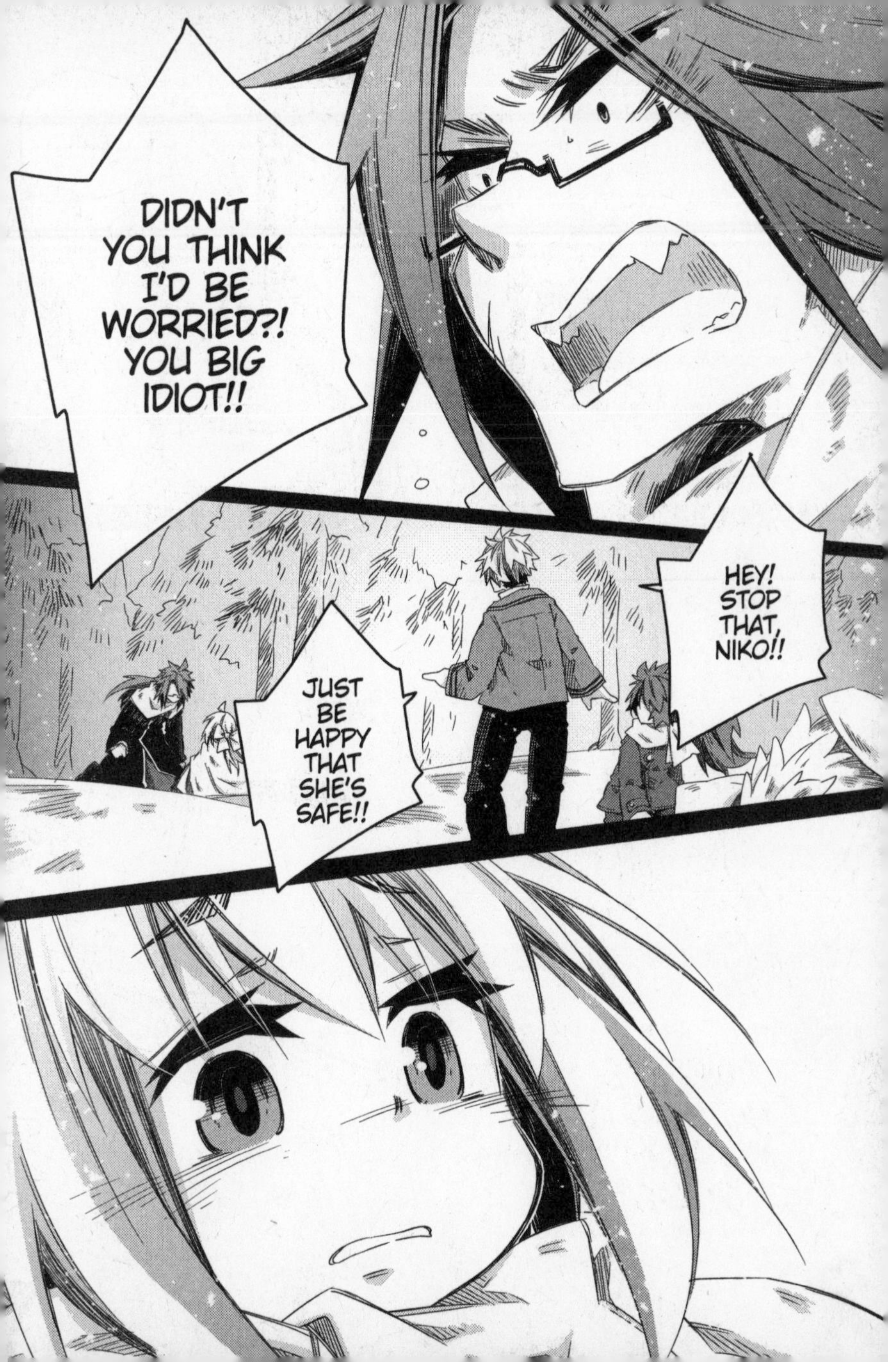
DIDN'T YOU THINK I'D BE WORRIED?! YOU BIG IDIOT!!
HEY! STOP THAT, NIKO!!
JUST BE HAPPY THAT SHE'S SAFE!!

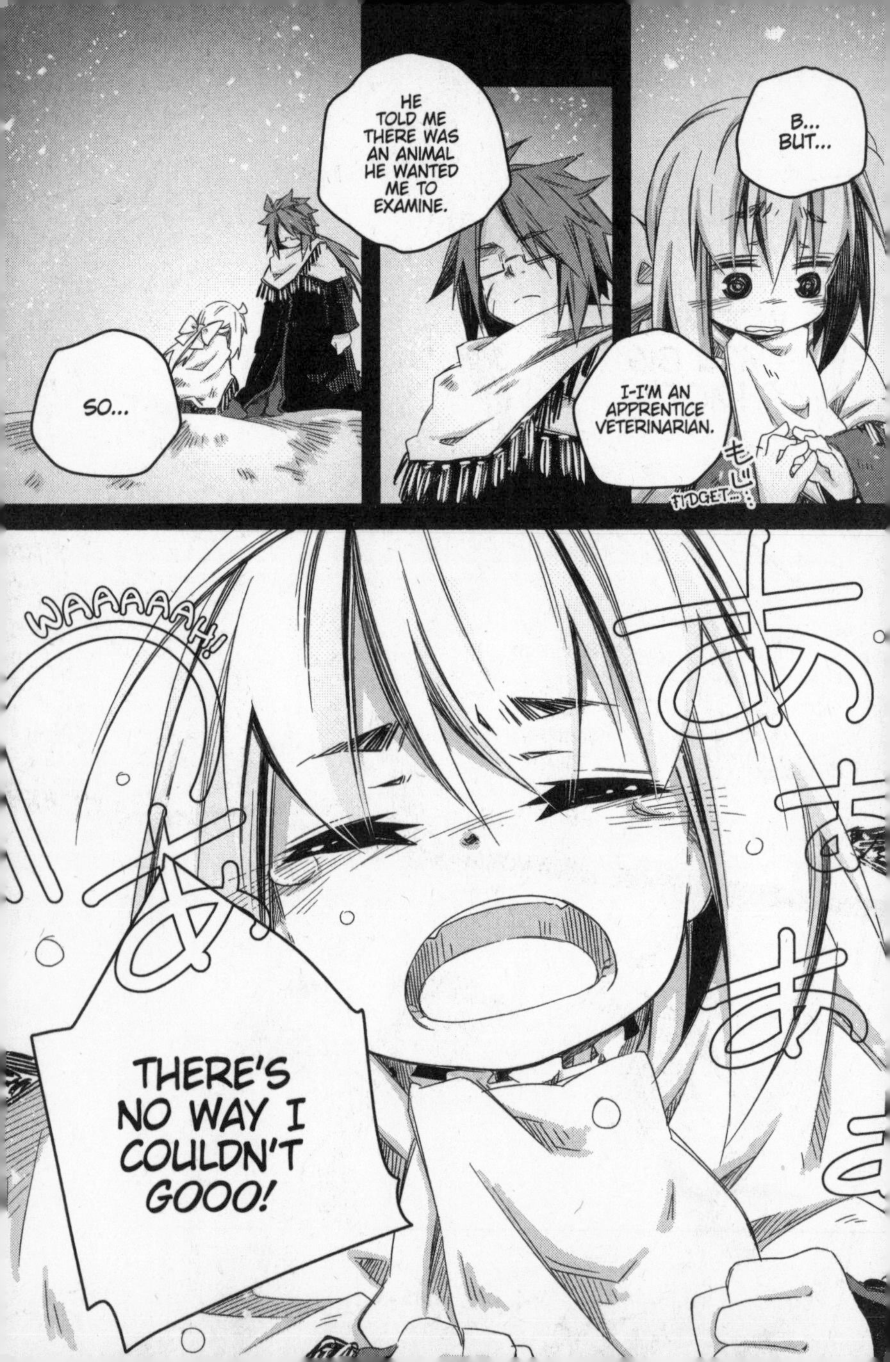
B... BUT...
I-I'M AN APPRENTICE VETERINARIAN.
FIDGET...
HE TOLD ME THERE WAS AN ANIMAL HE WANTED ME TO EXAMINE.
SO...
WAAAAAH!!
THERE'S NO WAY I COULDN'T GOOO!

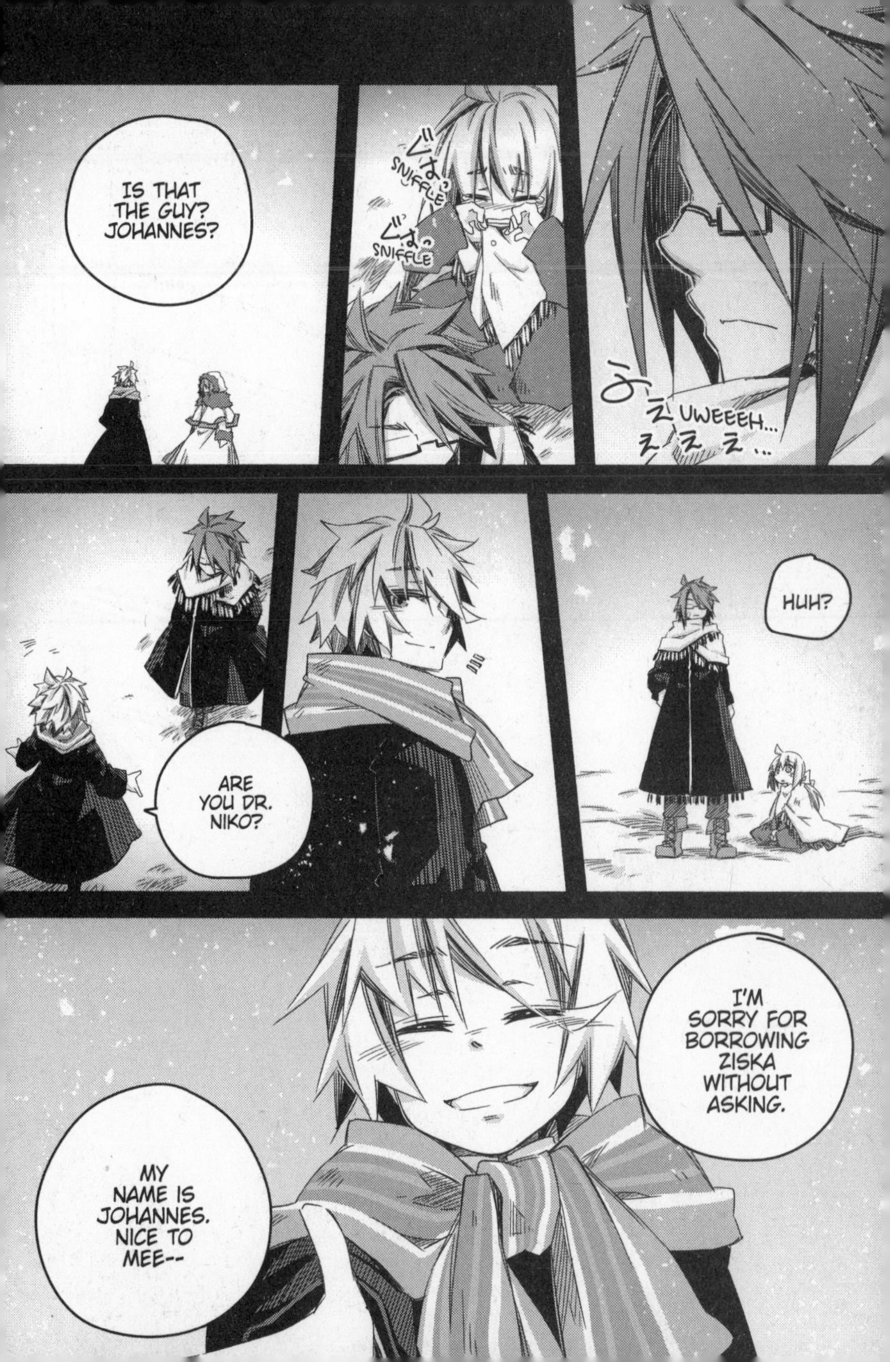
UWEEEH...
SNIFFLE
SNIFFLE
IS THAT THE GUY? JOHANNES?
HUH?
ARE YOU DR. NIKO?
I'M SORRY FOR BORROWING ZISKA WITHOUT ASKING.
MY NAME IS JOHANNES. NICE TO MEE--

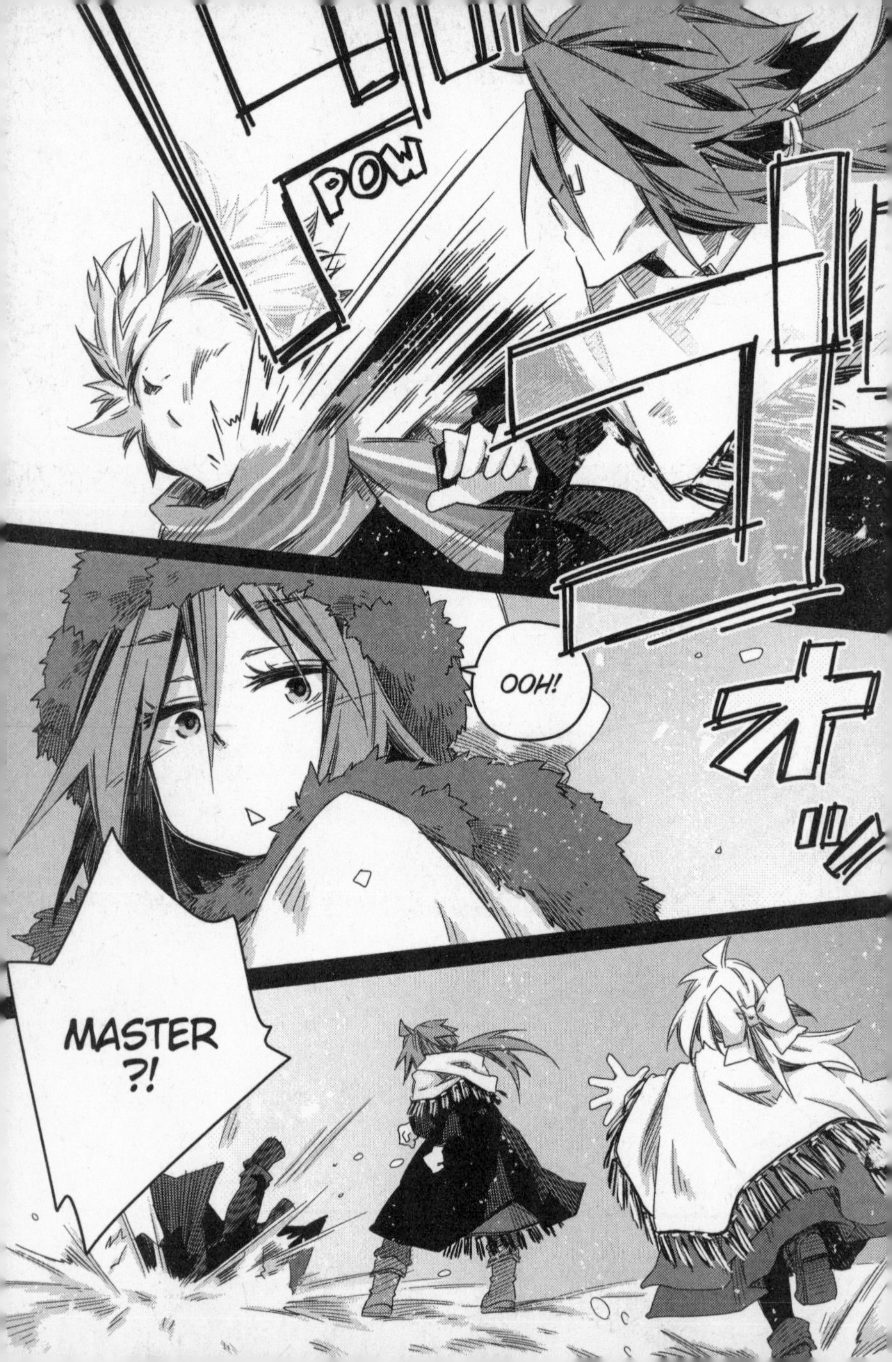
POW
OOH!
MASTER ?!

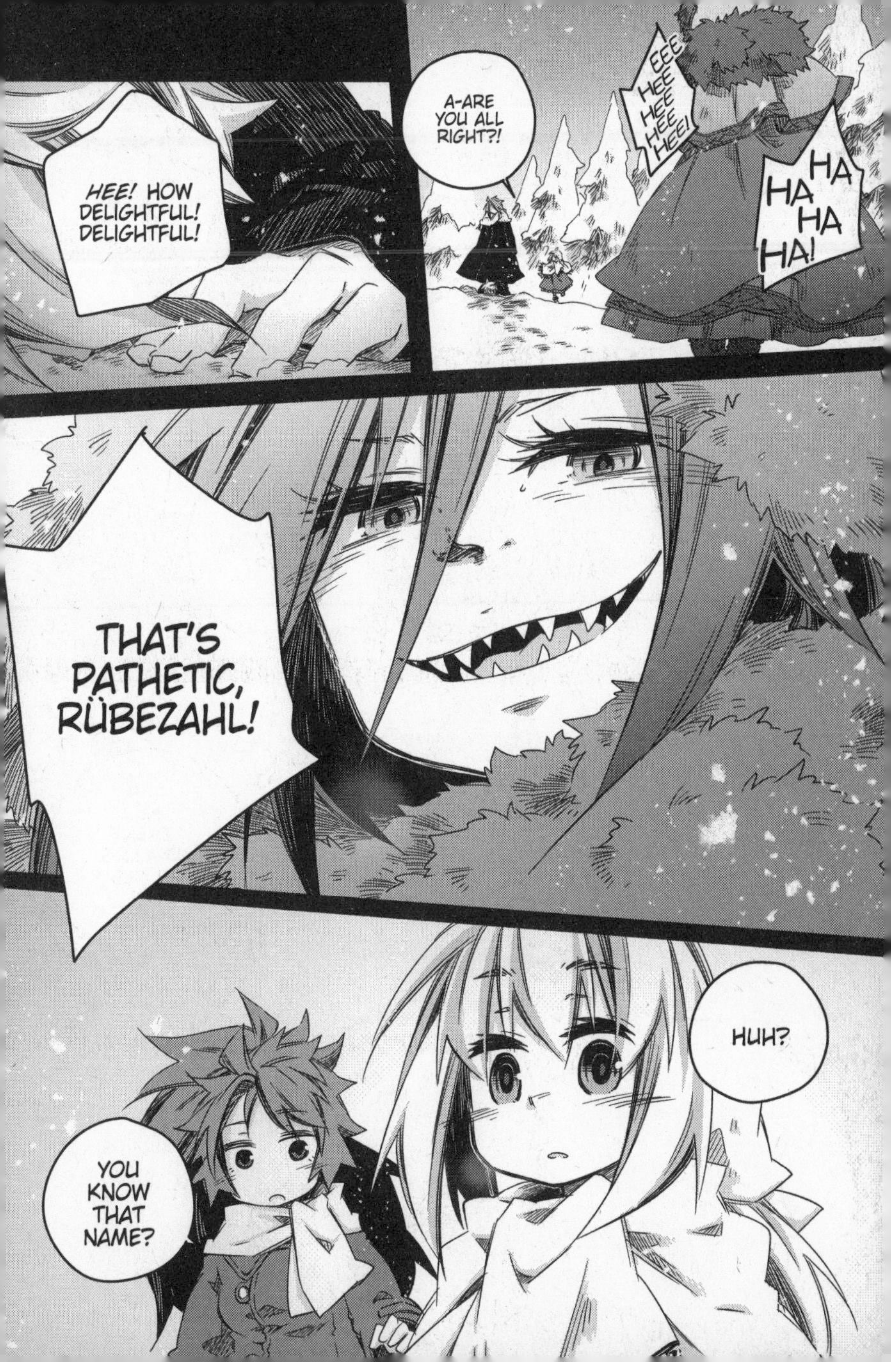
EEE HEE HEE HEE HEE!
HA HA HA HA!
A-ARE YOU ALL RIGHT?!
HEE! HOW DELIGHTFUL! DELIGHTFUL!
THAT'S PATHETIC, RÜBEZAHL!
HUH?
YOU KNOW THAT NAME?

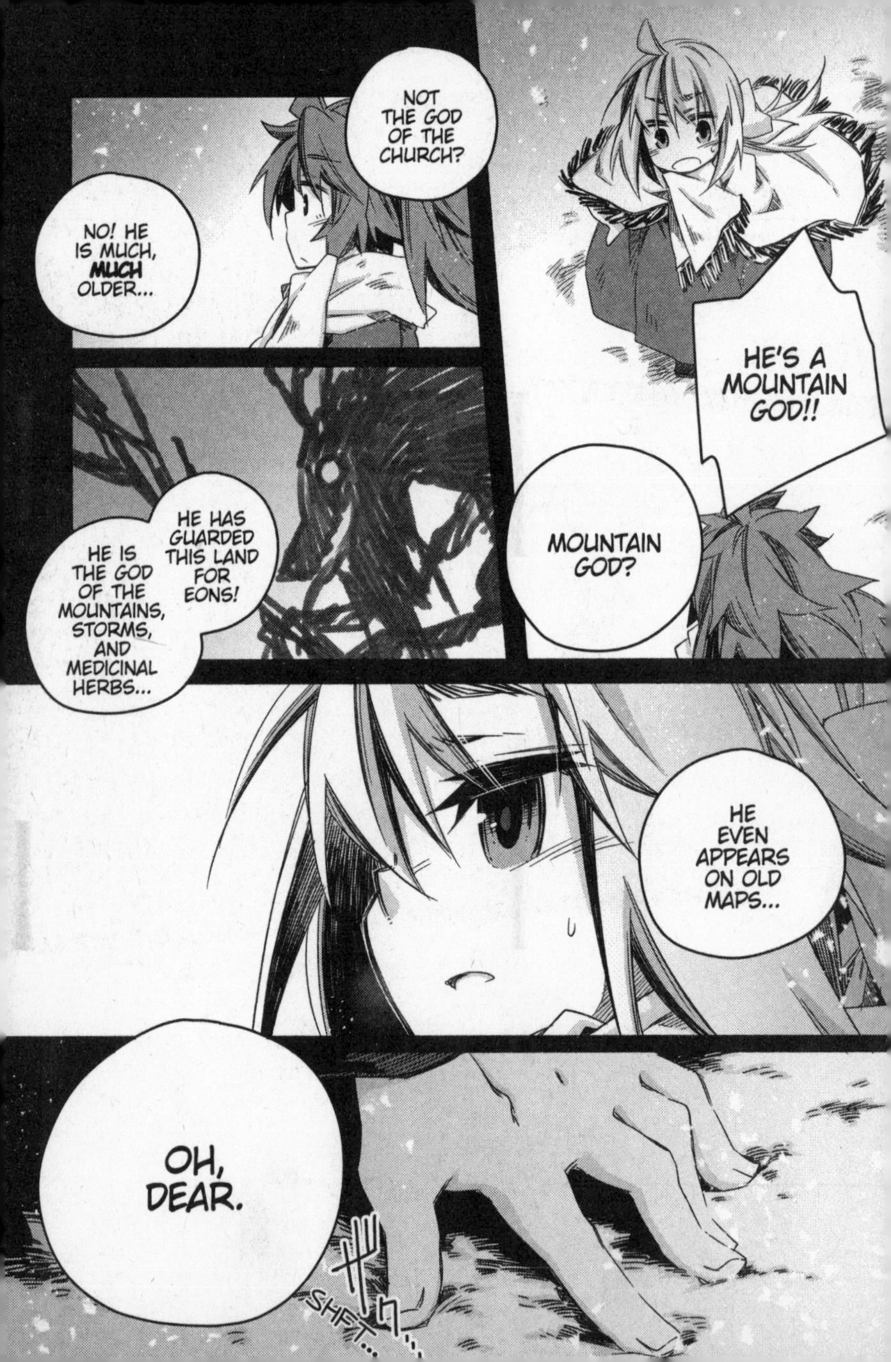
NOT THE GOD OF THE CHURCH?
NO! HE IS MUCH, **MUCH** OLDER...
HE'S A MOUNTAIN GOD!!
MOUNTAIN GOD?
HE HAS GUARDED THIS LAND FOR EONS!
HE IS THE GOD OF THE MOUNTAINS, STORMS, AND MEDICINAL HERBS...
HE EVEN APPEARS ON OLD MAPS...
OH, DEAR.
SHFT...

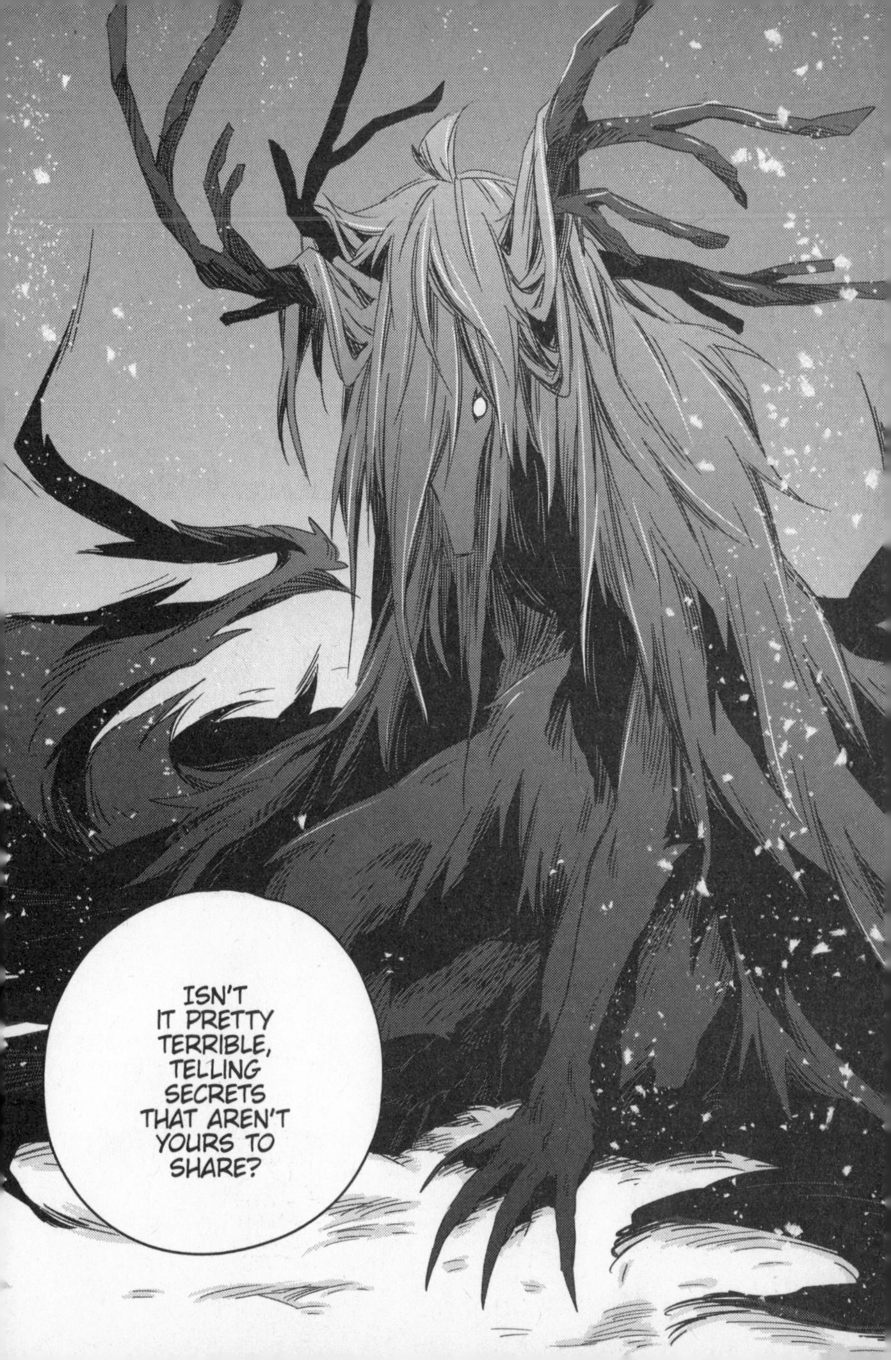
ISN'T IT PRETTY TERRIBLE, TELLING SECRETS THAT AREN'T YOURS TO SHARE?

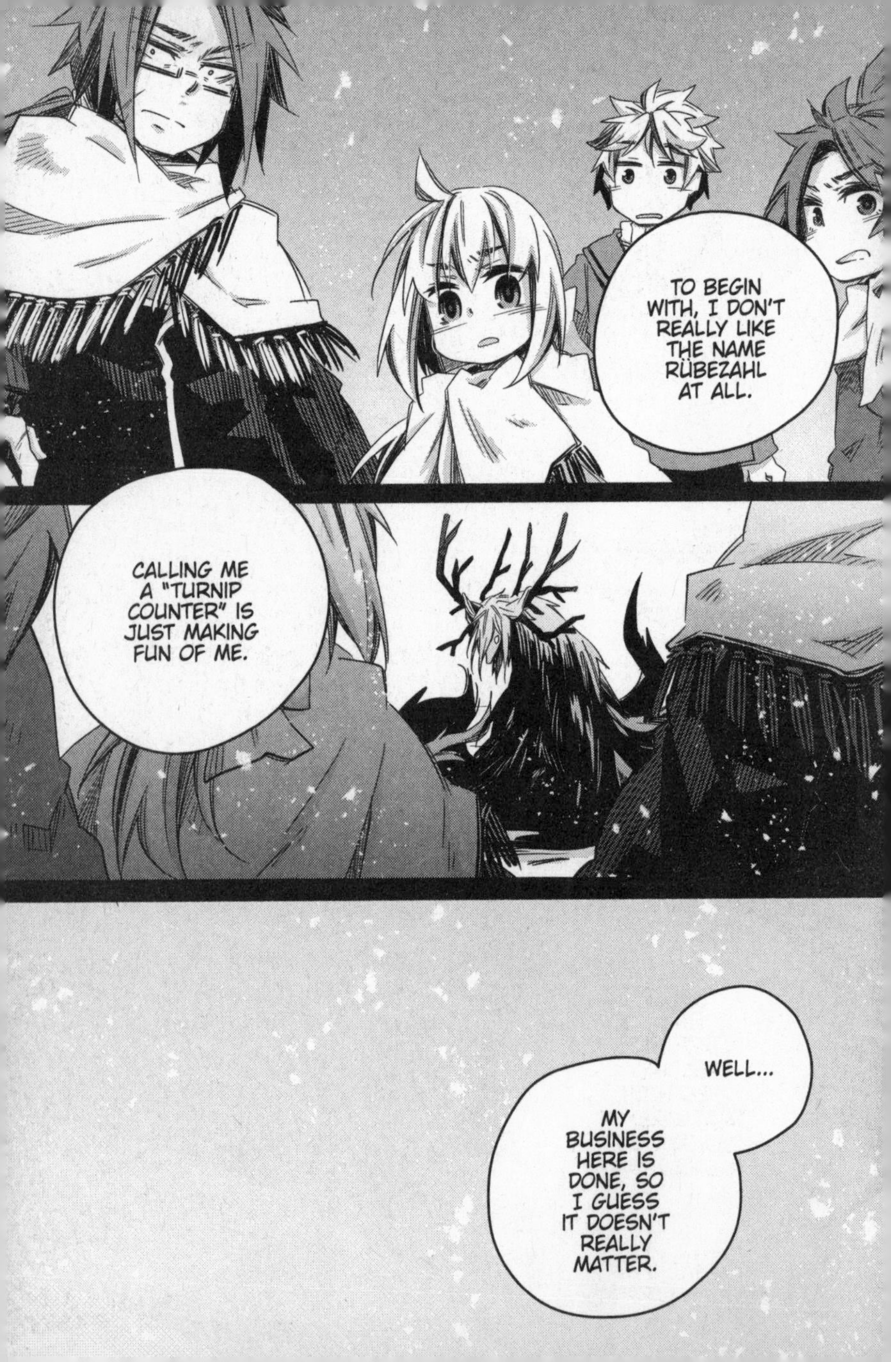
TO BEGIN WITH, I DON'T REALLY LIKE THE NAME RÜBEZAHL AT ALL.
CALLING ME A "TURNIP COUNTER" IS JUST MAKING FUN OF ME.
WELL...
MY BUSINESS HERE IS DONE, SO I GUESS IT DOESN'T REALLY MATTER.

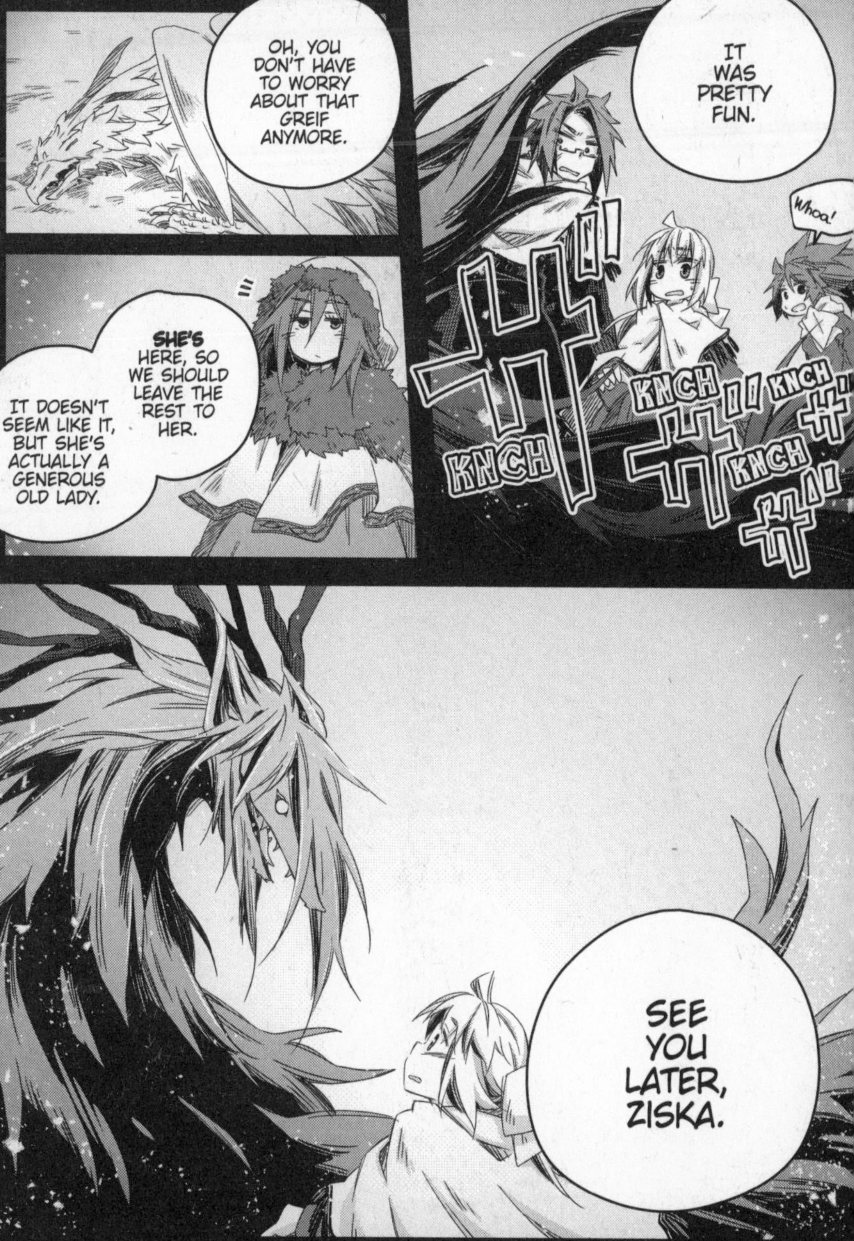
IT WAS PRETTY FUN.
Whoa!
KNCH
KNCH
KNCH
KNCH
OH, YOU DON'T HAVE TO WORRY ABOUT THAT GREIF ANYMORE.
SHE'S HERE, SO WE SHOULD LEAVE THE REST TO HER.
IT DOESN'T SEEM LIKE IT, BUT SHE'S ACTUALLY A GENEROUS OLD LADY.
SEE YOU LATER, ZISKA.

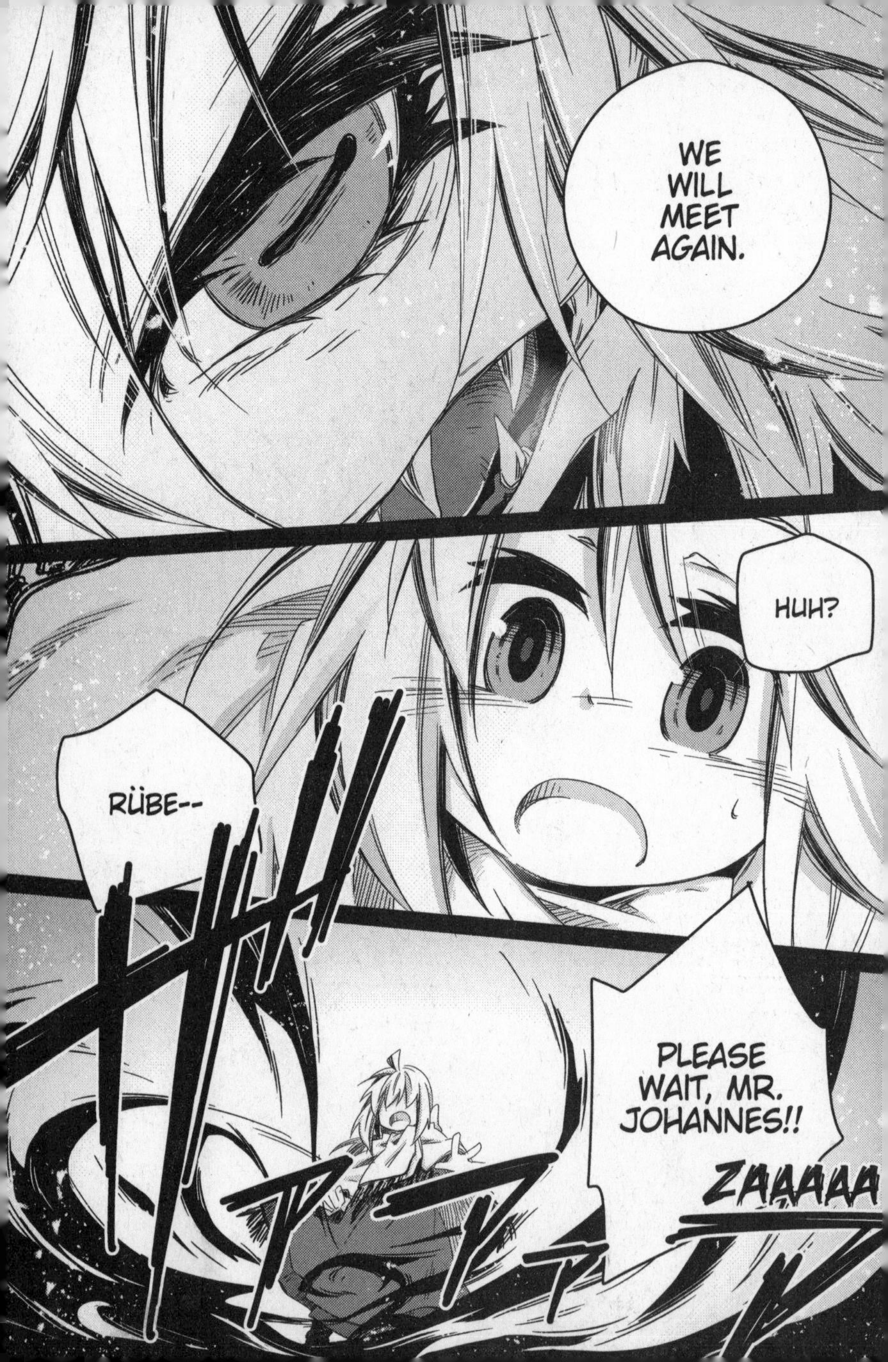
WE WILL MEET AGAIN.
HUH?
RÜBE--
PLEASE WAIT, MR. JOHANNES!!
ZAAAAA

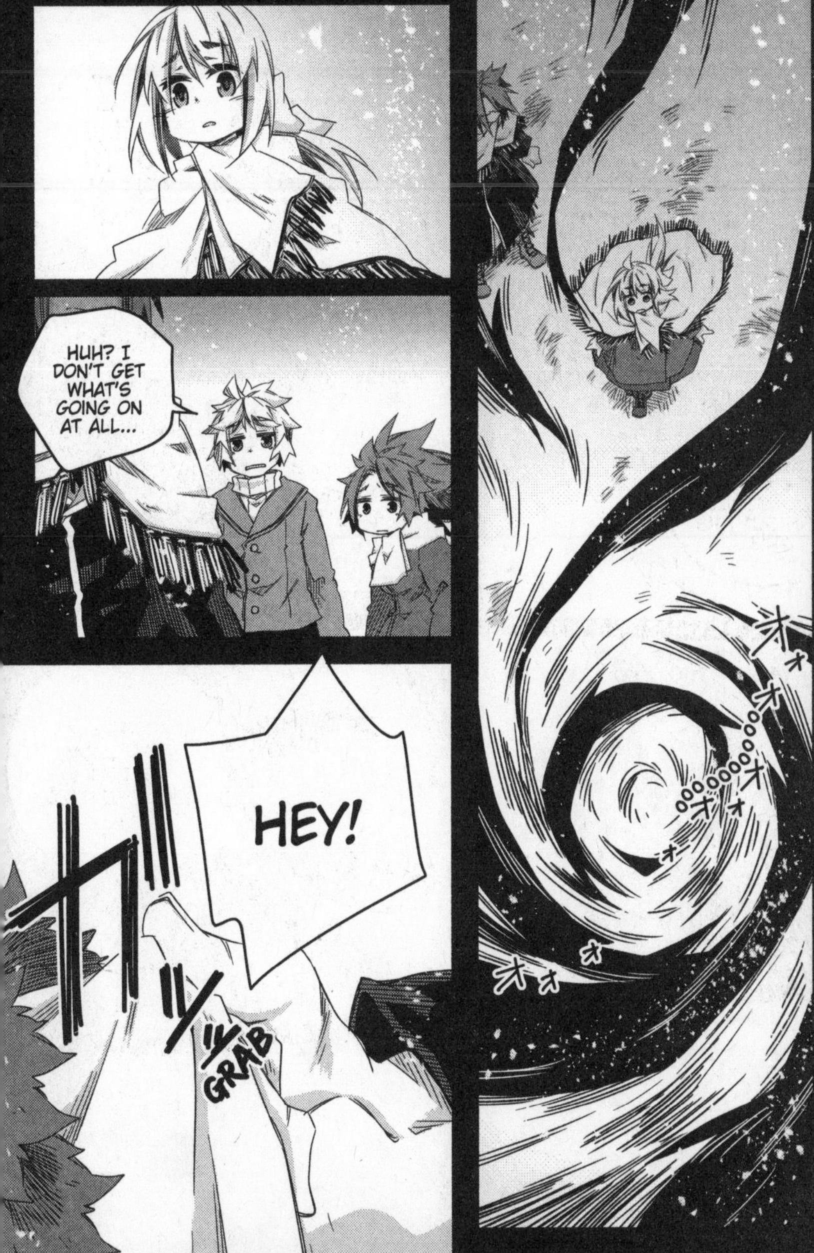
HUH? I DON'T GET WHAT'S GOING ON AT ALL...
HEY!
GRAB

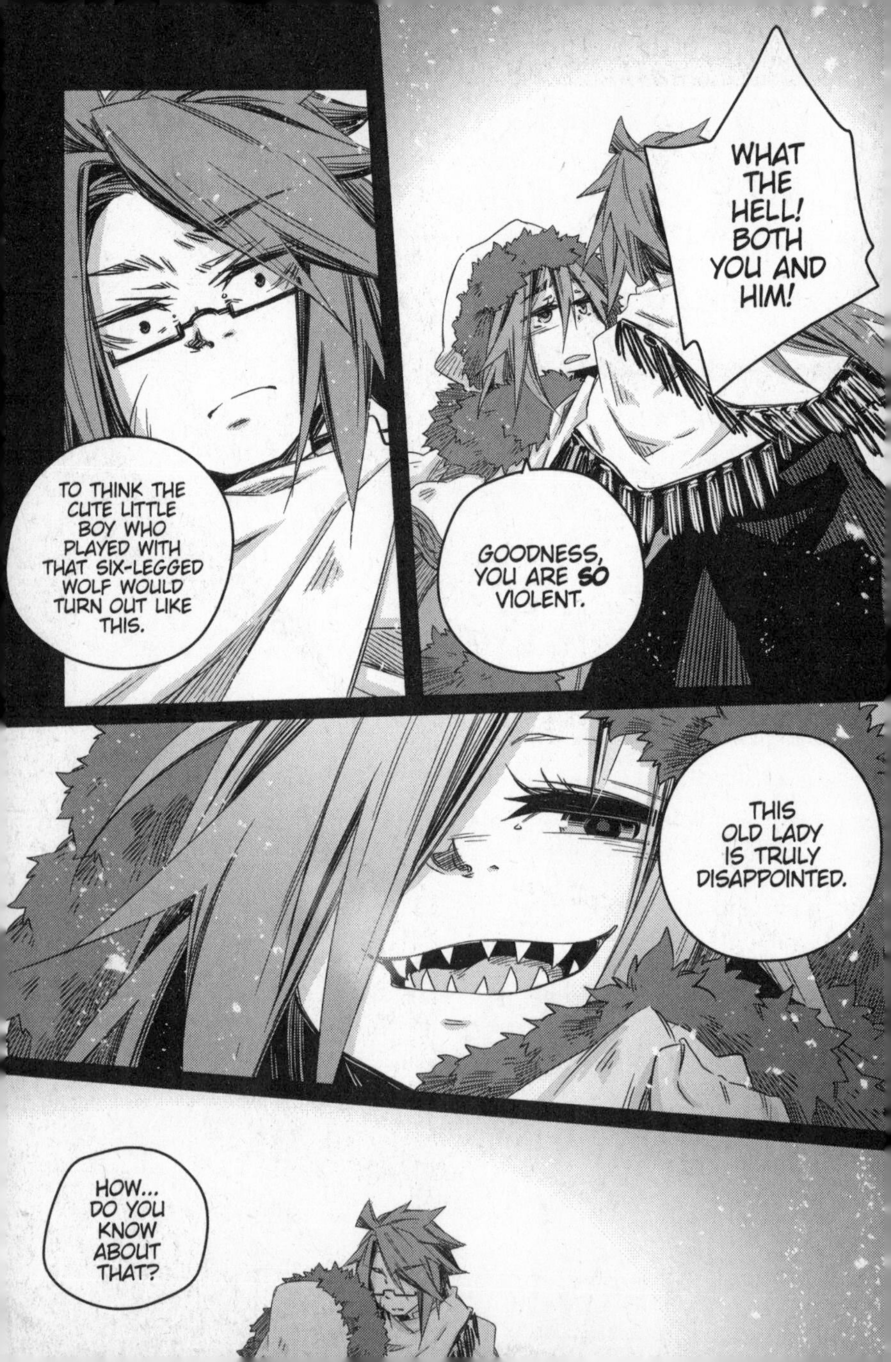
WHAT THE HELL! BOTH YOU AND HIM!
GOODNESS, YOU ARE **SO** VIOLENT.
TO THINK THE CUTE LITTLE BOY WHO PLAYED WITH THAT SIX-LEGGED WOLF WOULD TURN OUT LIKE THIS.
THIS OLD LADY IS TRULY DISAPPOINTED.
HOW... DO YOU KNOW ABOUT THAT?

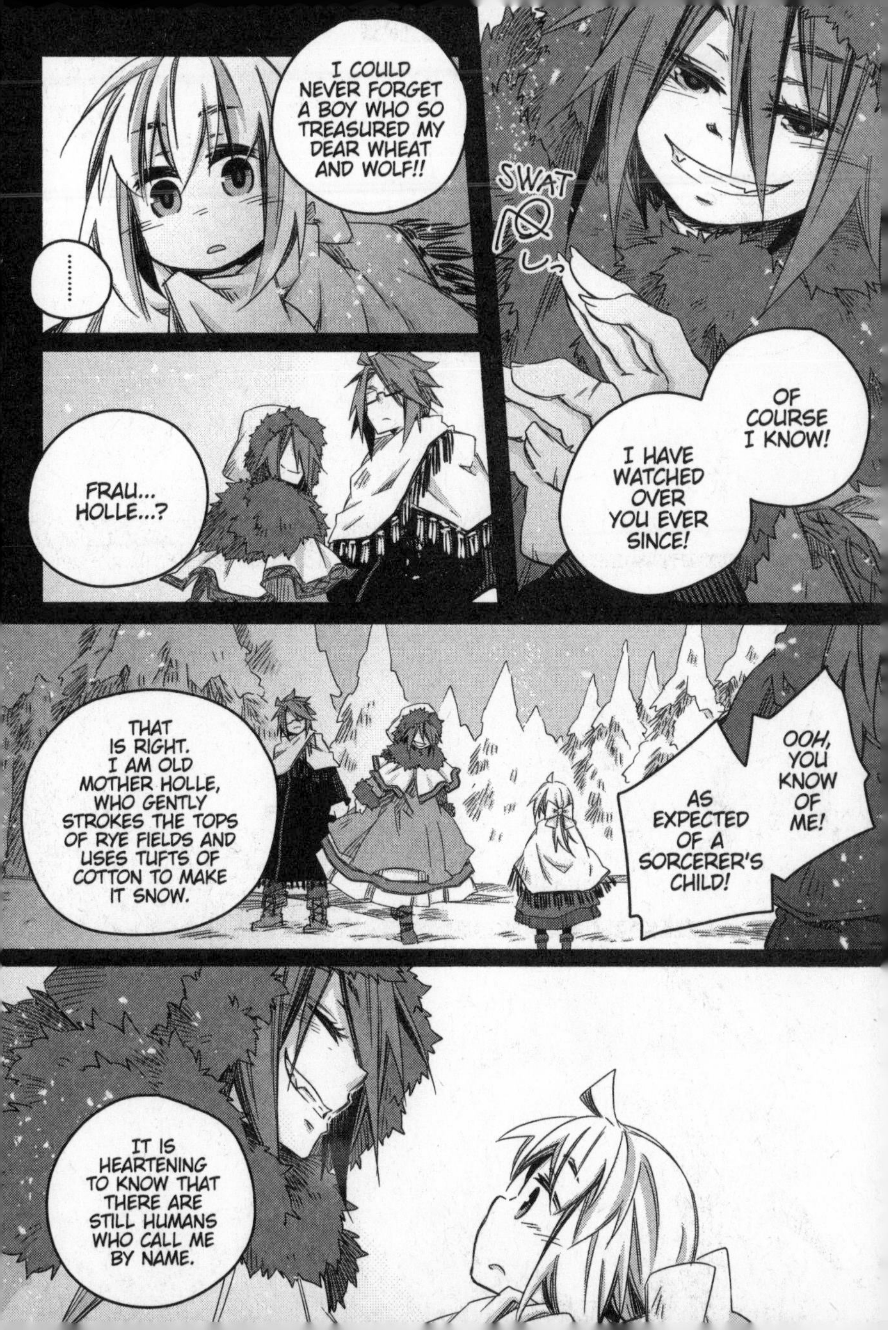
SWAT
OF COURSE I KNOW!
I HAVE WATCHED OVER YOU EVER SINCE!
I COULD NEVER FORGET A BOY WHO SO TREASURED MY DEAR WHEAT AND WOLF!!
......
FRAU... HOLLE...?
OOH, YOU KNOW OF ME!
AS EXPECTED OF A SORCERER'S CHILD!
THAT IS RIGHT. I AM OLD MOTHER HOLLE, WHO GENTLY STROKES THE TOPS OF RYE FIELDS AND USES TUFTS OF COTTON TO MAKE IT SNOW.
IT IS HEARTENING TO KNOW THAT THERE ARE STILL HUMANS WHO CALL ME BY NAME.

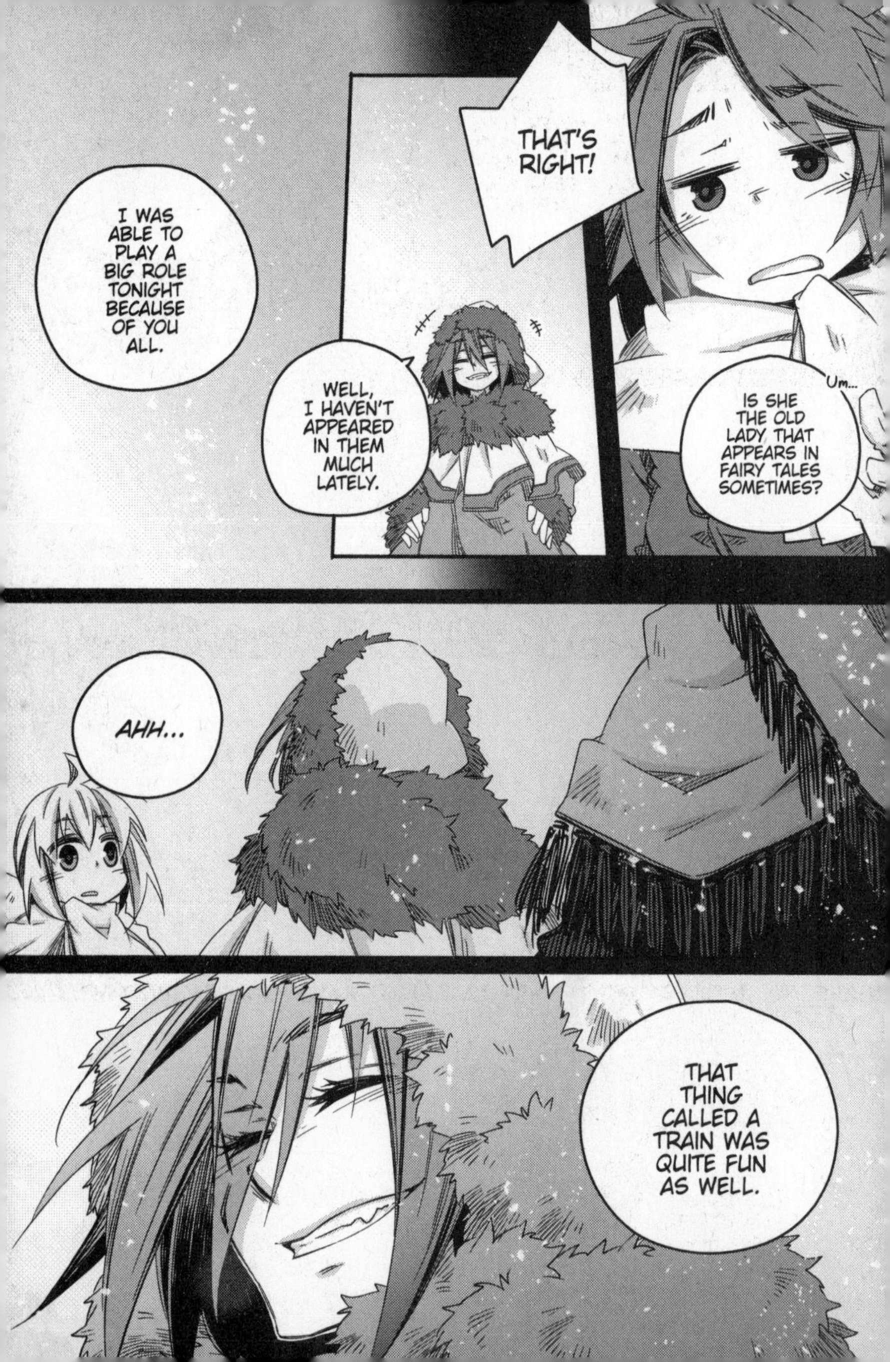

Um...
IS SHE THE OLD LADY THAT APPEARS IN FAIRY TALES SOMETIMES?
THAT'S RIGHT!
WELL, I HAVEN'T APPEARED IN THEM MUCH LATELY.
I WAS ABLE TO PLAY A BIG ROLE TONIGHT BECAUSE OF YOU ALL.
AHH...
THAT THING CALLED A TRAIN WAS QUITE FUN AS WELL.

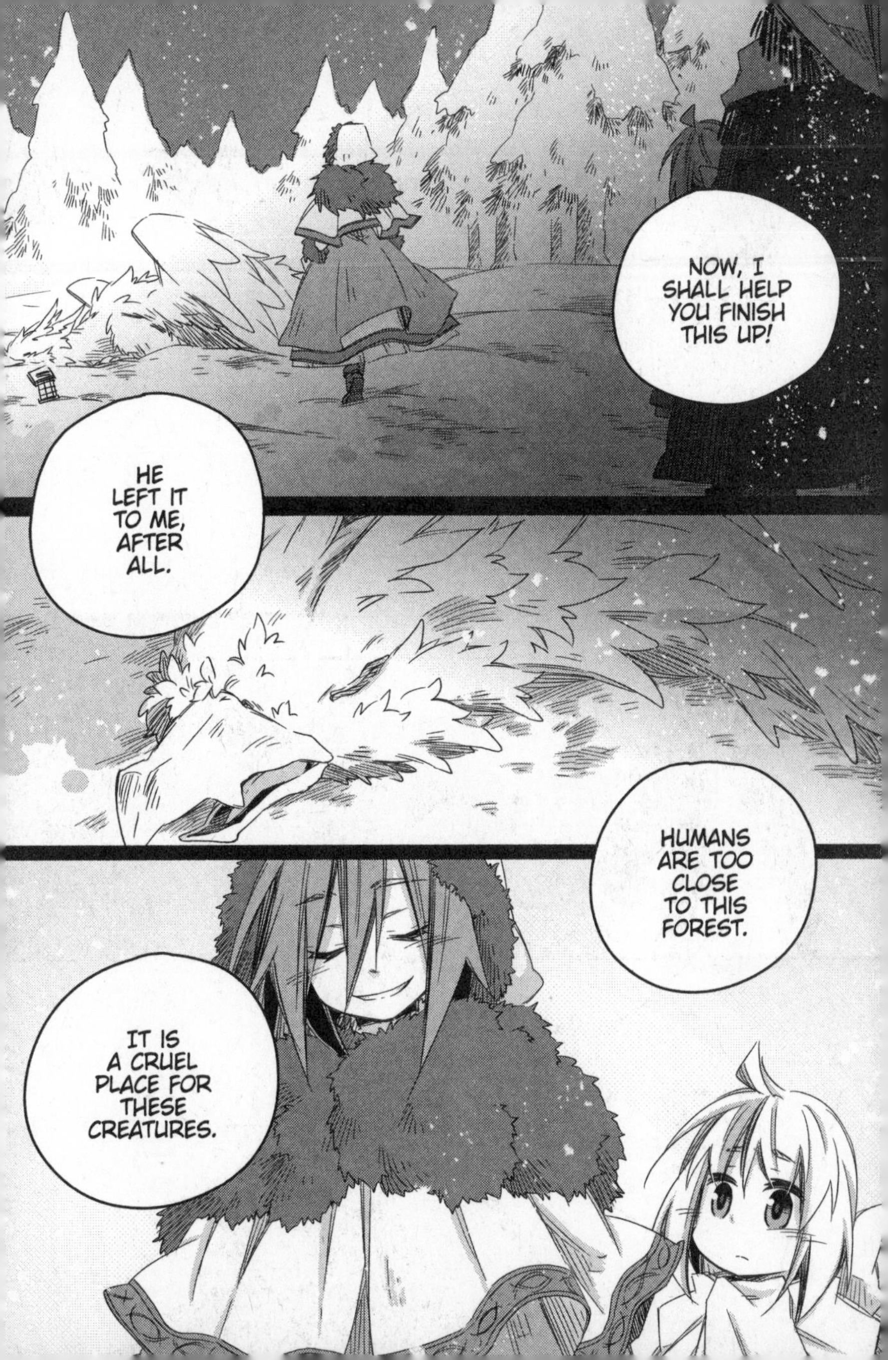
NOW, I SHALL HELP YOU FINISH THIS UP!
HE LEFT IT TO ME, AFTER ALL.
HUMANS ARE TOO CLOSE TO THIS FOREST.
IT IS A CRUEL PLACE FOR THESE CREATURES.

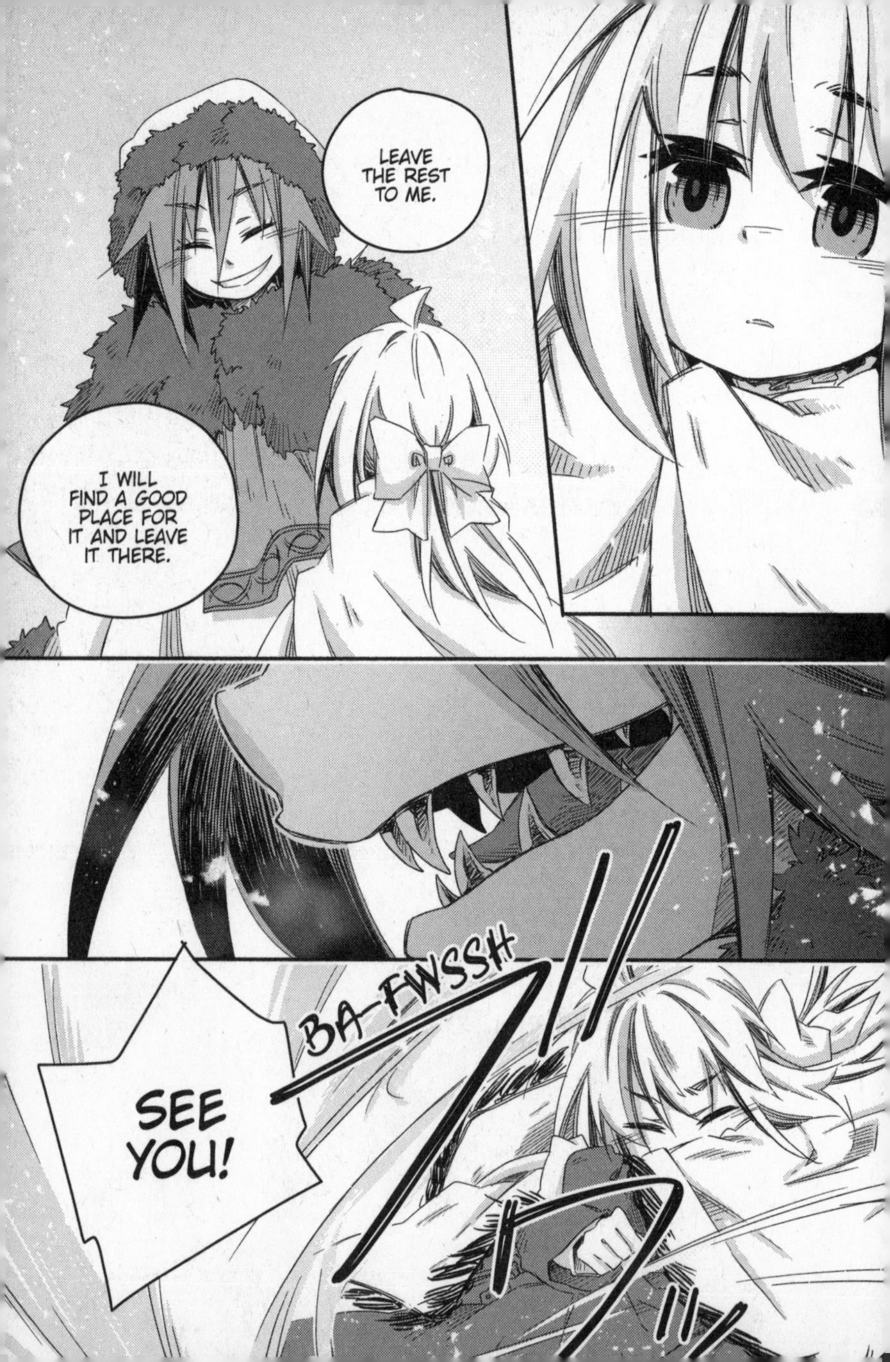
LEAVE THE REST TO ME.
I WILL FIND A GOOD PLACE FOR IT AND LEAVE IT THERE.
BA-FWSSH
SEE YOU!

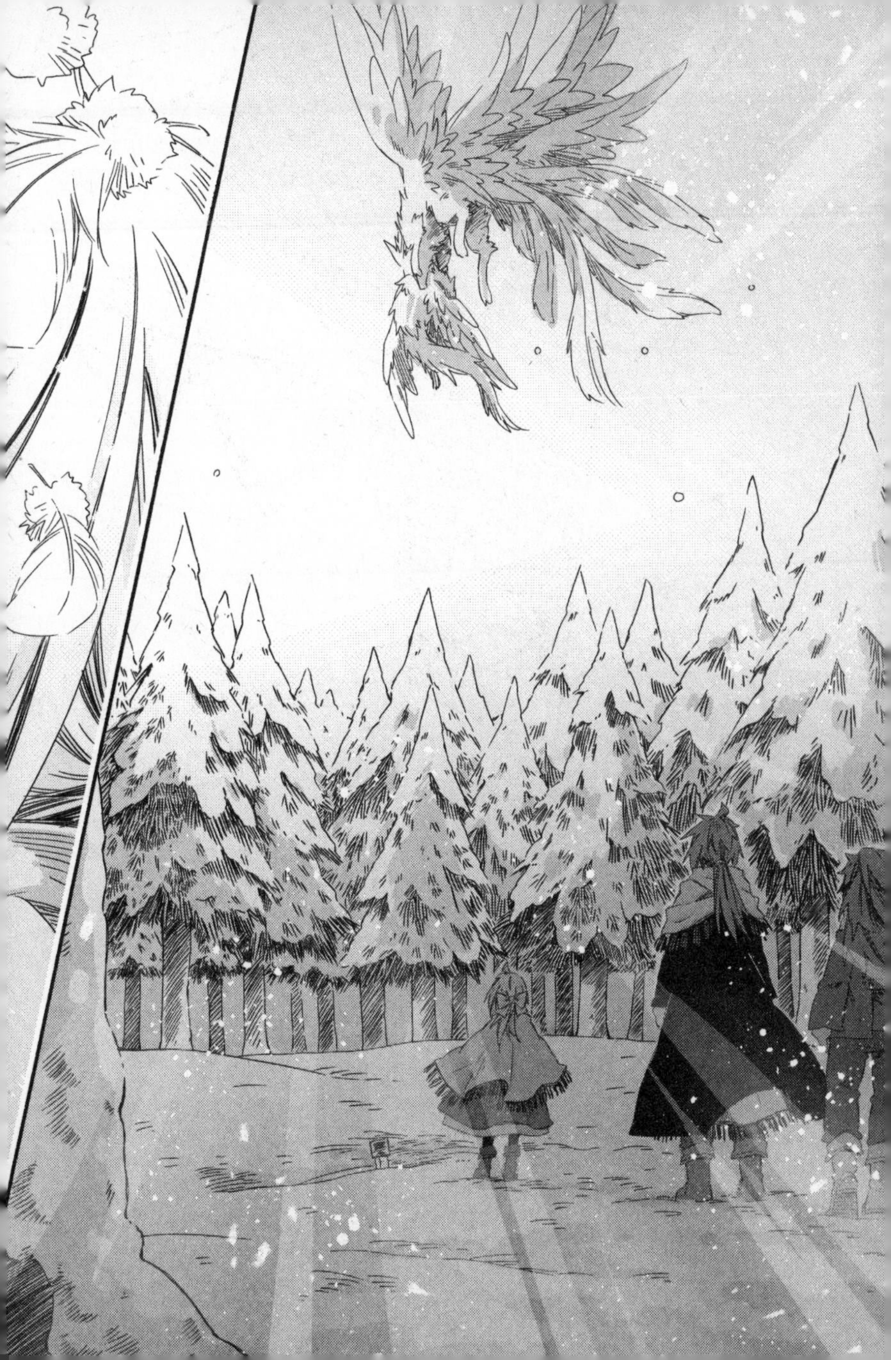

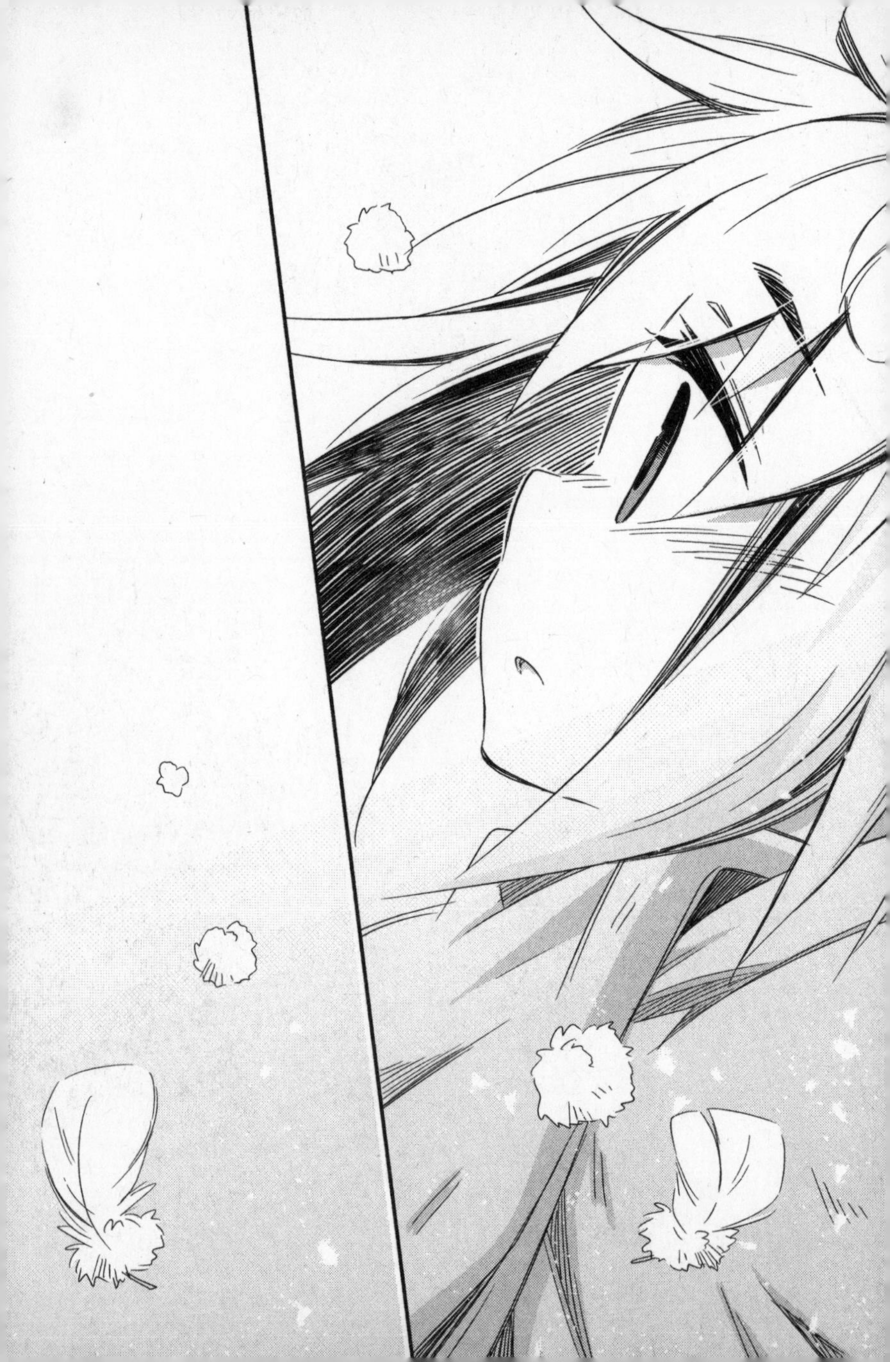

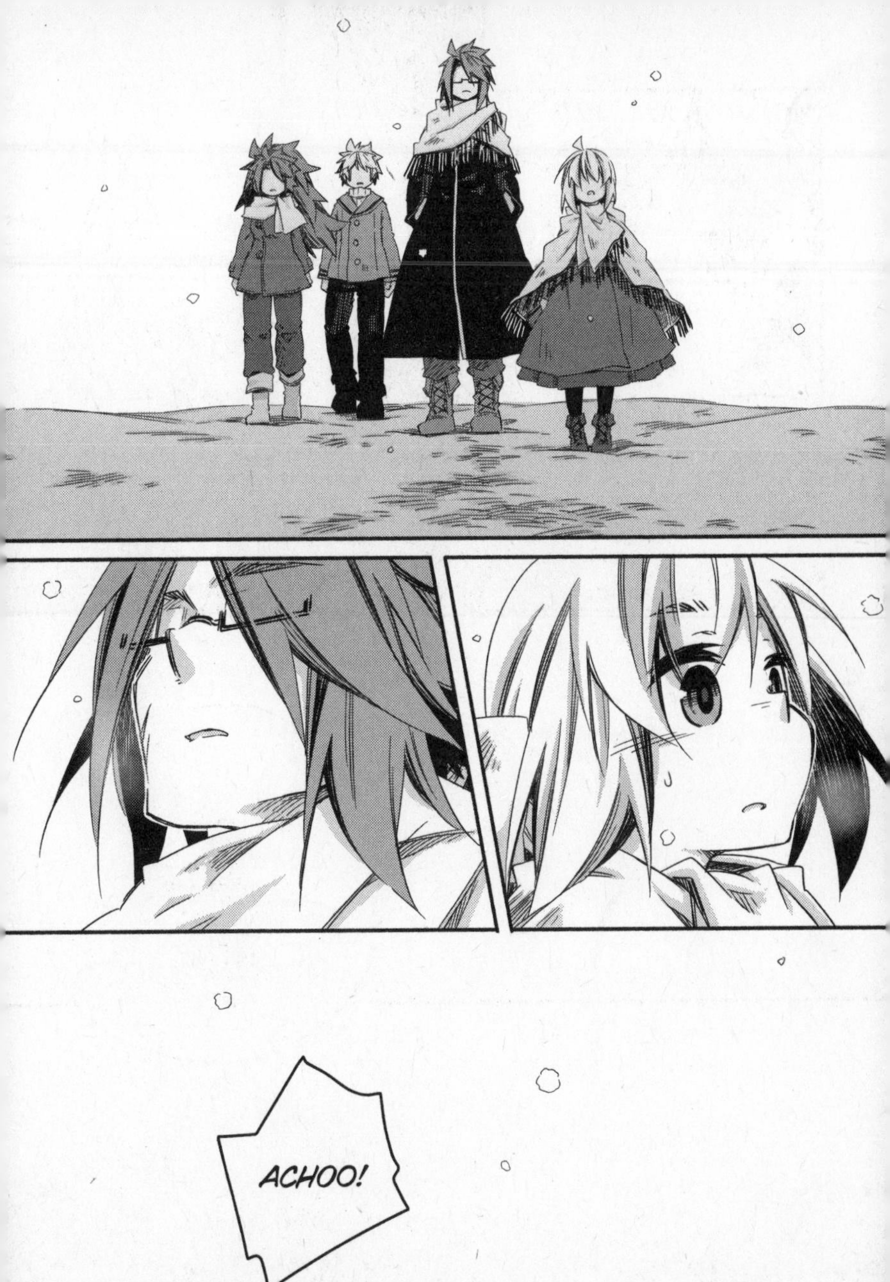
ACHOO!

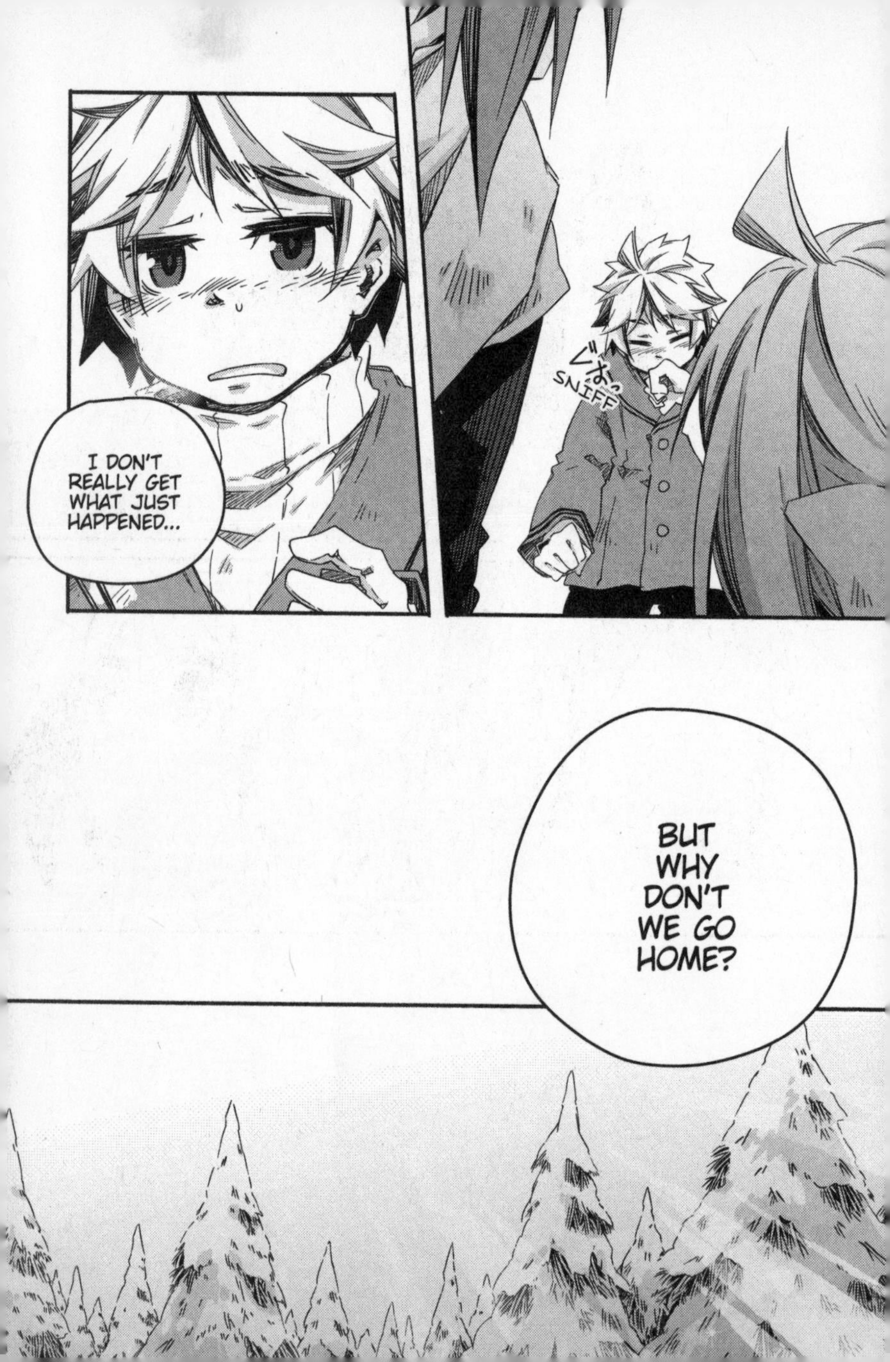
ぐおっ
SNIFF
I DON'T REALLY GET WHAT JUST HAPPENED...
BUT WHY DON'T WE GO HOME?

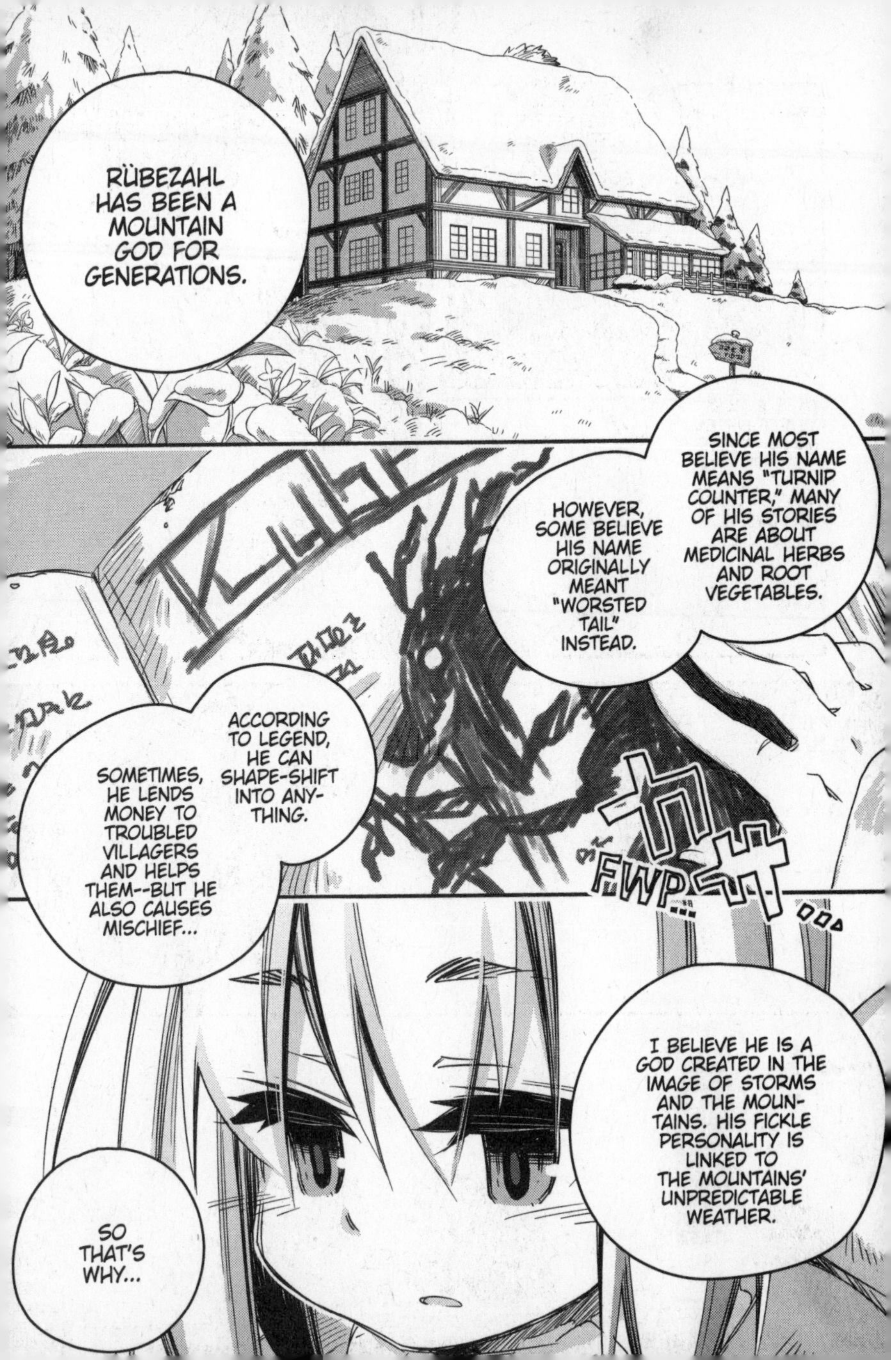
RÜBEZAHL HAS BEEN A MOUNTAIN GOD FOR GENERATIONS.
SINCE MOST BELIEVE HIS NAME MEANS "TURNIP COUNTER," MANY OF HIS STORIES ARE ABOUT MEDICINAL HERBS AND ROOT VEGETABLES.
HOWEVER, SOME BELIEVE HIS NAME ORIGINALLY MEANT "WORSTED TAIL" INSTEAD.
ACCORDING TO LEGEND, HE CAN SHAPE-SHIFT INTO ANY-THING.
SOMETIMES, HE LENDS MONEY TO TROUBLED VILLAGERS AND HELPS THEM--BUT HE ALSO CAUSES MISCHIEF...
FWP...
I BELIEVE HE IS A GOD CREATED IN THE IMAGE OF STORMS AND THE MOUN-TAINS. HIS FICKLE PERSONALITY IS LINKED TO THE MOUNTAINS' UNPREDICTABLE WEATHER.
SO THAT'S WHY...

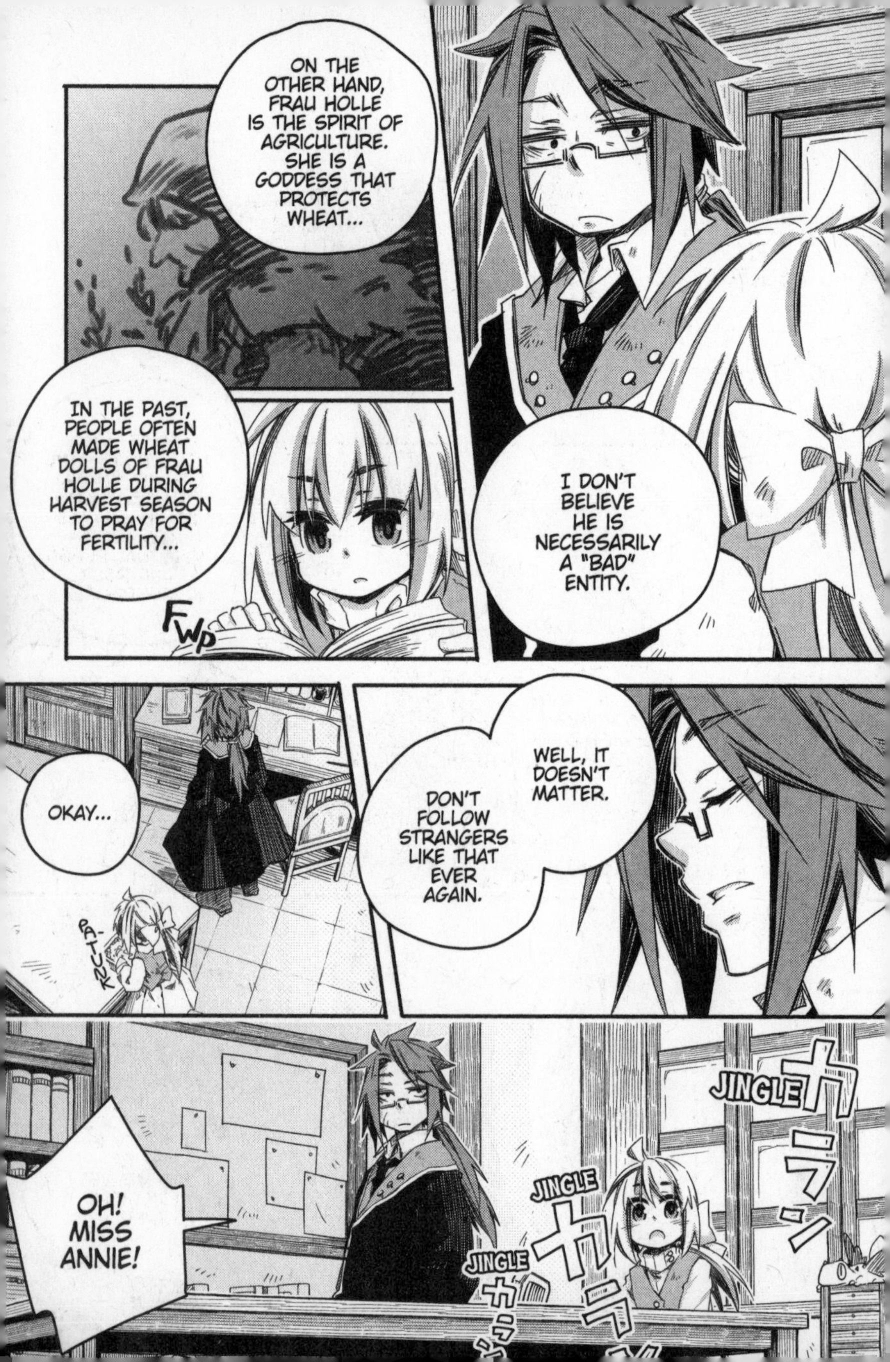
ON THE OTHER HAND, FRAU HOLLE IS THE SPIRIT OF AGRICULTURE. SHE IS A GODDESS THAT PROTECTS WHEAT...
IN THE PAST, PEOPLE OFTEN MADE WHEAT DOLLS OF FRAU HOLLE DURING HARVEST SEASON TO PRAY FOR FERTILITY...
FWP
I DON'T BELIEVE HE IS NECESSARILY A "BAD" ENTITY.
WELL, IT DOESN'T MATTER.
DON'T FOLLOW STRANGERS LIKE THAT EVER AGAIN.
OKAY...
PA-TUNK
JINGLE
JINGLE
JINGLE
OH! MISS ANNIE!

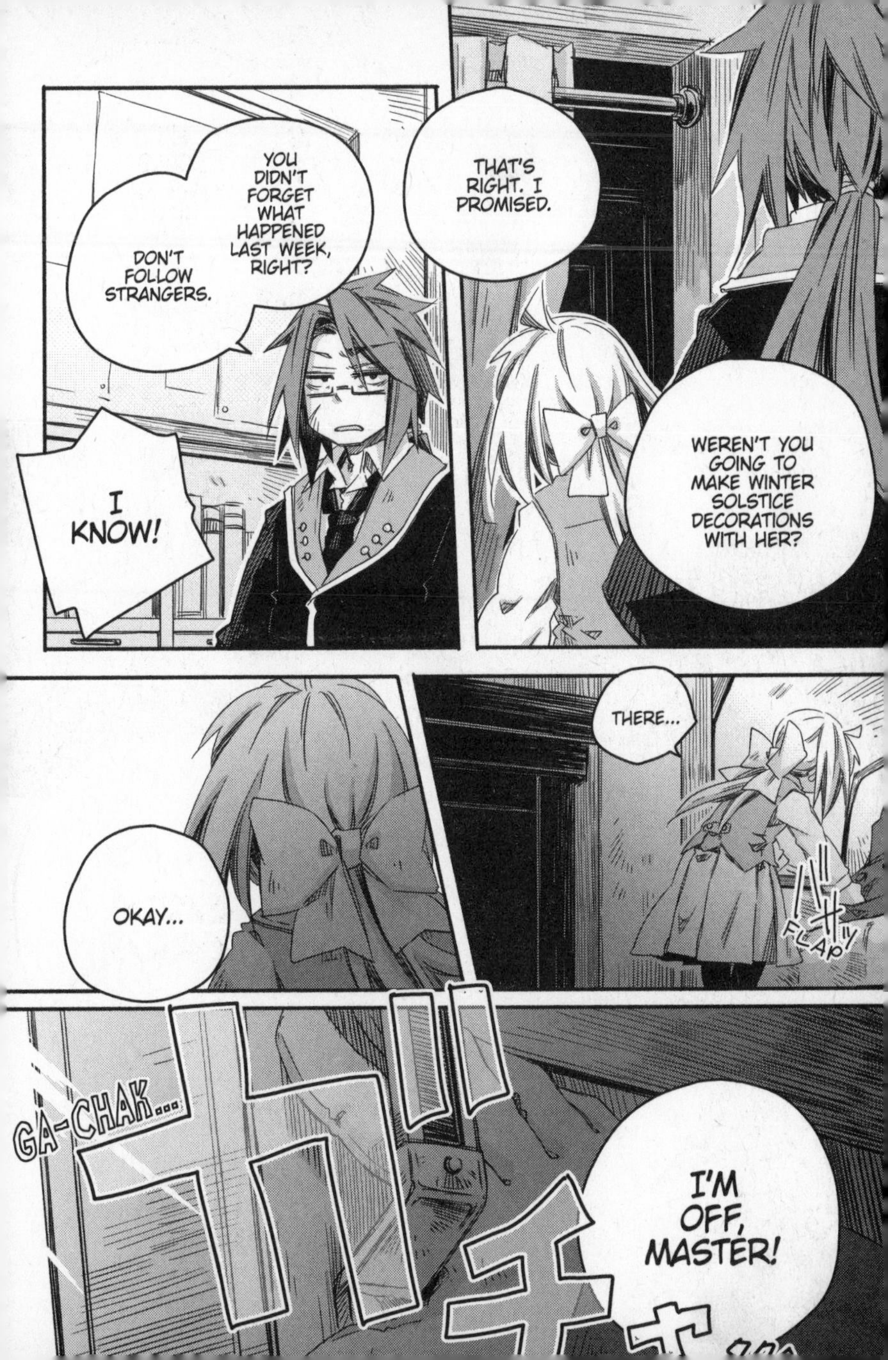
THAT'S RIGHT. I PROMISED.
WEREN'T YOU GOING TO MAKE WINTER SOLSTICE DECORATIONS WITH HER?
YOU DIDN'T FORGET WHAT HAPPENED LAST WEEK, RIGHT?
DON'T FOLLOW STRANGERS.
I KNOW!
THERE...
FLAP
OKAY...
I'M OFF, MASTER!
GA-CHAK...

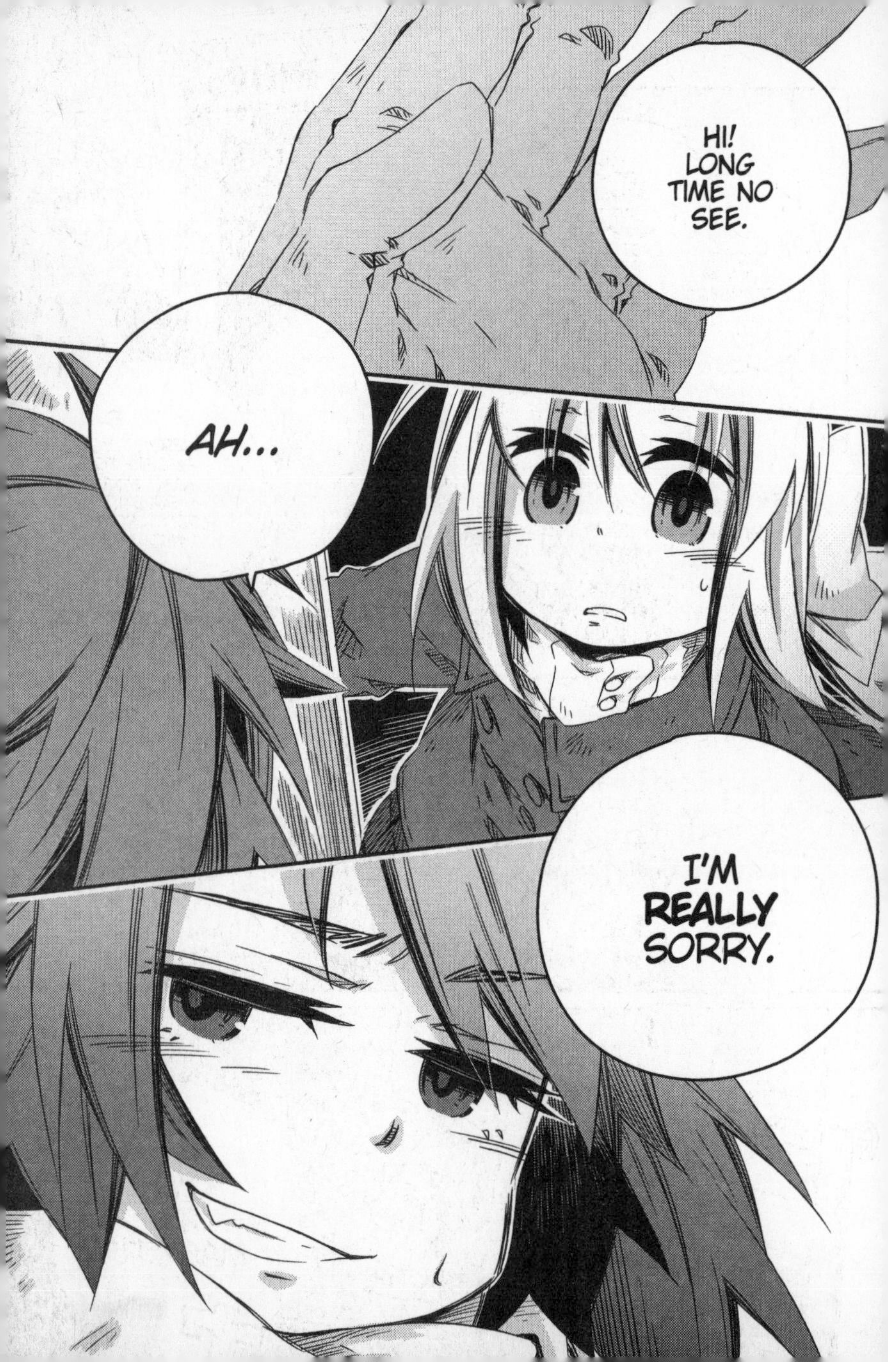
HI! LONG TIME NO SEE.
AH...
I'M **REALLY** SORRY.

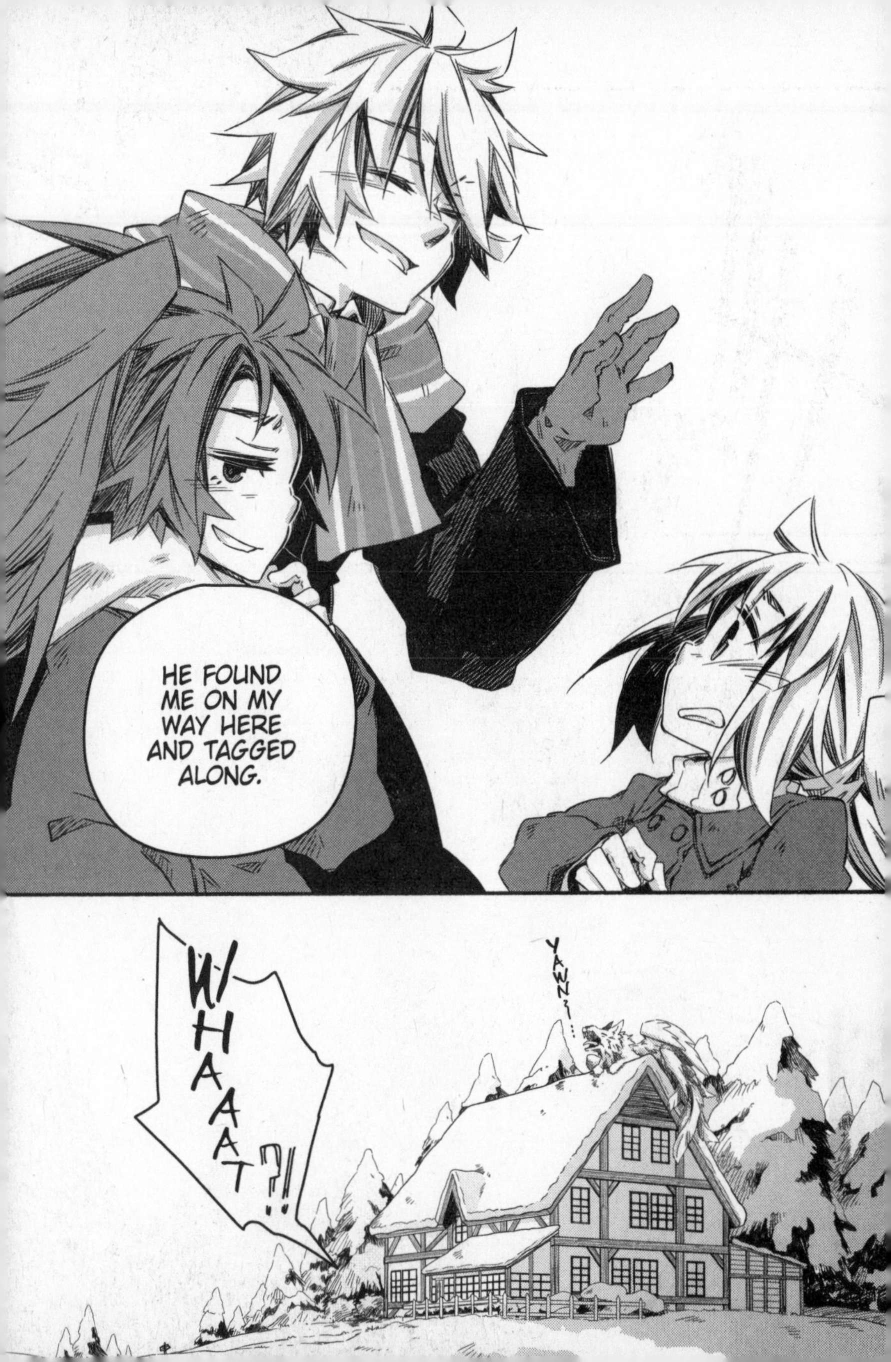
HE FOUND ME ON MY WAY HERE AND TAGGED ALONG.
YAWN~...
W-WHAAAT?!!

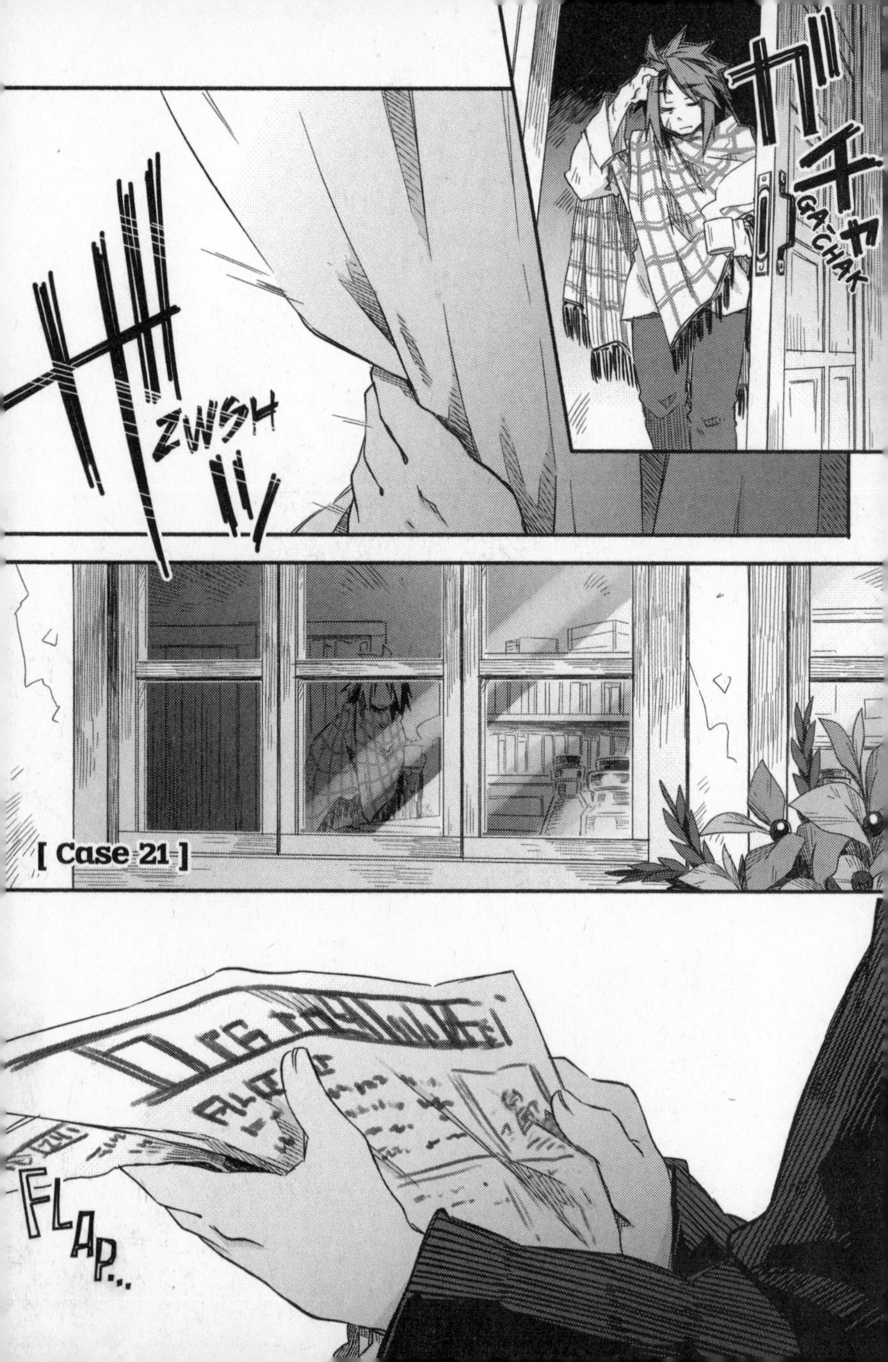
ガチャ
GA-CHAK
ZWSH
[Case 21]
FLAP...

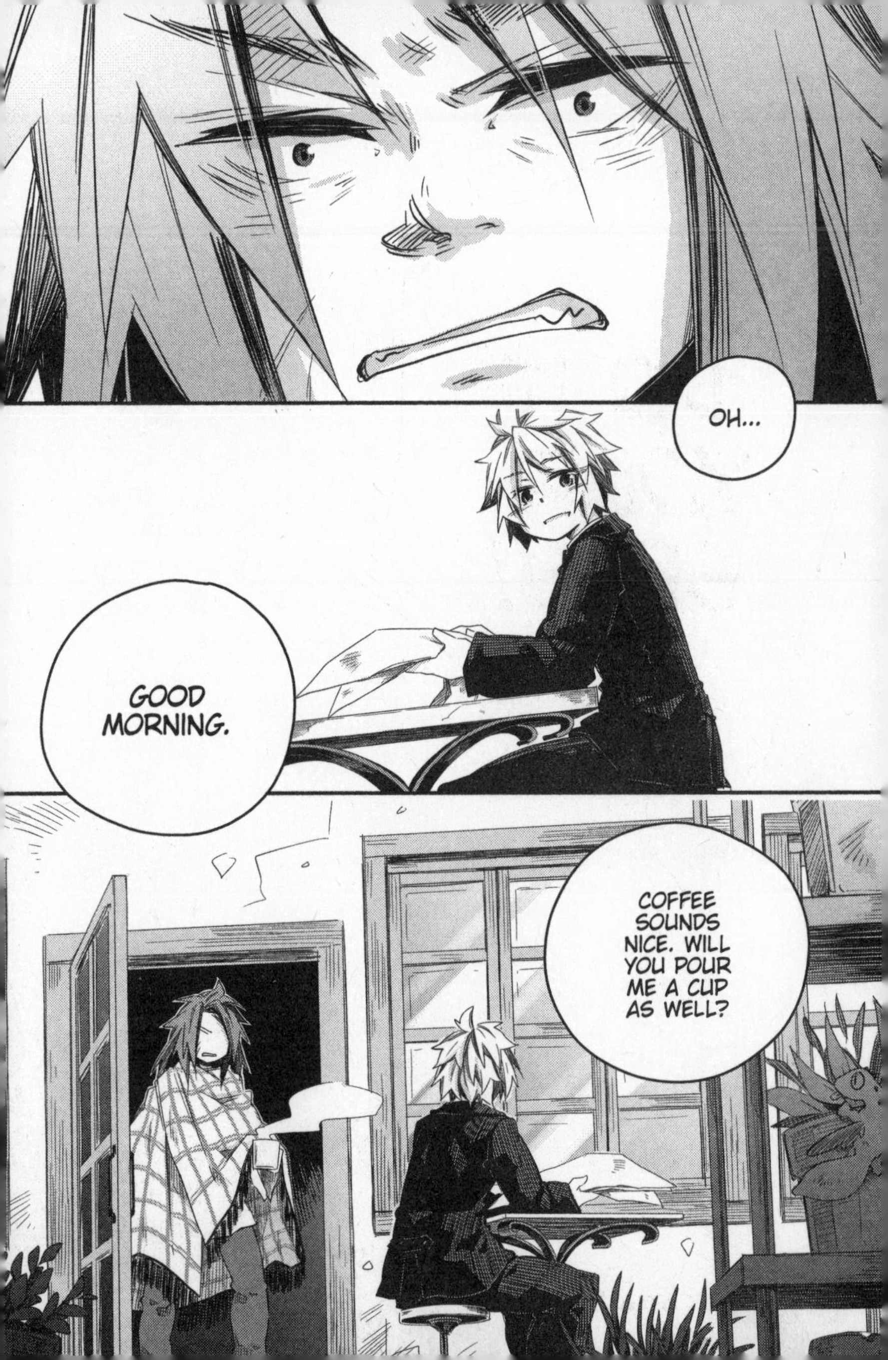
OH...
GOOD MORNING.
COFFEE SOUNDS NICE. WILL YOU POUR ME A CUP AS WELL?

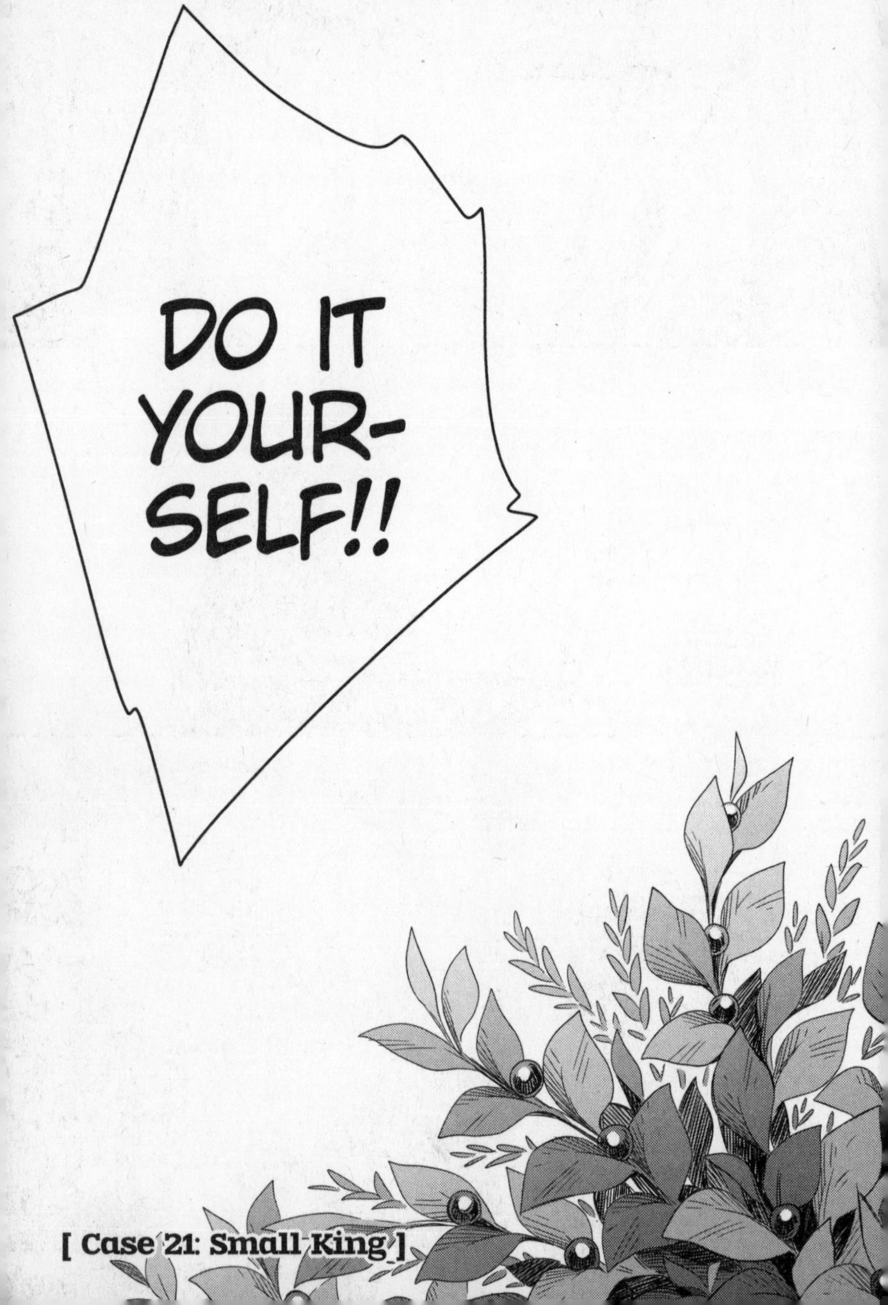
DO IT YOURSELF!!

[Case 21: Small King]

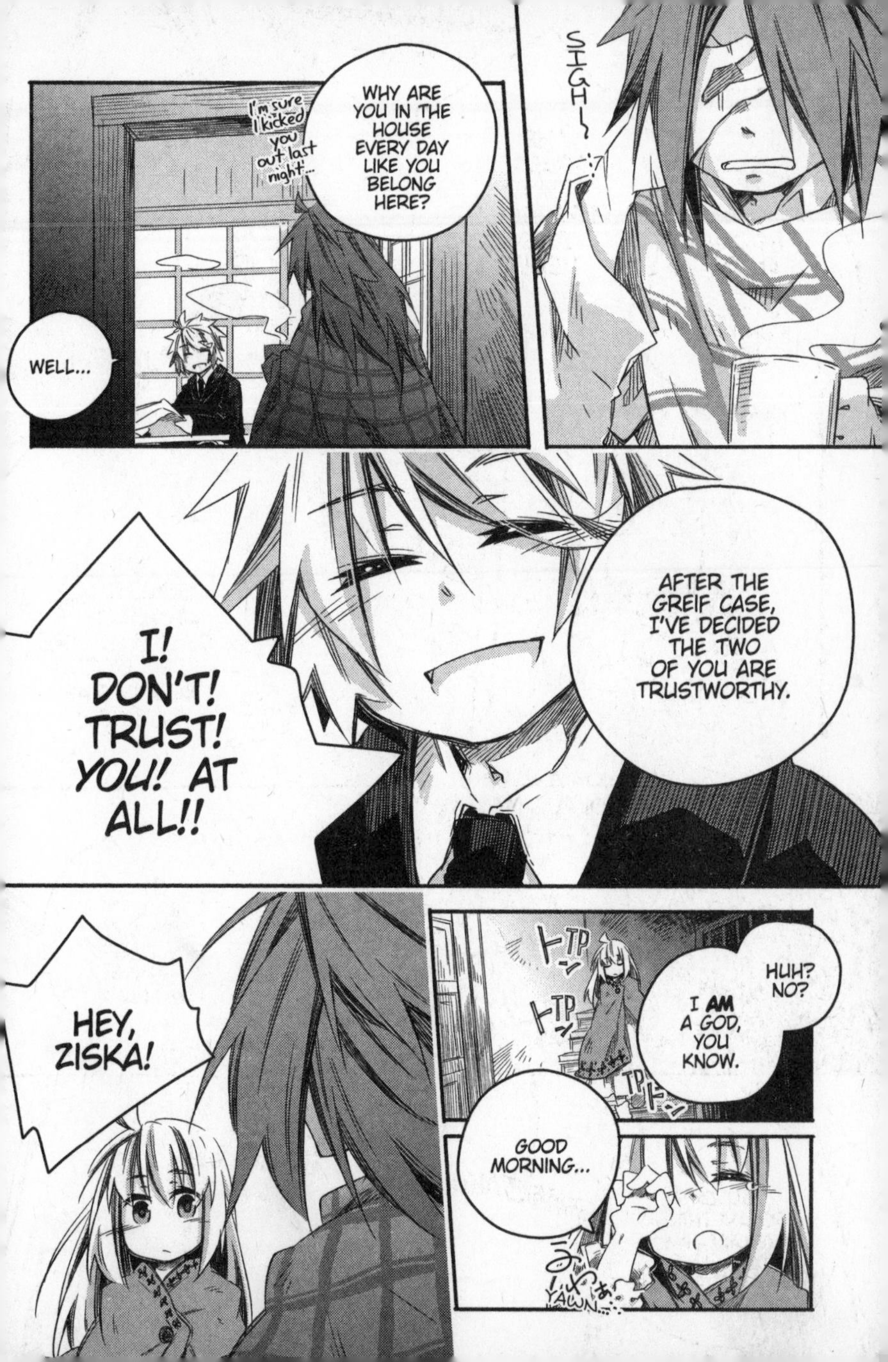
SIGH~
WHY ARE YOU IN THE HOUSE EVERY DAY LIKE YOU BELONG HERE?
I'm sure I kicked you out last night...
WELL...
AFTER THE GREIF CASE, I'VE DECIDED THE TWO OF YOU ARE TRUSTWORTHY.
I! DON'T! TRUST! YOU! AT ALL!!
HUH? NO?
I AM A GOD, YOU KNOW.
TP
TP
TP
GOOD MORNING...
YAWN...
HEY, ZISKA!

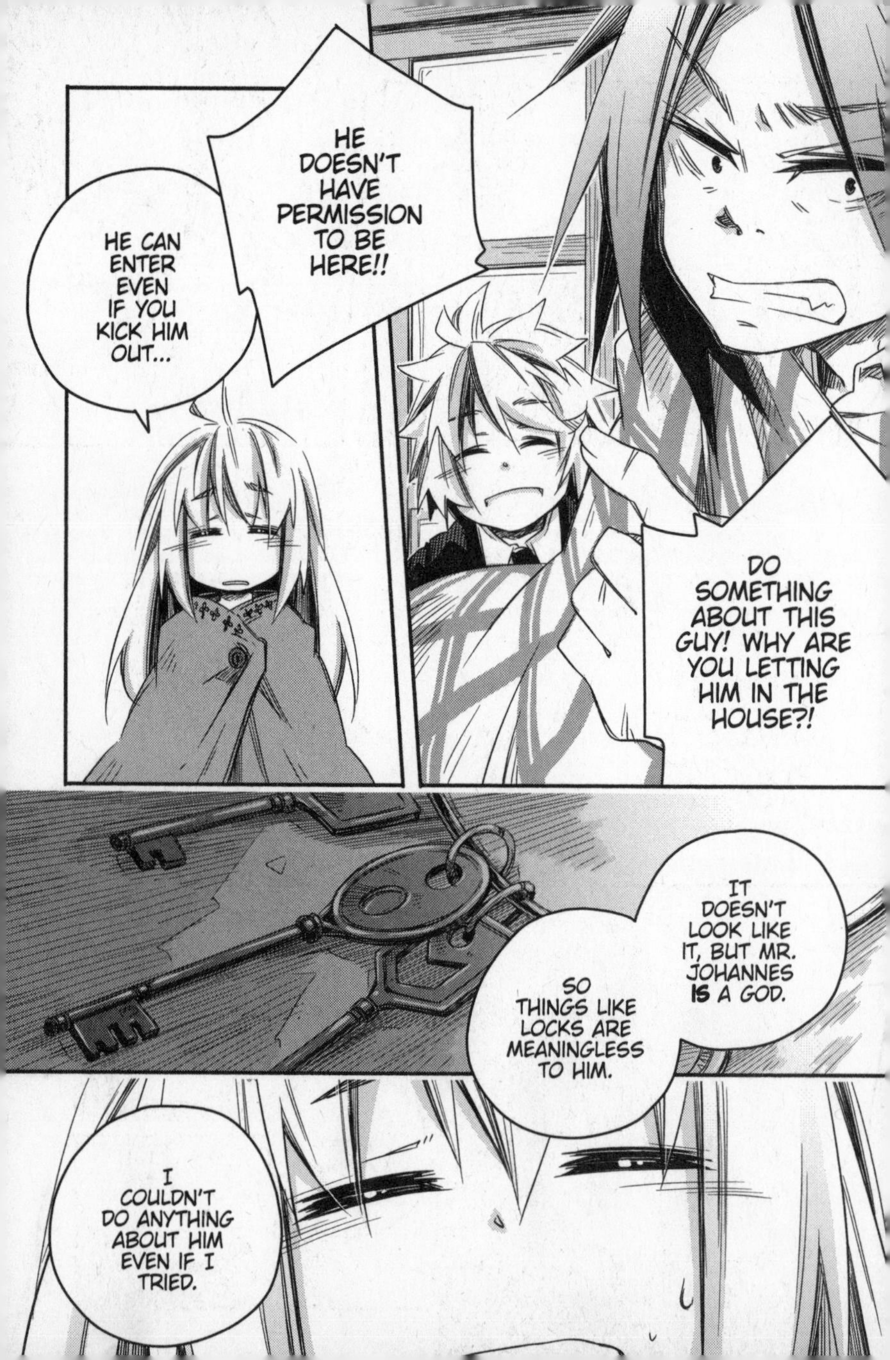
HE DOESN'T HAVE PERMISSION TO BE HERE!!
DO SOMETHING ABOUT THIS GUY! WHY ARE YOU LETTING HIM IN THE HOUSE?!
HE CAN ENTER EVEN IF YOU KICK HIM OUT...
IT DOESN'T LOOK LIKE IT, BUT MR. JOHANNES **IS** A GOD.
SO THINGS LIKE LOCKS ARE MEANINGLESS TO HIM.
I COULDN'T DO ANYTHING ABOUT HIM EVEN IF I TRIED.

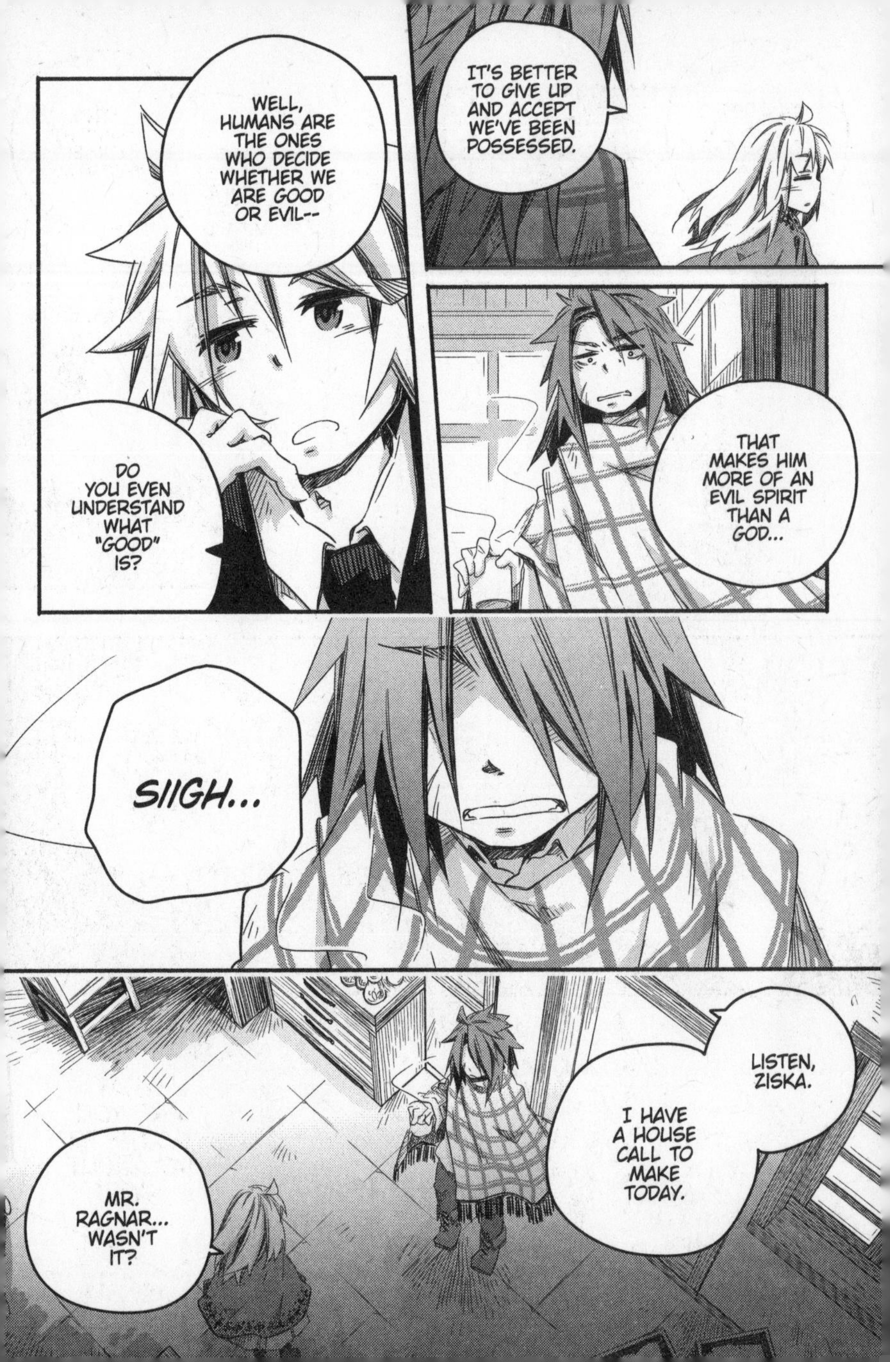
IT'S BETTER TO GIVE UP AND ACCEPT WE'VE BEEN POSSESSED.
THAT MAKES HIM MORE OF AN EVIL SPIRIT THAN A GOD...
WELL, HUMANS ARE THE ONES WHO DECIDE WHETHER WE ARE GOOD OR EVIL--
DO YOU EVEN UNDERSTAND WHAT "GOOD" IS?
SIIGH...
LISTEN, ZISKA.
I HAVE A HOUSE CALL TO MAKE TODAY.
MR. RAGNAR... WASN'T IT?

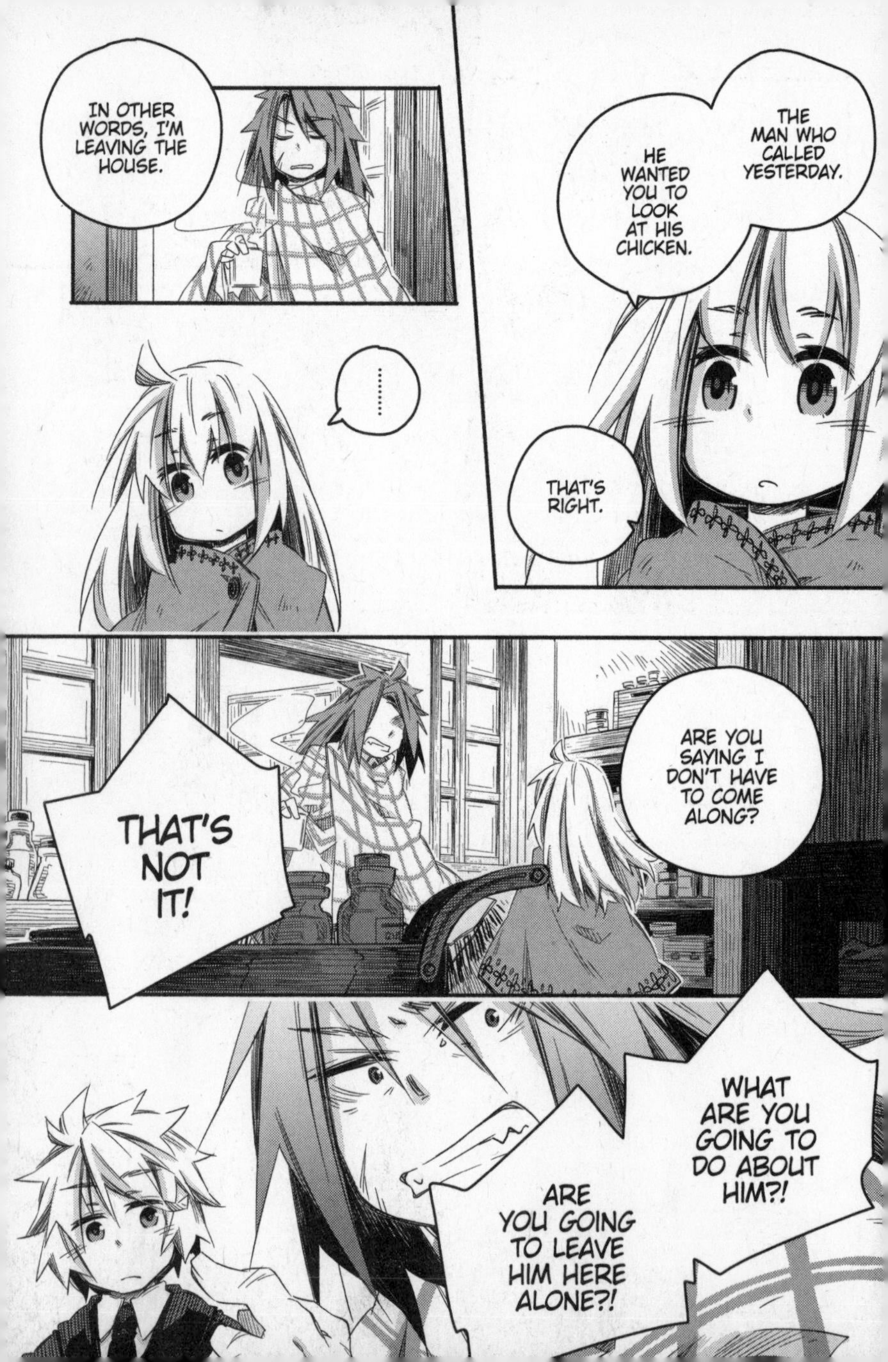
THE MAN WHO CALLED YESTERDAY.
HE WANTED YOU TO LOOK AT HIS CHICKEN.
THAT'S RIGHT.
IN OTHER WORDS, I'M LEAVING THE HOUSE.
……
ARE YOU SAYING I DON'T HAVE TO COME ALONG?
THAT'S NOT IT!
WHAT ARE YOU GOING TO DO ABOUT HIM?!
ARE YOU GOING TO LEAVE HIM HERE ALONE?!

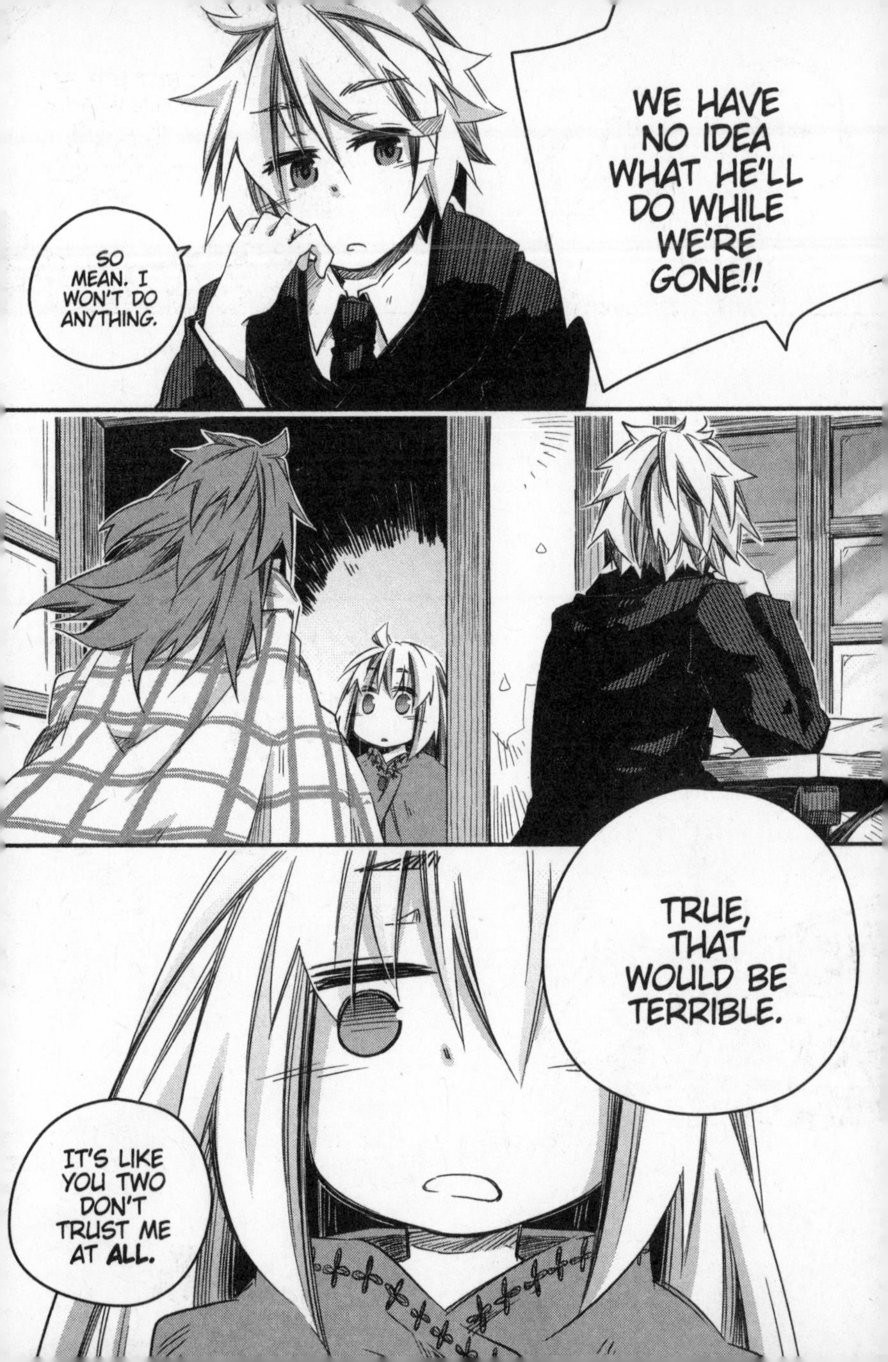
WE HAVE NO IDEA WHAT HE'LL DO WHILE WE'RE GONE!!
SO MEAN. I WON'T DO ANYTHING.
TRUE, THAT WOULD BE TERRIBLE.
IT'S LIKE YOU TWO DON'T TRUST ME AT ALL.

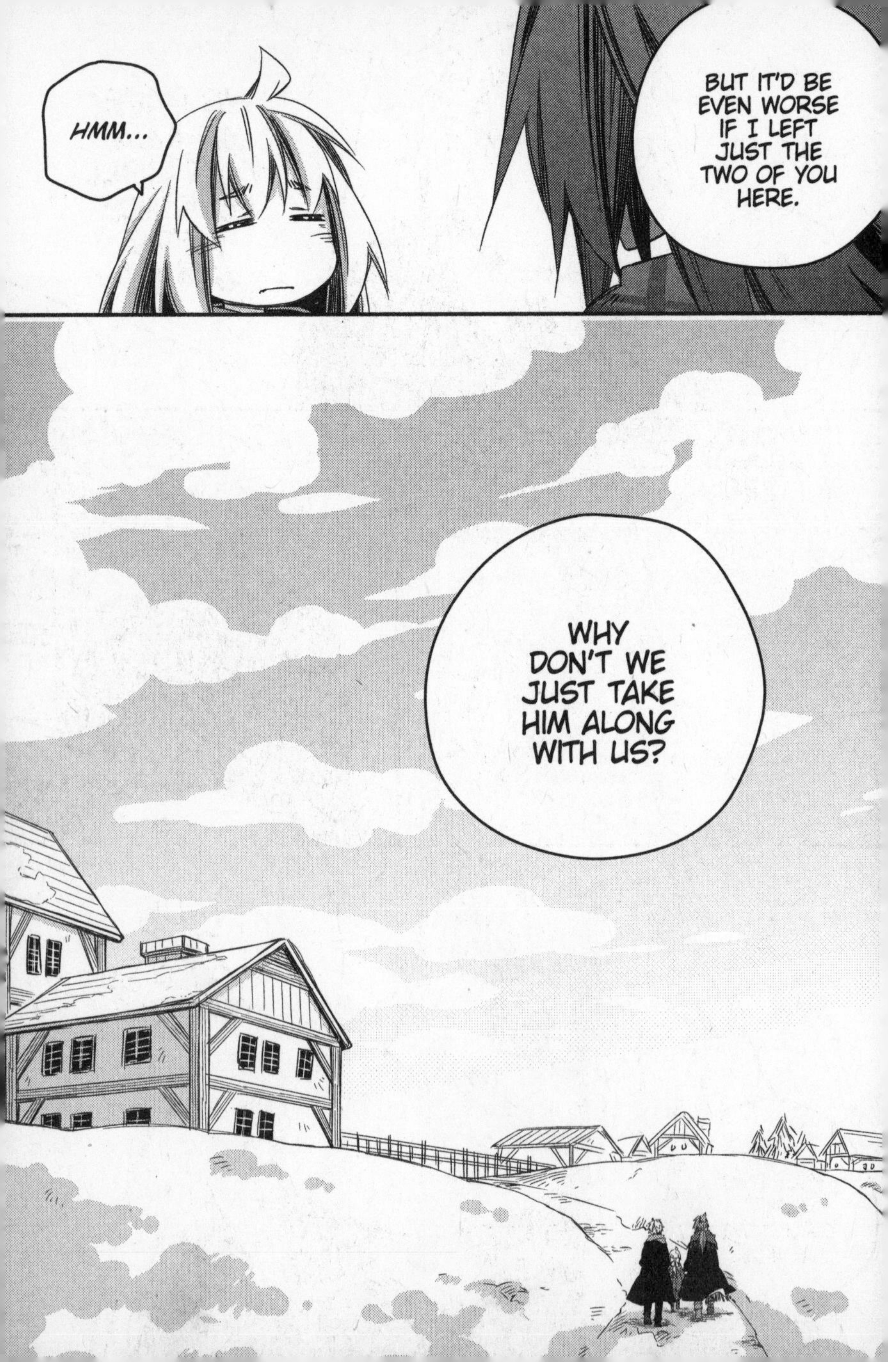
BUT IT'D BE EVEN WORSE IF I LEFT JUST THE TWO OF YOU HERE.
HMM...
WHY DON'T WE JUST TAKE HIM ALONG WITH US?

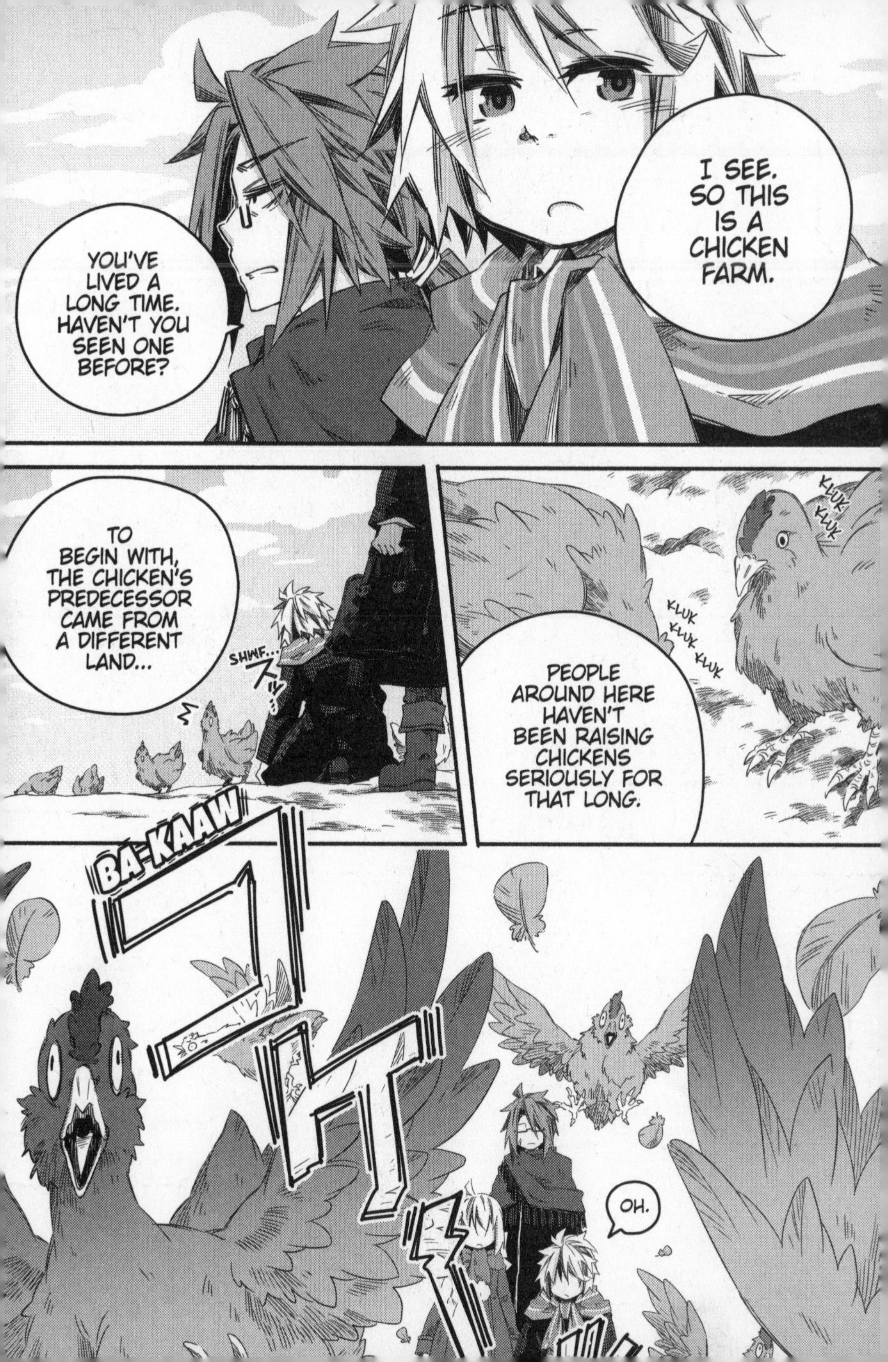
I SEE. SO THIS IS A CHICKEN FARM.
YOU'VE LIVED A LONG TIME. HAVEN'T YOU SEEN ONE BEFORE?
KLUK KLUK
KLUK KLUK KLUK
PEOPLE AROUND HERE HAVEN'T BEEN RAISING CHICKENS SERIOUSLY FOR THAT LONG.
TO BEGIN WITH, THE CHICKEN'S PREDECESSOR CAME FROM A DIFFERENT LAND...
SHWF...
BA-KAAW
OH.

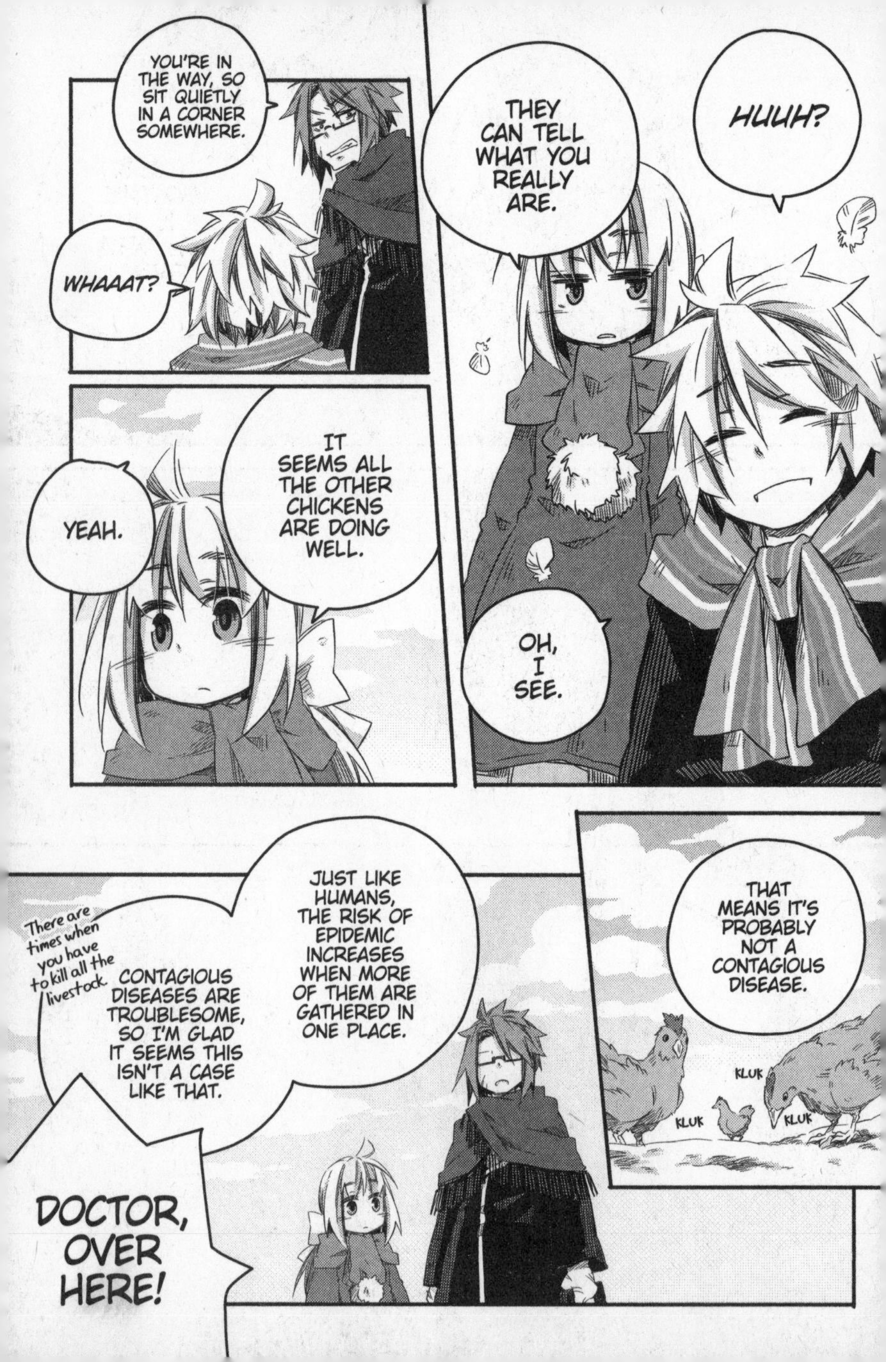
HUUH?
THEY CAN TELL WHAT YOU REALLY ARE.
OH, I SEE.
YOU'RE IN THE WAY, SO SIT QUIETLY IN A CORNER SOMEWHERE.
WHAAAT?
IT SEEMS ALL THE OTHER CHICKENS ARE DOING WELL.
YEAH.
THAT MEANS IT'S PROBABLY NOT A CONTAGIOUS DISEASE.
KLUK
KLUK
KLUK
JUST LIKE HUMANS, THE RISK OF EPIDEMIC INCREASES WHEN MORE OF THEM ARE GATHERED IN ONE PLACE.
CONTAGIOUS DISEASES ARE TROUBLESOME, SO I'M GLAD IT SEEMS THIS ISN'T A CASE LIKE THAT.
There are times when you have to kill all the livestock.
DOCTOR, OVER HERE!

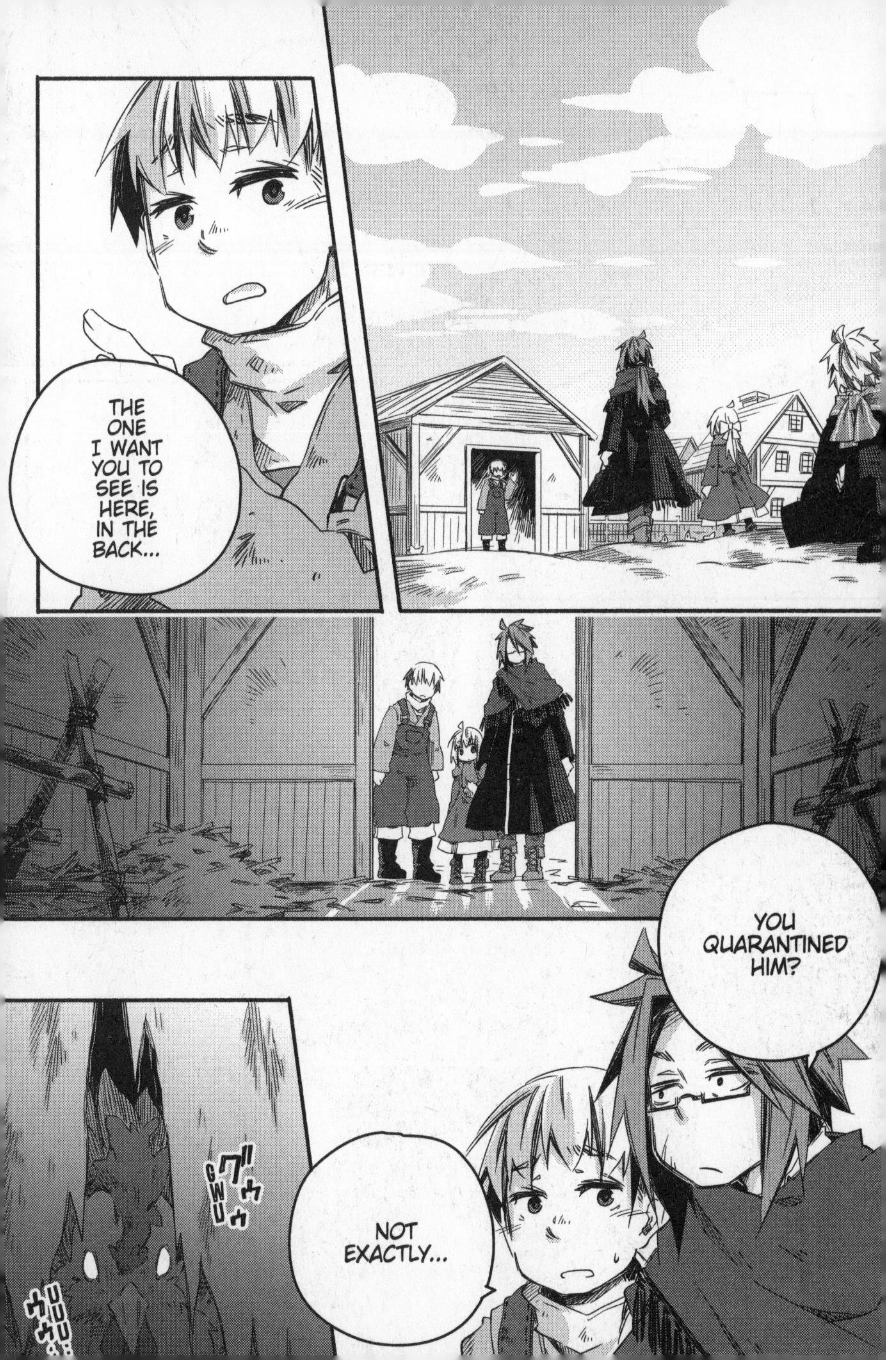
THE ONE I WANT YOU TO SEE IS HERE, IN THE BACK...
YOU QUARANTINED HIM?
NOT EXACTLY...
GWU
UUU

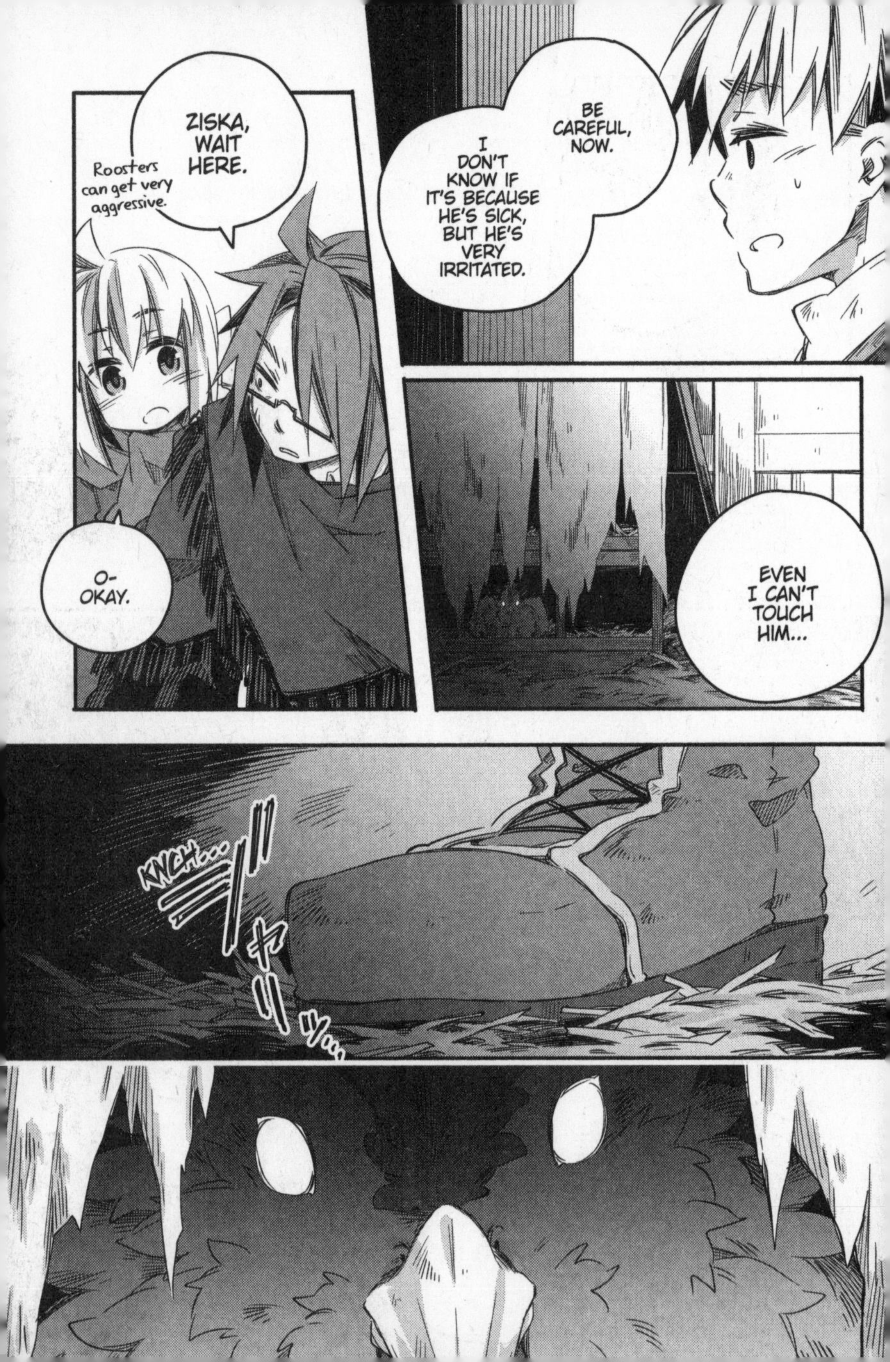

BE CAREFUL, NOW.
I DON'T KNOW IF IT'S BECAUSE HE'S SICK, BUT HE'S VERY IRRITATED.
EVEN I CAN'T TOUCH HIM...
ZISKA, WAIT HERE.
Roosters can get very aggressive.
O-OKAY.
KNCH...

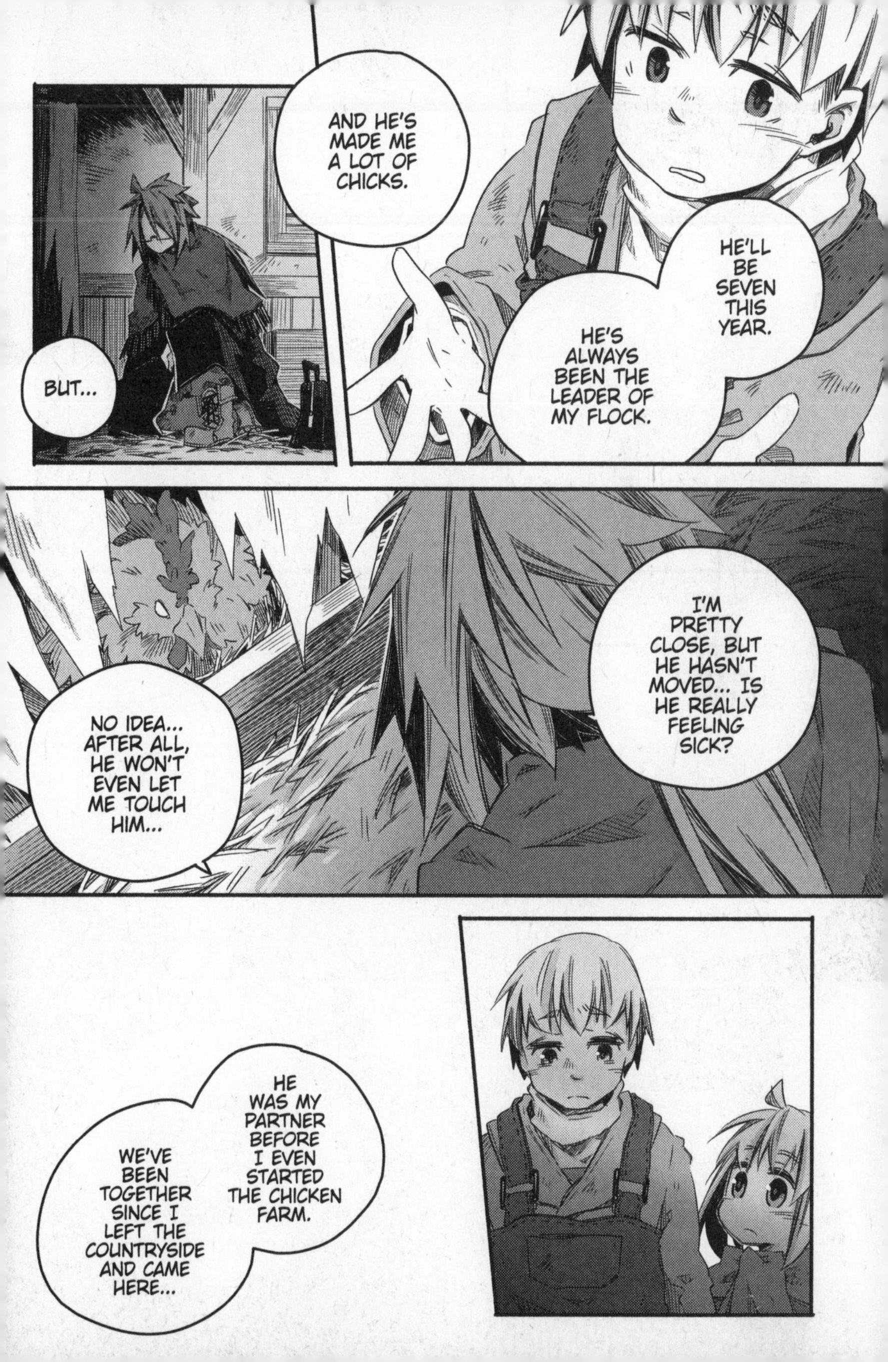

HE'LL BE SEVEN THIS YEAR.
HE'S ALWAYS BEEN THE LEADER OF MY FLOCK.
AND HE'S MADE ME A LOT OF CHICKS.
BUT...
I'M PRETTY CLOSE, BUT HE HASN'T MOVED... IS HE REALLY FEELING SICK?
NO IDEA... AFTER ALL, HE WON'T EVEN LET ME TOUCH HIM...
HE WAS MY PARTNER BEFORE I EVEN STARTED THE CHICKEN FARM.
WE'VE BEEN TOGETHER SINCE I LEFT THE COUNTRYSIDE AND CAME HERE...

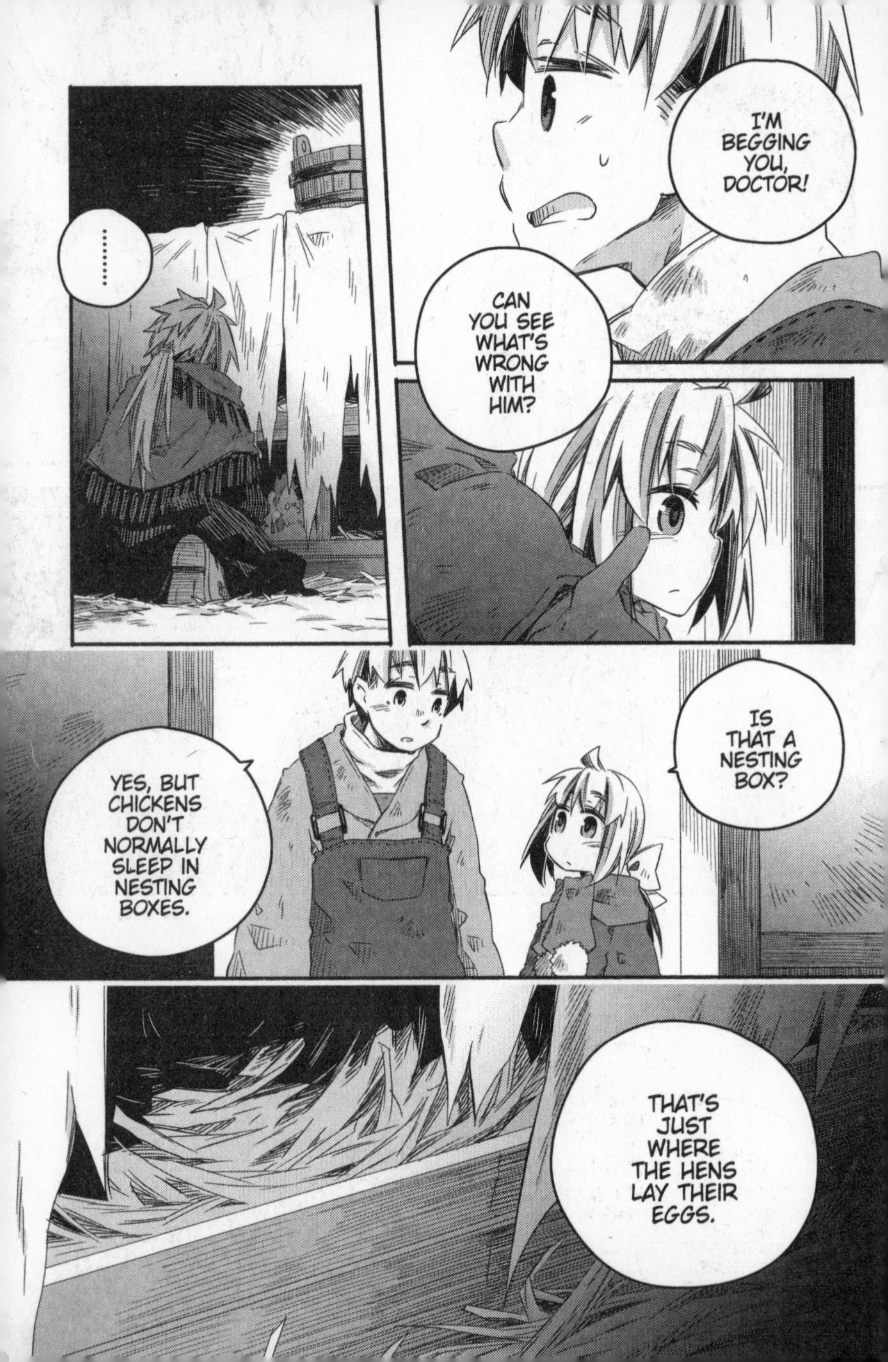
I'M BEGGING YOU, DOCTOR!
CAN YOU SEE WHAT'S WRONG WITH HIM?
......
IS THAT A NESTING BOX?
YES, BUT CHICKENS DON'T NORMALLY SLEEP IN NESTING BOXES.
THAT'S JUST WHERE THE HENS LAY THEIR EGGS.

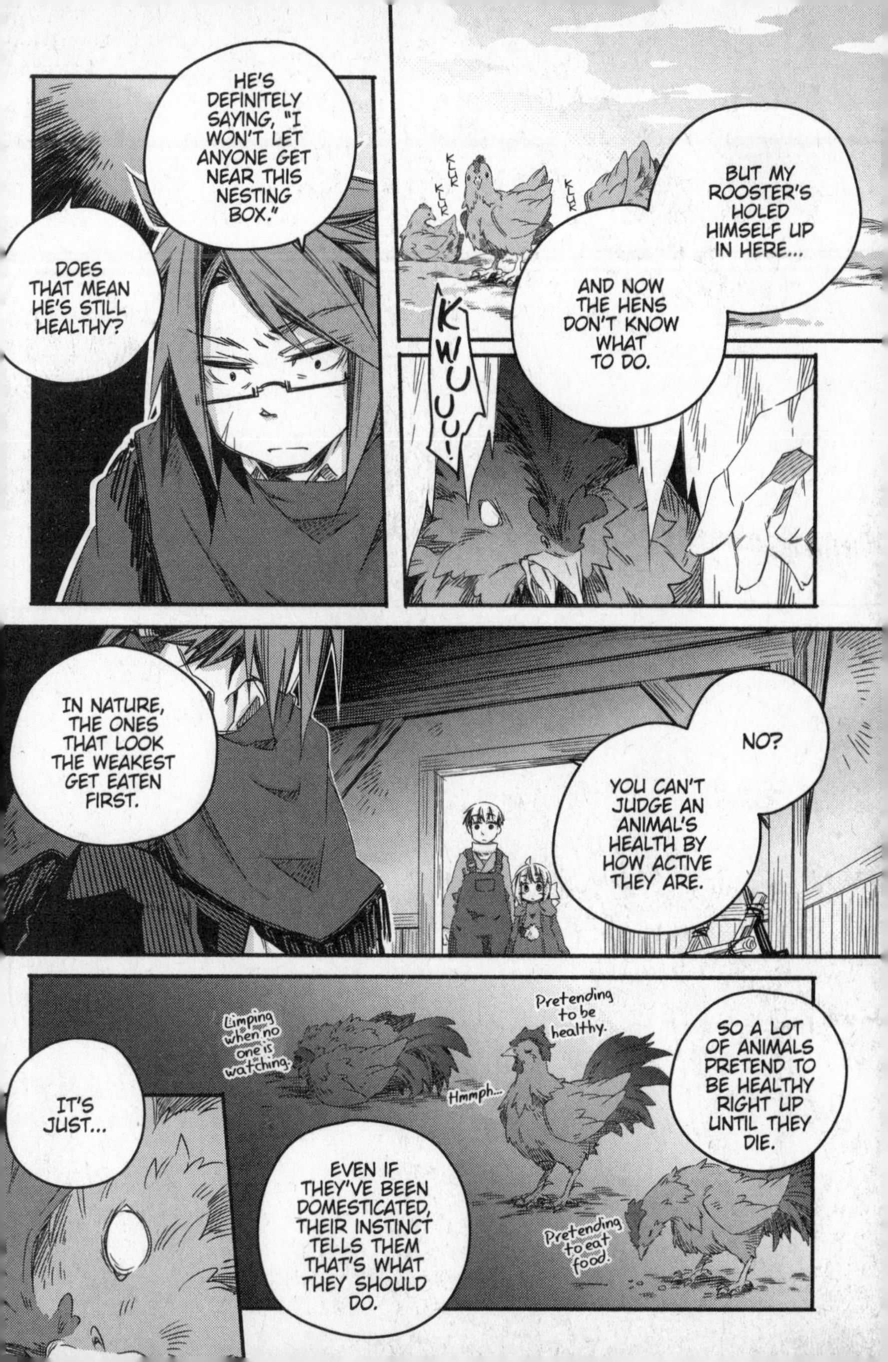
BUT MY ROOSTER'S HOLED HIMSELF UP IN HERE...
AND NOW THE HENS DON'T KNOW WHAT TO DO.
KLUK
KLUK
KLUK
KWUUUU!
HE'S DEFINITELY SAYING, "I WON'T LET ANYONE GET NEAR THIS NESTING BOX."
DOES THAT MEAN HE'S STILL HEALTHY?
NO?
YOU CAN'T JUDGE AN ANIMAL'S HEALTH BY HOW ACTIVE THEY ARE.
IN NATURE, THE ONES THAT LOOK THE WEAKEST GET EATEN FIRST.
SO A LOT OF ANIMALS PRETEND TO BE HEALTHY RIGHT UP UNTIL THEY DIE.
Pretending to be healthy.
Limping when no one is watching.
Hmmph...
EVEN IF THEY'VE BEEN DOMESTICATED, THEIR INSTINCT TELLS THEM THAT'S WHAT THEY SHOULD DO.
Pretending to eat food.
IT'S JUST...

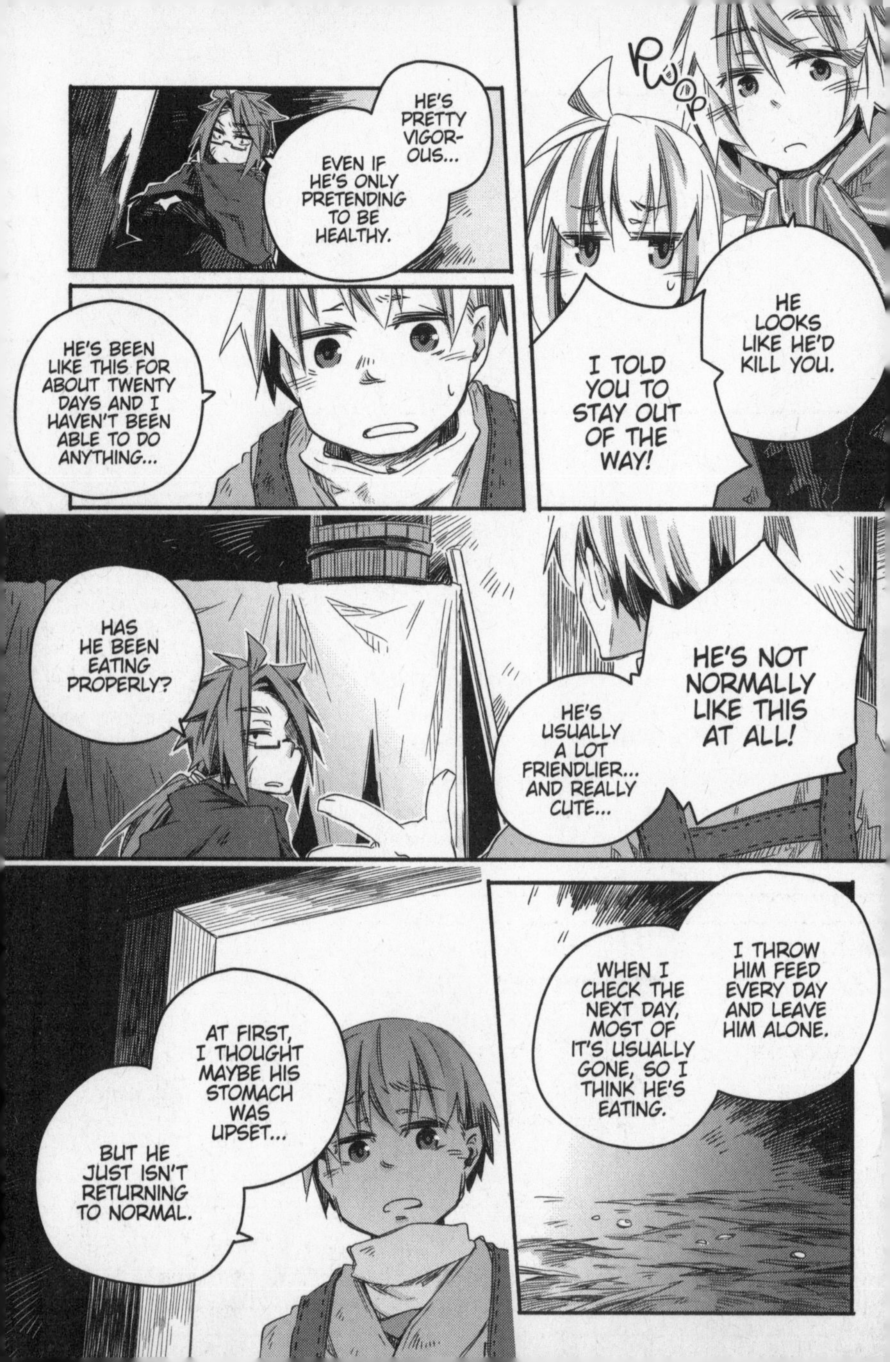
PWOP
HE LOOKS LIKE HE'D KILL YOU.
I TOLD YOU TO STAY OUT OF THE WAY!
HE'S PRETTY VIGOR-OUS...
EVEN IF HE'S ONLY PRETENDING TO BE HEALTHY.
HE'S BEEN LIKE THIS FOR ABOUT TWENTY DAYS AND I HAVEN'T BEEN ABLE TO DO ANYTHING...
HE'S NOT NORMALLY LIKE THIS AT ALL!
HE'S USUALLY A LOT FRIENDLIER... AND REALLY CUTE...
HAS HE BEEN EATING PROPERLY?
I THROW HIM FEED EVERY DAY AND LEAVE HIM ALONE.
WHEN I CHECK THE NEXT DAY, MOST OF IT'S USUALLY GONE, SO I THINK HE'S EATING.
AT FIRST, I THOUGHT MAYBE HIS STOMACH WAS UPSET...
BUT HE JUST ISN'T RETURNING TO NORMAL.

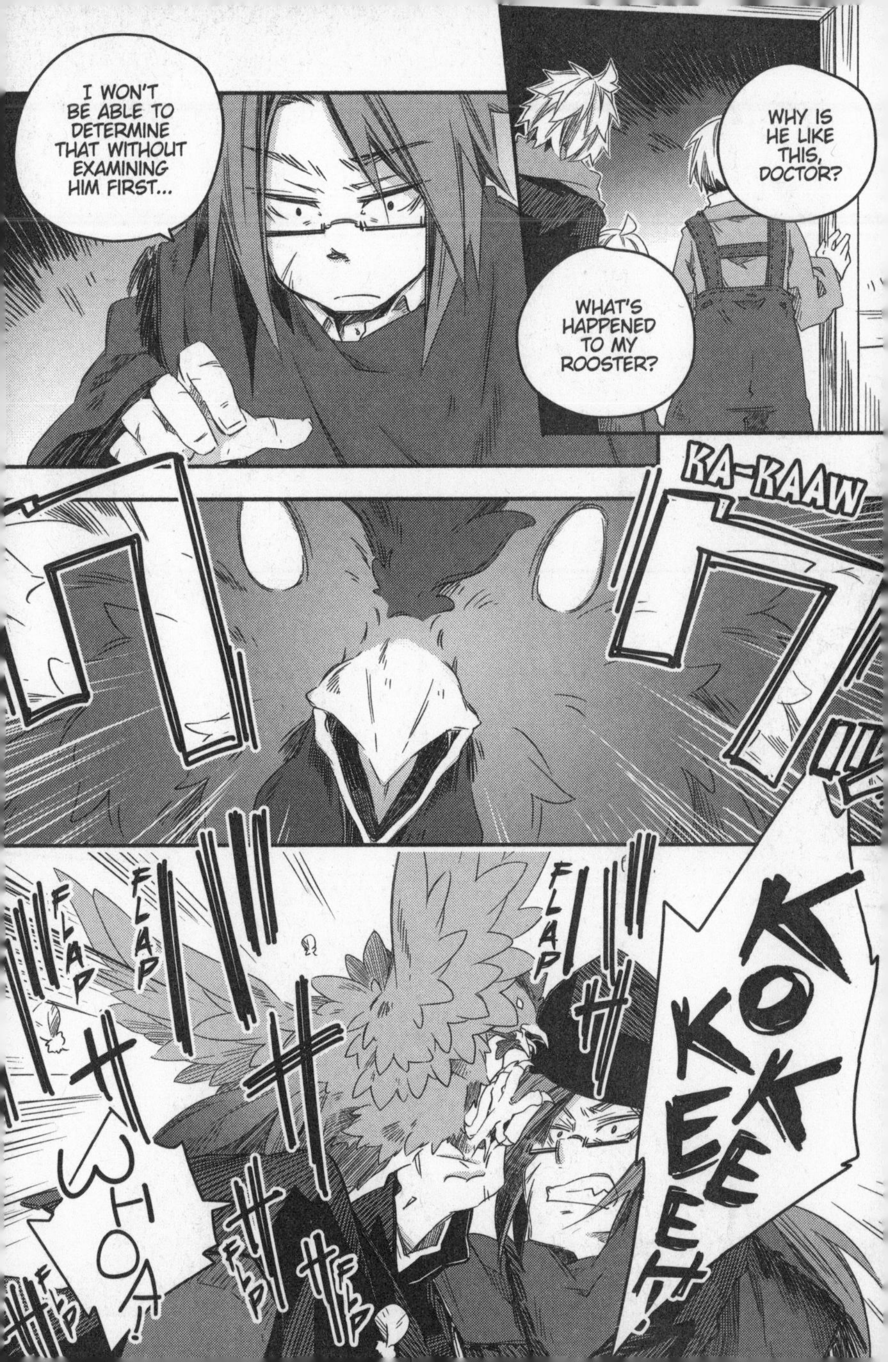
WHY IS HE LIKE THIS, DOCTOR?
WHAT'S HAPPENED TO MY ROOSTER?
I WON'T BE ABLE TO DETERMINE THAT WITHOUT EXAMINING HIM FIRST...
KA-KAAW
KOKEEEEH!
FLAP
FLAP
FLAP
WHOA!

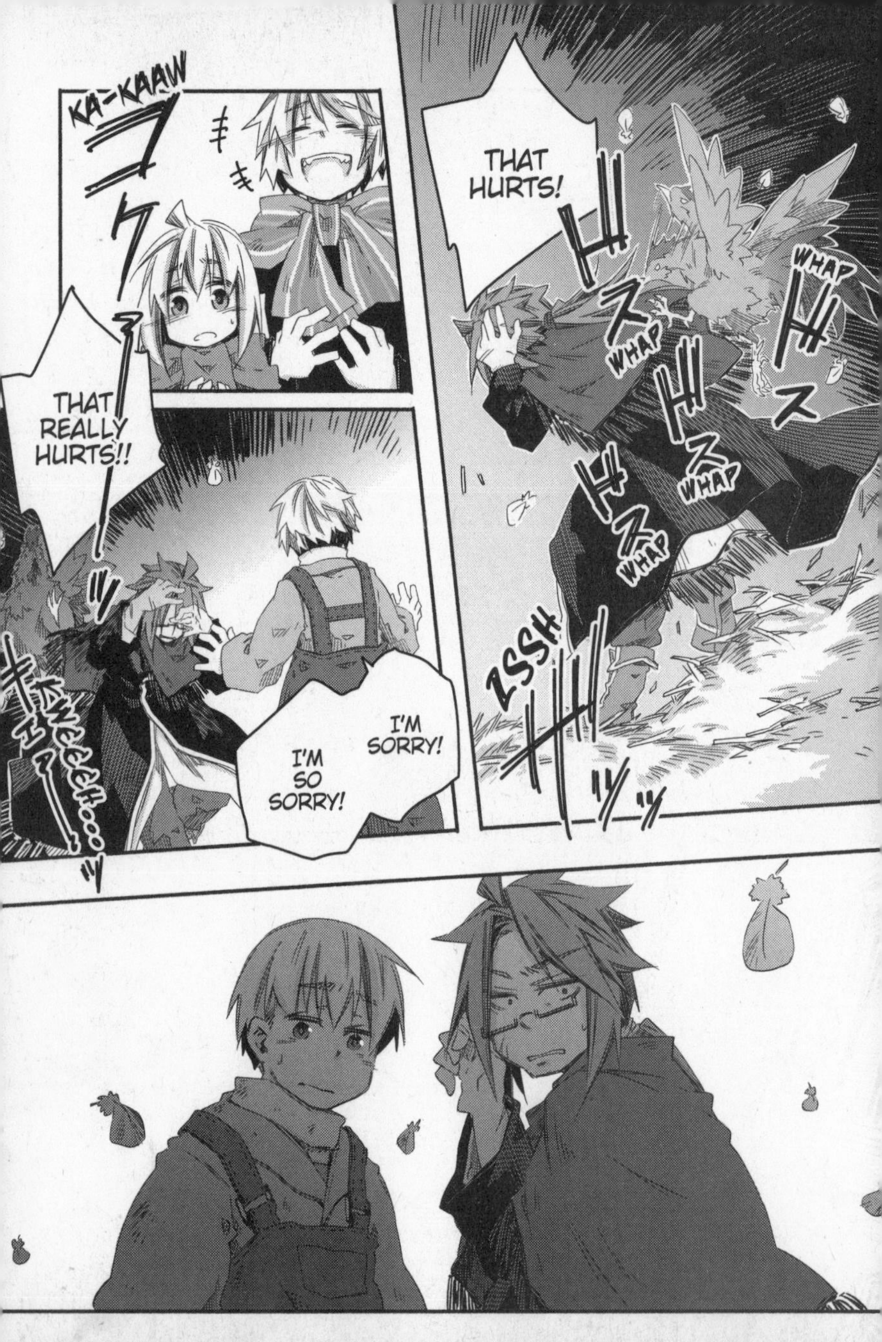
THAT HURTS!
WHAP
WHAP
WHAP
WHAP
ZSSH
KA-KAAW
THAT REALLY HURTS!!
I'M SORRY!
I'M SO SORRY!
KWEEEEHooo

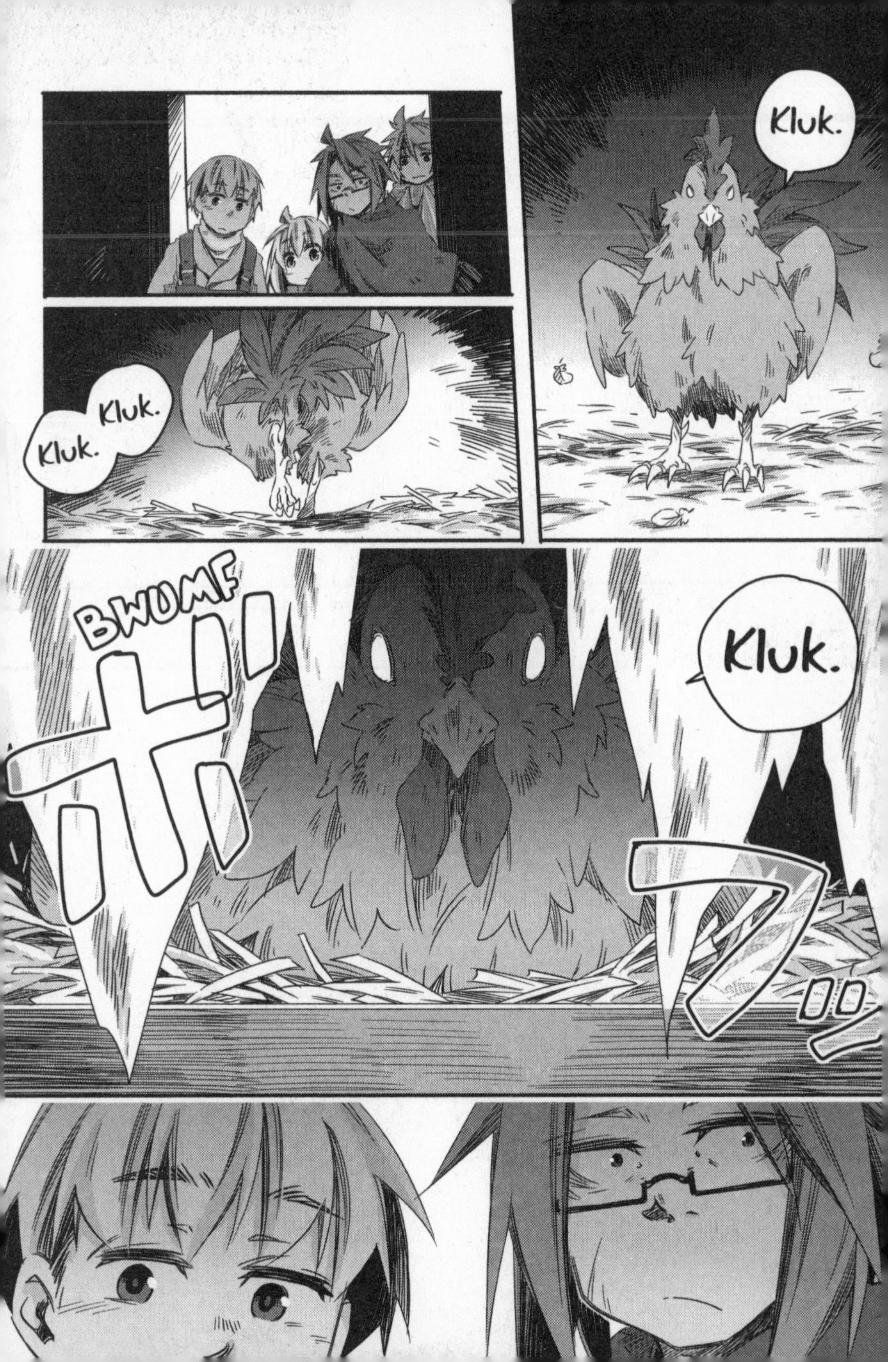
Kluk.
Kluk.
Kluk.
Kluk.
BWOMF
ボフッ

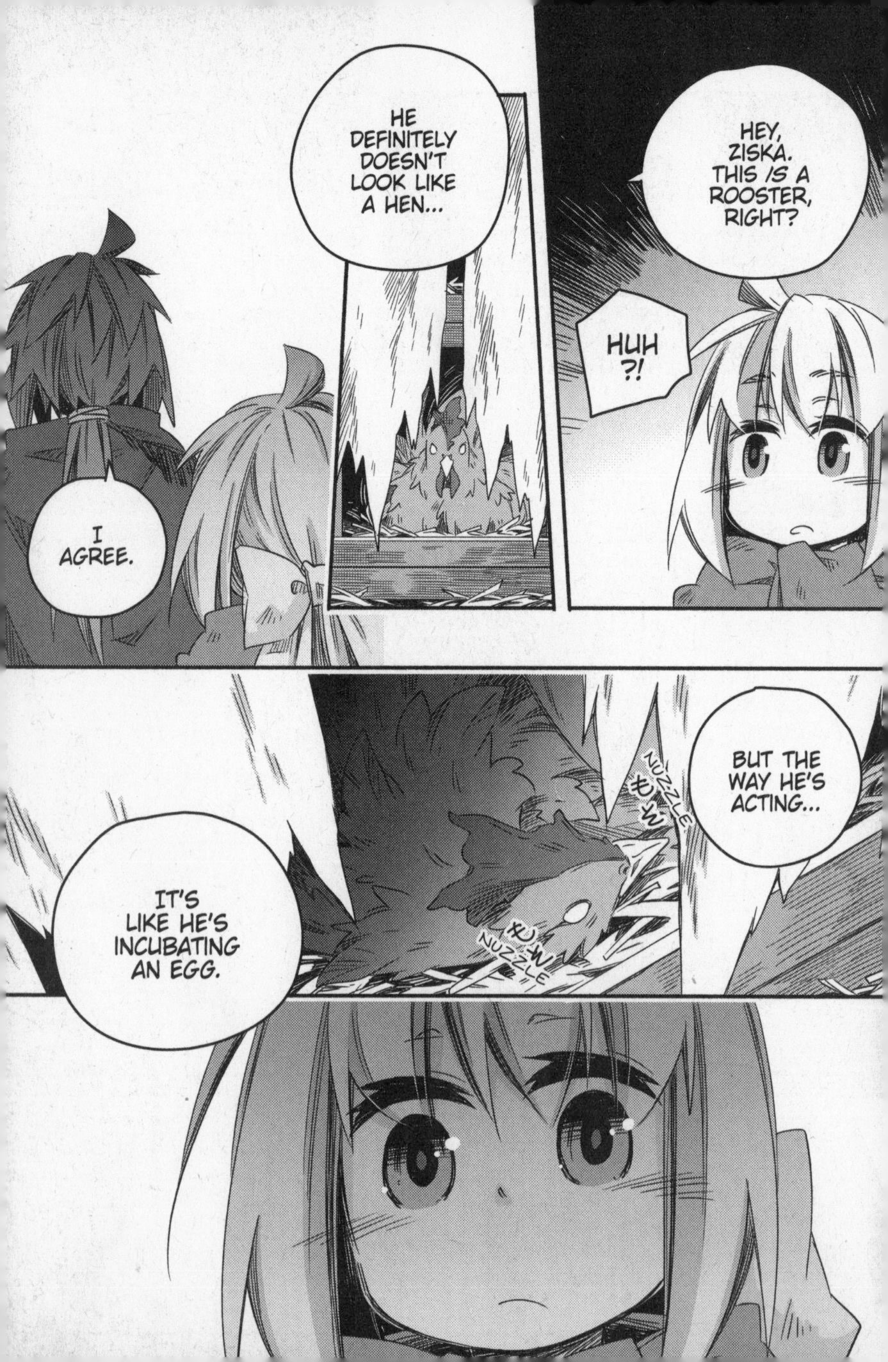
HEY, ZISKA. THIS *IS* A ROOSTER, RIGHT?
HUH ?!
HE DEFINITELY DOESN'T LOOK LIKE A HEN...
I AGREE.
BUT THE WAY HE'S ACTING...
NUZZLE
NUZZLE
IT'S LIKE HE'S INCUBATING AN EGG.

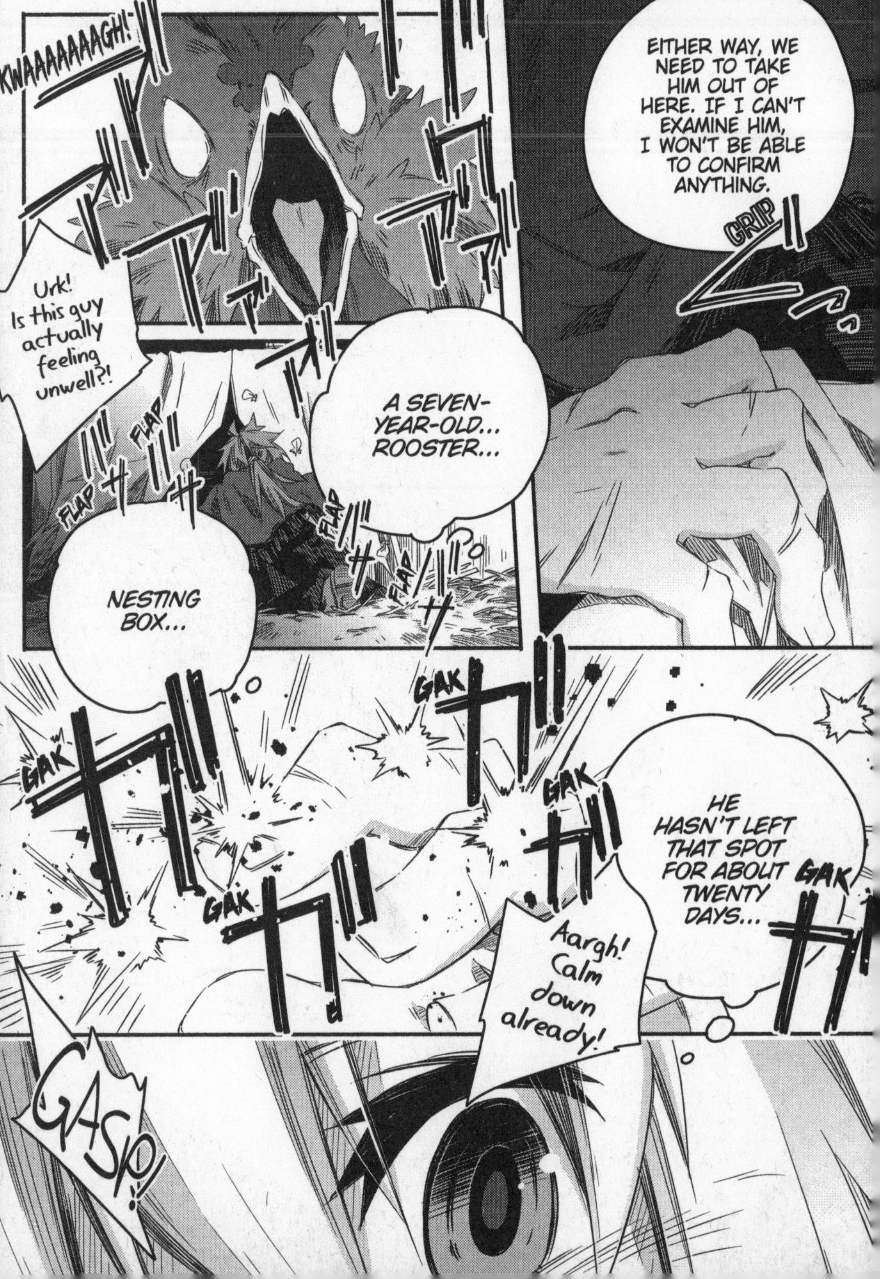
EITHER WAY, WE NEED TO TAKE HIM OUT OF HERE. IF I CAN'T EXAMINE HIM, I WON'T BE ABLE TO CONFIRM ANYTHING.
GRIP
KWAAAAAAGH!
Urk! Is this guy actually feeling unwell?!
FLAP
FLAP
A SEVEN-YEAR-OLD... ROOSTER...
FLAP
FLAP
NESTING BOX...
HE HASN'T LEFT THAT SPOT FOR ABOUT TWENTY DAYS...
GAK
GAK
GAK
GAK
GAK
Aargh! Calm down already!
GASP!

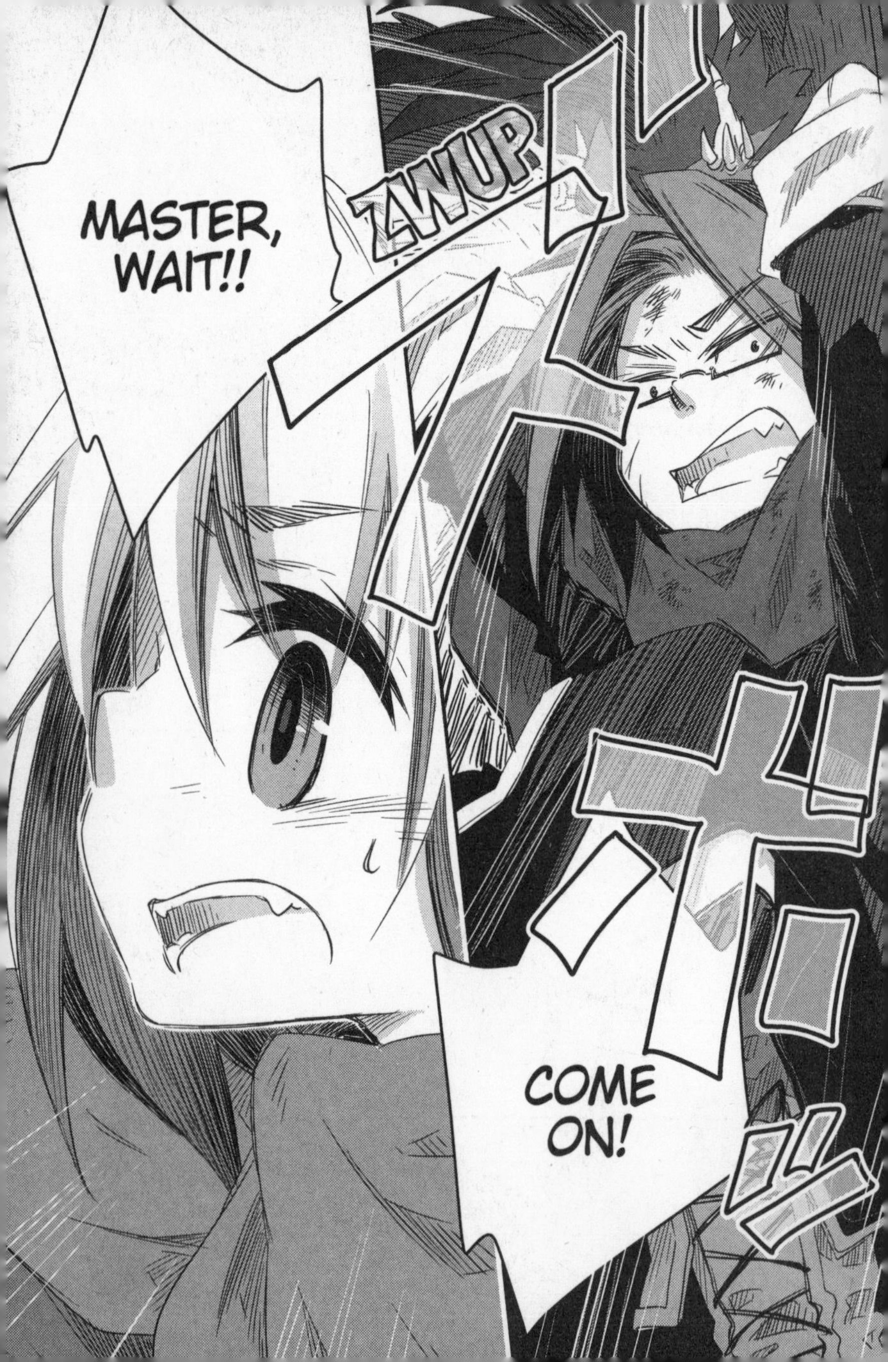
ZWUP
MASTER, WAIT!!
COME ON!

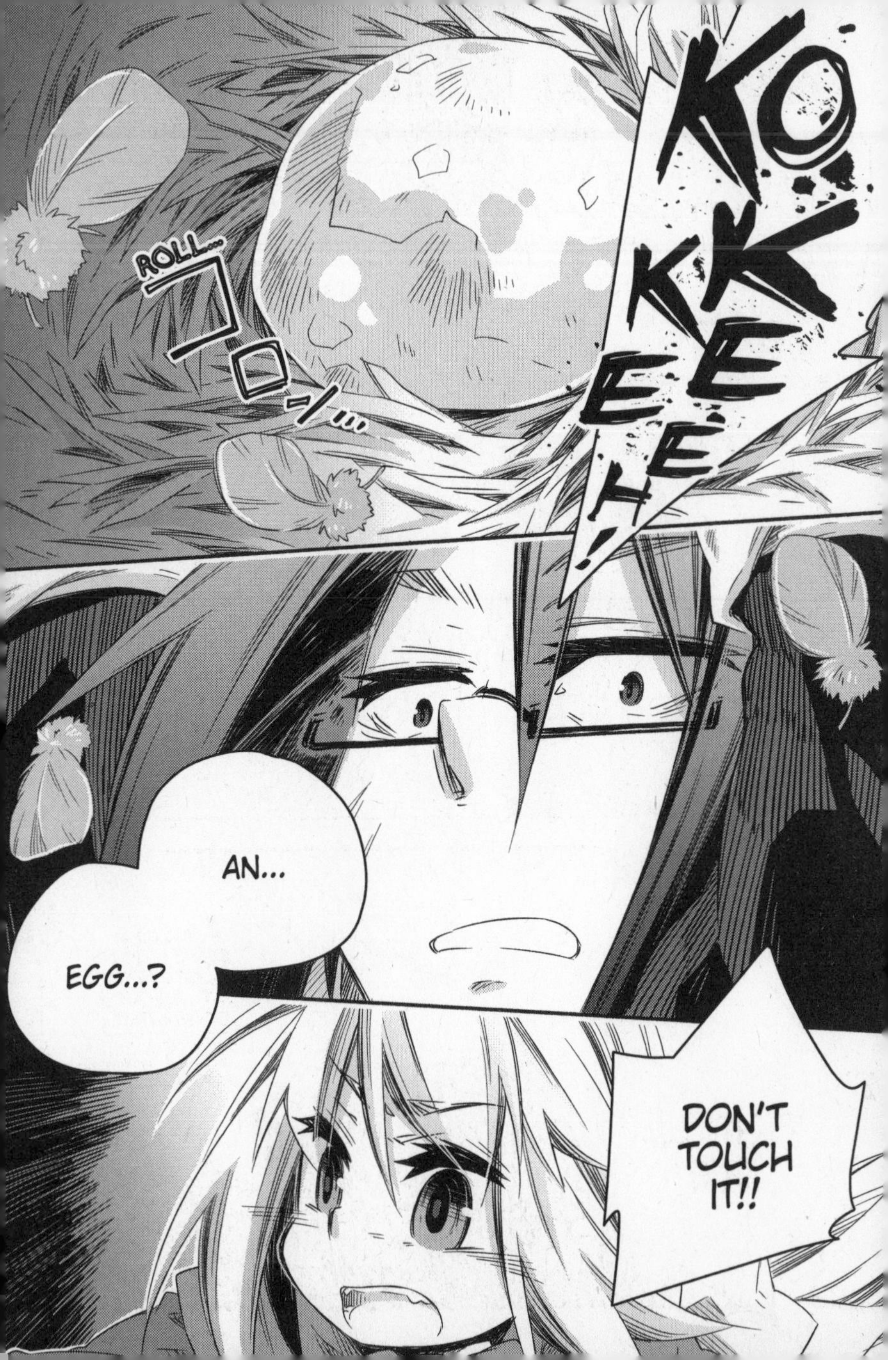
KOKKEEEEH!
ROLL...
AN...
EGG...?
DON'T TOUCH IT!!

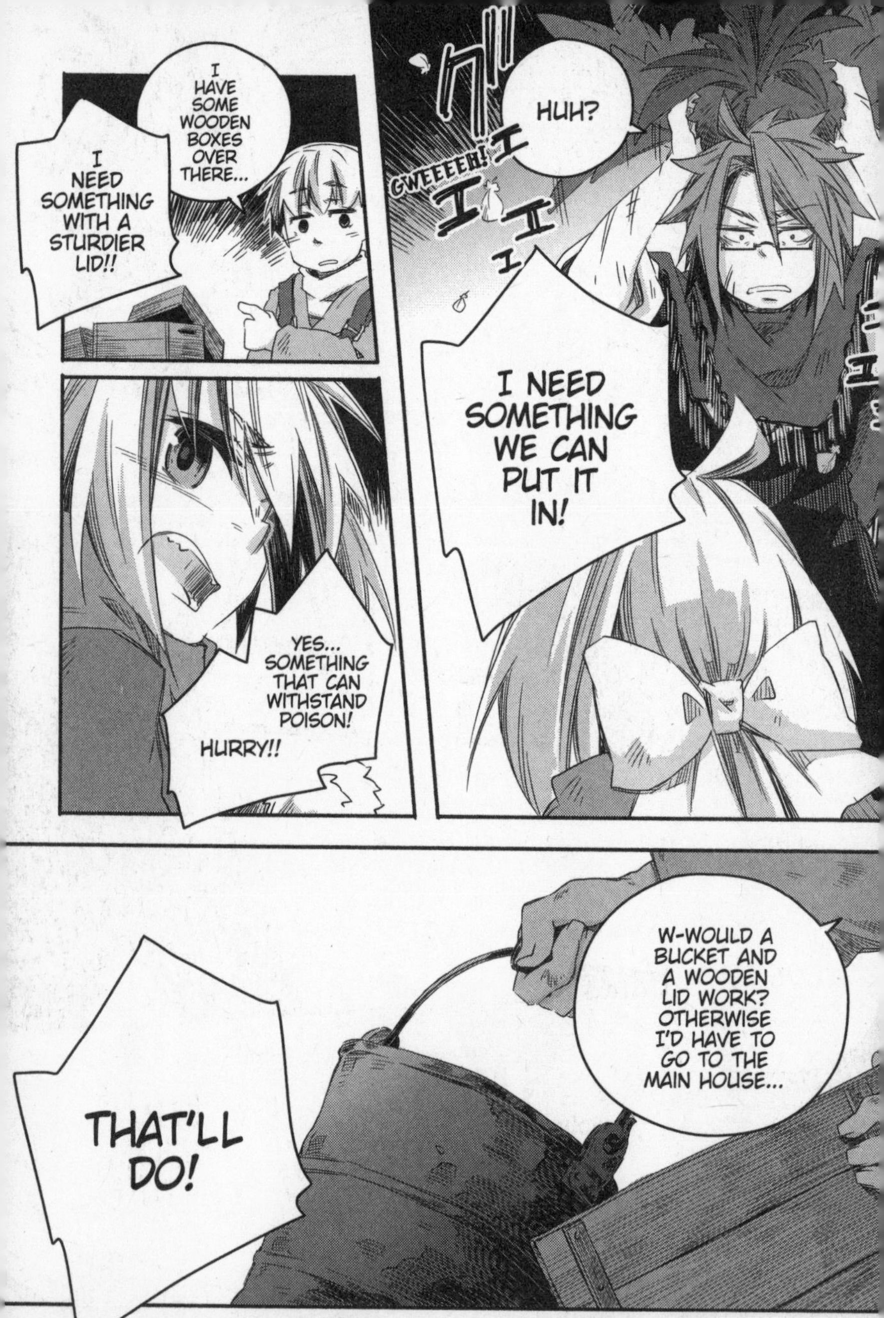
HUH?
GWEEEEH!
I NEED SOMETHING WE CAN PUT IT IN!
I HAVE SOME WOODEN BOXES OVER THERE...
I NEED SOMETHING WITH A STURDIER LID!!
YES... SOMETHING THAT CAN WITHSTAND POISON!
HURRY!!
W-WOULD A BUCKET AND A WOODEN LID WORK? OTHERWISE I'D HAVE TO GO TO THE MAIN HOUSE...
THAT'LL DO!

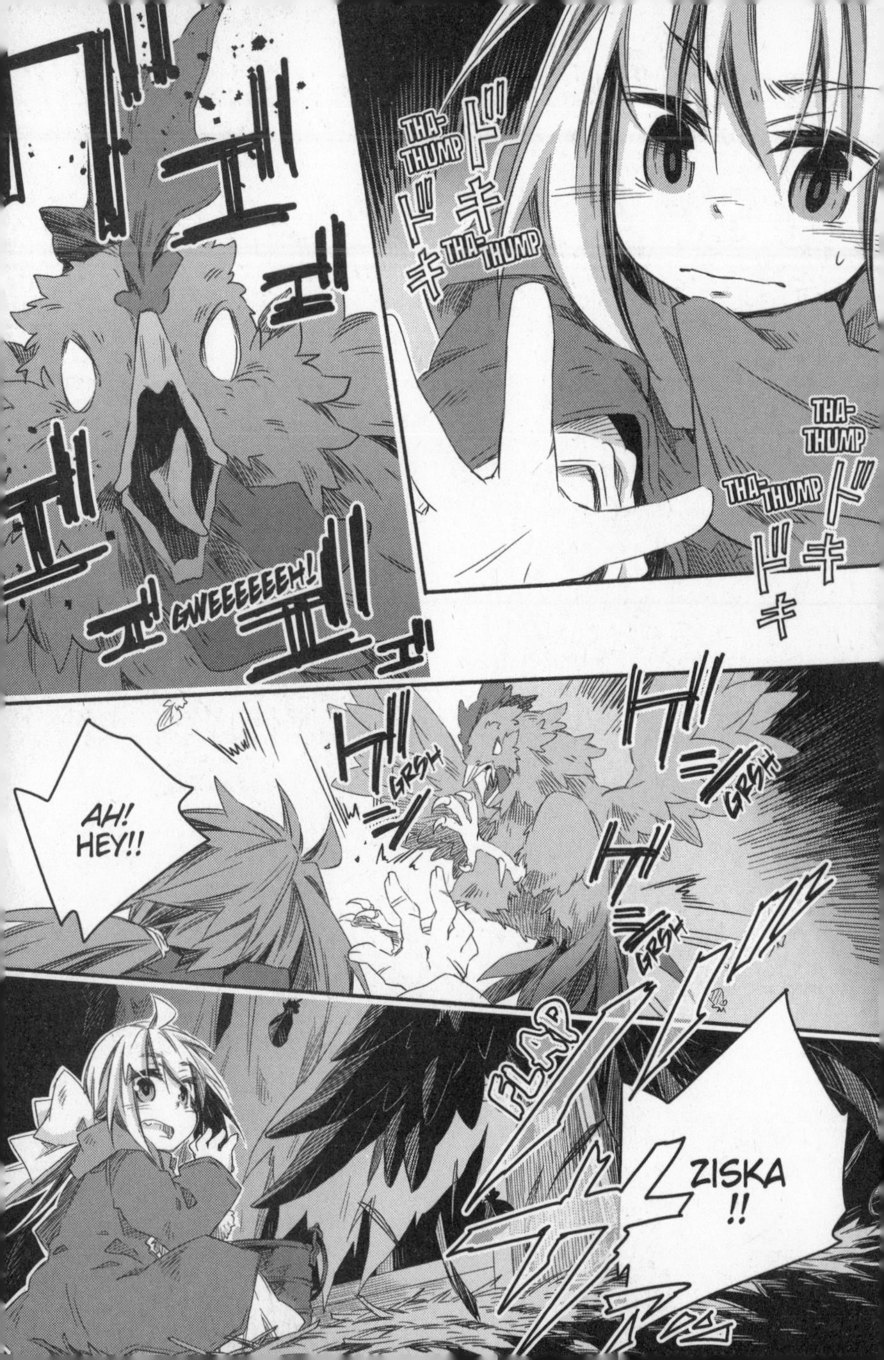

THA-THUMP
ドキ
ドキ
THA-THUMP
THA-THUMP
THA-THUMP
ドキ
ドキ
GWEEEEEEH!
GRSH
GRSH
GRSH
AH! HEY!!
FLAP
ZISKA !!

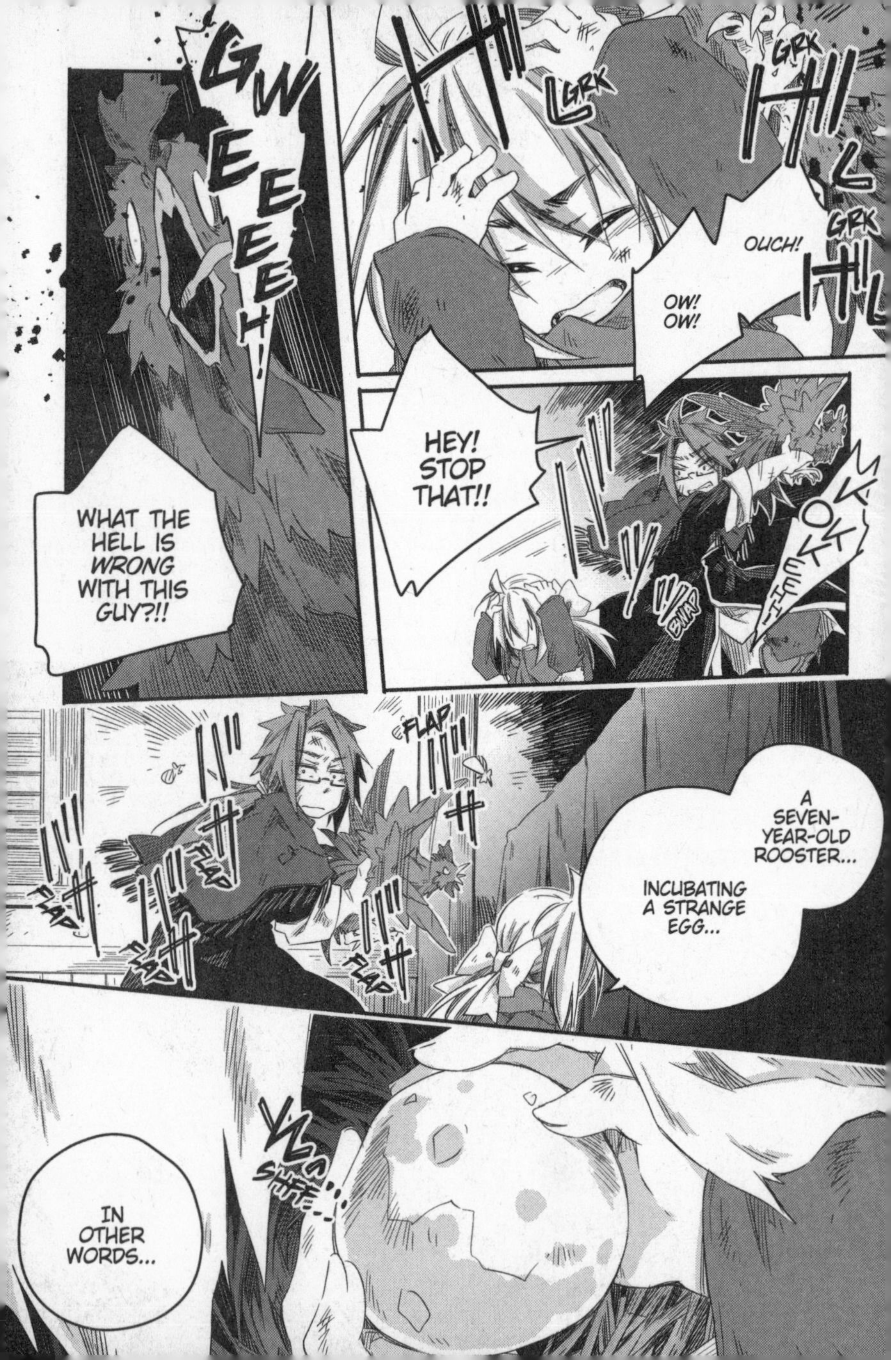
GRK
GRK
OUCH!
OW! OW!
HEY! STOP THAT!!
KOKKEH!
BWAP
GWEEEEH!
WHAT THE HELL IS *WRONG* WITH THIS GUY?!!
FLAP
FLAP
FLAP
FLAP
FLAP
A SEVEN-YEAR-OLD ROOSTER...
INCUBATING A STRANGE EGG...
SHUFF...
IN OTHER WORDS...

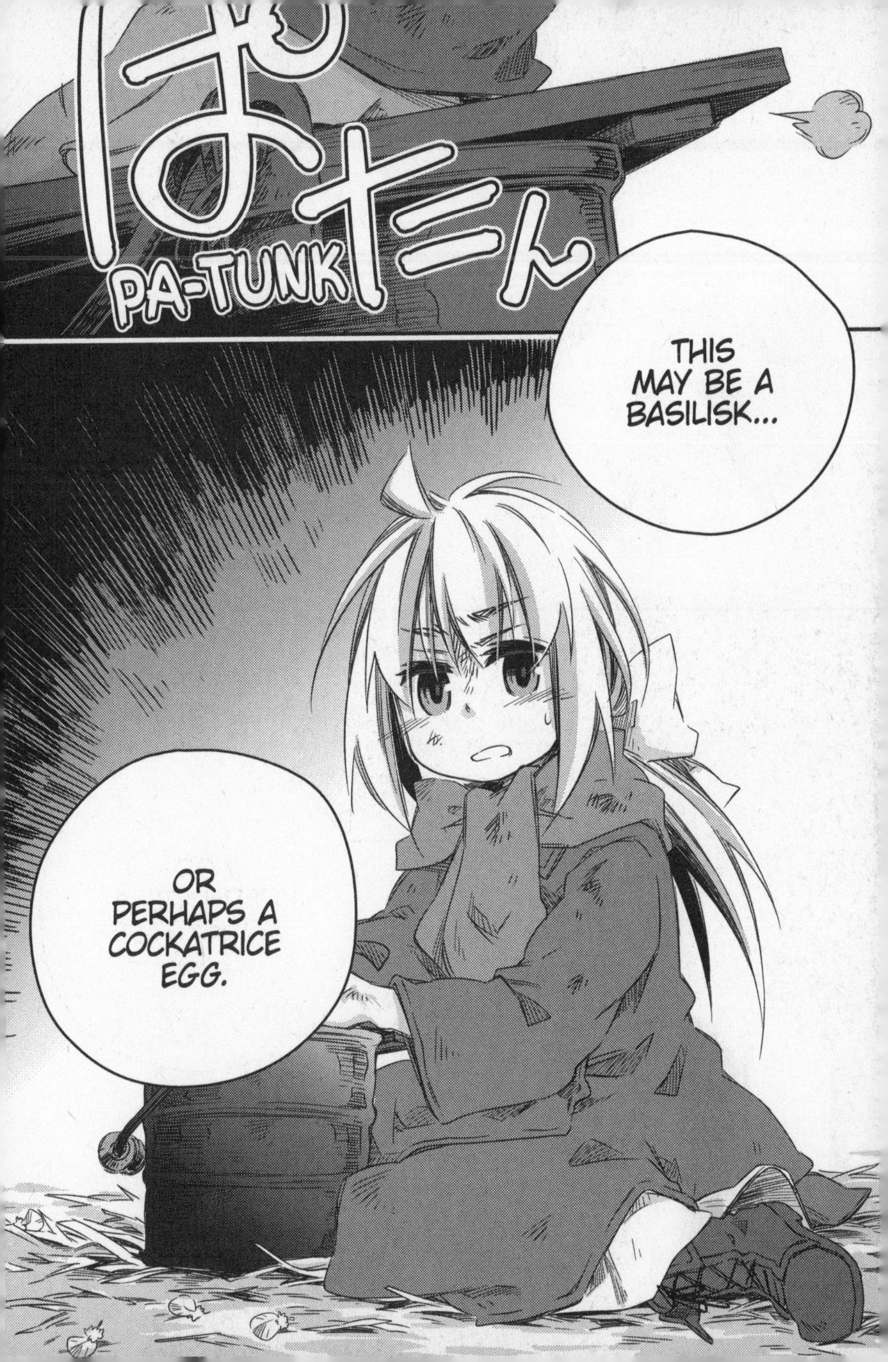
ぱたーん
PA-TUNK
THIS MAY BE A BASILISK...
OR PERHAPS A COCKATRICE EGG.

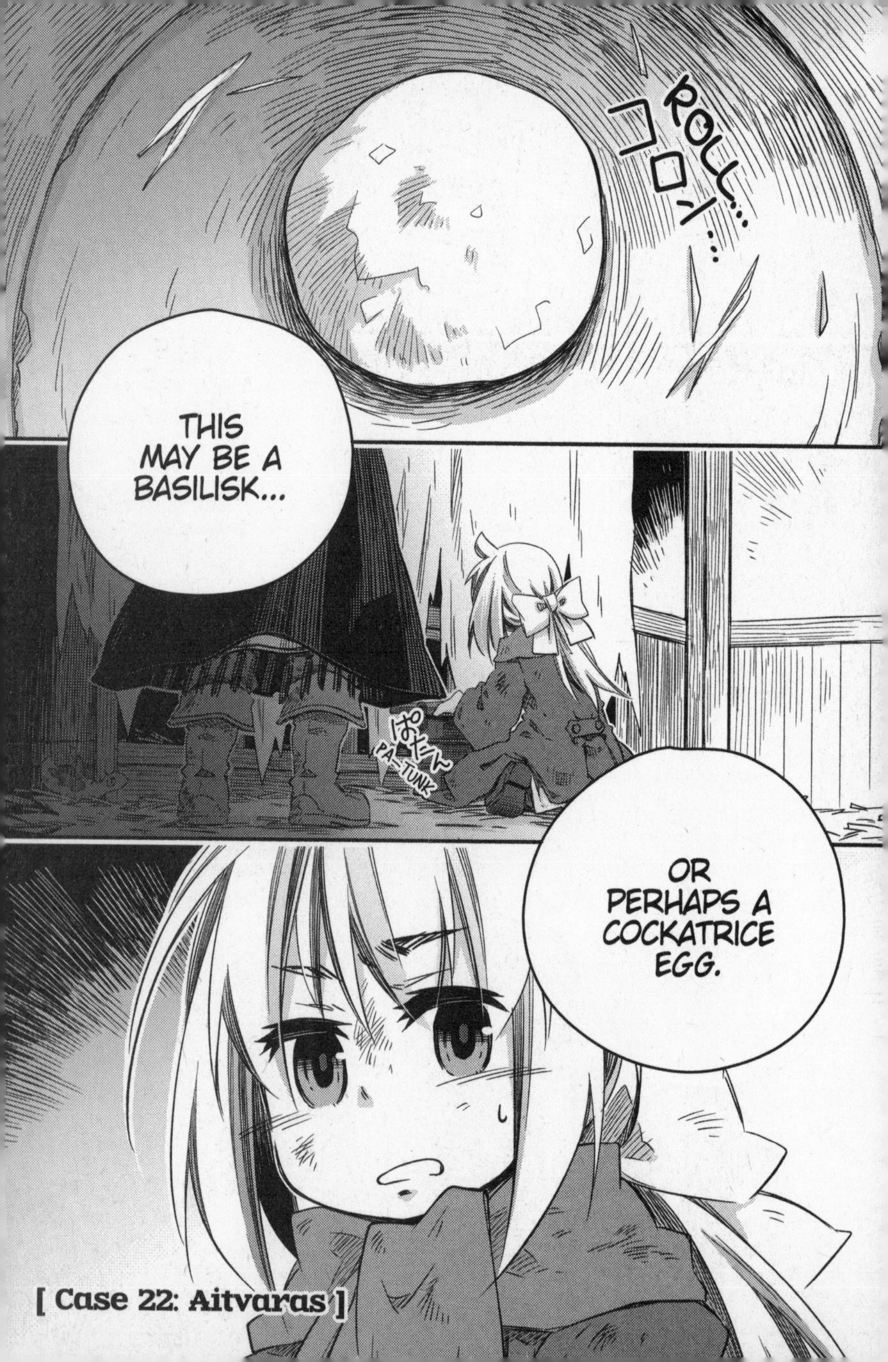
ROLL...
コロン...
THIS MAY BE A BASILISK...
ぽたん
PA-TUNK
OR PERHAPS A COCKATRICE EGG.
[Case 22: Aitvaras]

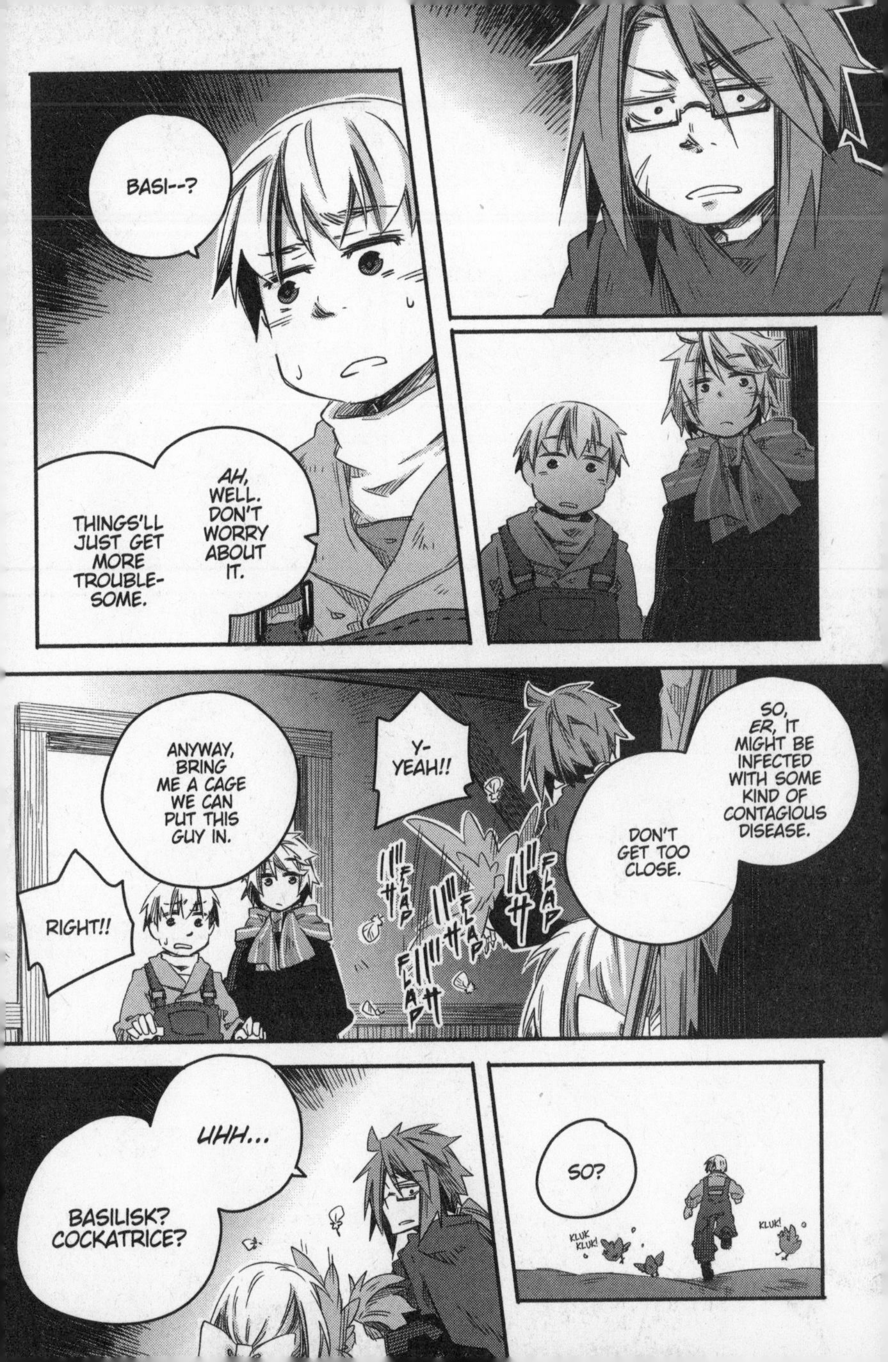
BASI--?
AH, WELL. DON'T WORRY ABOUT IT.
THINGS'LL JUST GET MORE TROUBLE-SOME.
SO, ER, IT MIGHT BE INFECTED WITH SOME KIND OF CONTAGIOUS DISEASE.
DON'T GET TOO CLOSE.
FLAP
FLAP
FLAP
FLAP
Y-YEAH!!
ANYWAY, BRING ME A CAGE WE CAN PUT THIS GUY IN.
RIGHT!!
SO?
KLUK!
KLUK KLUK!
UHH...
BASILISK? COCKATRICE?

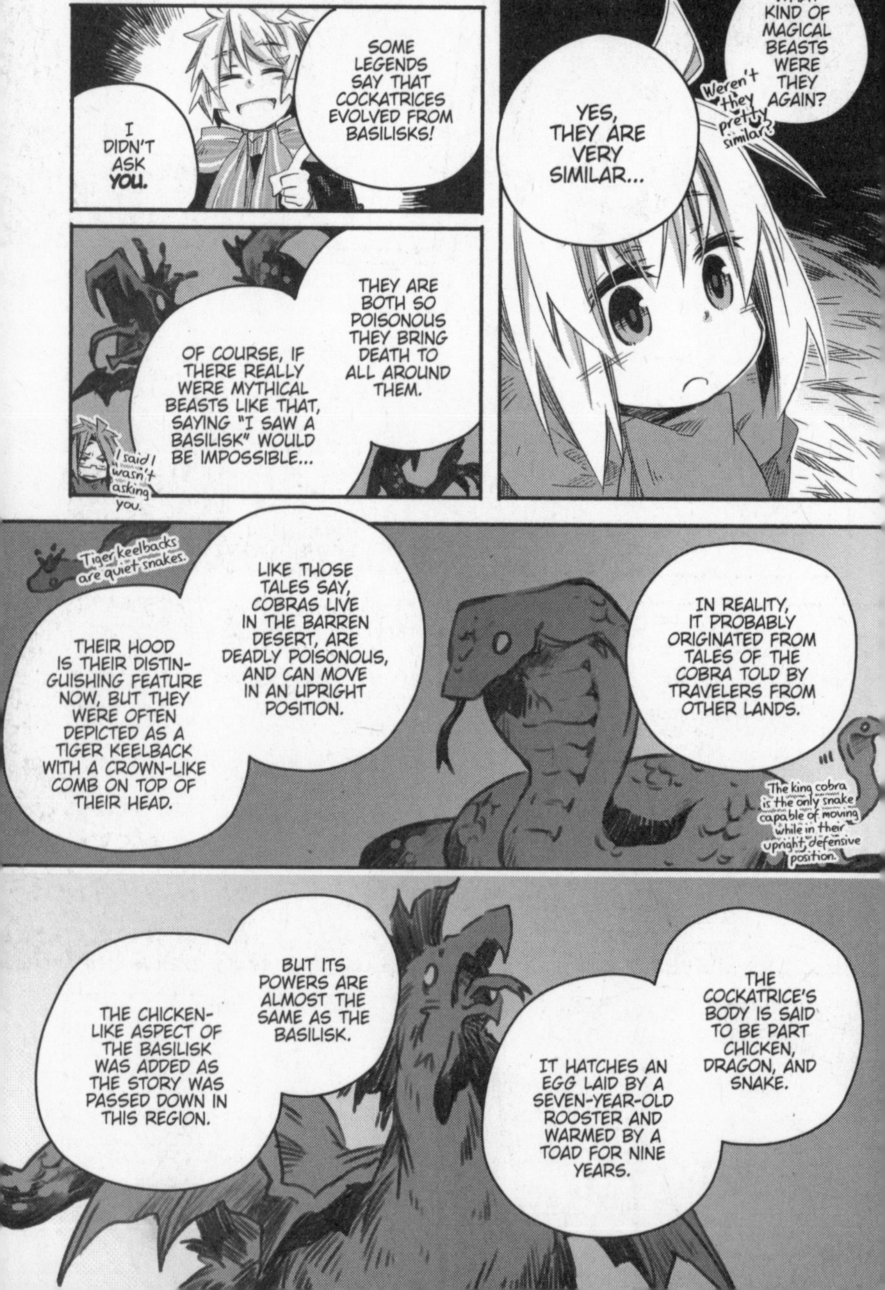
WHAT KIND OF MAGICAL BEASTS WERE THEY AGAIN?
Weren't they pretty similar?
YES, THEY ARE VERY SIMILAR...
SOME LEGENDS SAY THAT COCKATRICES EVOLVED FROM BASILISKS!
I DIDN'T ASK **YOU.**
THEY ARE BOTH SO POISONOUS THEY BRING DEATH TO ALL AROUND THEM.
OF COURSE, IF THERE REALLY WERE MYTHICAL BEASTS LIKE THAT, SAYING "I SAW A BASILISK" WOULD BE IMPOSSIBLE...
I said I wasn't asking you.
IN REALITY, IT PROBABLY ORIGINATED FROM TALES OF THE COBRA TOLD BY TRAVELERS FROM OTHER LANDS.
The king cobra is the only snake capable of moving while in their upright, defensive position.
LIKE THOSE TALES SAY, COBRAS LIVE IN THE BARREN DESERT, ARE DEADLY POISONOUS, AND CAN MOVE IN AN UPRIGHT POSITION.
THEIR HOOD IS THEIR DISTIN-GUISHING FEATURE NOW, BUT THEY WERE OFTEN DEPICTED AS A TIGER KEELBACK WITH A CROWN-LIKE COMB ON TOP OF THEIR HEAD.
Tiger keelbacks are quiet snakes.
THE COCKATRICE'S BODY IS SAID TO BE PART CHICKEN, DRAGON, AND SNAKE.
IT HATCHES AN EGG LAID BY A SEVEN-YEAR-OLD ROOSTER AND WARMED BY A TOAD FOR NINE YEARS.
BUT ITS POWERS ARE ALMOST THE SAME AS THE BASILISK.
THE CHICKEN-LIKE ASPECT OF THE BASILISK WAS ADDED AS THE STORY WAS PASSED DOWN IN THIS REGION.

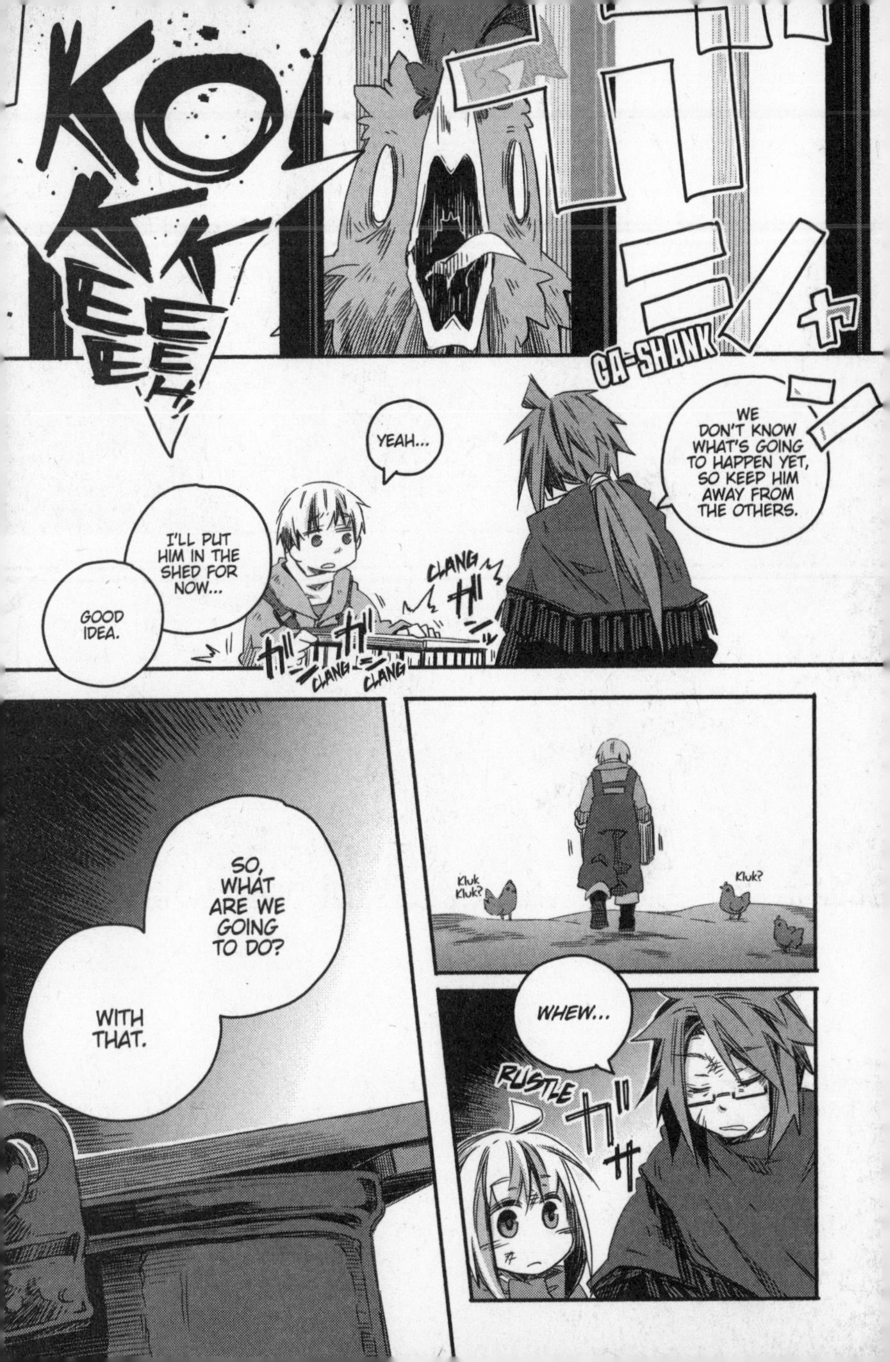
KOKKEEEEEH!!
CA-SHANK
WE DON'T KNOW WHAT'S GOING TO HAPPEN YET, SO KEEP HIM AWAY FROM THE OTHERS.
YEAH...
I'LL PUT HIM IN THE SHED FOR NOW...
GOOD IDEA.
CLANG
CLANG
CLANG
Kluk?
Kluk Kluk?
WHEW...
RUSTLE
SO, WHAT ARE WE GOING TO DO?
WITH THAT.

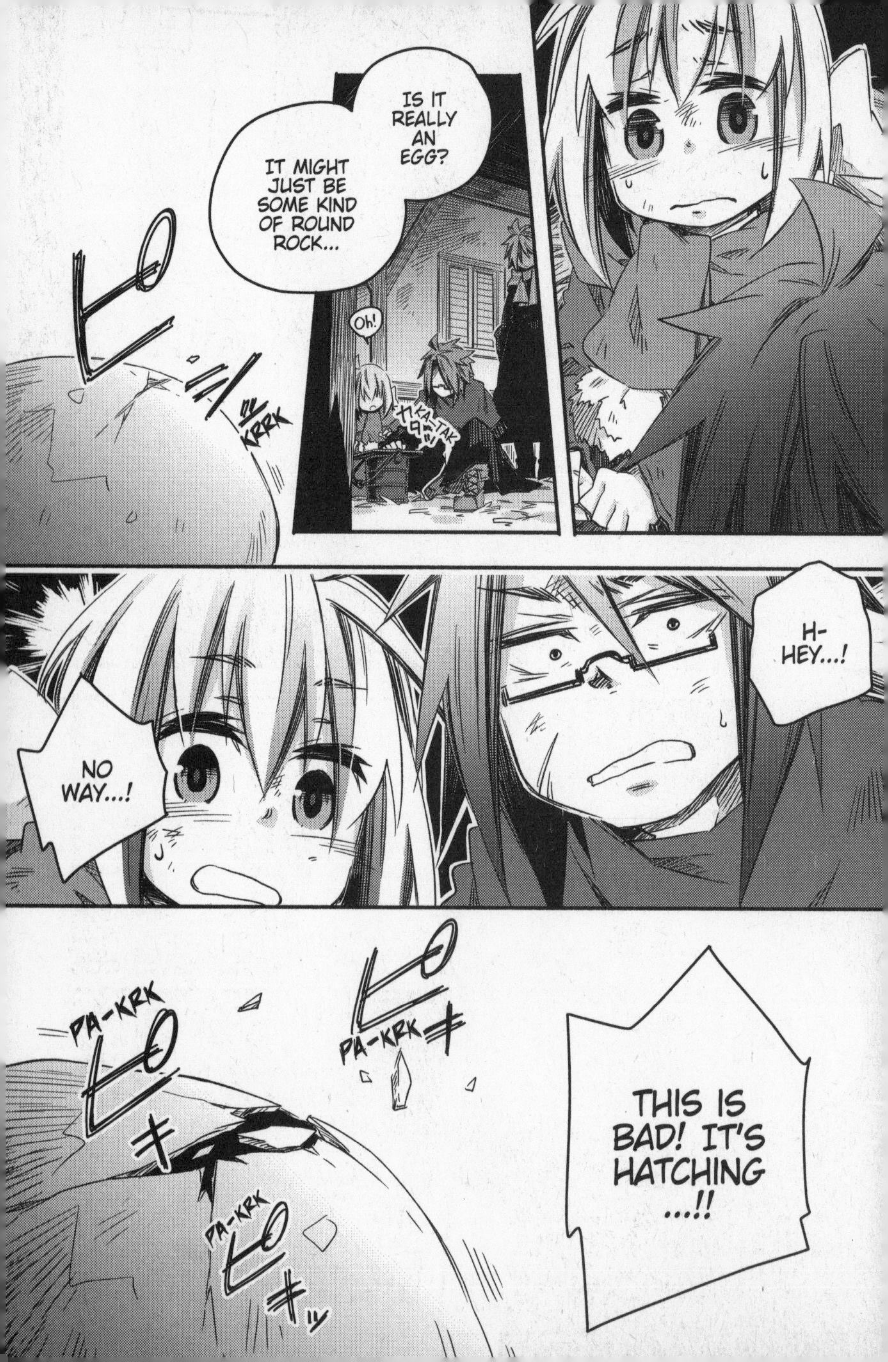
IS IT REALLY AN EGG?
IT MIGHT JUST BE SOME KIND OF ROUND ROCK...
Oh!
KA-TAK
KRRK
H-HEY...!
NO WAY...!
THIS IS BAD! IT'S HATCHING ...!!
PA-KRK
PA-KRK
PA-KRK

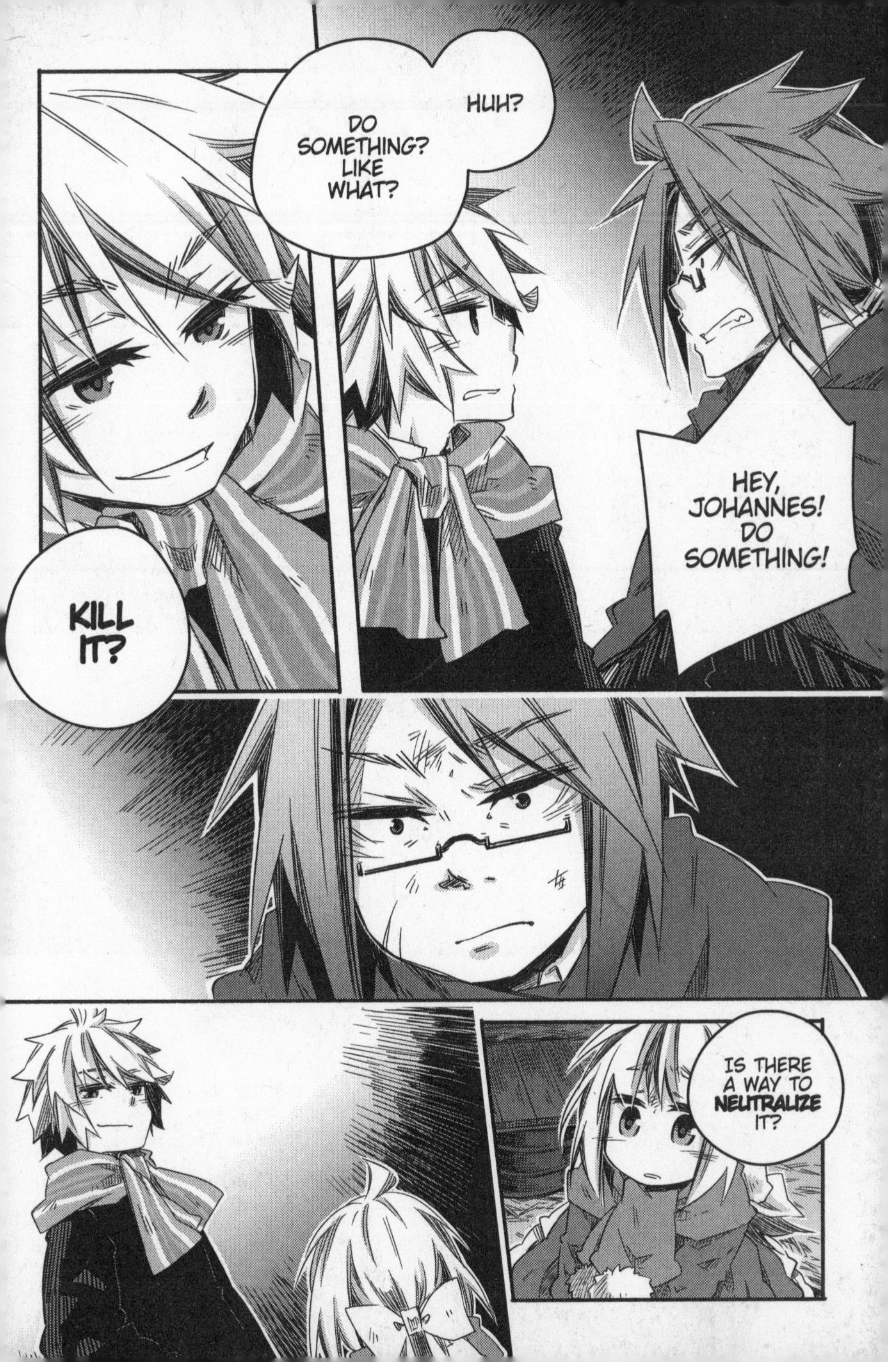
HEY, JOHANNES! DO SOMETHING!
HUH?
DO SOMETHING? LIKE WHAT?
KILL IT?
IS THERE A WAY TO NEUTRALIZE IT?

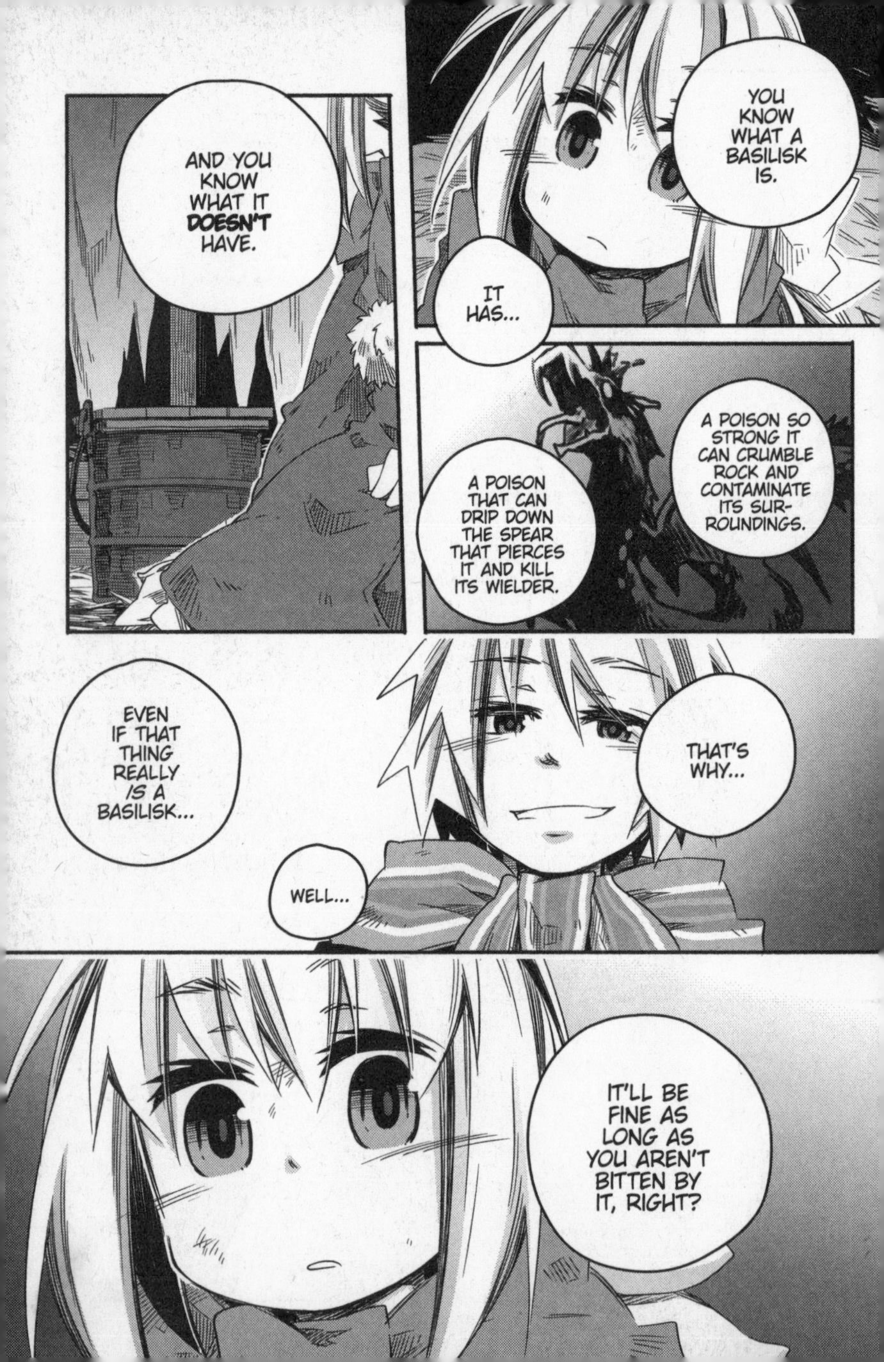
YOU KNOW WHAT A BASILISK IS.
IT HAS...
A POISON SO STRONG IT CAN CRUMBLE ROCK AND CONTAMINATE ITS SUR-ROUNDINGS.
A POISON THAT CAN DRIP DOWN THE SPEAR THAT PIERCES IT AND KILL ITS WIELDER.
AND YOU KNOW WHAT IT **DOESN'T** HAVE.
THAT'S WHY...
EVEN IF THAT THING REALLY *IS* A BASILISK...
WELL...
IT'LL BE FINE AS LONG AS YOU AREN'T BITTEN BY IT, RIGHT?

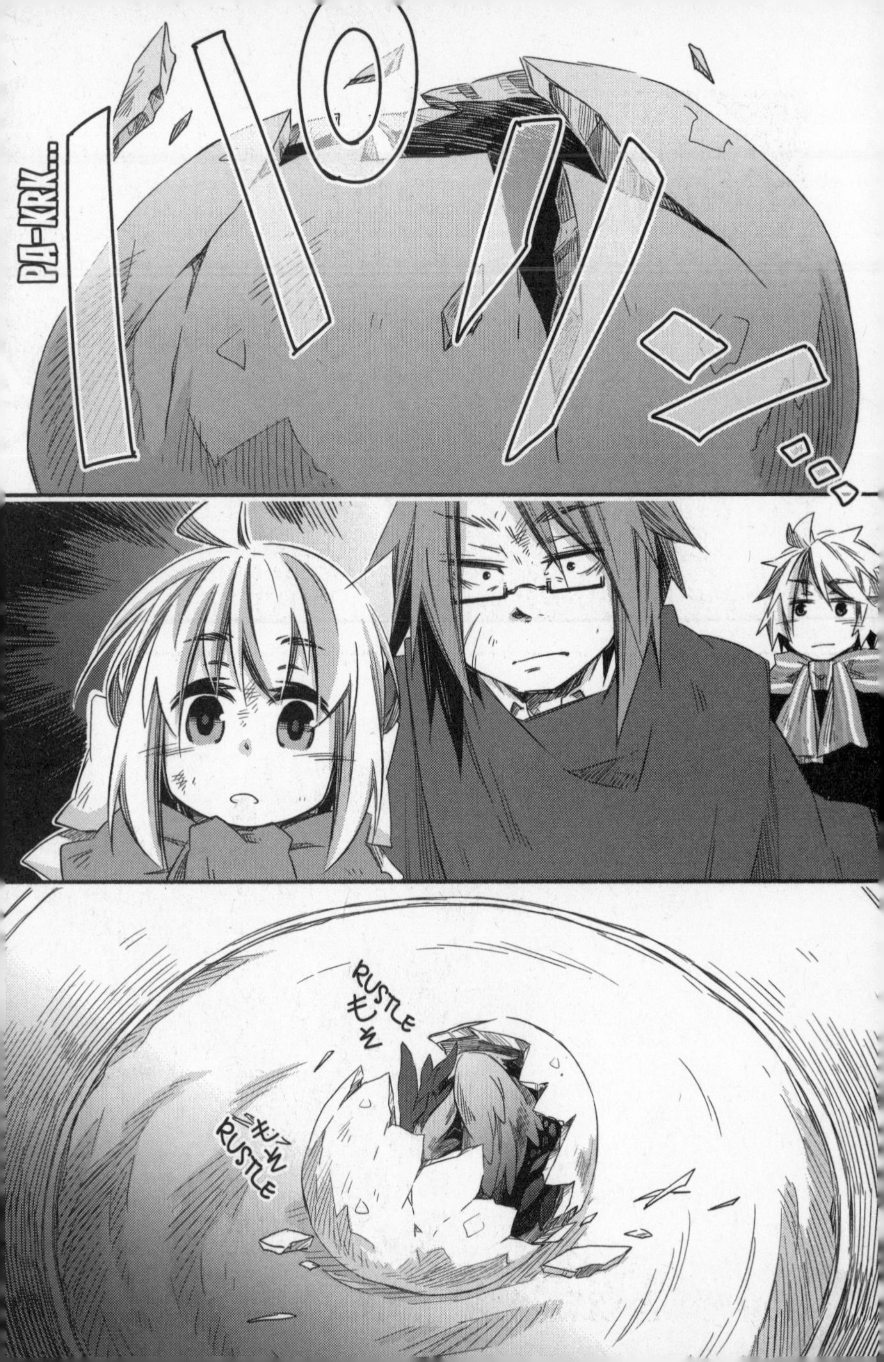
PA-KRK...
RUSTLE
RUSTLE

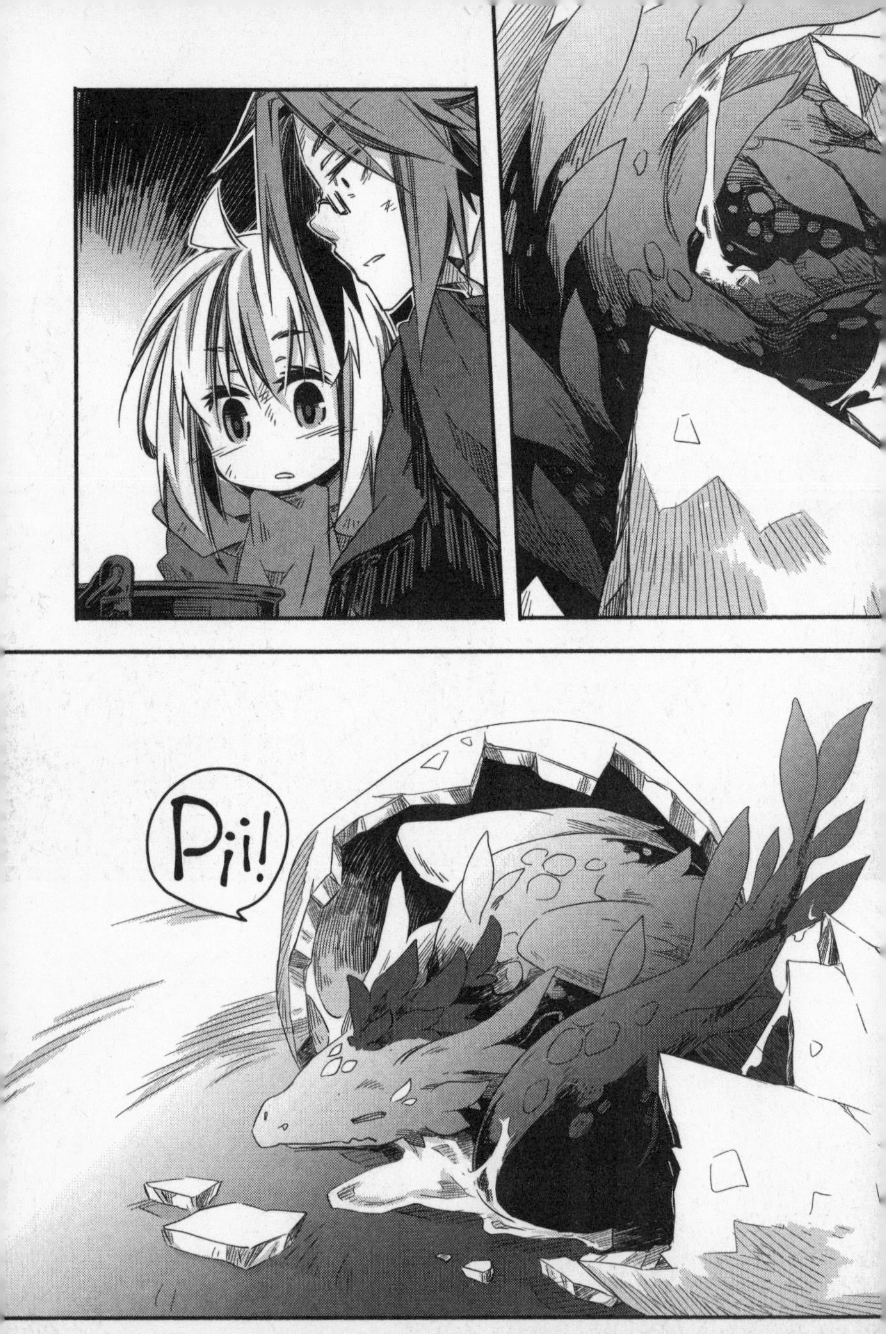
Pii!

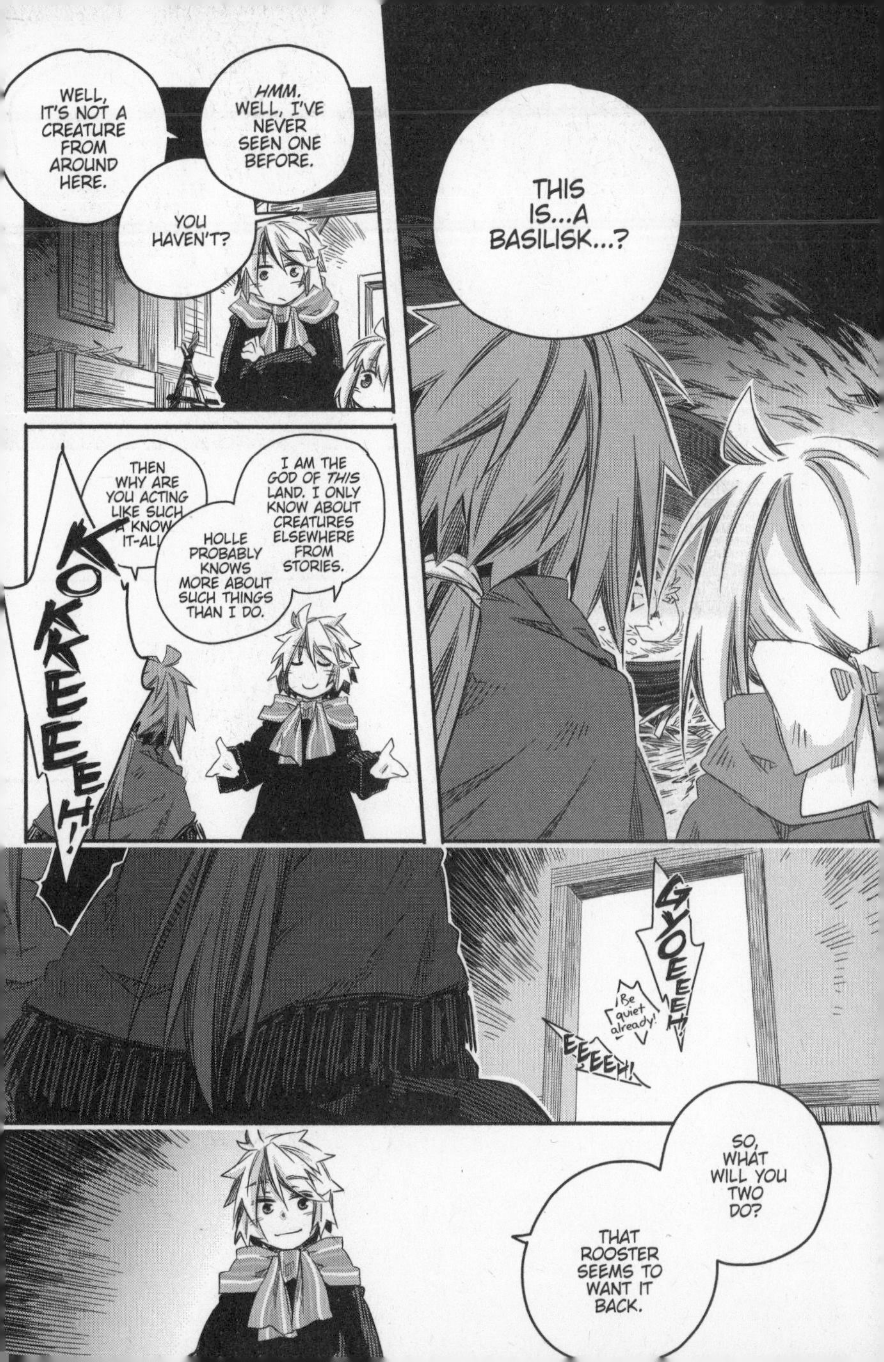
THIS IS...A BASILISK...?
HMM. WELL, I'VE NEVER SEEN ONE BEFORE.
YOU HAVEN'T?
WELL, IT'S NOT A CREATURE FROM AROUND HERE.
I AM THE GOD OF THIS LAND. I ONLY KNOW ABOUT CREATURES ELSEWHERE FROM STORIES.
HOLLE PROBABLY KNOWS MORE ABOUT SUCH THINGS THAN I DO.
THEN WHY ARE YOU ACTING LIKE SUCH A KNOW-IT-ALL?
KOKKEEEEH!
GYOEEEEH!
Be quiet already!
EEEEH!
SO, WHAT WILL YOU TWO DO?
THAT ROOSTER SEEMS TO WANT IT BACK.

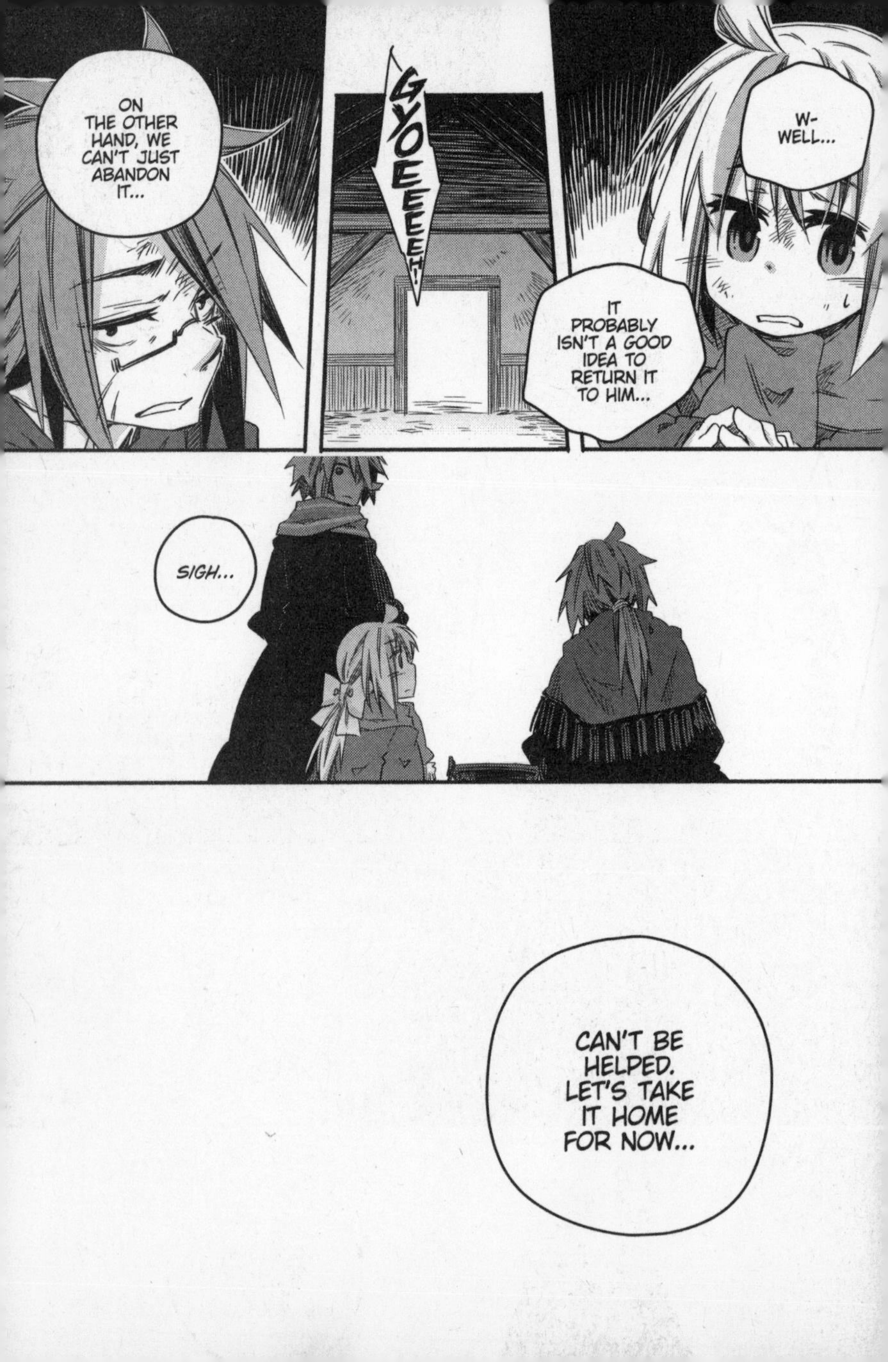
W-WELL...
IT PROBABLY ISN'T A GOOD IDEA TO RETURN IT TO HIM...
GYOEEEEEH!
ON THE OTHER HAND, WE CAN'T JUST ABANDON IT...
SIGH...
CAN'T BE HELPED. LET'S TAKE IT HOME FOR NOW...

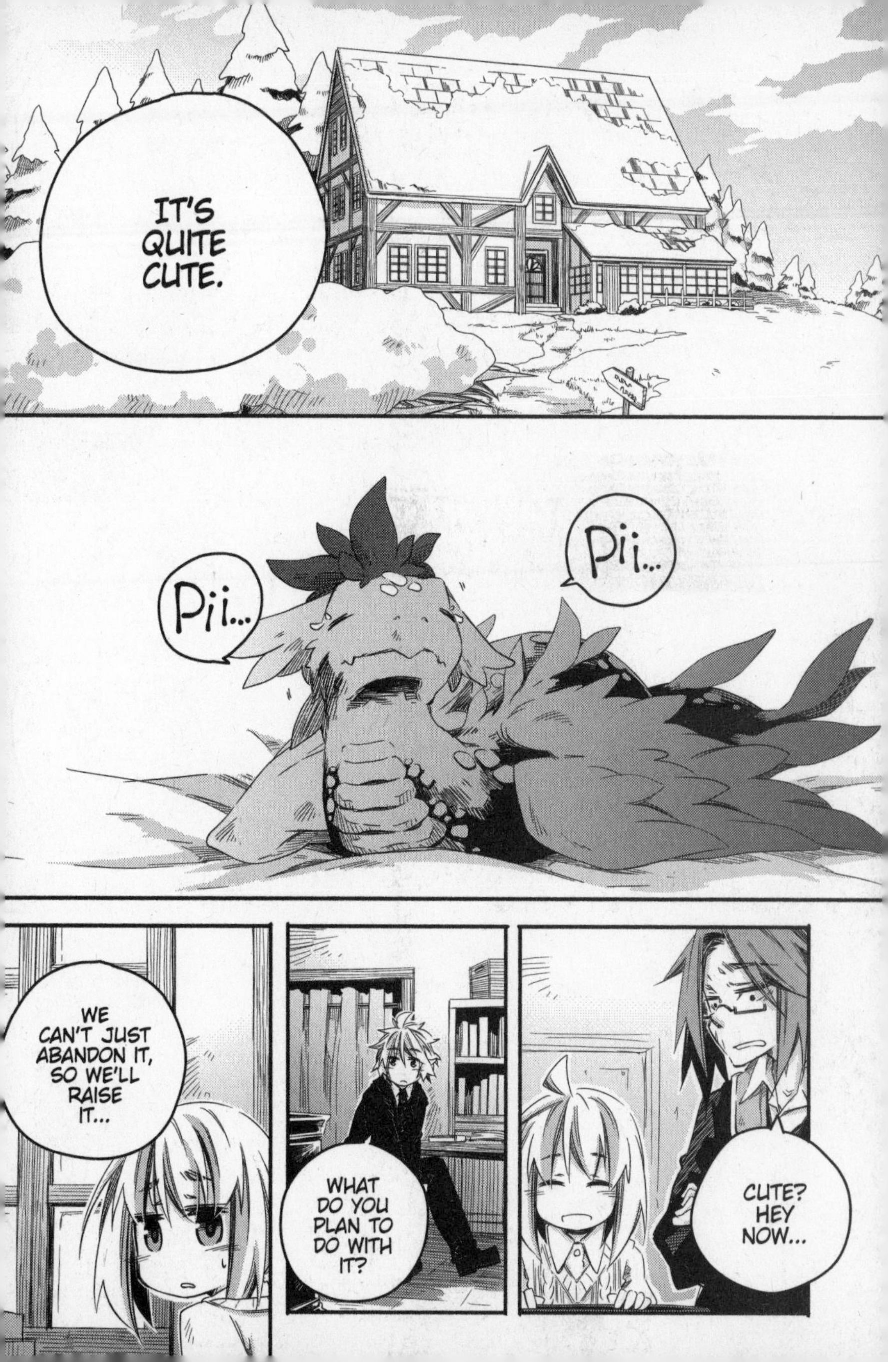
IT'S QUITE CUTE.
Pii...
Pii...
CUTE? HEY NOW...
WHAT DO YOU PLAN TO DO WITH IT?
WE CAN'T JUST ABANDON IT, SO WE'LL RAISE IT...

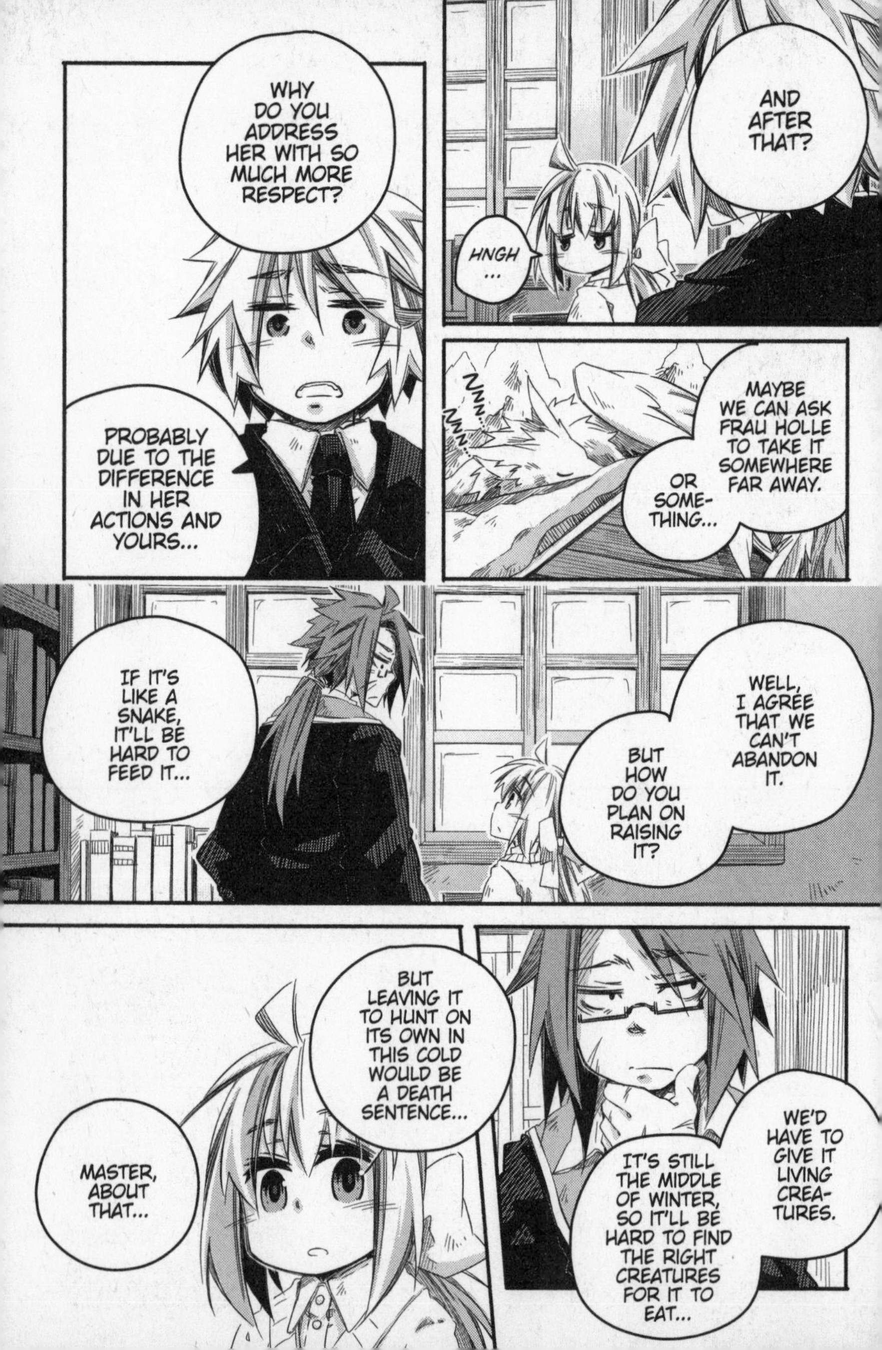
AND AFTER THAT?
HNGH...
MAYBE WE CAN ASK FRAU HOLLE TO TAKE IT SOMEWHERE FAR AWAY.
OR SOMETHING...
WHY DO YOU ADDRESS HER WITH SO MUCH MORE RESPECT?
PROBABLY DUE TO THE DIFFERENCE IN HER ACTIONS AND YOURS...
WELL, I AGREE THAT WE CAN'T ABANDON IT.
BUT HOW DO YOU PLAN ON RAISING IT?
IF IT'S LIKE A SNAKE, IT'LL BE HARD TO FEED IT...
WE'D HAVE TO GIVE IT LIVING CREATURES.
IT'S STILL THE MIDDLE OF WINTER, SO IT'LL BE HARD TO FIND THE RIGHT CREATURES FOR IT TO EAT...
BUT LEAVING IT TO HUNT ON ITS OWN IN THIS COLD WOULD BE A DEATH SENTENCE...
MASTER, ABOUT THAT...

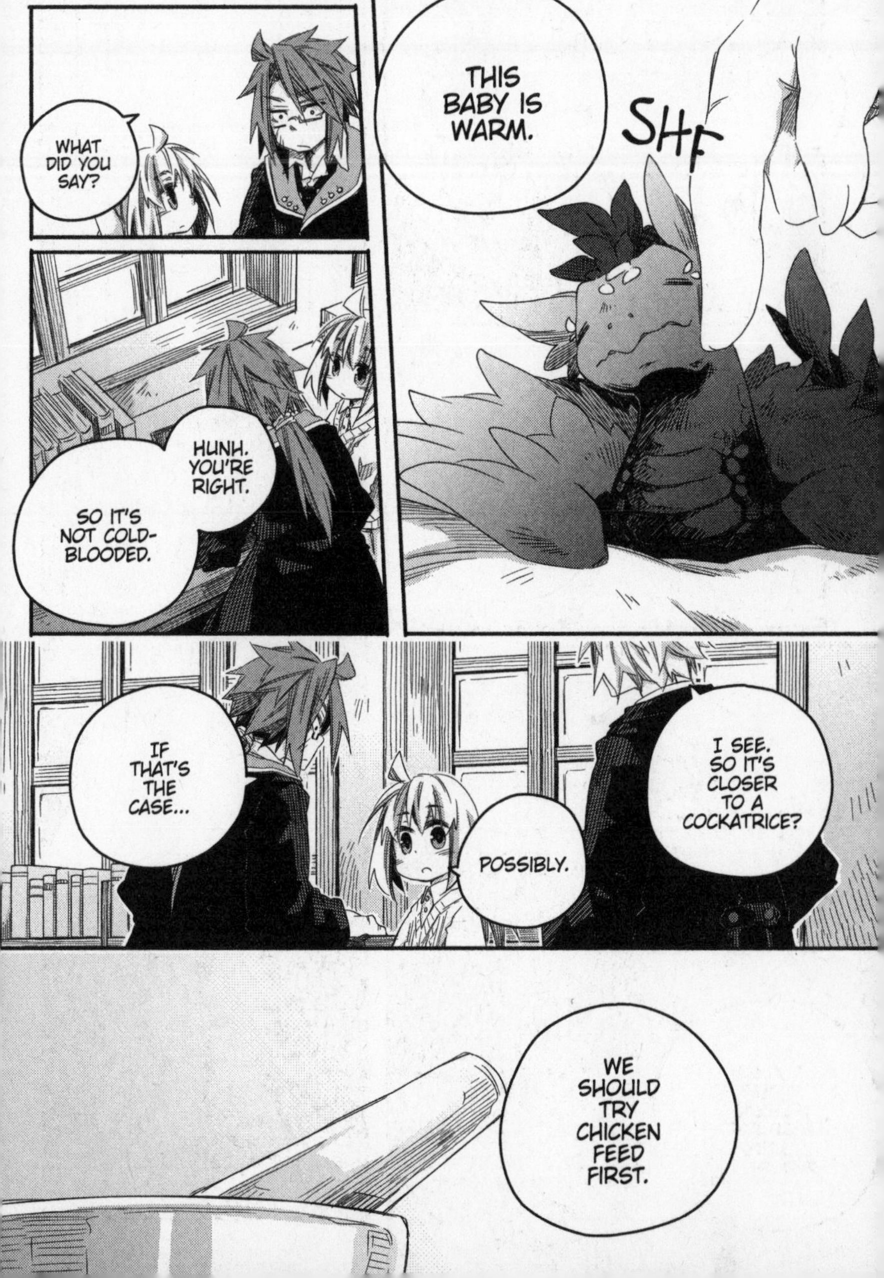
THIS BABY IS WARM.
SHF
WHAT DID YOU SAY?
HUNH. YOU'RE RIGHT.
SO IT'S NOT COLD-BLOODED.
I SEE. SO IT'S CLOSER TO A COCKATRICE?
POSSIBLY.
IF THAT'S THE CASE...
WE SHOULD TRY CHICKEN FEED FIRST.

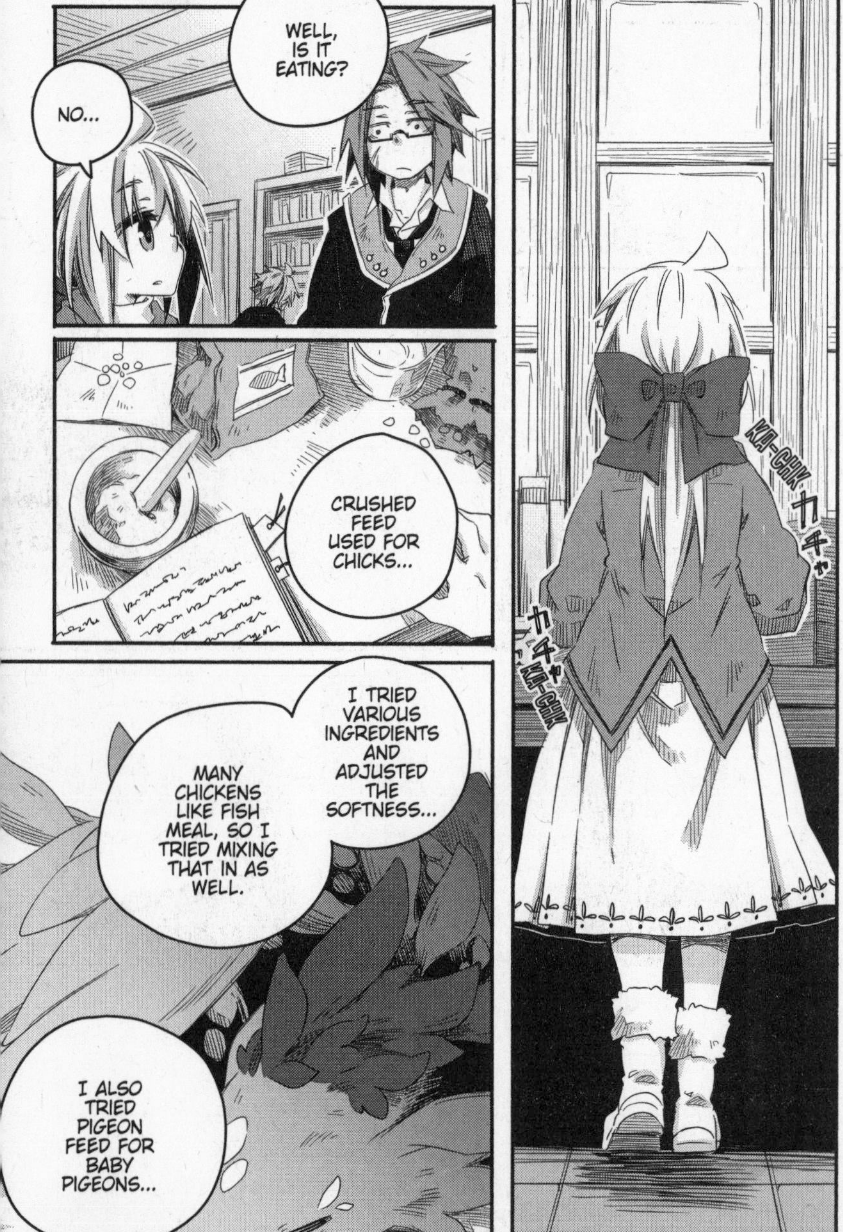
KA-CHIK
カチャ
カチャ
KA-CHIK
WELL, IS IT EATING?
NO...
CRUSHED FEED USED FOR CHICKS...
I TRIED VARIOUS INGREDIENTS AND ADJUSTED THE SOFTNESS...
MANY CHICKENS LIKE FISH MEAL, SO I TRIED MIXING THAT IN AS WELL.
I ALSO TRIED PIGEON FEED FOR BABY PIGEONS...

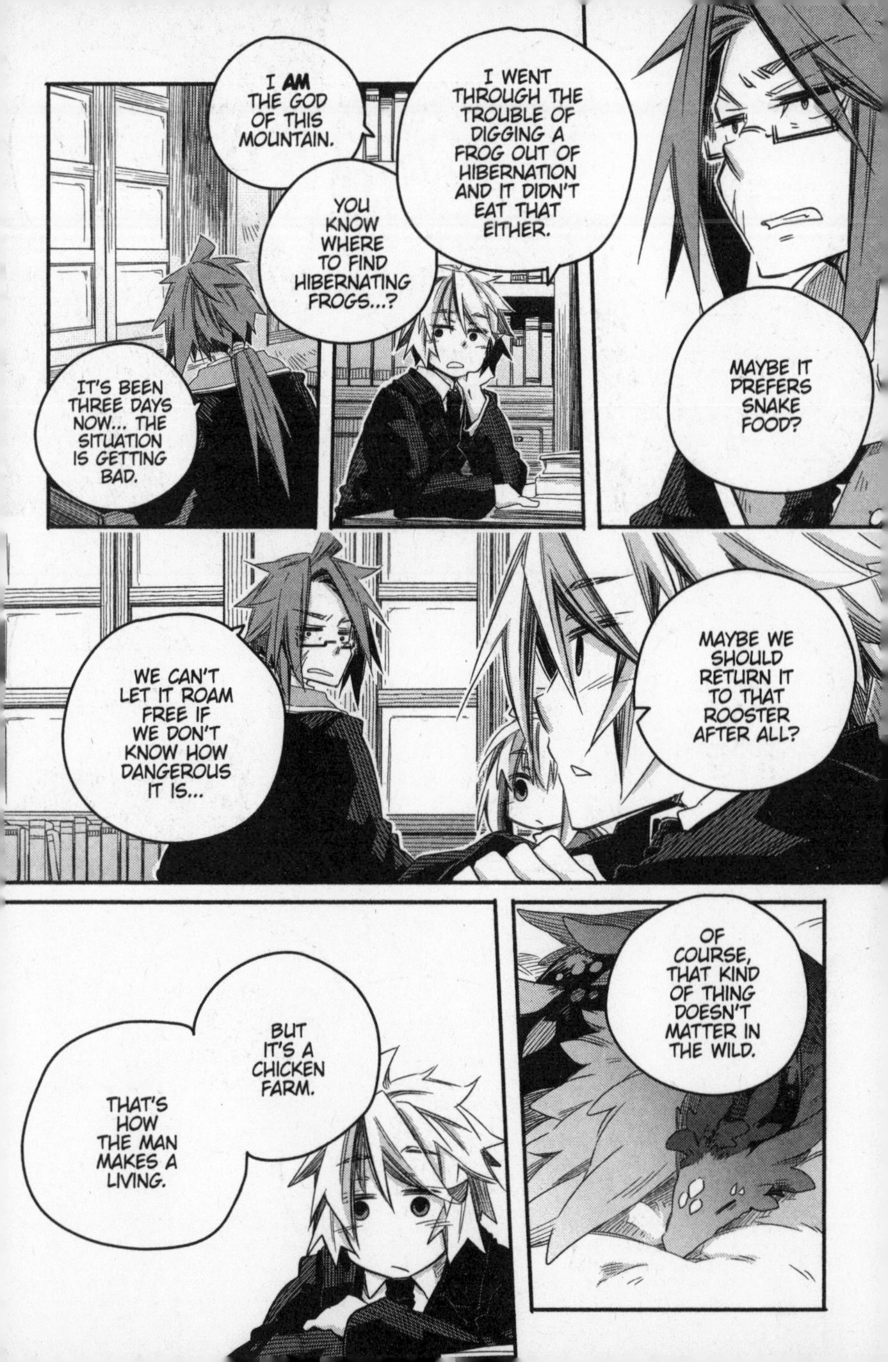
MAYBE IT PREFERS SNAKE FOOD?
I WENT THROUGH THE TROUBLE OF DIGGING A FROG OUT OF HIBERNATION AND IT DIDN'T EAT THAT EITHER.
YOU KNOW WHERE TO FIND HIBERNATING FROGS...?
I **AM** THE GOD OF THIS MOUNTAIN.
IT'S BEEN THREE DAYS NOW... THE SITUATION IS GETTING BAD.
MAYBE WE SHOULD RETURN IT TO THAT ROOSTER AFTER ALL?
WE CAN'T LET IT ROAM FREE IF WE DON'T KNOW HOW DANGEROUS IT IS...
OF COURSE, THAT KIND OF THING DOESN'T MATTER IN THE WILD.
BUT IT'S A CHICKEN FARM.
THAT'S HOW THE MAN MAKES A LIVING.

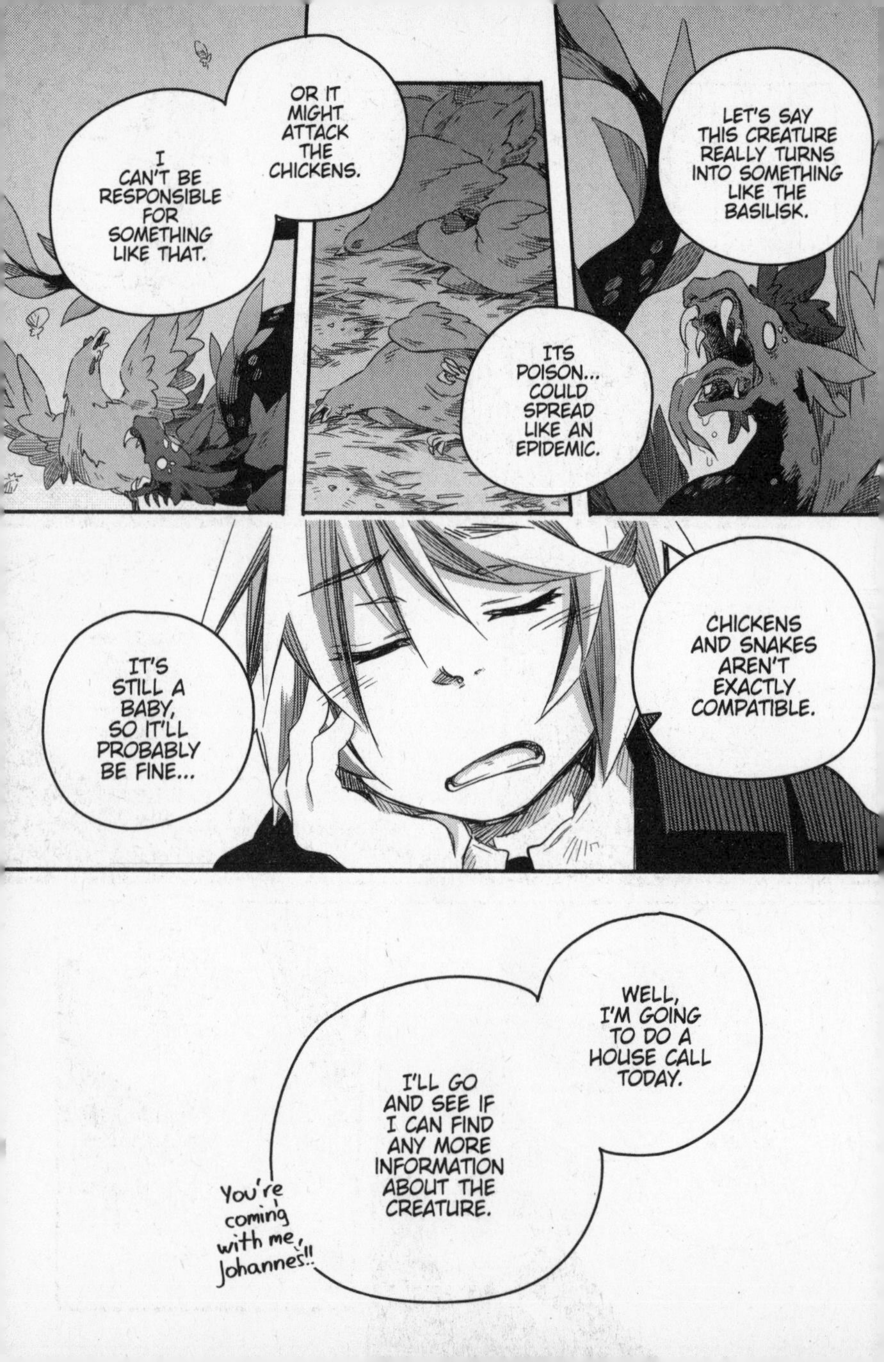
LET'S SAY THIS CREATURE REALLY TURNS INTO SOMETHING LIKE THE BASILISK.
ITS POISON... COULD SPREAD LIKE AN EPIDEMIC.
OR IT MIGHT ATTACK THE CHICKENS.
I CAN'T BE RESPONSIBLE FOR SOMETHING LIKE THAT.
CHICKENS AND SNAKES AREN'T EXACTLY COMPATIBLE.
IT'S STILL A BABY, SO IT'LL PROBABLY BE FINE...
WELL, I'M GOING TO DO A HOUSE CALL TODAY.
I'LL GO AND SEE IF I CAN FIND ANY MORE INFORMATION ABOUT THE CREATURE.
You're coming with me, Johannes!!

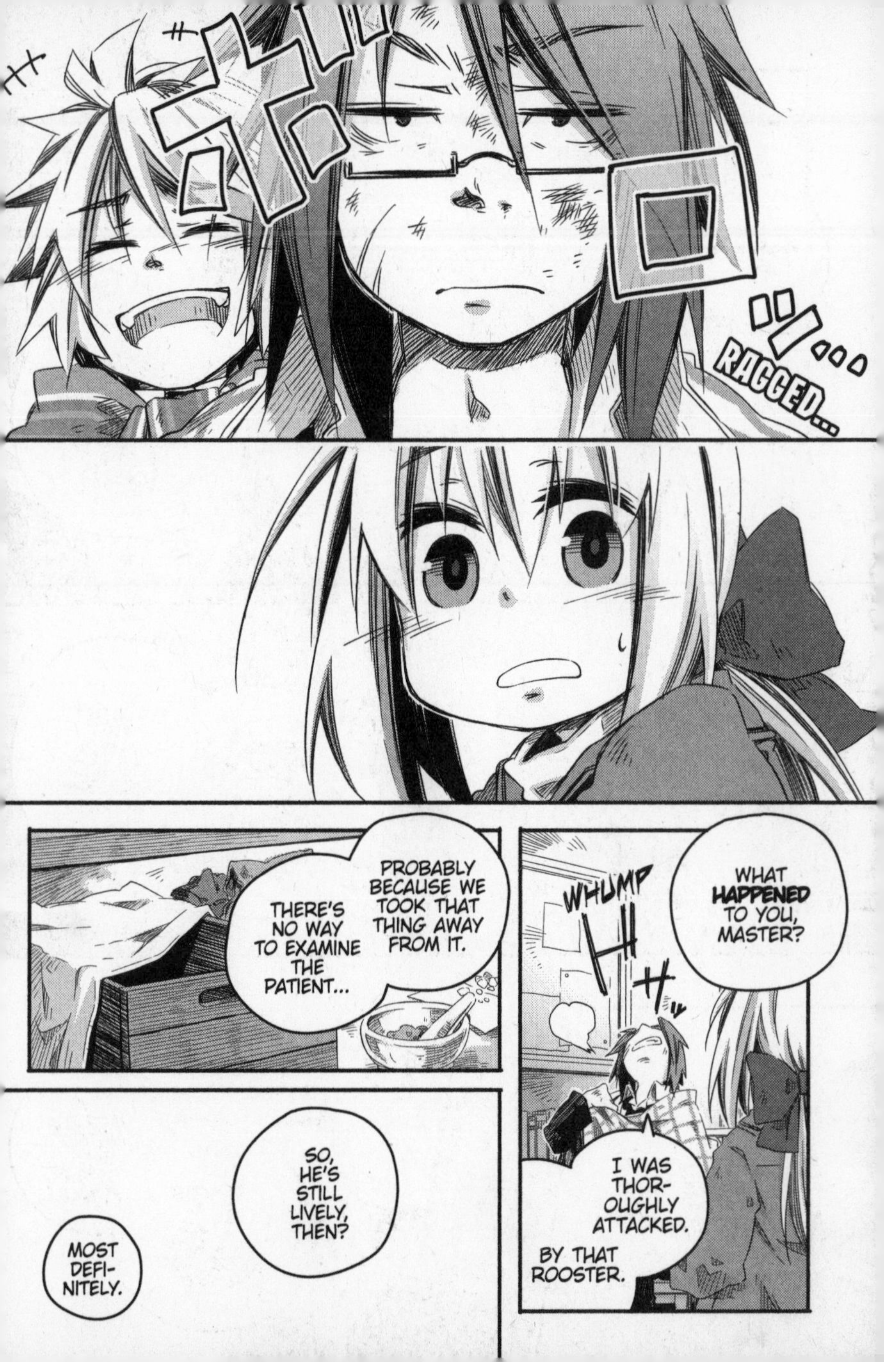
RAGGED...
WHUMP
WHAT HAPPENED TO YOU, MASTER?
I WAS THOROUGHLY ATTACKED.
BY THAT ROOSTER.
PROBABLY BECAUSE WE TOOK THAT THING AWAY FROM IT.
THERE'S NO WAY TO EXAMINE THE PATIENT...
SO, HE'S STILL LIVELY, THEN?
MOST DEFINITELY.

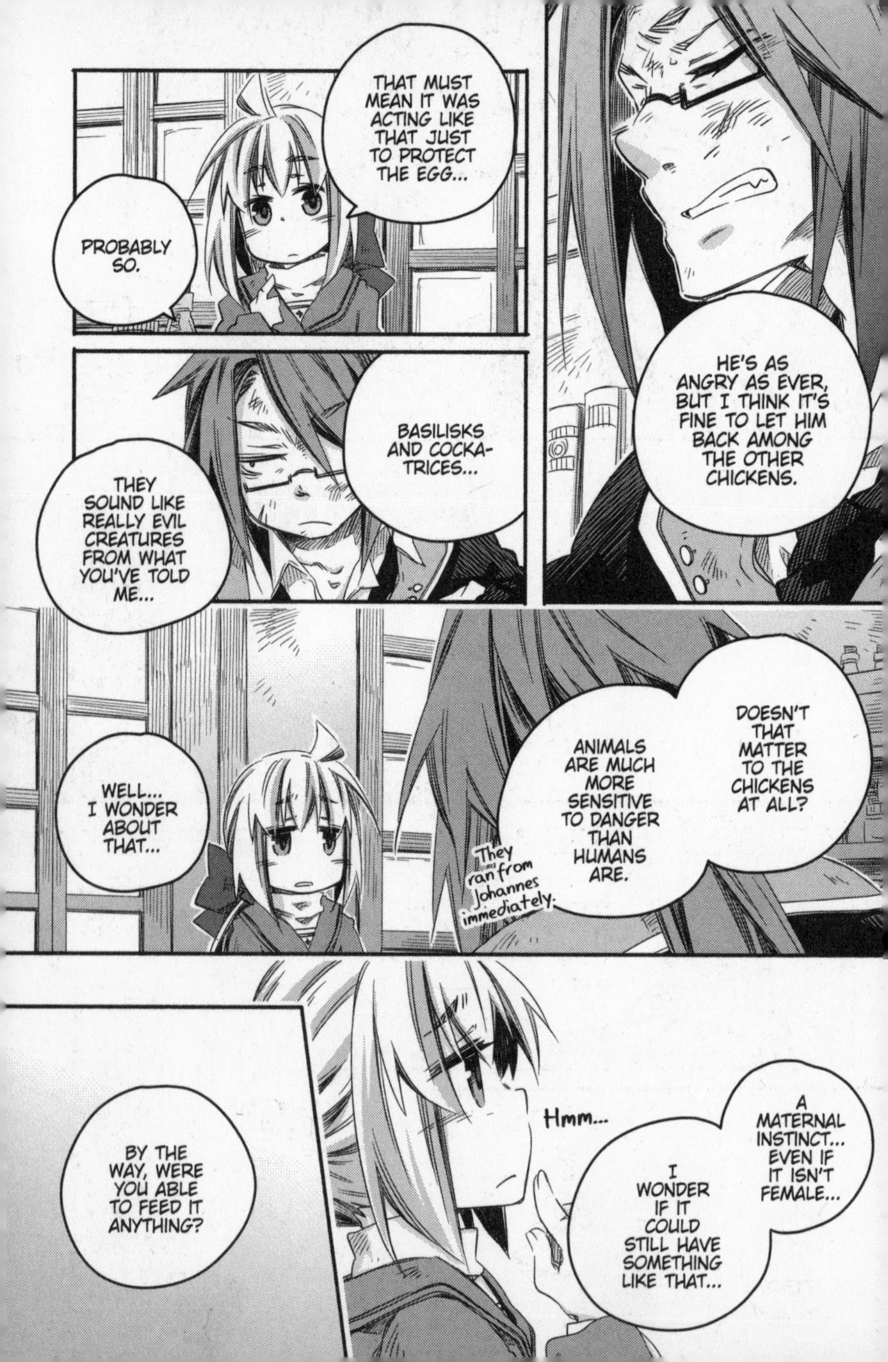
HE'S AS ANGRY AS EVER, BUT I THINK IT'S FINE TO LET HIM BACK AMONG THE OTHER CHICKENS.
THAT MUST MEAN IT WAS ACTING LIKE THAT JUST TO PROTECT THE EGG...
PROBABLY SO.
BASILISKS AND COCKA-TRICES...
THEY SOUND LIKE REALLY EVIL CREATURES FROM WHAT YOU'VE TOLD ME...
DOESN'T THAT MATTER TO THE CHICKENS AT ALL?
ANIMALS ARE MUCH MORE SENSITIVE TO DANGER THAN HUMANS ARE.
They ran from Johannes immediately.
WELL... I WONDER ABOUT THAT...
A MATERNAL INSTINCT... EVEN IF IT ISN'T FEMALE...
I WONDER IF IT COULD STILL HAVE SOMETHING LIKE THAT...
Hmm...
BY THE WAY, WERE YOU ABLE TO FEED IT ANYTHING?

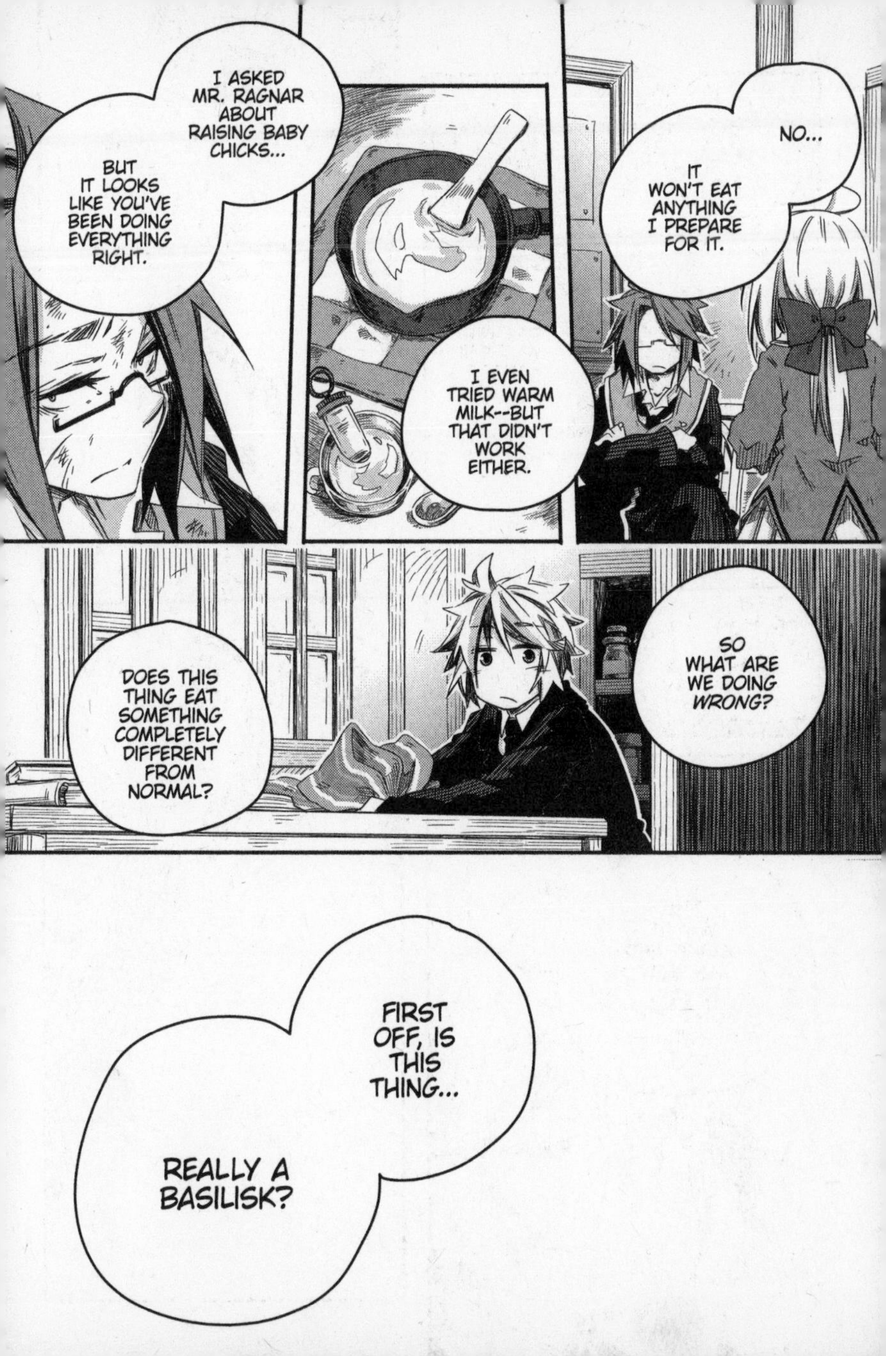
NO...
IT WON'T EAT ANYTHING I PREPARE FOR IT.
I EVEN TRIED WARM MILK--BUT THAT DIDN'T WORK EITHER.
I ASKED MR. RAGNAR ABOUT RAISING BABY CHICKS...
BUT IT LOOKS LIKE YOU'VE BEEN DOING EVERYTHING RIGHT.
SO WHAT ARE WE DOING *WRONG*?
DOES THIS THING EAT SOMETHING COMPLETELY DIFFERENT FROM NORMAL?
FIRST OFF, IS THIS THING...
REALLY A BASILISK?

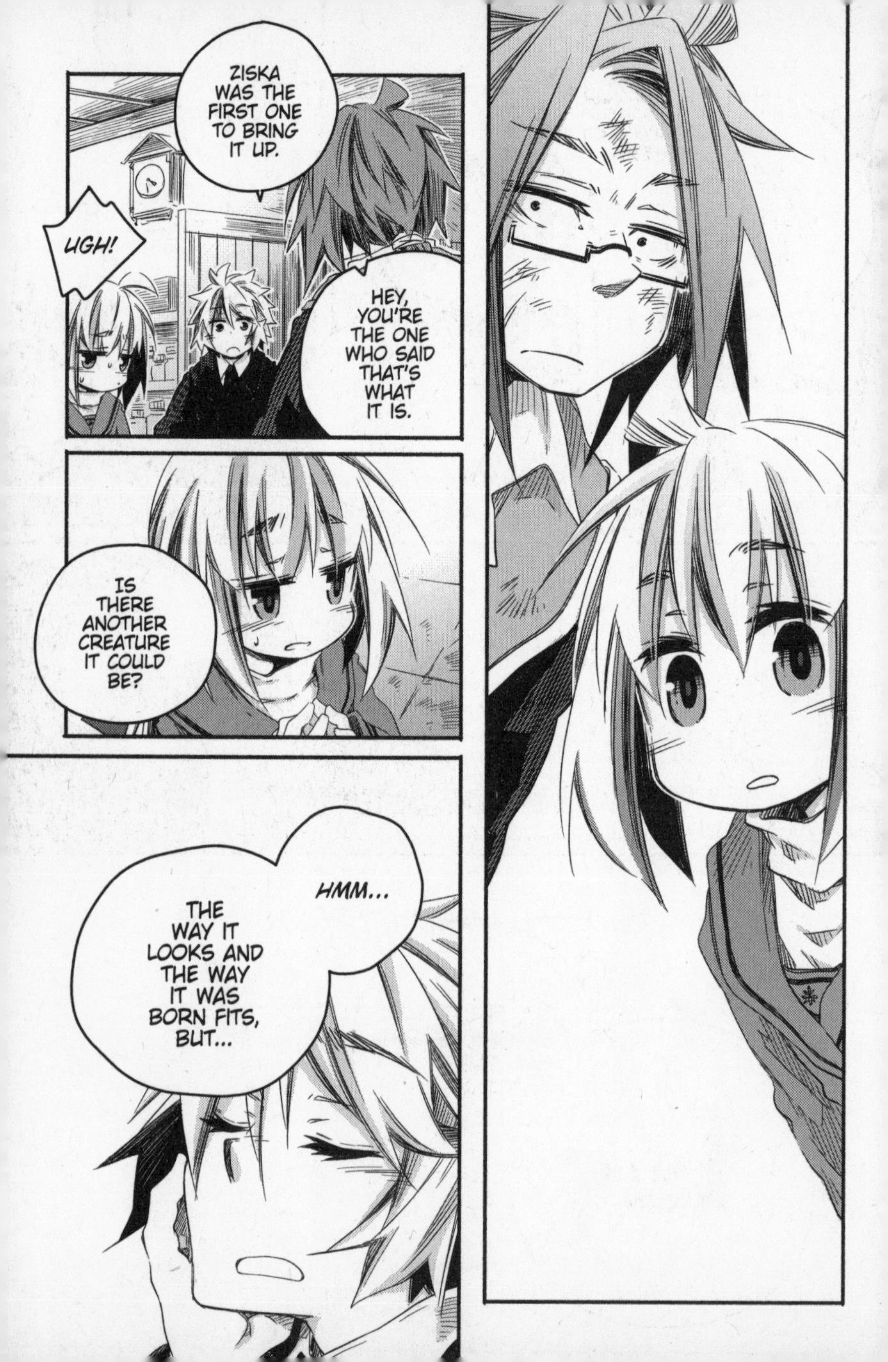
ZISKA WAS THE FIRST ONE TO BRING IT UP.
HEY, YOU'RE THE ONE WHO SAID THAT'S WHAT IT IS.
UGH!
IS THERE ANOTHER CREATURE IT COULD BE?
HMM...
THE WAY IT LOOKS AND THE WAY IT WAS BORN FITS, BUT...

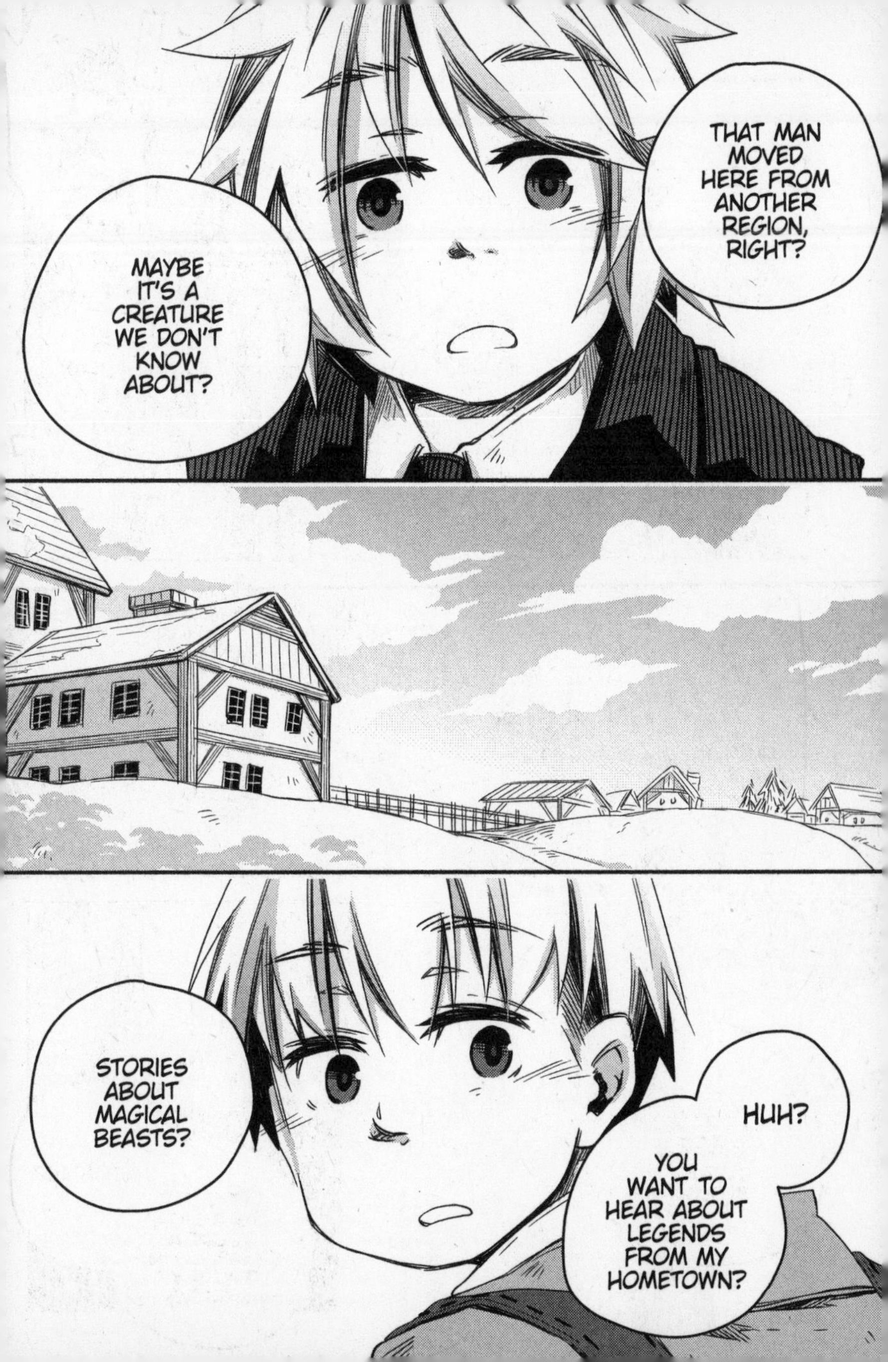
THAT MAN MOVED HERE FROM ANOTHER REGION, RIGHT?
MAYBE IT'S A CREATURE WE DON'T KNOW ABOUT?
HUH?
YOU WANT TO HEAR ABOUT LEGENDS FROM MY HOMETOWN?
STORIES ABOUT MAGICAL BEASTS?

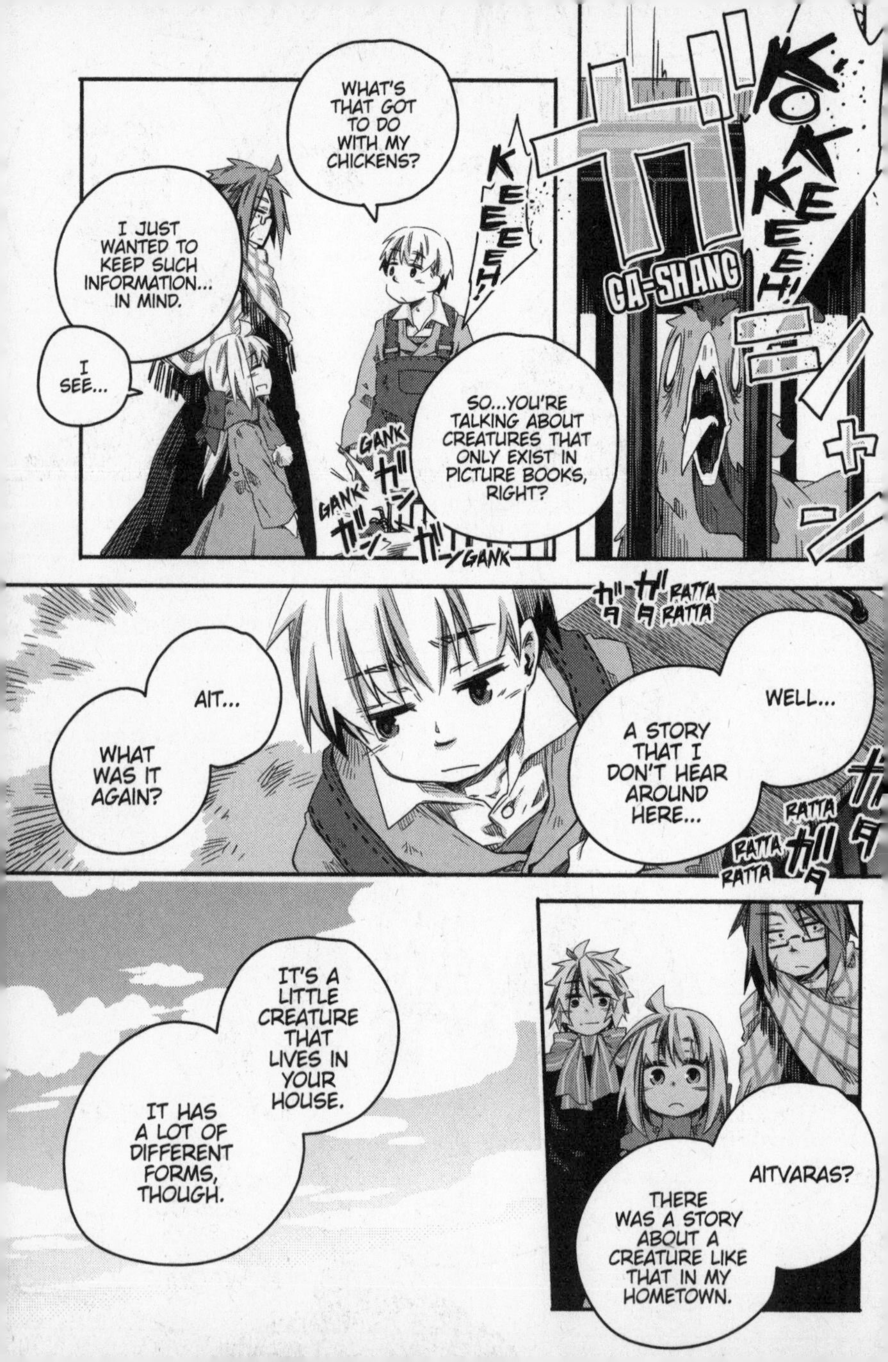
KOKKEEEH!
GA-SHANG
KEEEEH!
WHAT'S THAT GOT TO DO WITH MY CHICKENS?
I JUST WANTED TO KEEP SUCH INFORMATION... IN MIND.
SO...YOU'RE TALKING ABOUT CREATURES THAT ONLY EXIST IN PICTURE BOOKS, RIGHT?
I SEE...
GANK
GANK
GANK
RATTA RATTA
WELL...
A STORY THAT I DON'T HEAR AROUND HERE...
AIT...
WHAT WAS IT AGAIN?
RATTA RATTA RATTA
AITVARAS?
THERE WAS A STORY ABOUT A CREATURE LIKE THAT IN MY HOMETOWN.
IT'S A LITTLE CREATURE THAT LIVES IN YOUR HOUSE.
IT HAS A LOT OF DIFFERENT FORMS, THOUGH.

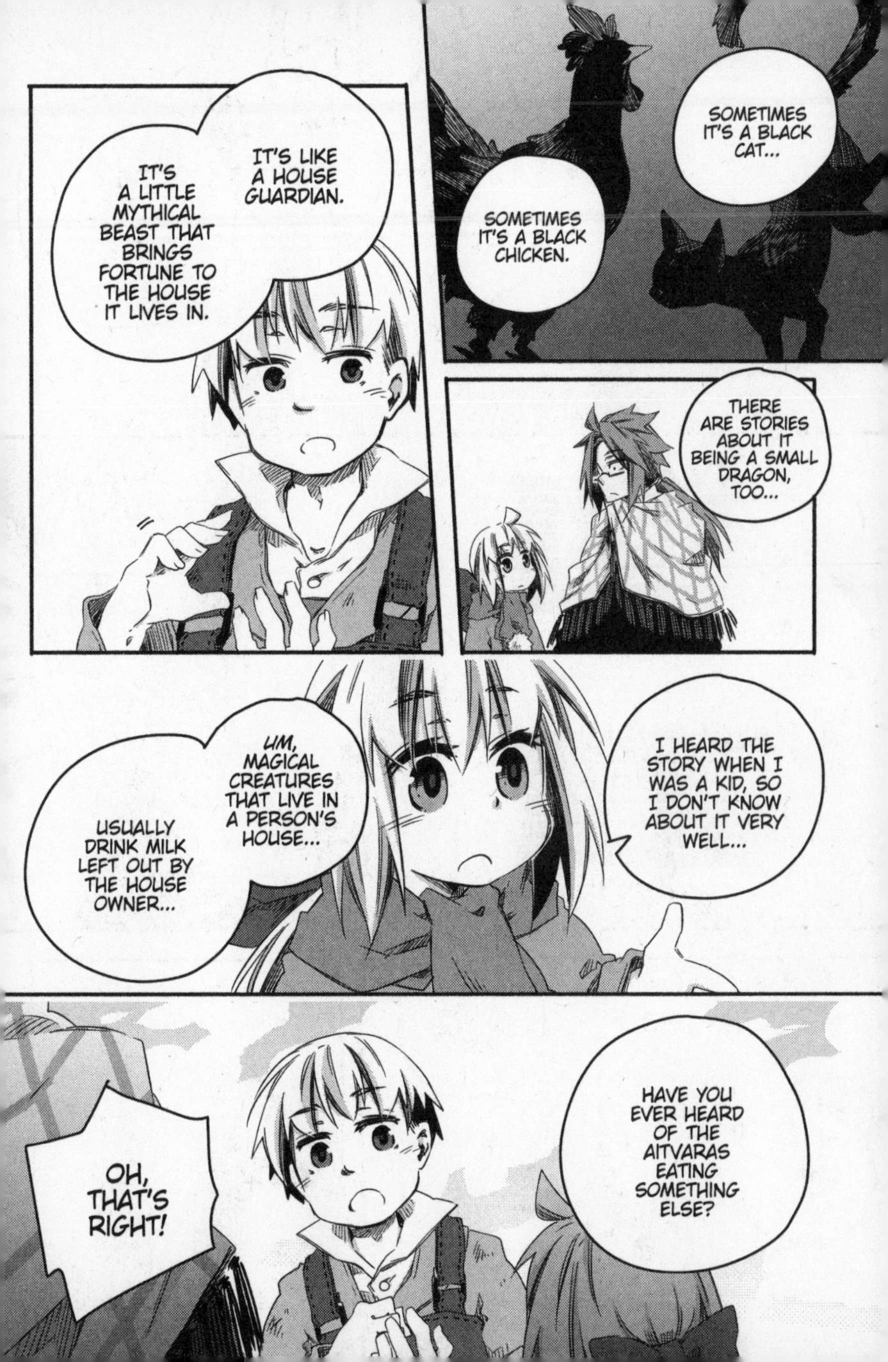
SOMETIMES IT'S A BLACK CAT...
SOMETIMES IT'S A BLACK CHICKEN.
THERE ARE STORIES ABOUT IT BEING A SMALL DRAGON, TOO...
IT'S LIKE A HOUSE GUARDIAN.
IT'S A LITTLE MYTHICAL BEAST THAT BRINGS FORTUNE TO THE HOUSE IT LIVES IN.
I HEARD THE STORY WHEN I WAS A KID, SO I DON'T KNOW ABOUT IT VERY WELL...
UM, MAGICAL CREATURES THAT LIVE IN A PERSON'S HOUSE...
USUALLY DRINK MILK LEFT OUT BY THE HOUSE OWNER...
HAVE YOU EVER HEARD OF THE AITVARAS EATING SOMETHING ELSE?
OH, THAT'S RIGHT!

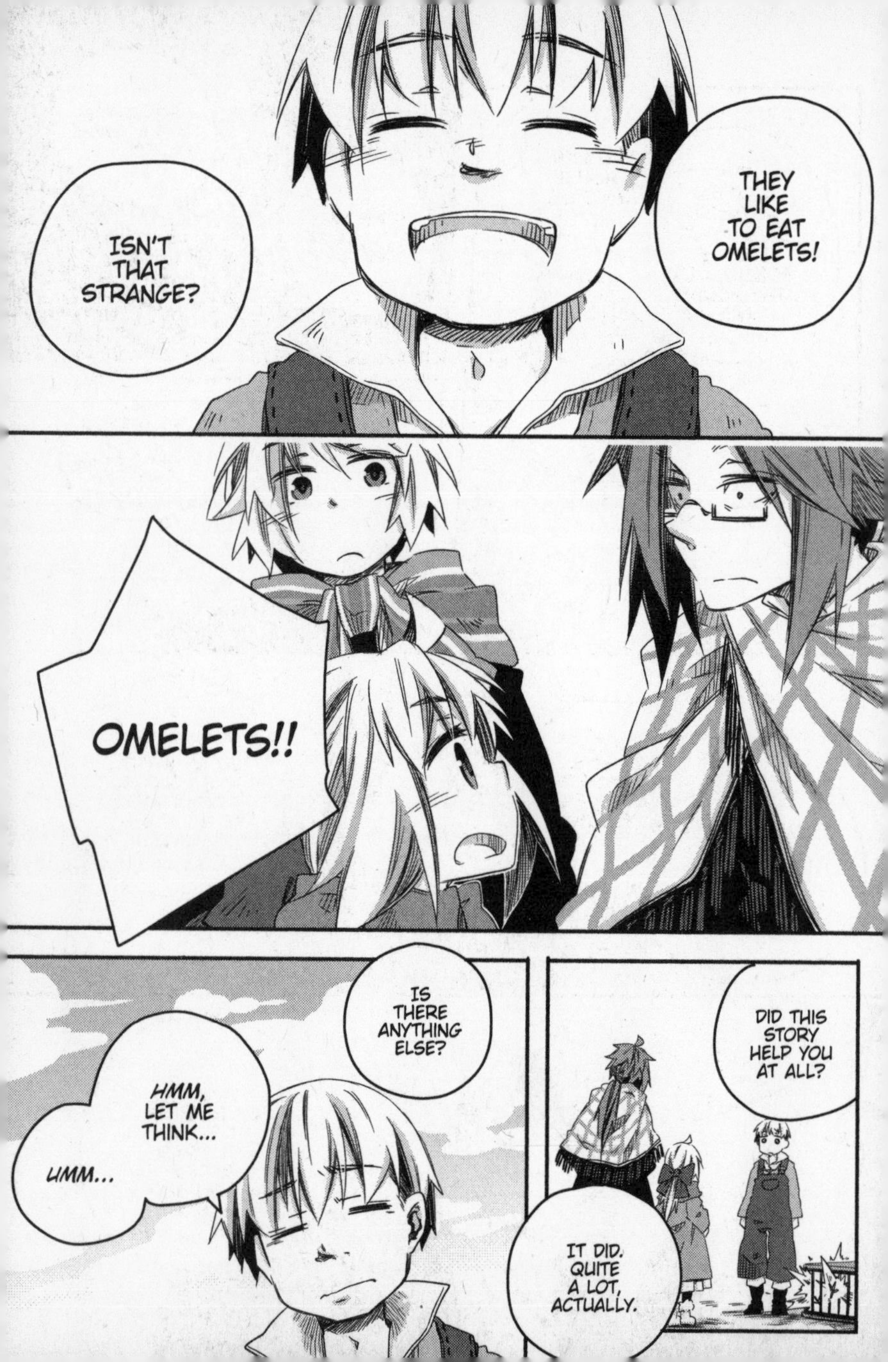
THEY LIKE TO EAT OMELETS!
ISN'T THAT STRANGE?
OMELETS!!
DID THIS STORY HELP YOU AT ALL?
IT DID. QUITE A LOT, ACTUALLY.
IS THERE ANYTHING ELSE?
HMM, LET ME THINK... UMM...

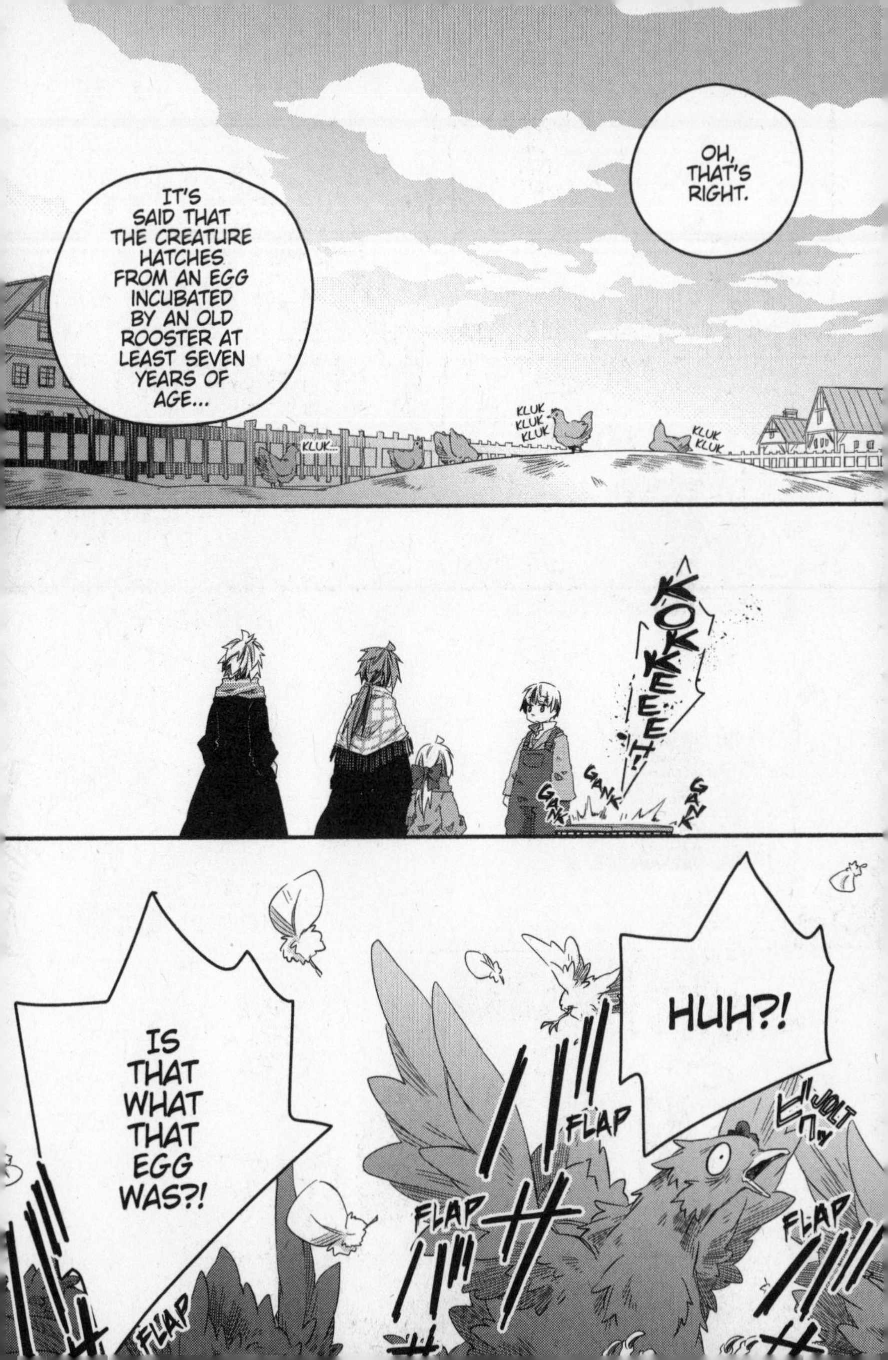
OH, THAT'S RIGHT.
IT'S SAID THAT THE CREATURE HATCHES FROM AN EGG INCUBATED BY AN OLD ROOSTER AT LEAST SEVEN YEARS OF AGE...
KLUK KLUK
KLUK KLUK KLUK
KLUK...
KOKKEEEH!
GANK
GANK
GANK
HUH?!
JOLT
FLAP
FLAP
FLAP
IS THAT WHAT THAT EGG WAS?!
FLAP

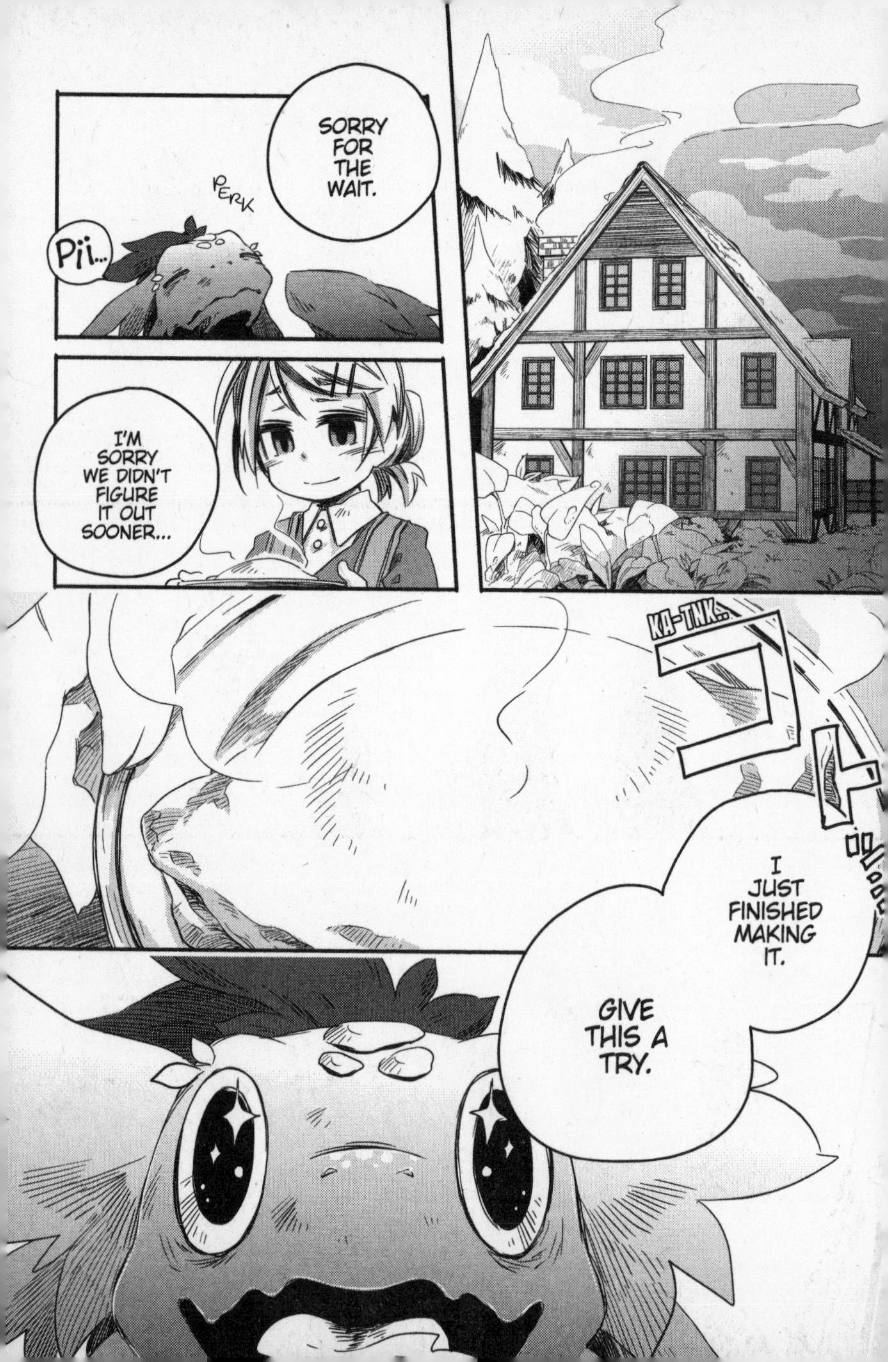
SORRY FOR THE WAIT.
PERK
Pii...
I'M SORRY WE DIDN'T FIGURE IT OUT SOONER...
KA-TNK..
I JUST FINISHED MAKING IT.
GIVE THIS A TRY.

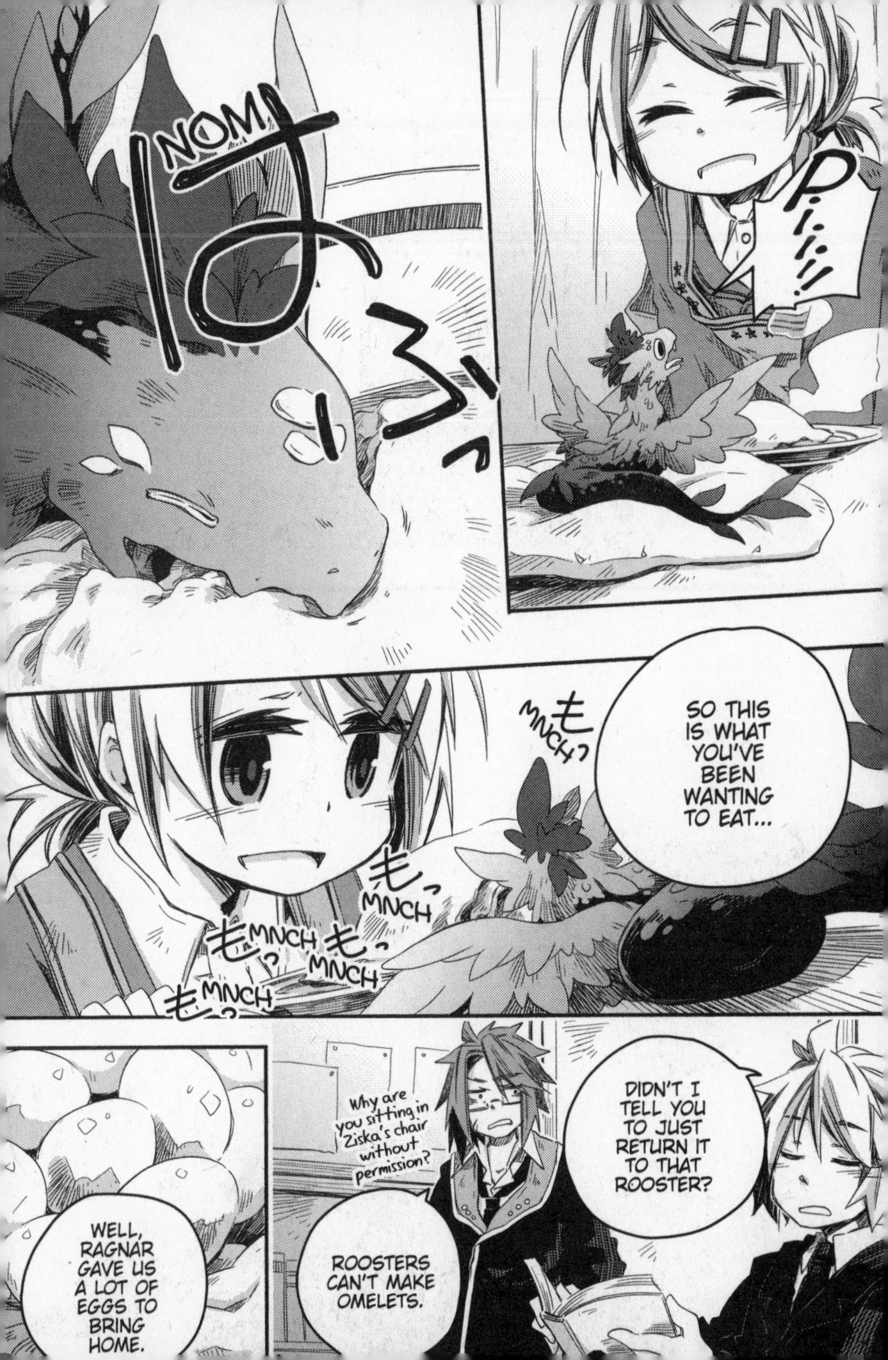
P!!!!
NOM
はふっ
SO THIS IS WHAT YOU'VE BEEN WANTING TO EAT...
も MNCH
もっ MNCH
もっ MNCH
も MNCH
も MNCH
DIDN'T I TELL YOU TO JUST RETURN IT TO THAT ROOSTER?
Why are you sitting in Ziska's chair without permission?
ROOSTERS CAN'T MAKE OMELETS.
WELL, RAGNAR GAVE US A LOT OF EGGS TO BRING HOME.

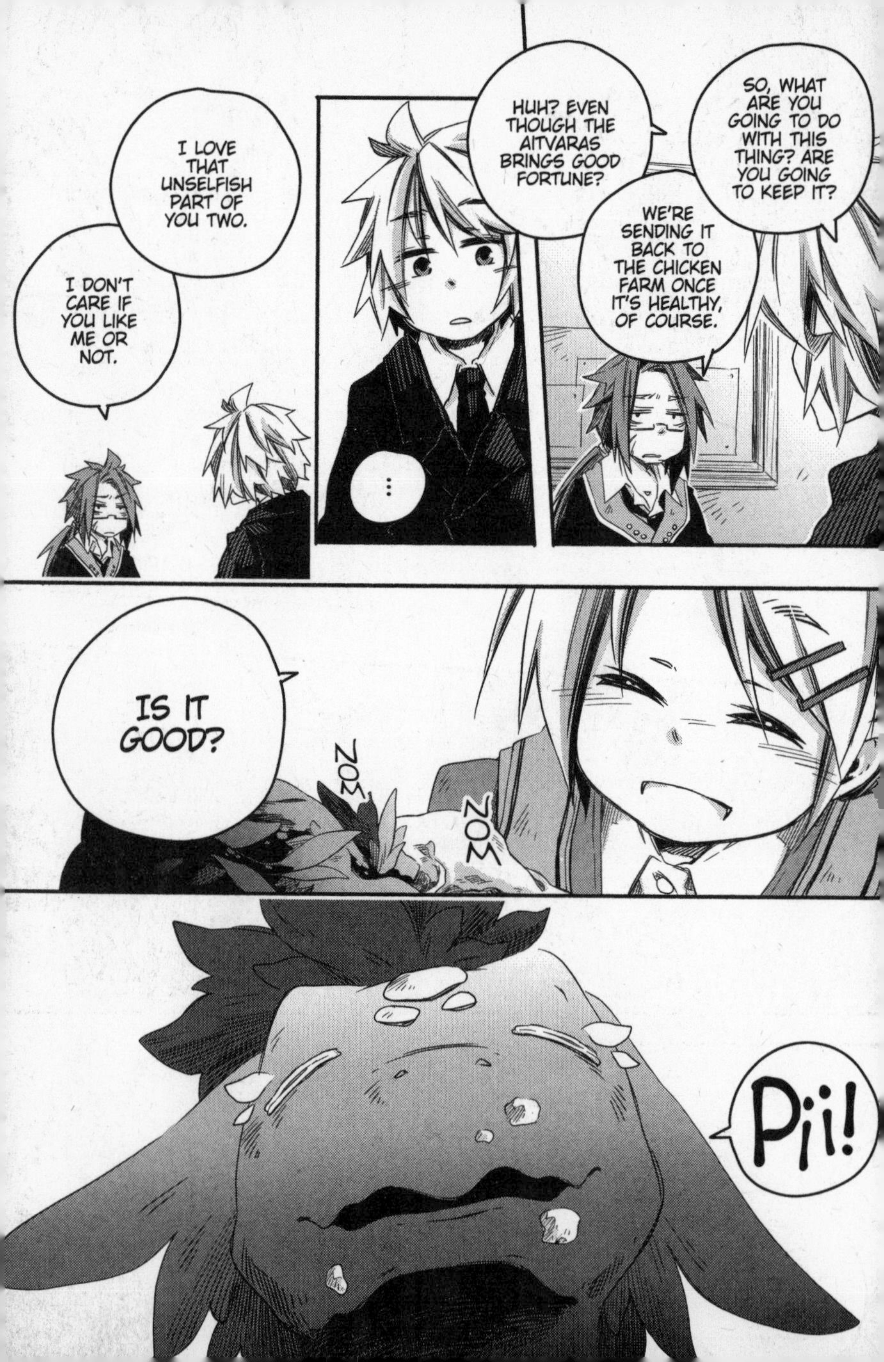
SO, WHAT ARE YOU GOING TO DO WITH THIS THING? ARE YOU GOING TO KEEP IT?
WE'RE SENDING IT BACK TO THE CHICKEN FARM ONCE IT'S HEALTHY, OF COURSE.
HUH? EVEN THOUGH THE AITVARAS BRINGS GOOD FORTUNE?
...
I LOVE THAT UNSELFISH PART OF YOU TWO.
I DON'T CARE IF YOU LIKE ME OR NOT.
IS IT GOOD?
NOM
NOM
Pii!

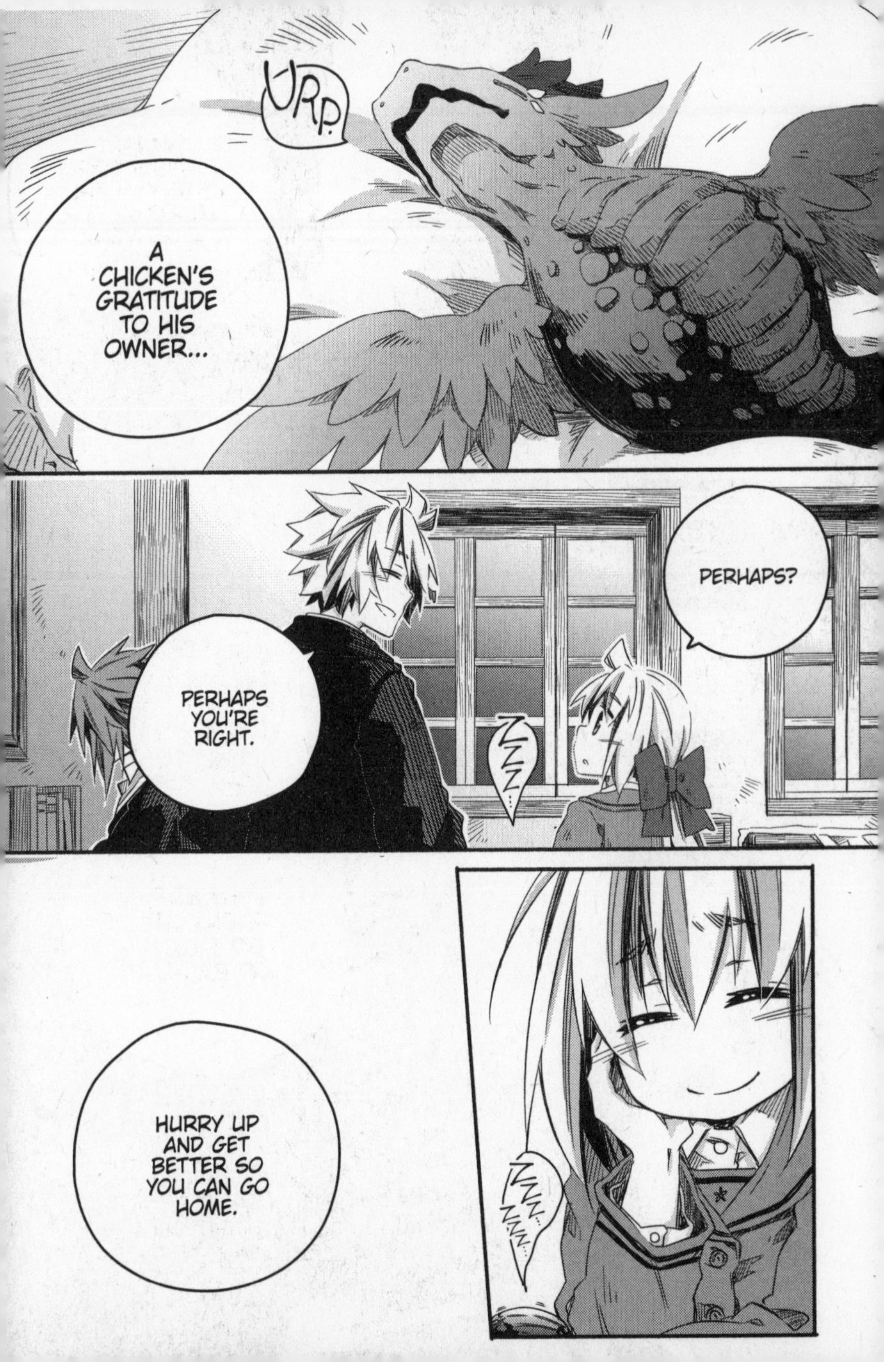
URP.
A CHICKEN'S GRATITUDE TO HIS OWNER...
PERHAPS?
ZZZ...
PERHAPS YOU'RE RIGHT.
ZZZ... ZZZ...
HURRY UP AND GET BETTER SO YOU CAN GO HOME.

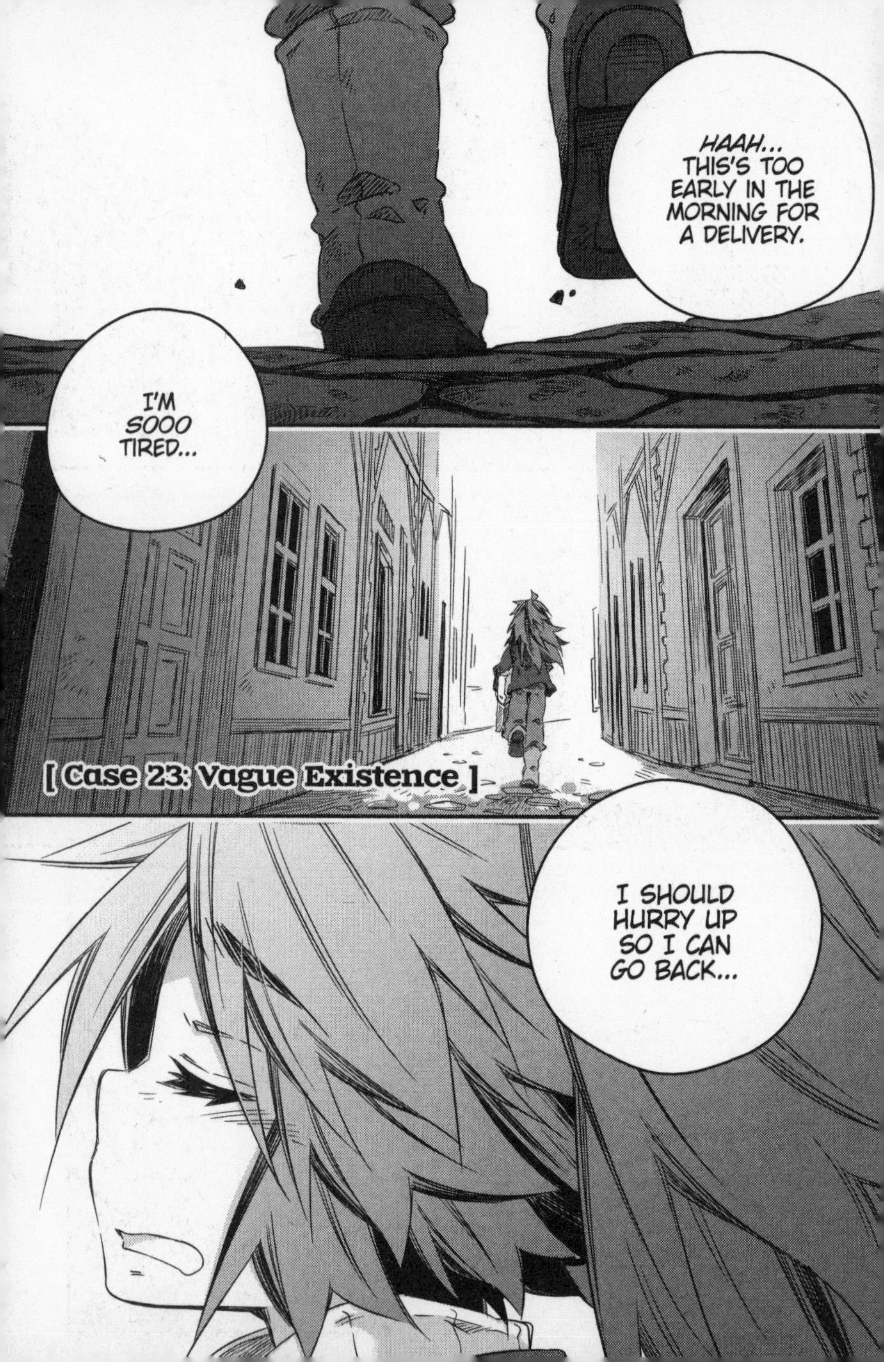
HAAH... THIS'S TOO EARLY IN THE MORNING FOR A DELIVERY.
I'M SOOO TIRED...
[Case 23: Vague Existence]
I SHOULD HURRY UP SO I CAN GO BACK...

MRAA...

RUSTLE...

A CAT?

PWOP

HERE, KITTY KITTY-- WANNA PLAY FOR A BIT?

I DON'T HAVE ANY SNACKS ON ME THOUGH...

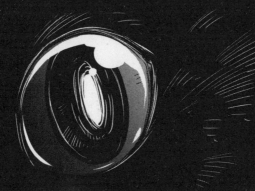

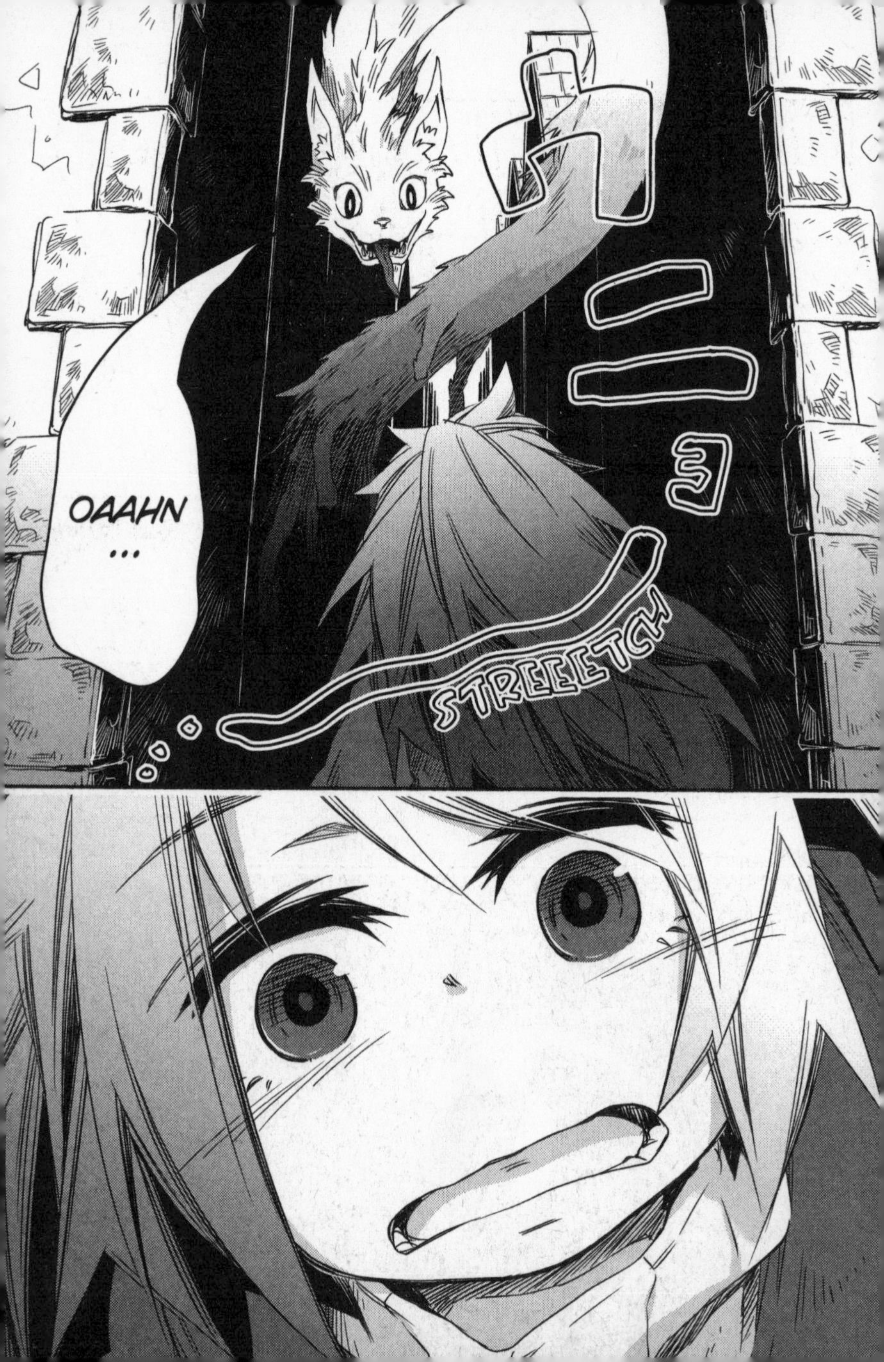
STREEETCH
OAAHN ...

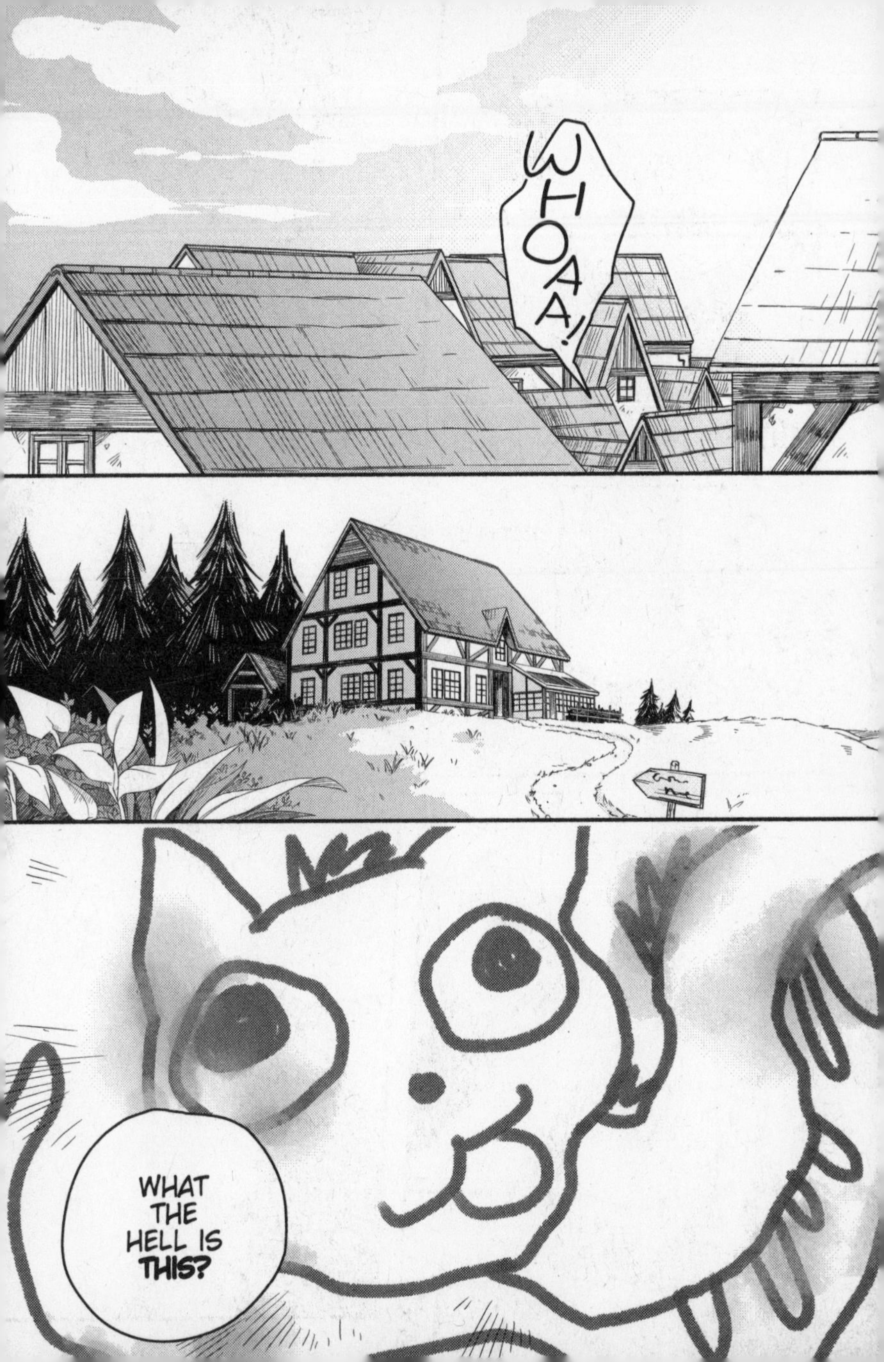
WHOA!
WHAT THE HELL IS THIS?

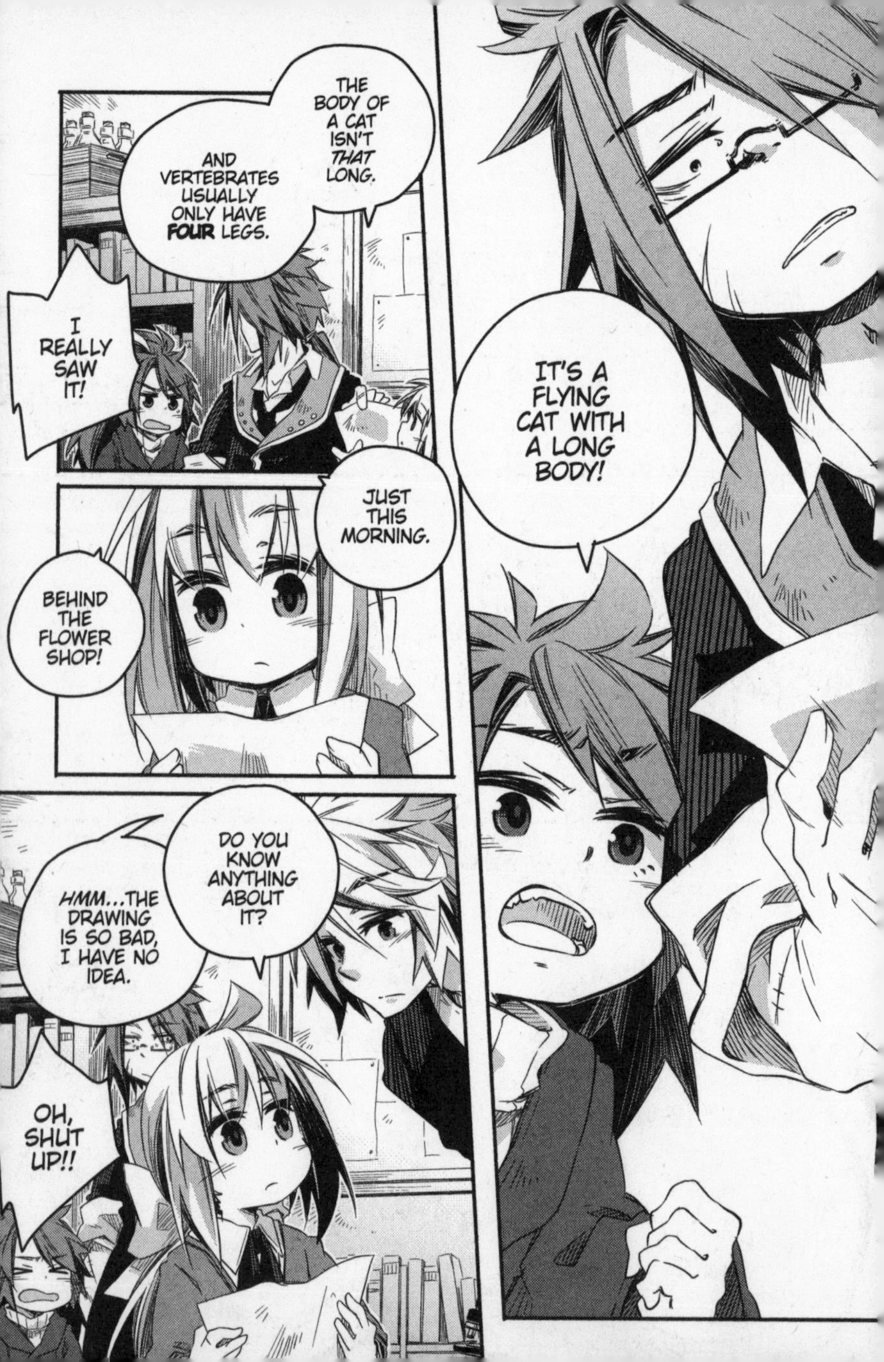

IT'S A FLYING CAT WITH A LONG BODY!
THE BODY OF A CAT ISN'T *THAT* LONG.
AND VERTEBRATES USUALLY ONLY HAVE **FOUR** LEGS.
I REALLY SAW IT!
JUST THIS MORNING.
BEHIND THE FLOWER SHOP!
DO YOU KNOW ANYTHING ABOUT IT?
HMM...THE DRAWING IS SO BAD, I HAVE NO IDEA.
OH, SHUT UP!!

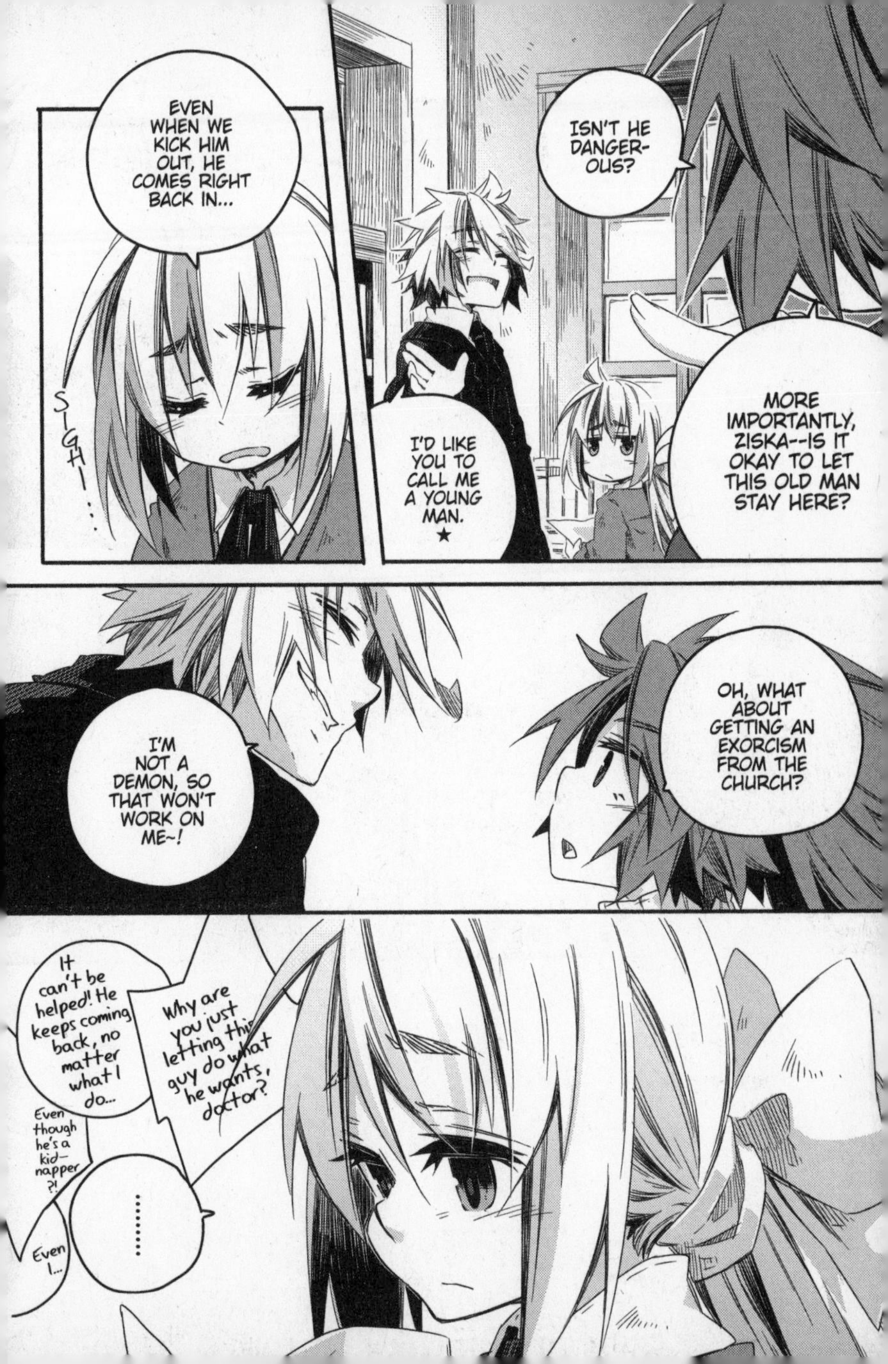
ISN'T HE DANGER-OUS?
MORE IMPORTANTLY, ZISKA--IS IT OKAY TO LET THIS OLD MAN STAY HERE?
I'D LIKE YOU TO CALL ME A YOUNG MAN. ★
EVEN WHEN WE KICK HIM OUT, HE COMES RIGHT BACK IN...
SIGH...
OH, WHAT ABOUT GETTING AN EXORCISM FROM THE CHURCH?
I'M NOT A DEMON, SO THAT WON'T WORK ON ME~!
Why are you just letting this guy do what he wants, doctor?
It can't be helped! He keeps coming back, no matter what I do...
Even though he's a kid-napper?!
......
Even I...

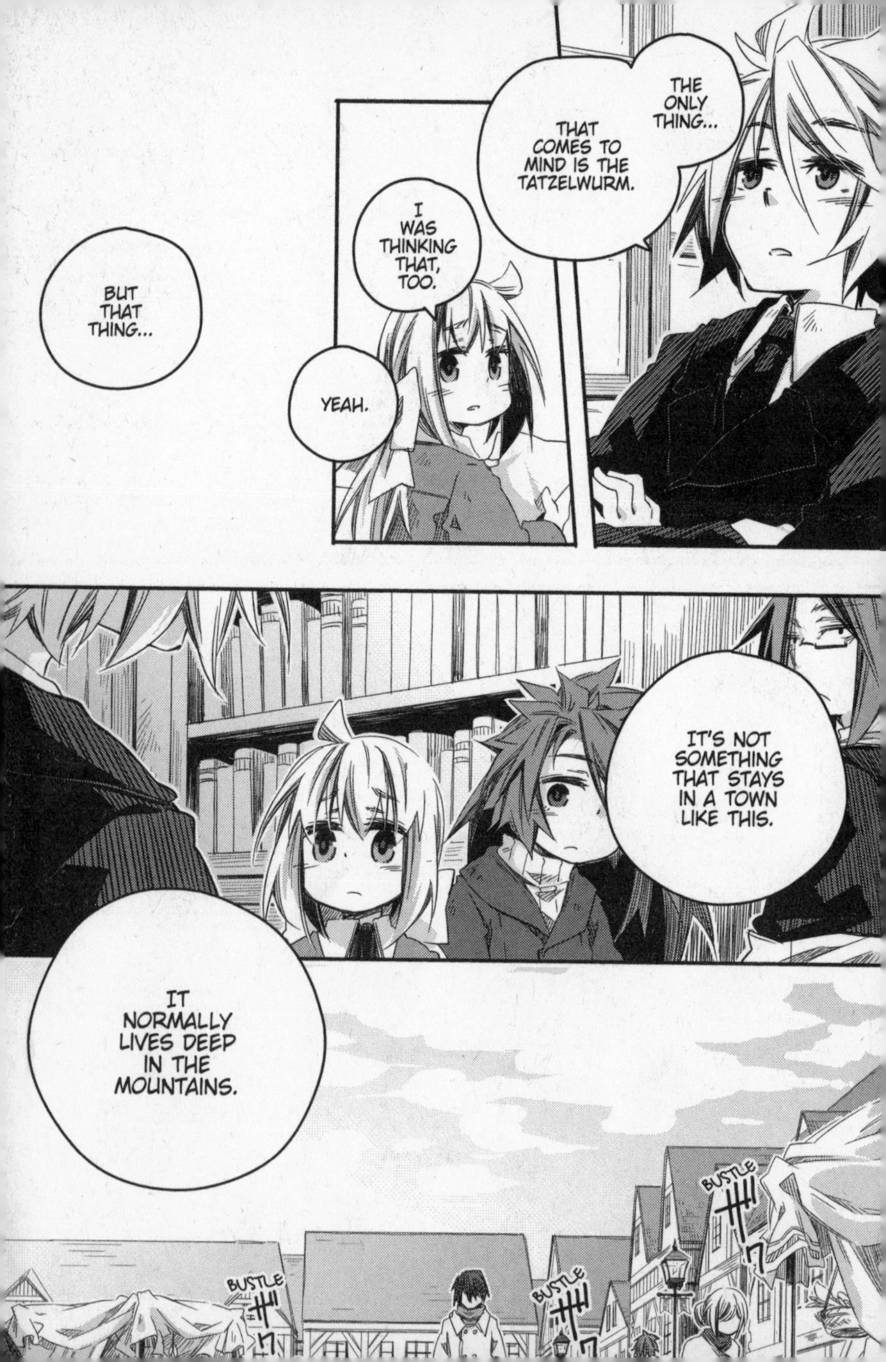
THE ONLY THING...
THAT COMES TO MIND IS THE TATZELWURM.
I WAS THINKING THAT, TOO.
YEAH.
BUT THAT THING...
IT'S NOT SOMETHING THAT STAYS IN A TOWN LIKE THIS.
IT NORMALLY LIVES DEEP IN THE MOUNTAINS.
BUSTLE
BUSTLE
BUSTLE

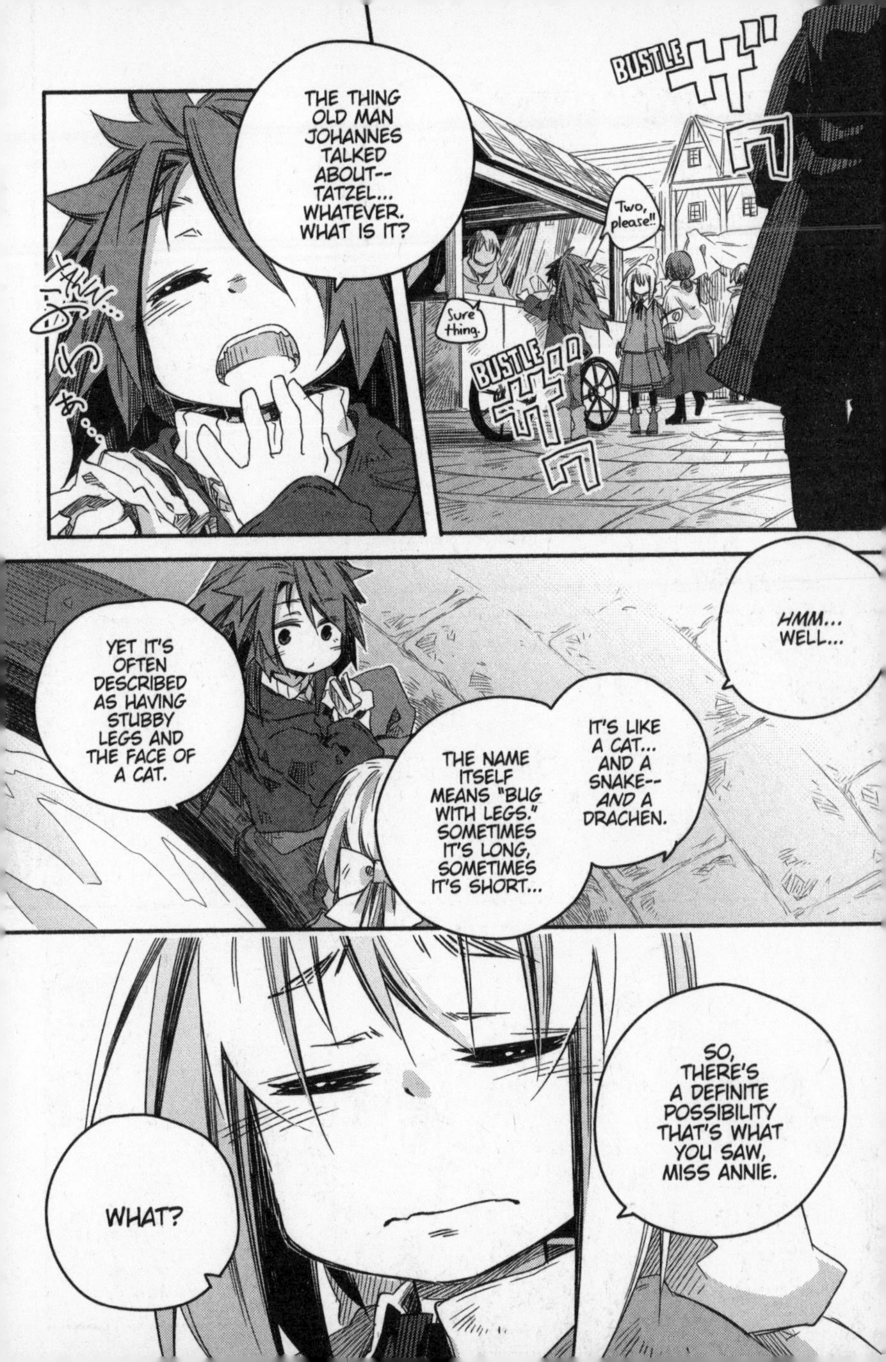
BUSTLE
Two, please!!
Sure thing.
BUSTLE
THE THING OLD MAN JOHANNES TALKED ABOUT-- TATZEL... WHATEVER. WHAT IS IT?
YAWN...
HMM... WELL...
IT'S LIKE A CAT... AND A SNAKE-- AND A DRACHEN.
THE NAME ITSELF MEANS "BUG WITH LEGS." SOMETIMES IT'S LONG, SOMETIMES IT'S SHORT...
YET IT'S OFTEN DESCRIBED AS HAVING STUBBY LEGS AND THE FACE OF A CAT.
SO, THERE'S A DEFINITE POSSIBILITY THAT'S WHAT YOU SAW, MISS ANNIE.
WHAT?

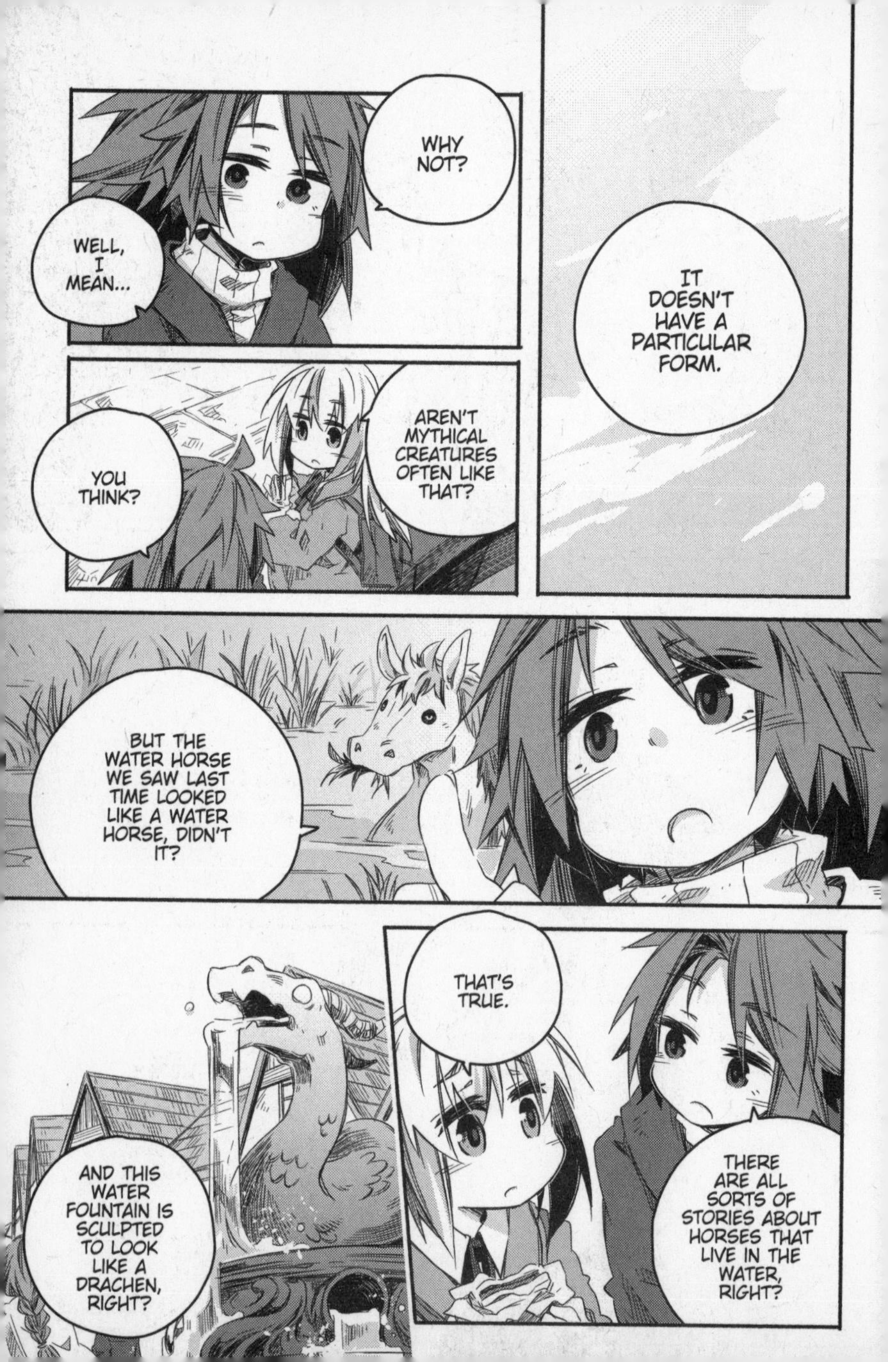
IT DOESN'T HAVE A PARTICULAR FORM.
WHY NOT?
WELL, I MEAN...
AREN'T MYTHICAL CREATURES OFTEN LIKE THAT?
YOU THINK?
BUT THE WATER HORSE WE SAW LAST TIME LOOKED LIKE A WATER HORSE, DIDN'T IT?
THAT'S TRUE.
THERE ARE ALL SORTS OF STORIES ABOUT HORSES THAT LIVE IN THE WATER, RIGHT?
AND THIS WATER FOUNTAIN IS SCULPTED TO LOOK LIKE A DRACHEN, RIGHT?

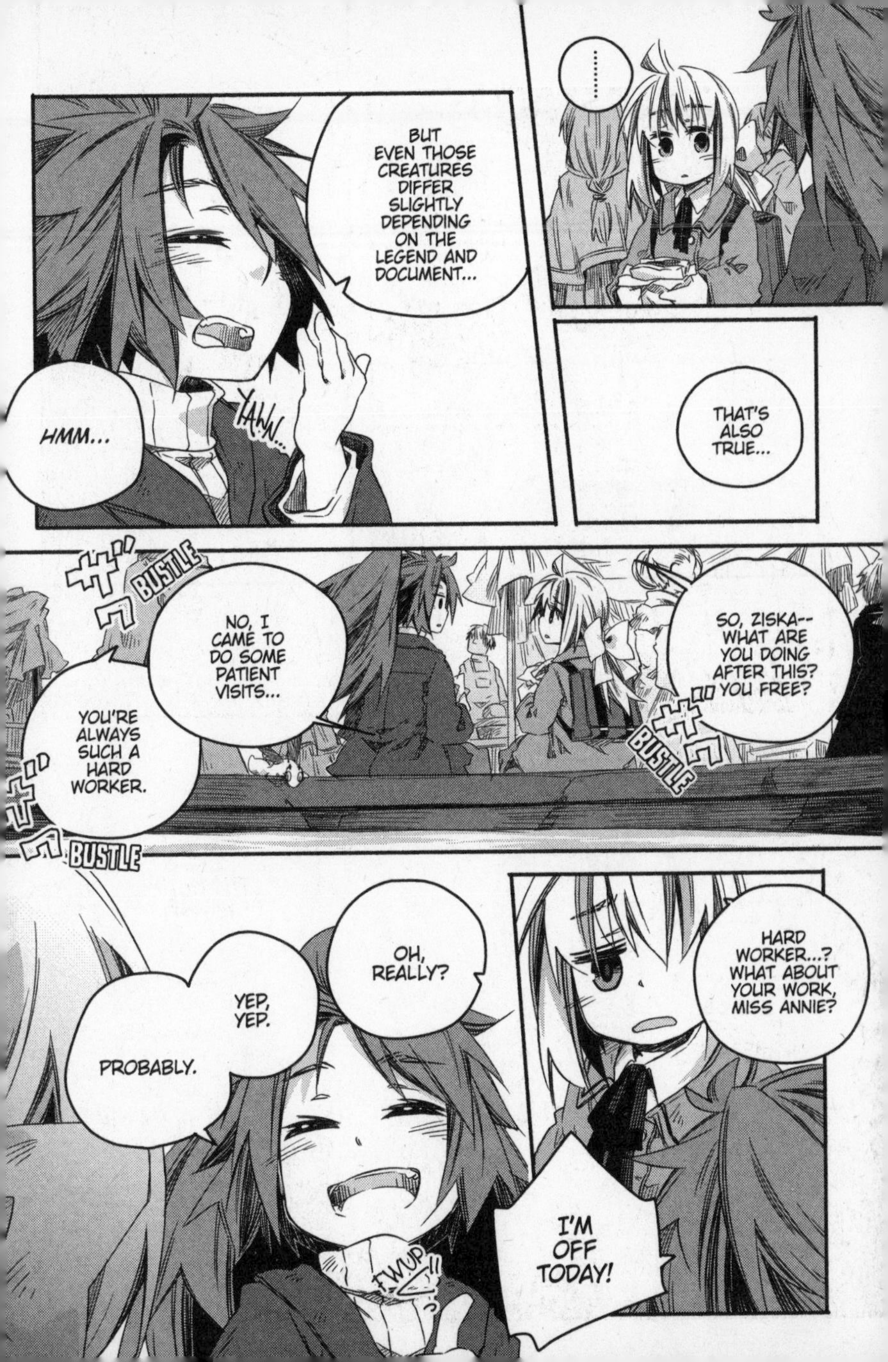
......
THAT'S ALSO TRUE...
BUT EVEN THOSE CREATURES DIFFER SLIGHTLY DEPENDING ON THE LEGEND AND DOCUMENT...
YAWN...
HMM...
BUSTLE
SO, ZISKA-- WHAT ARE YOU DOING AFTER THIS? YOU FREE?
NO, I CAME TO DO SOME PATIENT VISITS...
YOU'RE ALWAYS SUCH A HARD WORKER.
BUSTLE
BUSTLE
HARD WORKER...? WHAT ABOUT YOUR WORK, MISS ANNIE?
I'M OFF TODAY!
FWUP!!
OH, REALLY?
YEP, YEP.
PROBABLY.

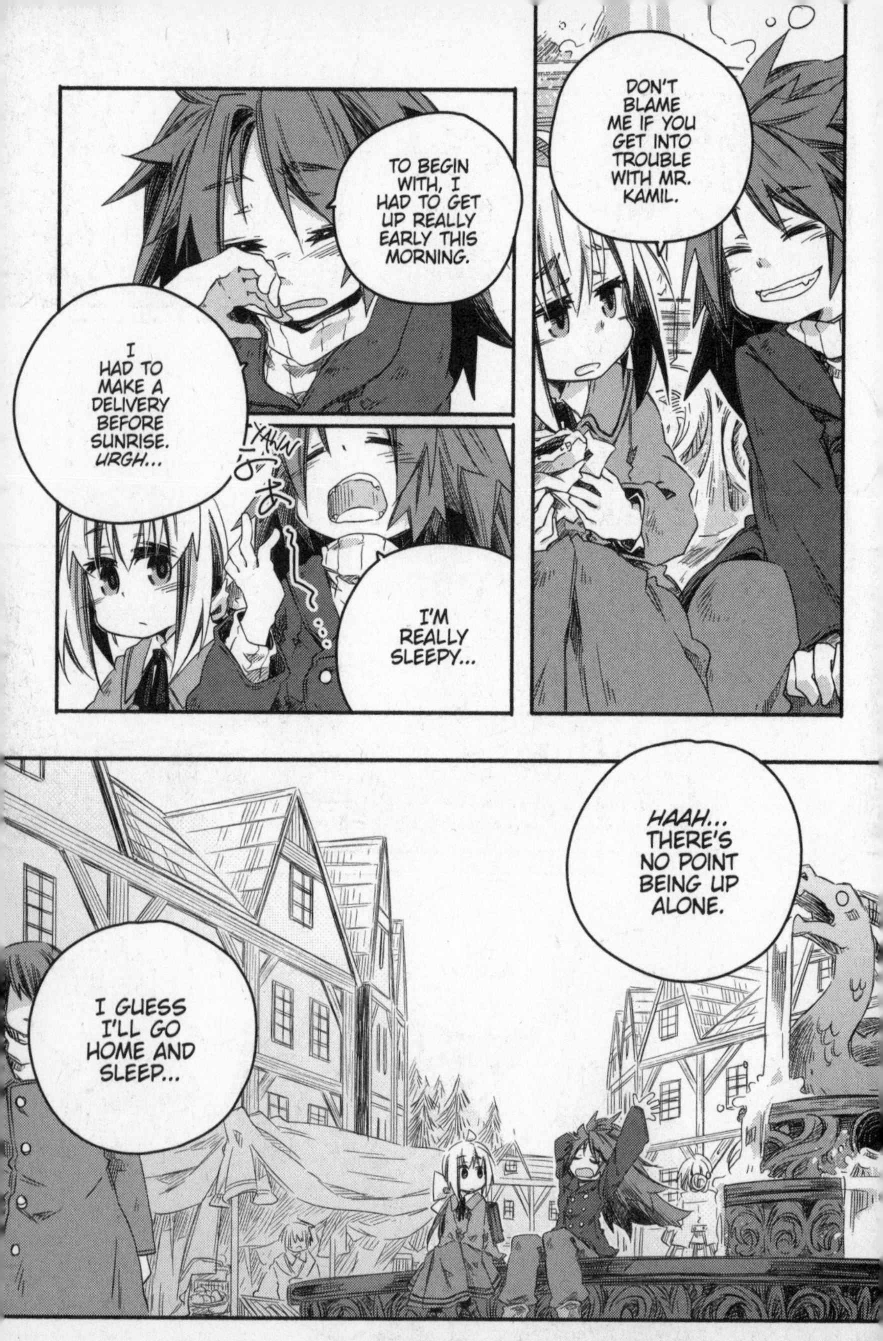
DON'T BLAME ME IF YOU GET INTO TROUBLE WITH MR. KAMIL.
TO BEGIN WITH, I HAD TO GET UP REALLY EARLY THIS MORNING.
I HAD TO MAKE A DELIVERY BEFORE SUNRISE. *URGH...*
YAWN
I'M REALLY SLEEPY...
HAAH... THERE'S NO POINT BEING UP ALONE.
I GUESS I'LL GO HOME AND SLEEP...

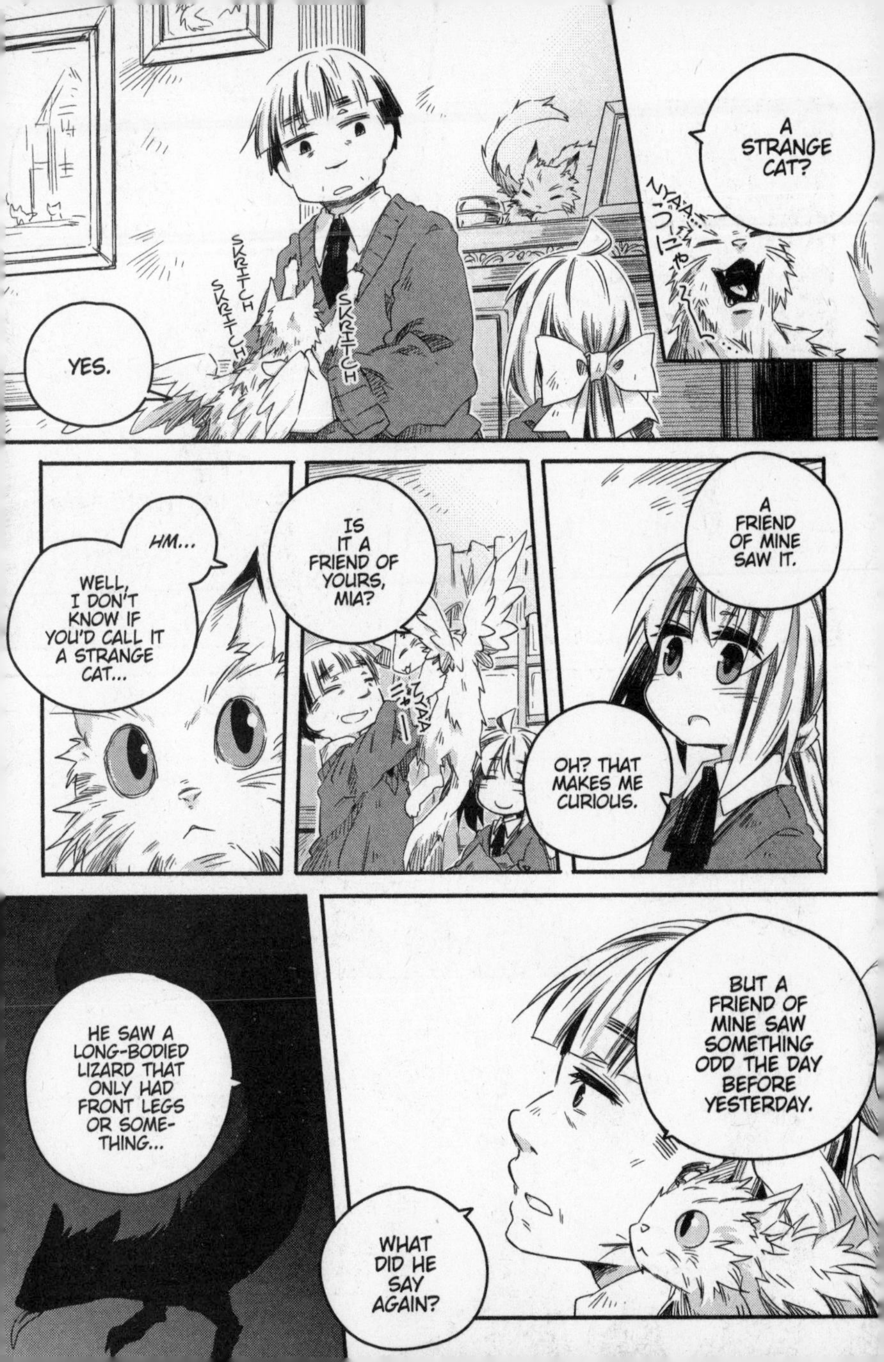
A STRANGE CAT?
NYAA...
YES.
SKRITCH
SKRITCH
SKRITCH
A FRIEND OF MINE SAW IT.
OH? THAT MAKES ME CURIOUS.
IS IT A FRIEND OF YOURS, MIA?
NYAA
HM...
WELL, I DON'T KNOW IF YOU'D CALL IT A STRANGE CAT...
BUT A FRIEND OF MINE SAW SOMETHING ODD THE DAY BEFORE YESTERDAY.
WHAT DID HE SAY AGAIN?
HE SAW A LONG-BODIED LIZARD THAT ONLY HAD FRONT LEGS OR SOME-THING...

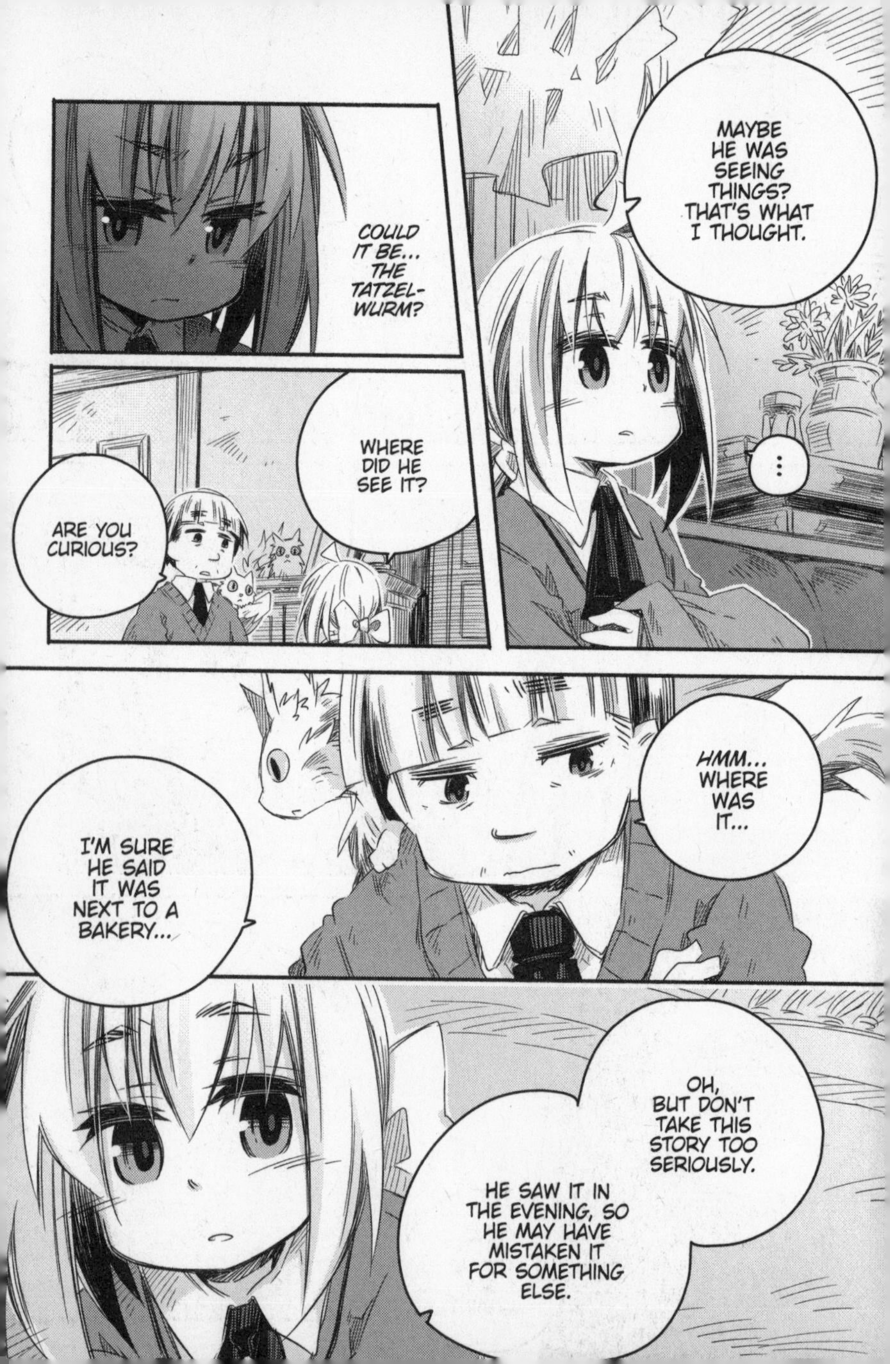
MAYBE HE WAS SEEING THINGS? THAT'S WHAT I THOUGHT.
...
COULD IT BE... THE TATZEL-WURM?
WHERE DID HE SEE IT?
ARE YOU CURIOUS?
HMM... WHERE WAS IT...
I'M SURE HE SAID IT WAS NEXT TO A BAKERY...
OH, BUT DON'T TAKE THIS STORY TOO SERIOUSLY.
HE SAW IT IN THE EVENING, SO HE MAY HAVE MISTAKEN IT FOR SOMETHING ELSE.

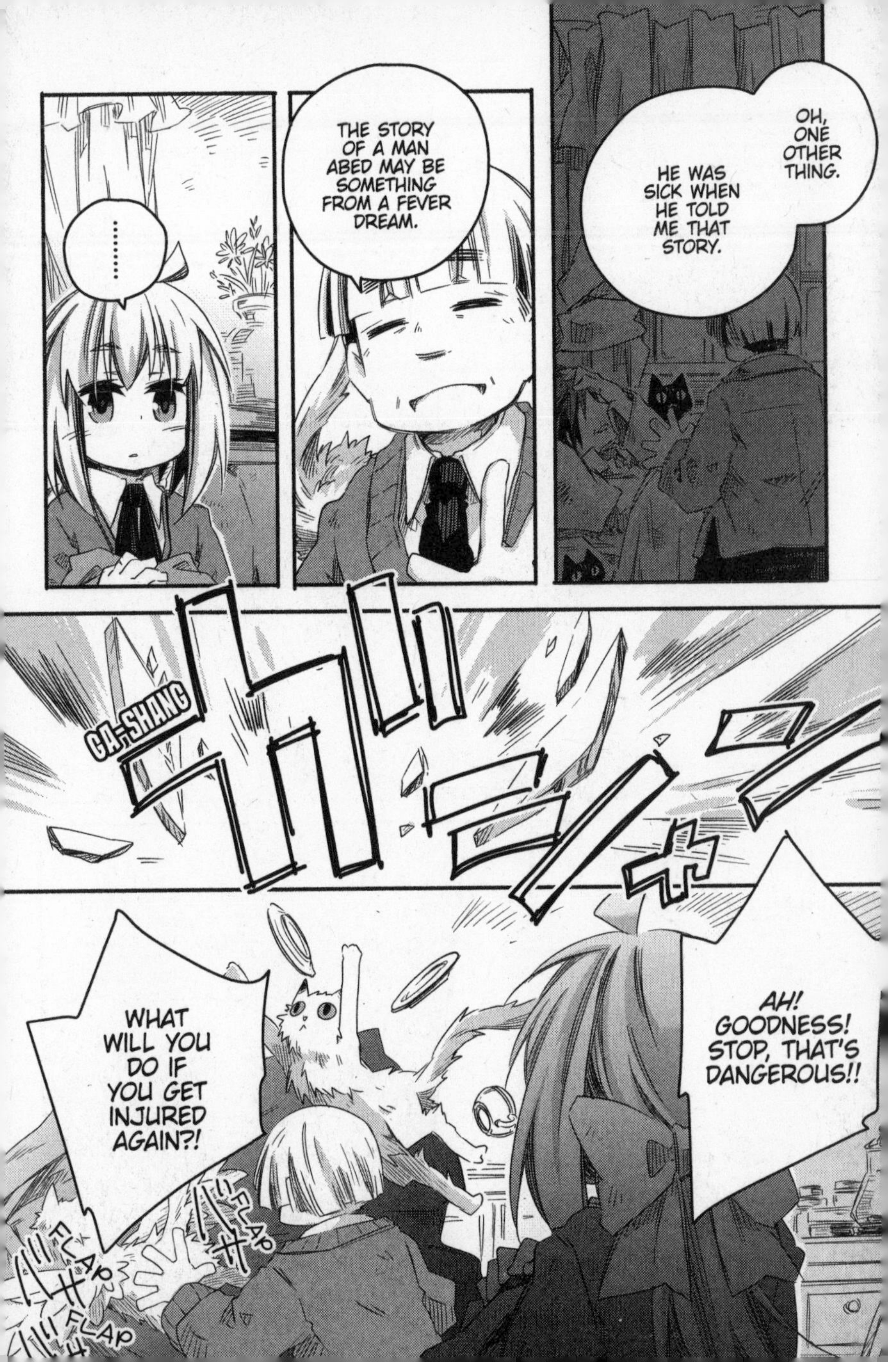
OH, ONE OTHER THING.
HE WAS SICK WHEN HE TOLD ME THAT STORY.
THE STORY OF A MAN ABED MAY BE SOMETHING FROM A FEVER DREAM.
……
GA-SHANG
AH! GOODNESS! STOP, THAT'S DANGEROUS!!
WHAT WILL YOU DO IF YOU GET INJURED AGAIN?!
FLAP
FLAP
FLAP

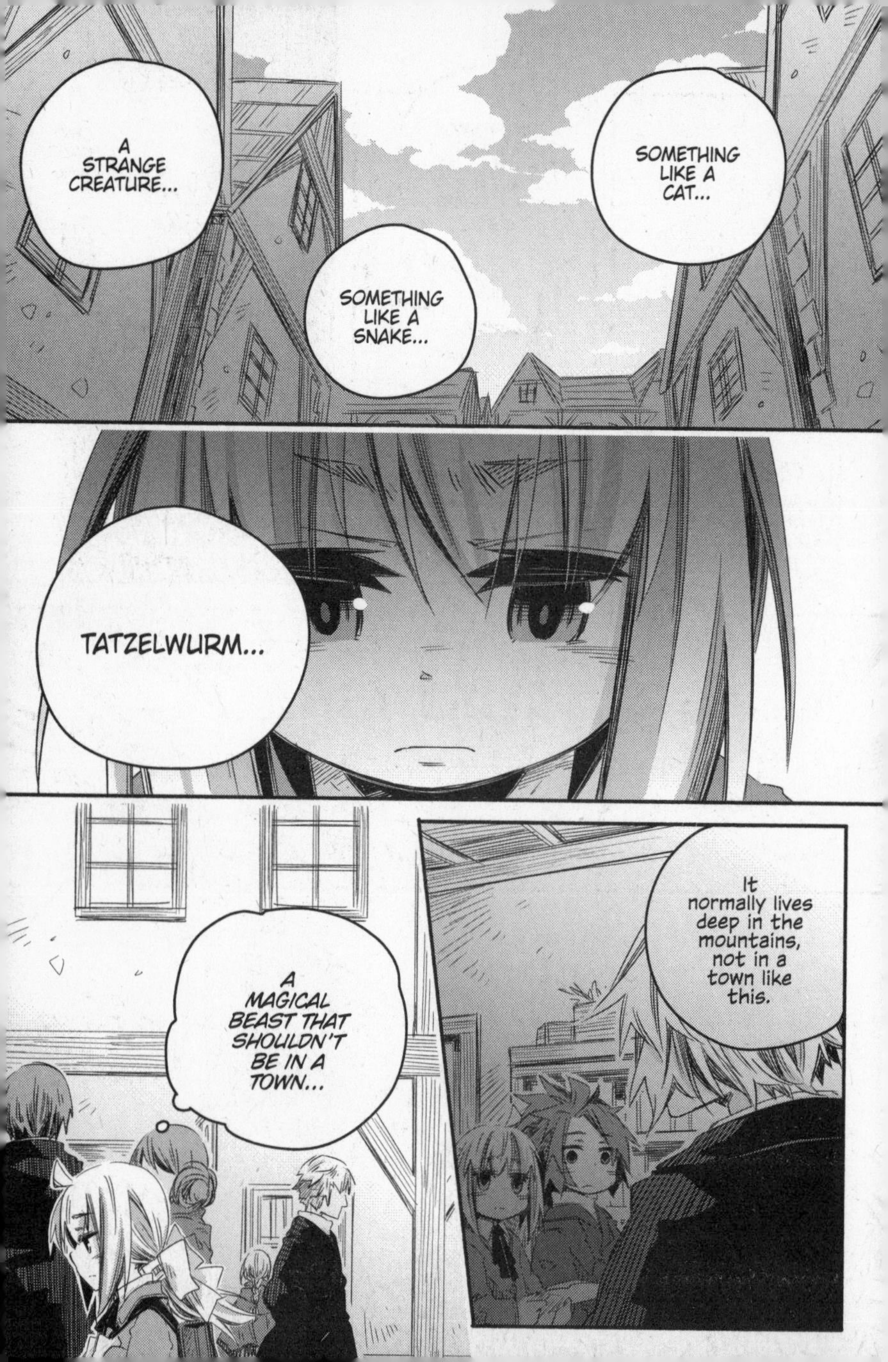
SOMETHING LIKE A CAT...
A STRANGE CREATURE...
SOMETHING LIKE A SNAKE...
TATZELWURM...
It normally lives deep in the mountains, not in a town like this.
A MAGICAL BEAST THAT SHOULDN'T BE IN A TOWN...

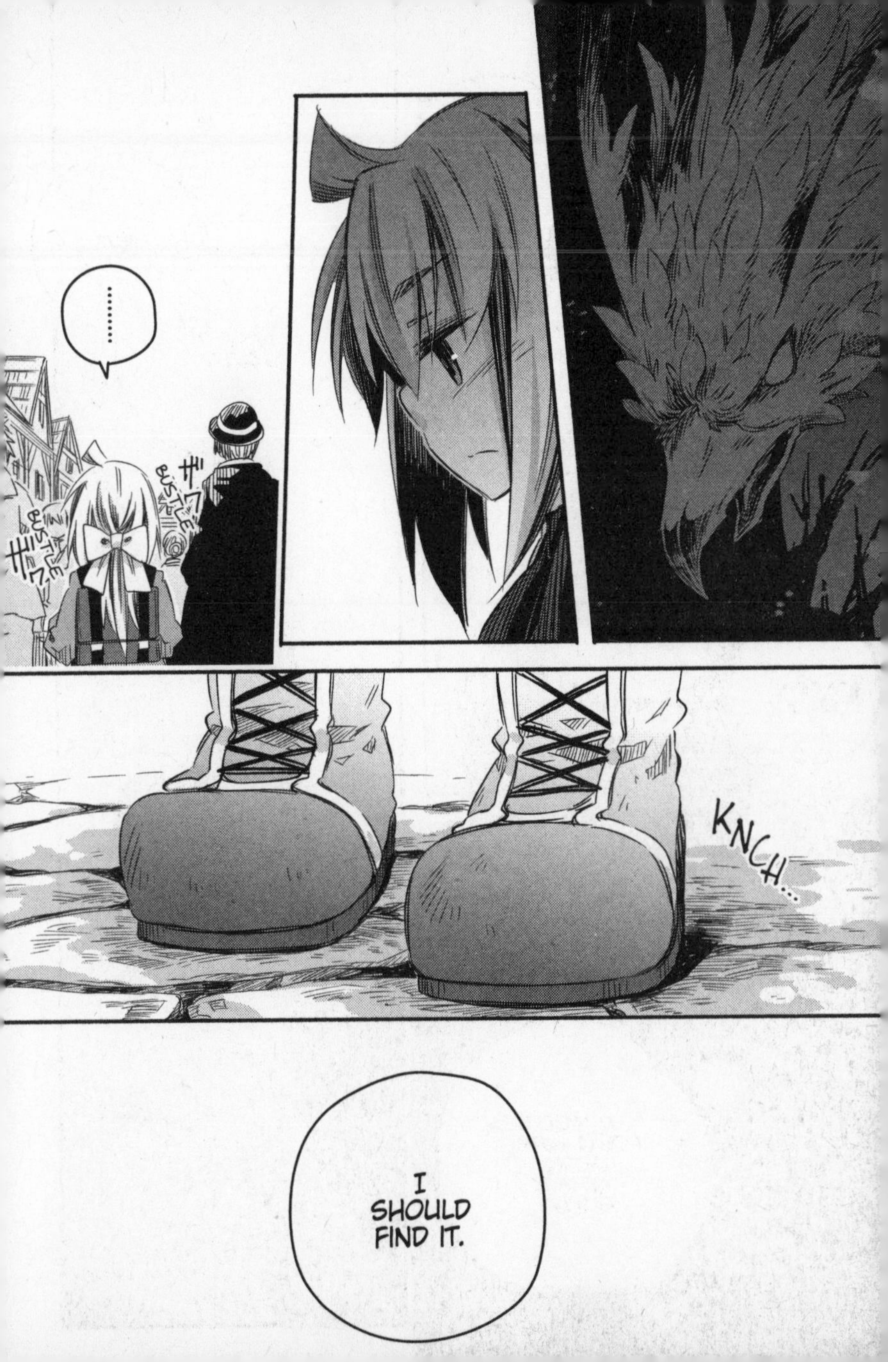
......
BUSTLE
BUSTLE
KNCH...
I SHOULD FIND IT.

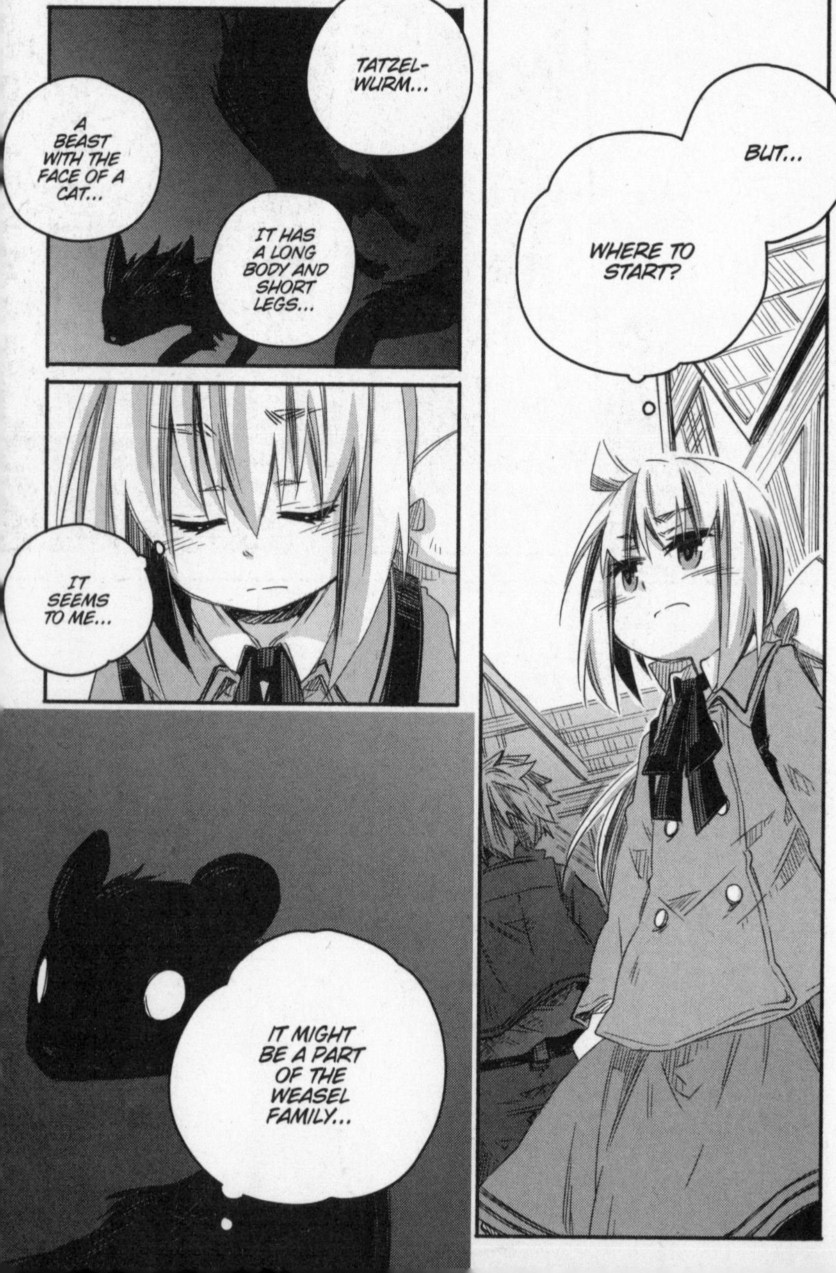
BUT...
WHERE TO START?
TATZEL-WURM...
A BEAST WITH THE FACE OF A CAT...
IT HAS A LONG BODY AND SHORT LEGS...
IT SEEMS TO ME...
IT MIGHT BE A PART OF THE WEASEL FAMILY...

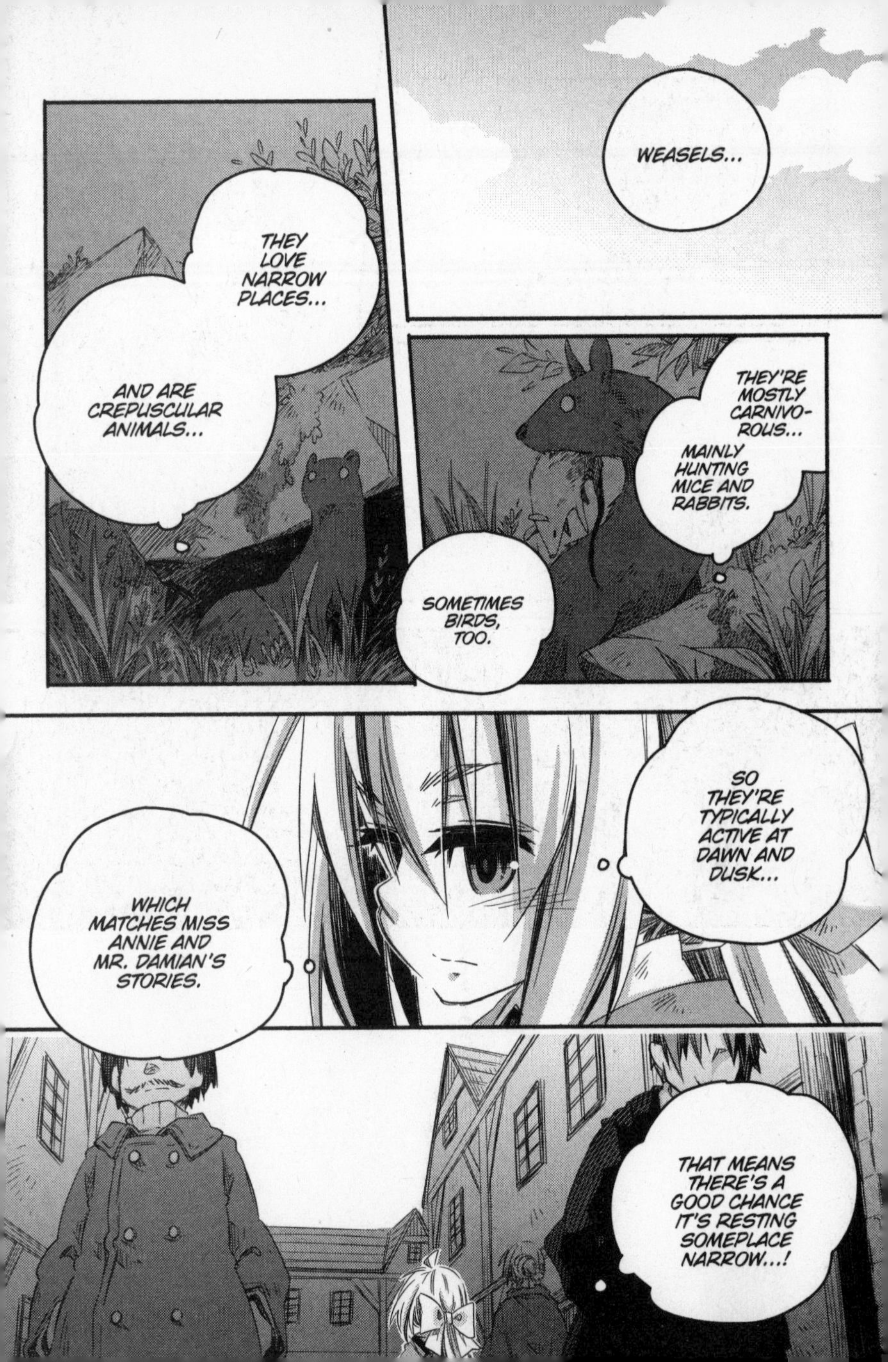
WEASELS...
THEY'RE MOSTLY CARNIVOROUS...
MAINLY HUNTING MICE AND RABBITS.
SOMETIMES BIRDS, TOO.
THEY LOVE NARROW PLACES...
AND ARE CREPUSCULAR ANIMALS...
SO THEY'RE TYPICALLY ACTIVE AT DAWN AND DUSK...
WHICH MATCHES MISS ANNIE AND MR. DAMIAN'S STORIES.
THAT MEANS THERE'S A GOOD CHANCE IT'S RESTING SOMEPLACE NARROW...!

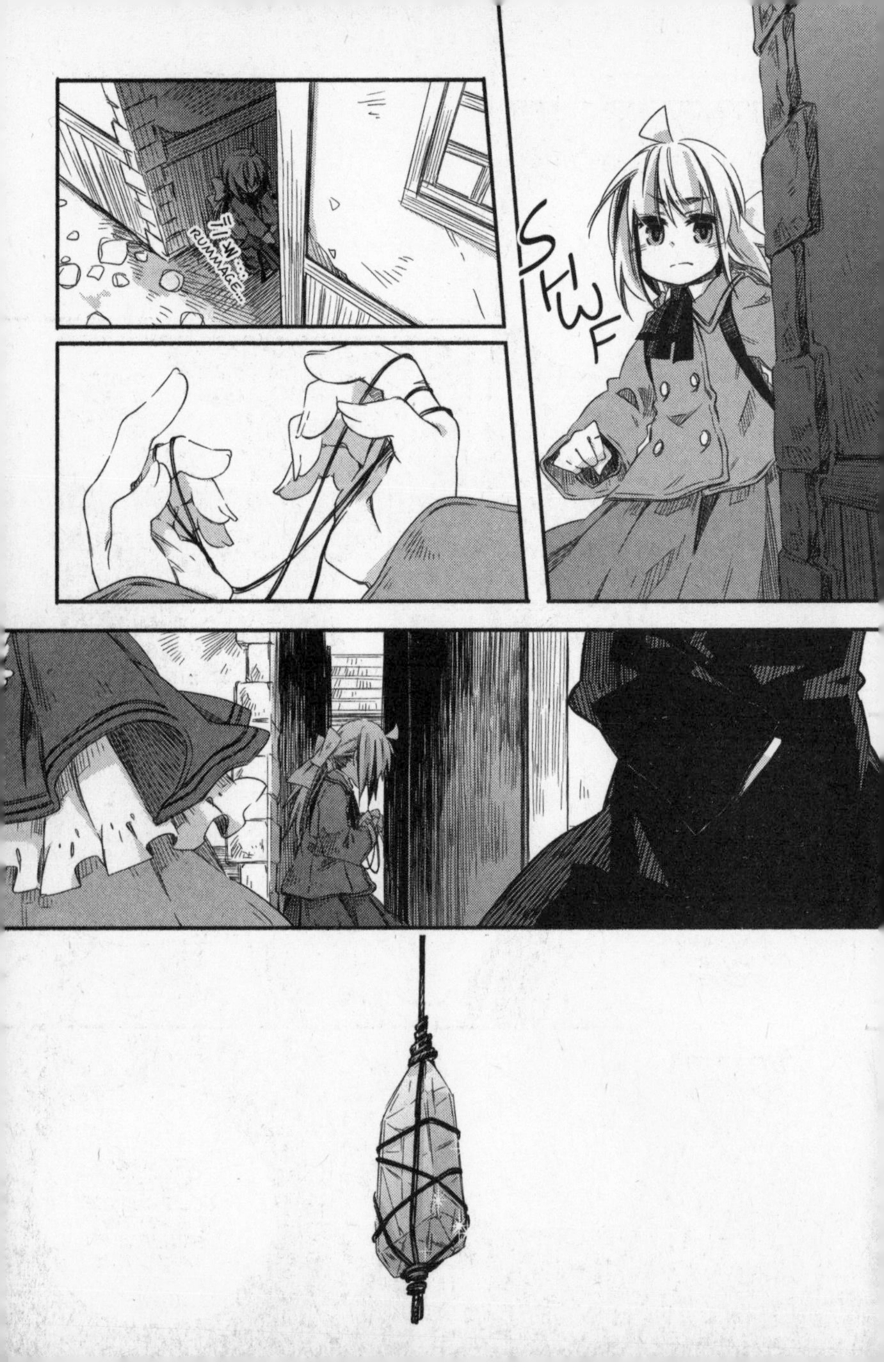
SHWF
RUMMAGE...

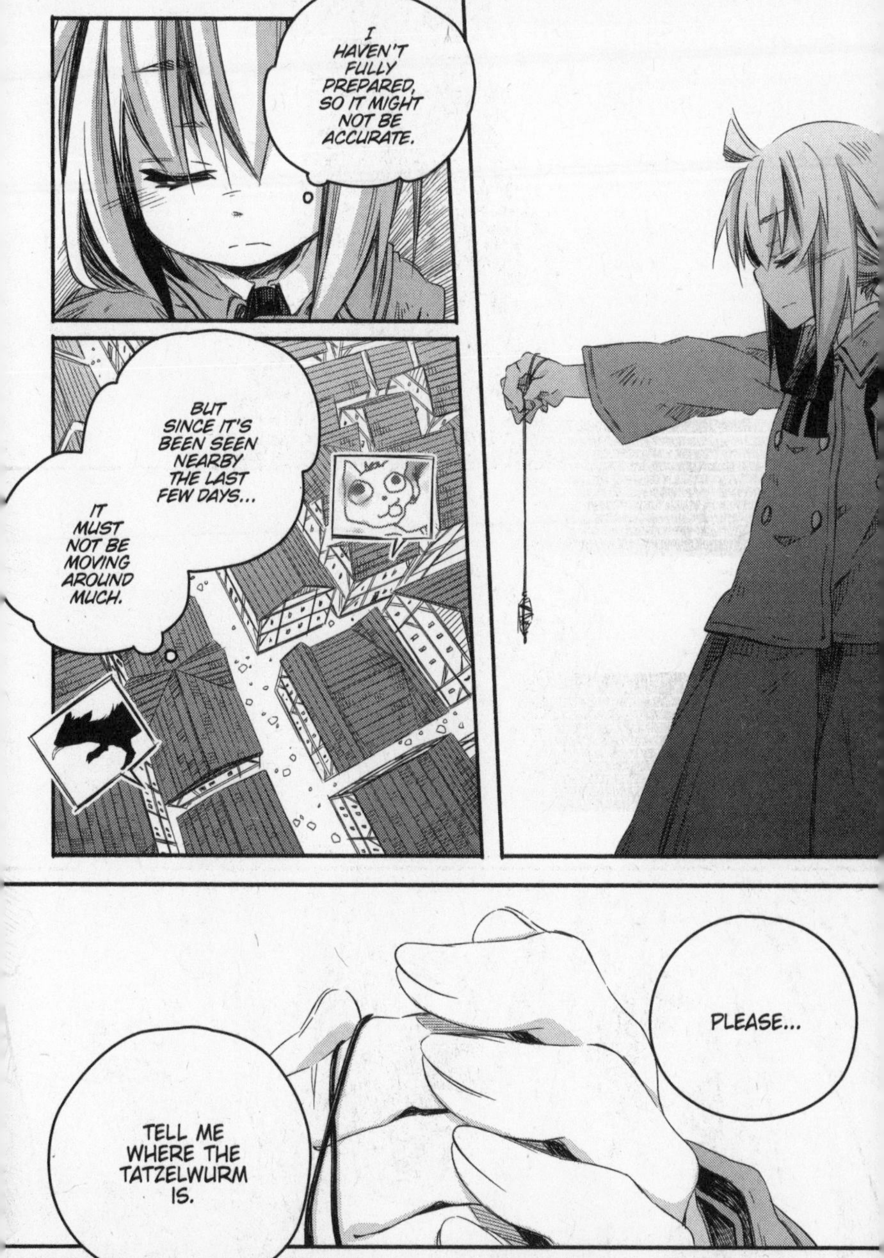
I HAVEN'T FULLY PREPARED, SO IT MIGHT NOT BE ACCURATE.
BUT SINCE IT'S BEEN SEEN NEARBY THE LAST FEW DAYS...
IT MUST NOT BE MOVING AROUND MUCH.
PLEASE...
TELL ME WHERE THE TATZELWURM IS.

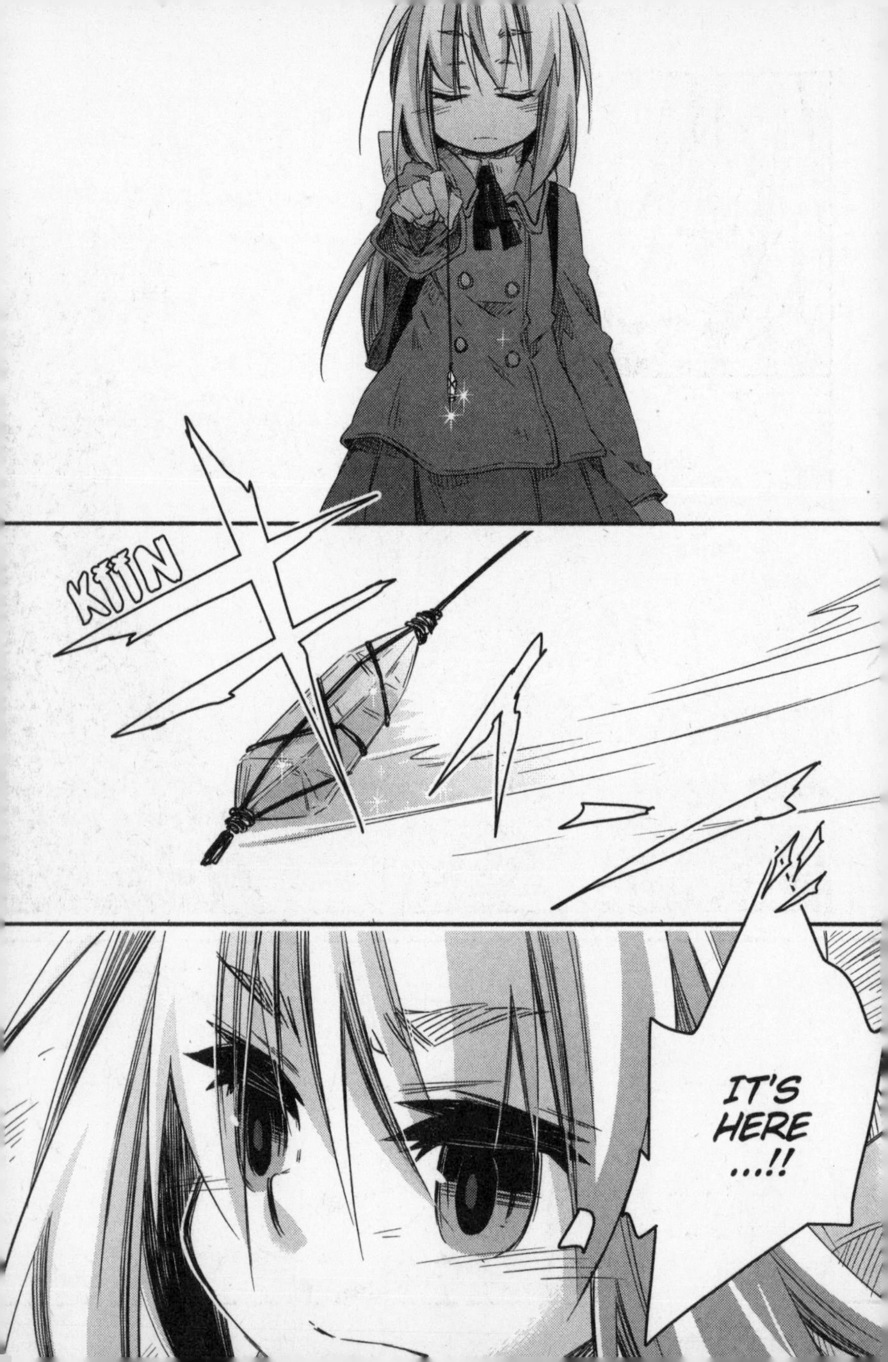
KIIN
IT'S HERE ...!!

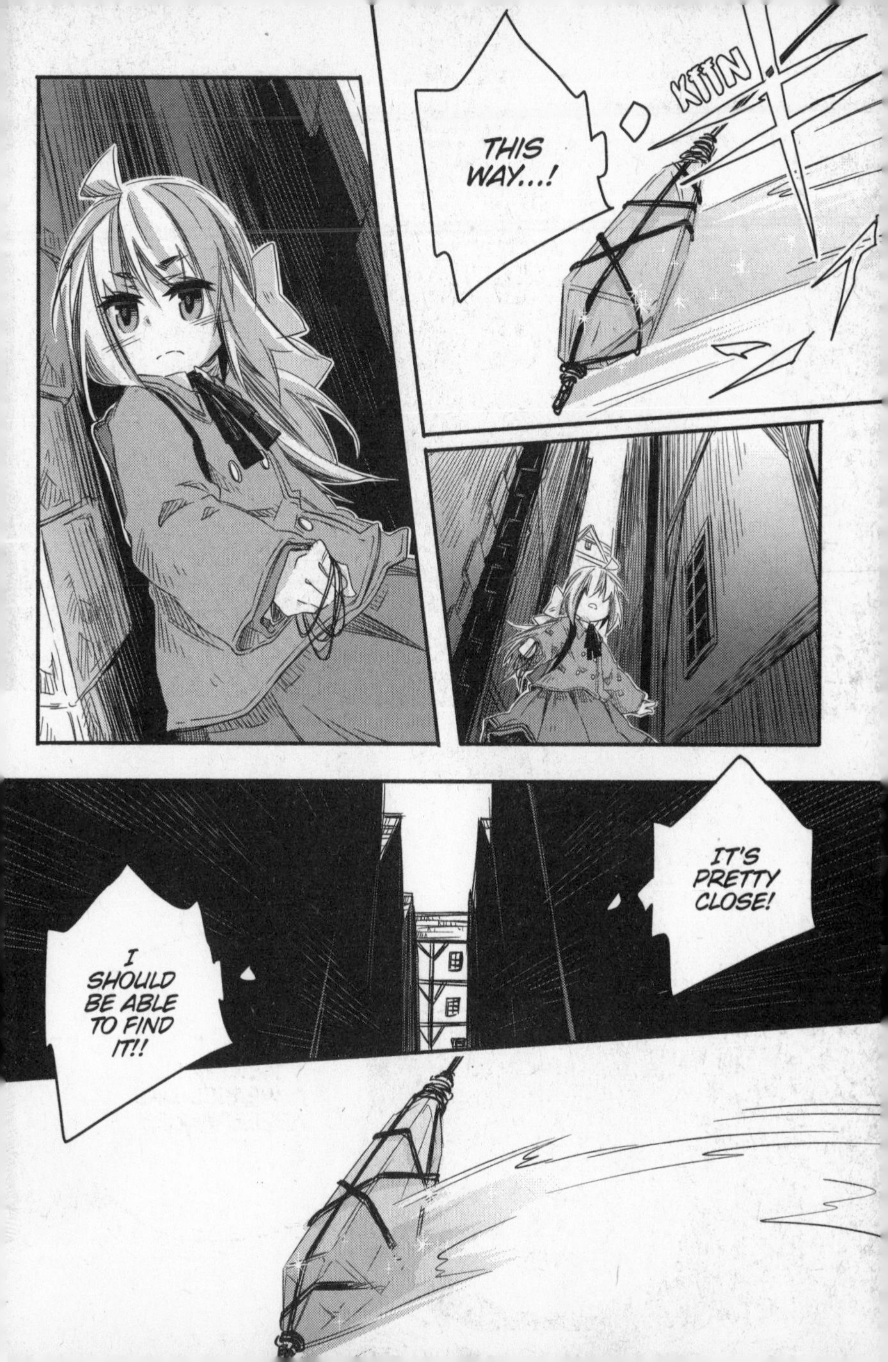
KIIIN
THIS WAY...!
IT'S PRETTY CLOSE!
I SHOULD BE ABLE TO FIND IT!!

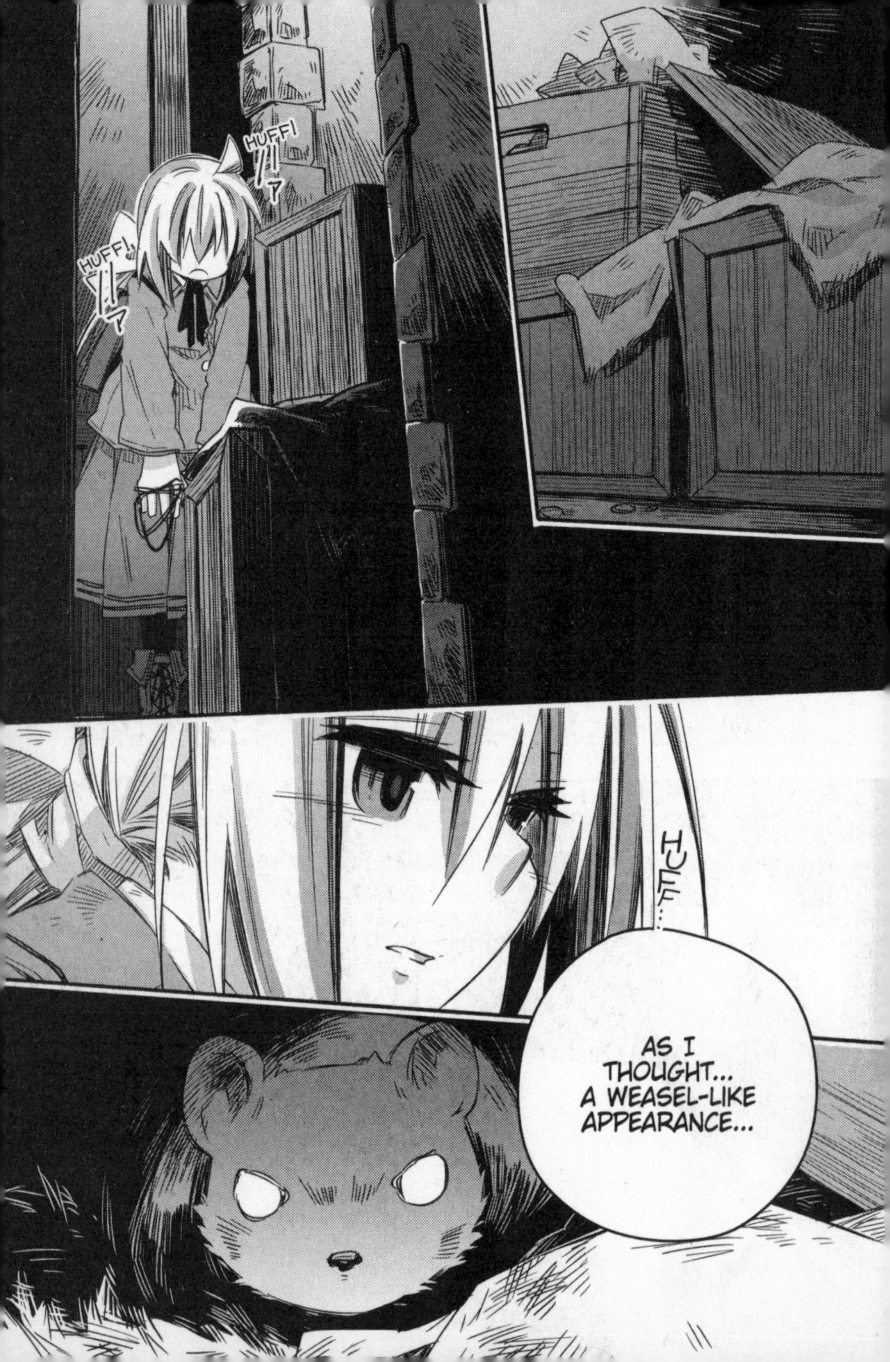
HUFF!
HUFF!
HUFF...
AS I THOUGHT... A WEASEL-LIKE APPEARANCE...

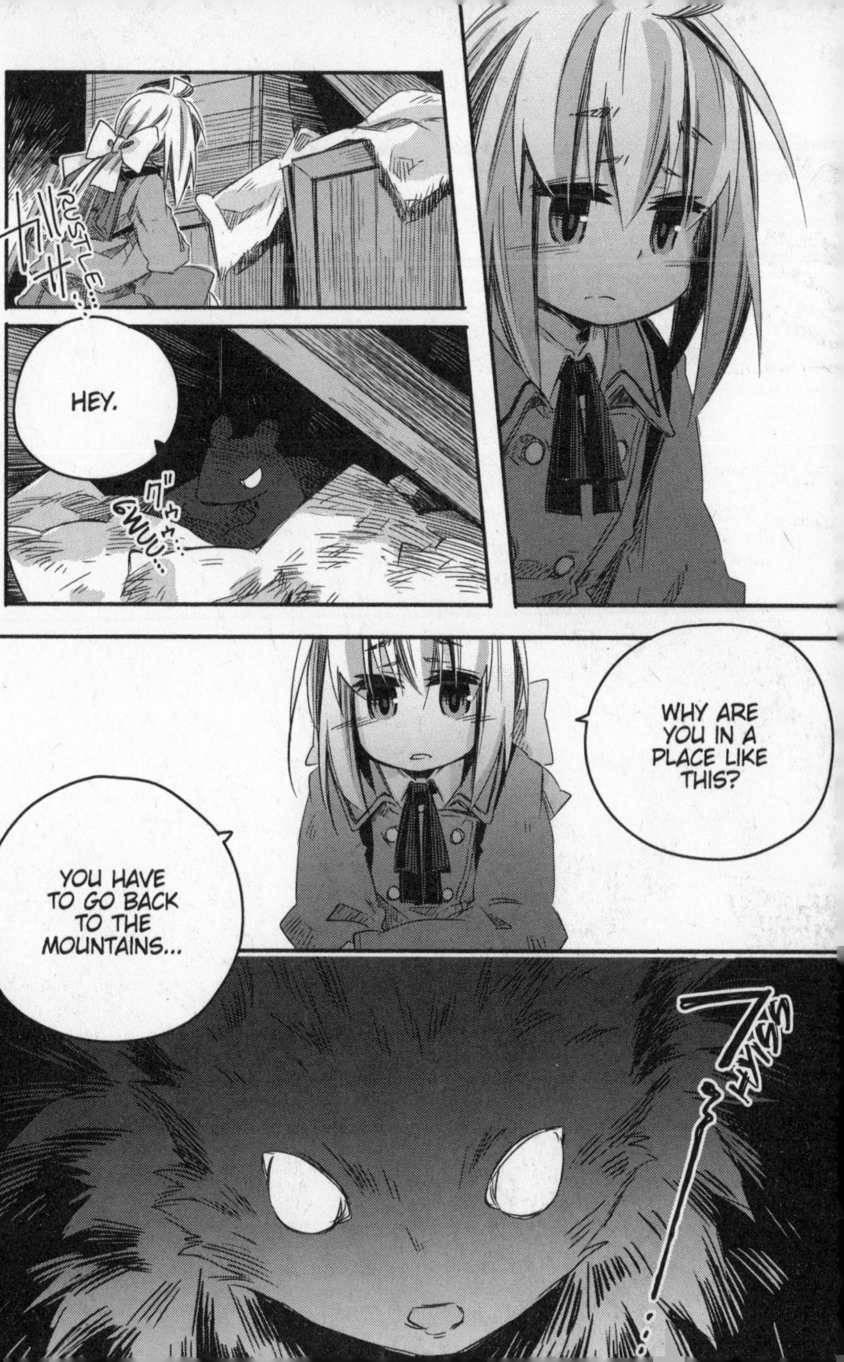
ガサ…
RUSTLE…
HEY.
グゥゥ…
GWUU…
WHY ARE YOU IN A PLACE LIKE THIS?
YOU HAVE TO GO BACK TO THE MOUNTAINS…

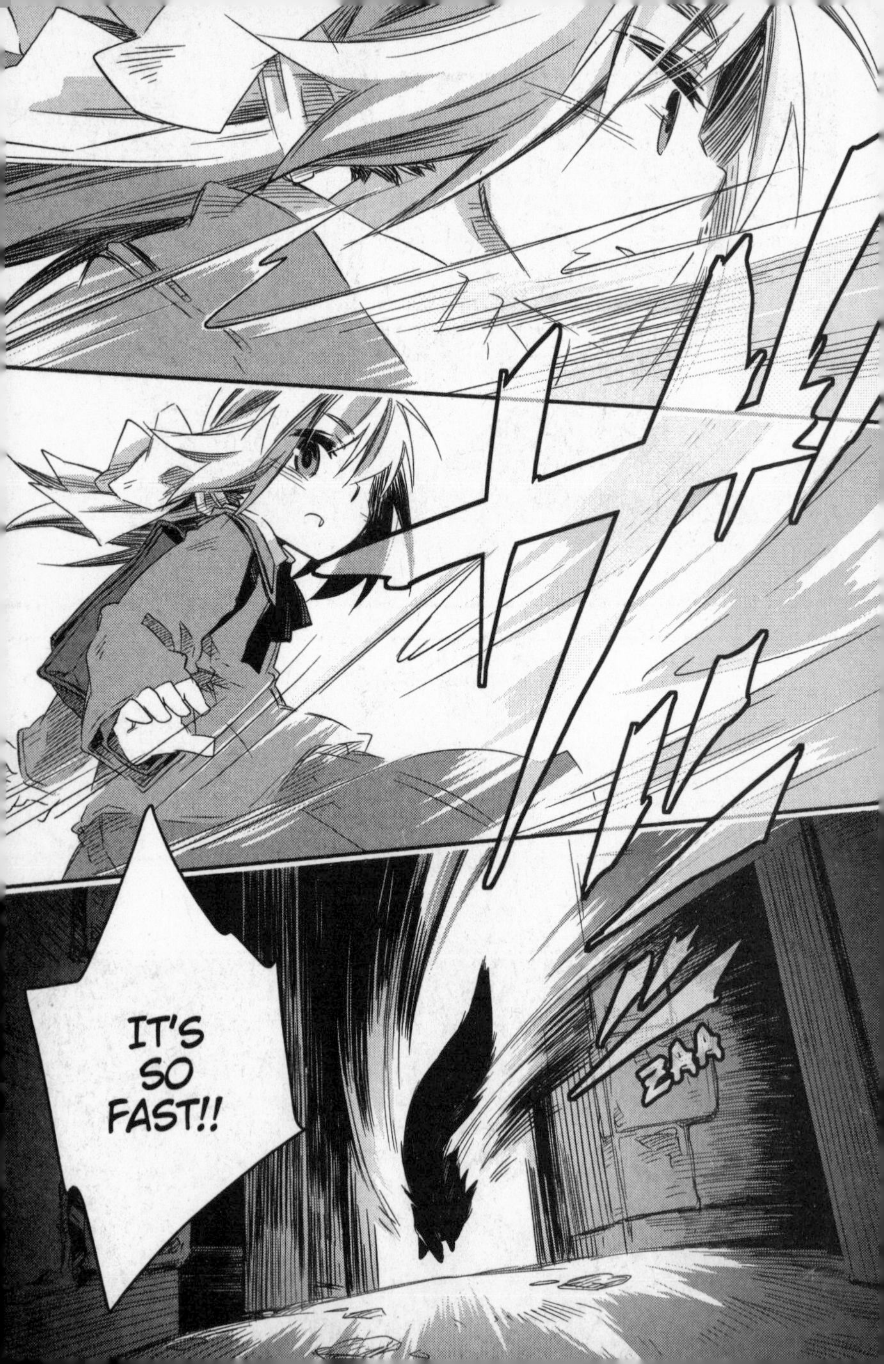
IT'S SO FAST!!
ZAA

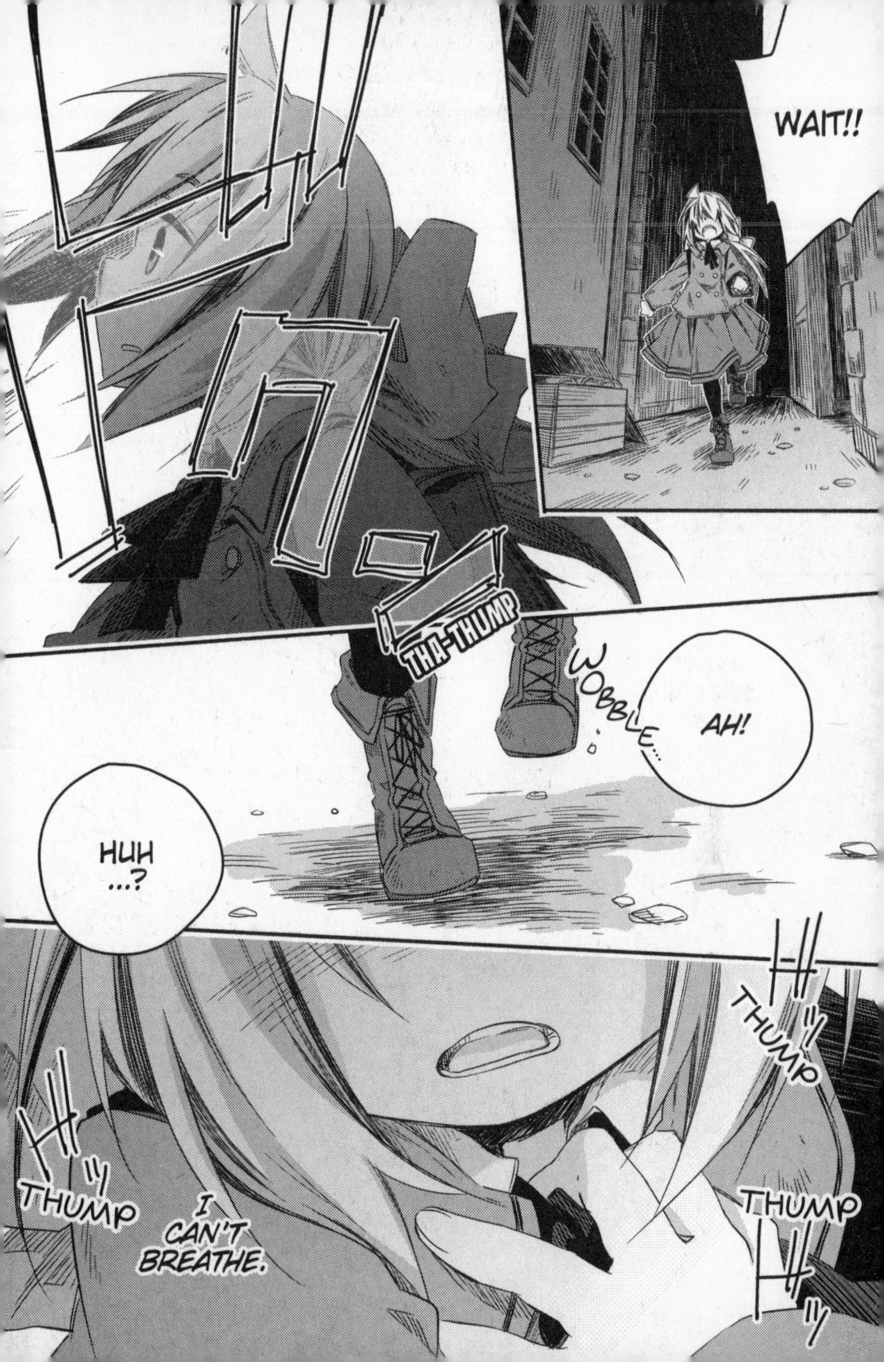
WAIT!!
THA-THUMP
AH!
WOBBLE...
HUH ...?
THUMP
THUMP
I CAN'T BREATHE.
THUMP

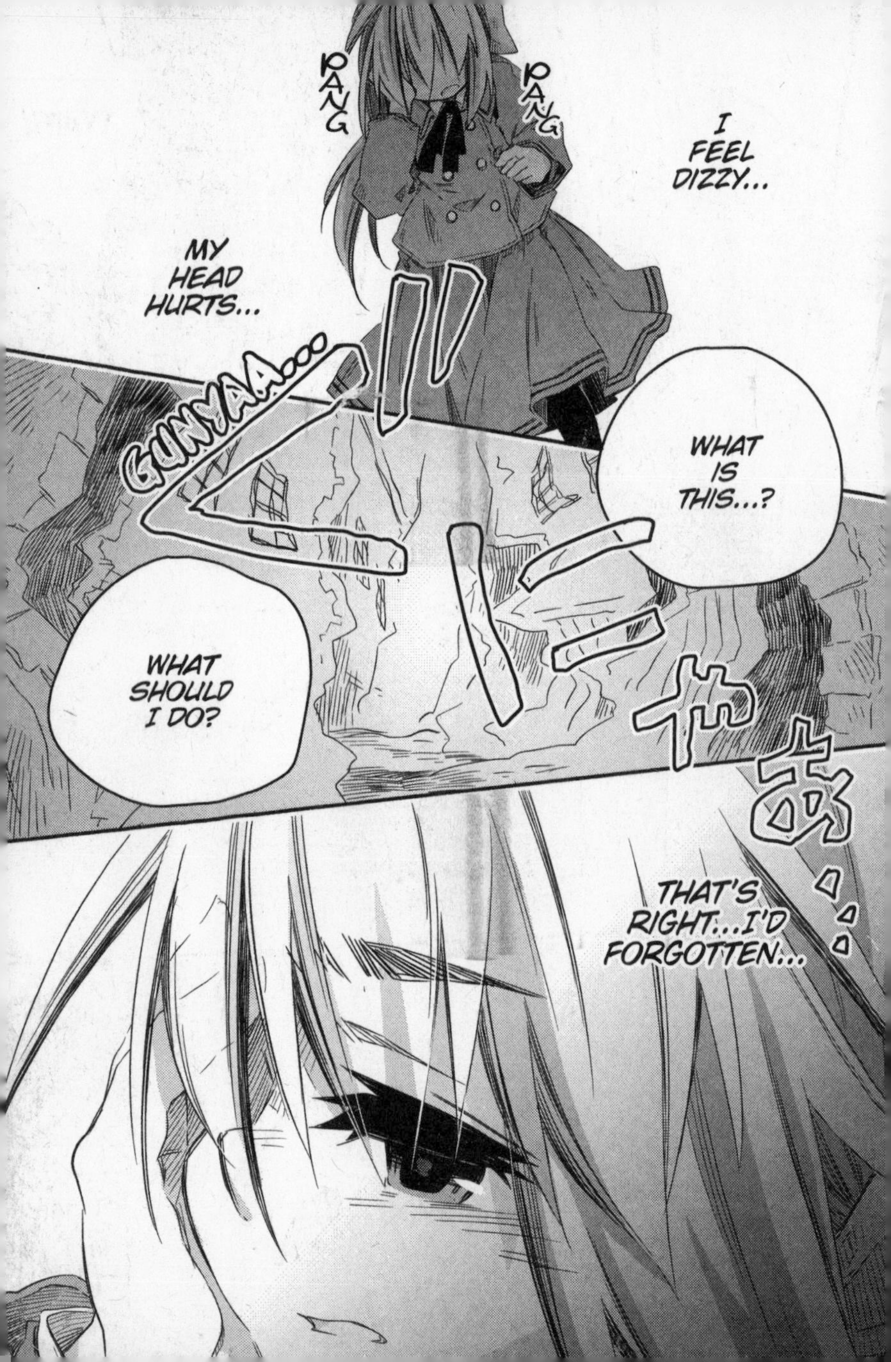
I FEEL DIZZY...
PANG
PANG
MY HEAD HURTS...
WHAT IS THIS...?
GUNYAA...
WHAT SHOULD I DO?
THAT'S RIGHT...I'D FORGOTTEN...

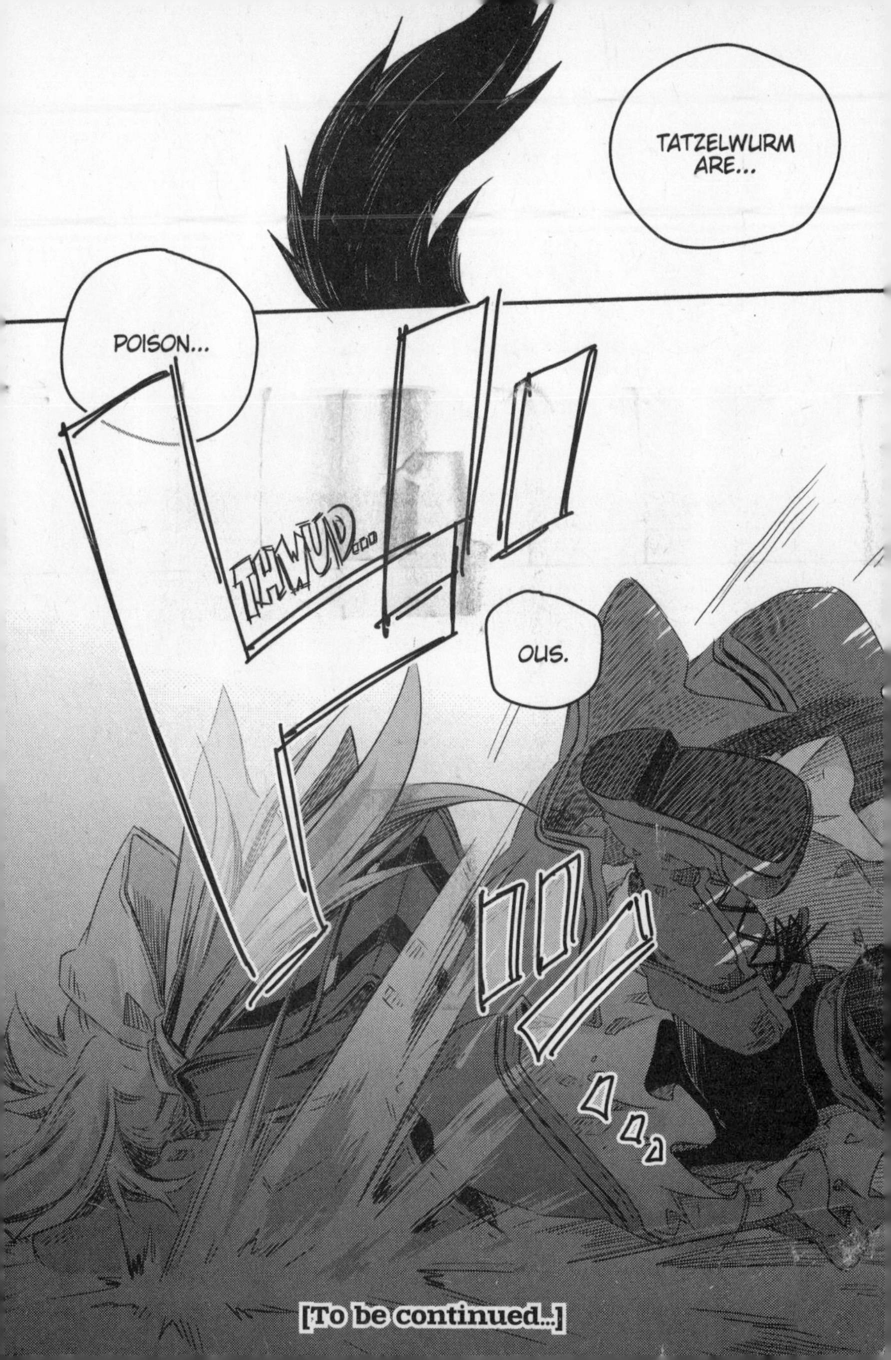
TATZELWURM ARE...
POISON...
THWUD...
OUS.
[To be continued...]

Informational Help:

Everyone from the Russian Folklore Association
Aiko Ishikawa-sensei, Yoko Kumanoya-sensei, Kiyomi Kobayashi-sensei
Yoko Naono-sensei, Tetsuya Yamada-sensei

Kanagawa University Institute of Japanese Folklore Culture
Special Researcher Kachiro Kobayashi-sensei

Thank you very much!

Mokuhata-san, Kashimura-sensei, Kobayashi-san
Thank you for all your help!

Assistants:
Hiroshi Morino-san (Chapter 18-22)
Koyuki Asakura-san (Chapter 23, Editing 20-22)
Funahana Satoumi-san (Chapter 23, Editing 20-22)
Thank you!

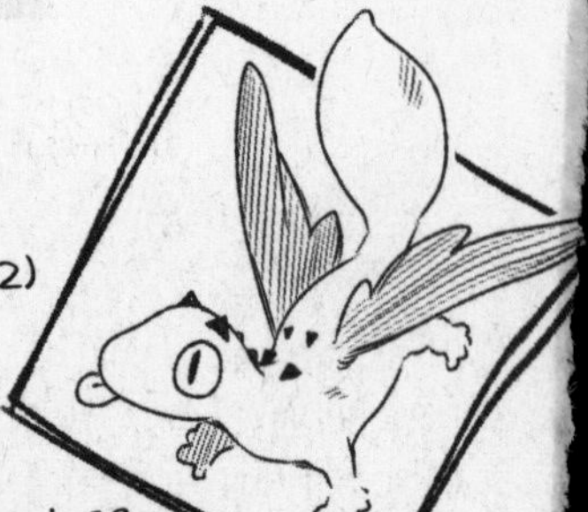

Each chapter has a puk hidden in it!! Try to find them all.

SEVEN SEAS ENTERTAINMENT PRESENTS

How to Treat Magical Beasts
Mine and Master's Medical Journal

story and art by **KAZIYA**

VOLUME 4

TRANSLATION
Angela Liu

ADAPTATION
Jaymee Goh

LETTERING AND RETOUCH
Annaliese Christman

COVER DESIGN
KC Fabellon

PROOFREADER
Kurestin Armada
Cae Hawksmoor

EDITOR
Jenn Grunigen

PREPRESS TECHNICIAN
Rhiannon Rasmussen-Silverstein

PRODUCTION MANAGER
Lissa Pattillo

MANAGING EDITOR
Julie Davis

ASSOCIATE PUBLISHER
Adam Arnold

PUBLISHER
Jason DeAngelis

WATASHI TO SENSEI NO GENJUU SHINRYOUROKU VOL. 4

Originally published in Japan in 2019 by MAG Garden Corporation, Tokyo.
English translation rights arranged through TOHAN CORPORATION, Tokyo.

Seven Seas press and purchase enquiries can be sent to Marketing Manager Lianne Sentar at press@gomanga.com. Information regarding the distribution and purchase of digital editions is available from Digital Manager CK Russell at digital@gomanga.com.

ISBN: 978-1-64275-335-6

Printed in Canada

First Printing: December 2019

10 9 8 7 6 5 4 3 2 1

FOLLOW US ONLINE: ***www.sevenseasentertainment.com***

READING DIRECTIONS

This book reads from ***right to left***, Japanese style. If this is your first time reading manga, you start reading from the top right panel on each page and take it from there. If you get lost, just follow the numbered diagram here. It may seem backwards at first, but you'll get the hang of it! Have fun!!

1
2
3
4
5
6
7
8
9

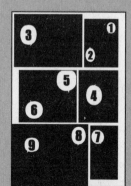

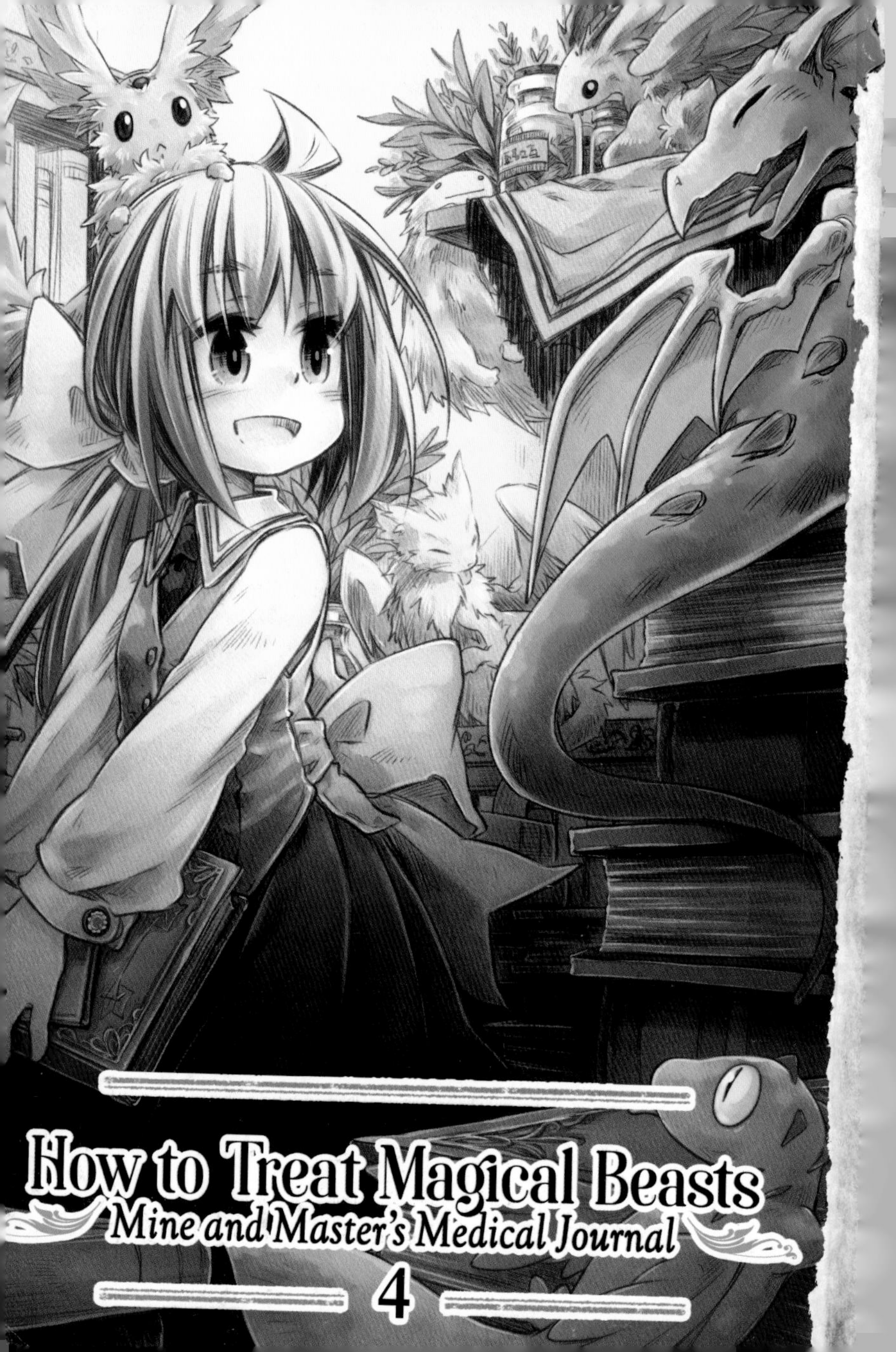
How to Treat Magical Beasts
Mine and Master's Medical Journal
4

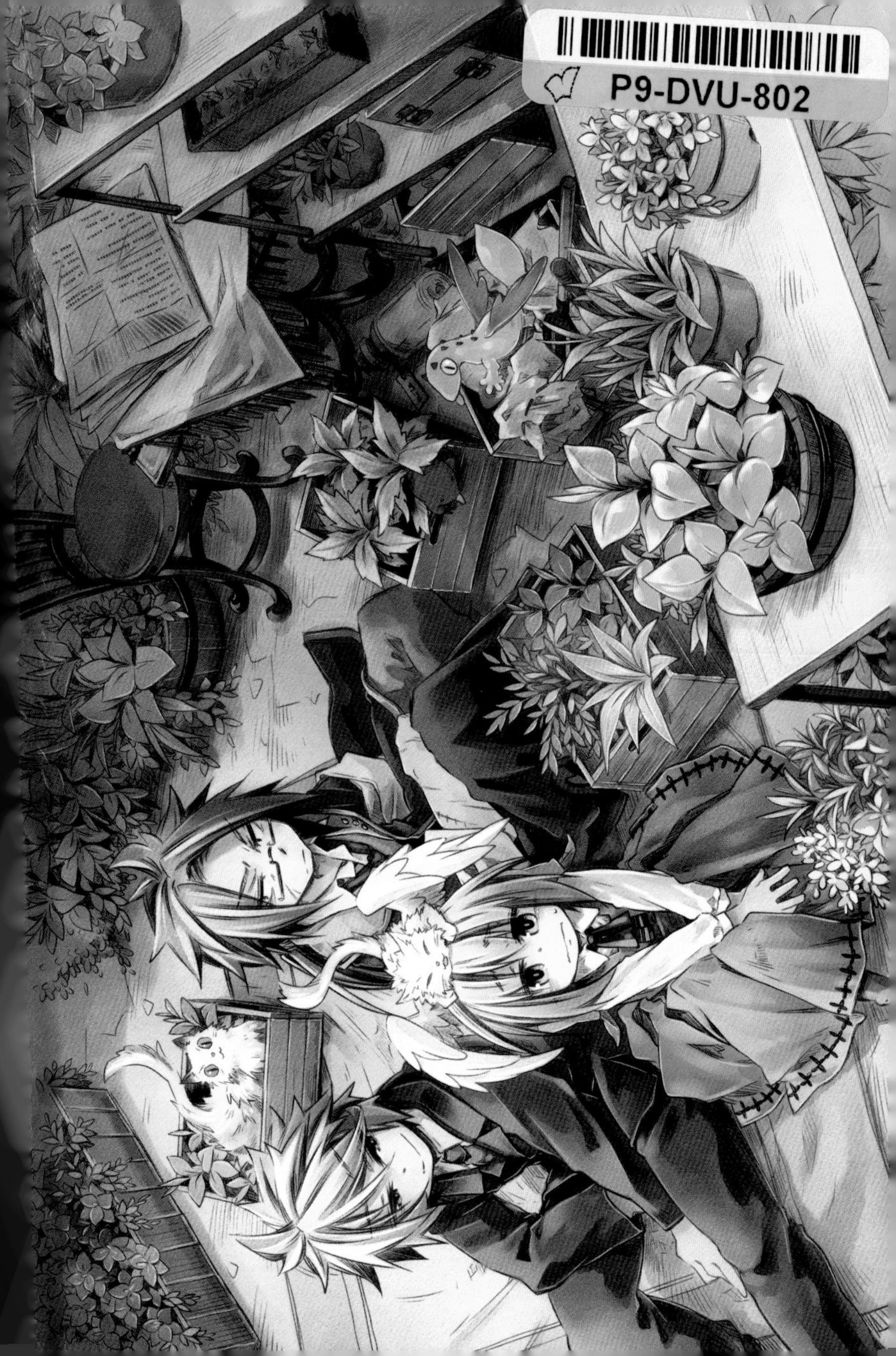